ENDING INCOME INEQUALITY

Income inequality in America has been on the rise for decades, but policy and legal thought has yet to catch up. Both parties in the United States have been hesitant to intervene in the market to address this problem, while the income tax system has been touted as a better and more efficient way to tackle income inequality. However, the tax system itself has failed to keep pace with the widening gaps in income. *Ending Income Inequality* challenges arguments made by legal scholars in the field of law and economics, who have supported the tax system over redistributive legal rules. By examining specific areas of the law such as minimum wage, collective bargaining, antitrust law, intellectual property, and housing regulation, the book argues that using legal rules, in addition to income taxes, is a promising path to reverse rising inequality.

Matthew Dimick is Professor of Law at the University at Buffalo School of Law and Director of the Baldy Center for Law & Social Policy.

Ending Income Inequality

A CRITICAL APPROACH TO THE LAW AND ECONOMICS OF REDISTRIBUTION

MATTHEW DIMICK
University at Buffalo School of Law

CAMBRIDGE
UNIVERSITY PRESS

CAMBRIDGE
UNIVERSITY PRESS

Shaftesbury Road, Cambridge CB2 8EA, United Kingdom

One Liberty Plaza, 20th Floor, New York, NY 10006, USA

477 Williamstown Road, Port Melbourne, VIC 3207, Australia

314–321, 3rd Floor, Plot 3, Splendor Forum, Jasola District Centre, New Delhi – 110025, India

103 Penang Road, #05–06/07, Visioncrest Commercial, Singapore 238467

Cambridge University Press is part of Cambridge University Press & Assessment, a department of the University of Cambridge.

We share the University's mission to contribute to society through the pursuit of education, learning and research at the highest international levels of excellence.

www.cambridge.org
Information on this title: www.cambridge.org/9781108842846
DOI: 10.1017/9781108906418

When citing this work, please include a reference to the DOI 10.1017/9781108906418

First published 2025

A catalogue record for this publication is available from the British Library

A Cataloging-in-Publication data record for this book is available from the Library of Congress

ISBN 978-1-108-84284-6 Hardback
ISBN 978-1-108-82284-8 Paperback

For Jan and David

Contents

PART II THE COMMON LAW

PART III REGULATION AND FUNCTIONAL LAW

Figures

Tables

Acknowledgments

First thanks are owed to my wonderfully supportive and smart colleagues at the University at Buffalo School of Law, past and present, who have shaped this book in more ways than they know: Heather Abraham, Dianne Avery, Mekonnen Ayano, Christine Bartholomew, Mark Bartholomew, Guyora Binder, Michael Boucai, Todd Brown, Luis Chiesa, Jorge Fabra Zamora, Lucinda Finley, Rebecca French, Jim Gardner, John Giammatteo, Paul Linden-Retek, Clayton Masterman, Lynn Mather, Martha McCluskey, Errol Meidinger, Athena Mutua, Tony O'Rourke, Jack Schlegel, Matt Steilen, Rob Steinfeld, Tico Taussig-Rubbo, Bert Westbrook, and Jim Wooten.

For their research assistance, I owe a debt of gratitude to Racquel Bozzelli, Michael Dolce, Jordan Einhorn, Simone Grande, Katherine Logan, and Jordan Mroczek.

For inspiration, encouragement, camaraderie, workshop comments, or all of the above, I wish to thank Matthew Adler, Kevin Banks, Pablo Beramendi, Catherine Fisk, Cindy Estlund, Nate Holdren, Mandy Hughett, Rob Hunter, Zachary Liscow, Guy Mundlak, Eric Posner, Brishen Rogers, César Rosado Marzán, David Rueda, Hila Shamir, Daniel Stegmueller, Dom Taylor, and Joshua Teitelbaum.

A big thanks goes to my editor, Jana Riess, and to my commissioning editor at Cambridge University Press, Matt Gallaway.

Most importantly, for their love, support, and patience, I wish to thank my companion in body, spirit, and mind, Kristen Howey Dimick; my children, Liam and Normandie; and my parents, to whom this book is dedicated, Jan and David Dimick.

PART I

Introduction

1

Orienting the Argument

Efficiency has long been the most important – if not the *exclusive* – normative principle guiding the economic analysis of law. In other words, which legal rule will maximize society's total wealth? However, the problem with efficiency is that total wealth is indifferent to the way it is distributed. According to efficiency, a bigger pie where almost everyone gets a very small slice and only a small handful of people get very large slices is better than a slightly smaller pie where everyone gets the same-sized slice. Adherents and detractors of the economic analysis of law have therefore often tangled over the competing goals of efficiency – the size of the pie – and its distribution – how the pie is divvied up.

Consider the following statements from some well-known representatives of the field. In a widely cited article, Kaplow and Shavell (1994) conclude, "[I]t is appropriate for economic analysis of legal rules to focus on efficiency and to ignore the distribution of income in offering normative judgments" (677). Or, in one of the core textbooks and introductions to law and economics, Cooter and Ulen (2016) reject "the redistributive approach to private law. Pursuing redistributive goals is an exceptional use of private law that special circumstances may justify but that ought not be the usual use of private law." (7). Finally, Weisbach (2003) agrees, writing, "The overwhelming majority of law and economics scholarship looks solely to efficiency to evaluate legal rules" (439). What all of these scholars have in common is a commitment to efficiency as a guiding principle in economics, a worldview that affects how they approach legal and policy challenges in the real-world. Thus, whether we are deciding how long an invention should be protected by patent, whether a merger of two giant corporations should be approved or denied, whether a factory has the right to pollute or the nearby residents a right to clean air, whether to adopt the negligence or strict liability rule in tort, or whether the minimum wage should be increased or abolished, the question always reduces to the distributively indifferent measure of efficiency: Which legal rule would maximize benefits and minimize costs for all of society?

The purpose of this book is to critically examine one of the central, intellectual pillars supporting the primacy of efficiency over distribution in the economic analysis of law. This is Kaplow and Shavell's (1994) argument that the income tax is a more efficient method than the legal system for redistributing income. Kaplow and Shavell's argument has been called the "double-distortion argument" (Sanchirico 2000, 799), a phrase which does indeed succinctly capture its basic reasoning. To put the arugment simply, using legal rules creates two economic "distortions" – losses of wealth in economists' parlance – while the tax system only generates one. Taxes regulate a person's income-earning activities; redistributive legal rules also do that, but in addition they regulate the activity that is the subject of the legal rule – for example, precautionary behavior in the case of torts, substantial performance in the case of contracts, or research and development in the case of intellectual property law. Because one distortion is better than two, the tax system accomplishes redistribution with the least amount of economic waste. We will have the opportunity to look at Kaplow and Shavell's thesis in a bit more detail in Chapter 2. For now, we should note how this argument supports law and economics' broader contention highlighted in the previous paragraph, and is narrowly about the most efficient method of redistribution. If legal rules are a more costly method of redistributing income, then it follows that we should not be concerned about whether or how legal rules affect the distribution of income.

Kaplow and Shavell's article is without question a scholarly success, accumulating over 1,000 citations when I last checked Google Scholar. But more than that, their argument for the superiority of taxation over legal rules is also a uniquely specific articulation and defense of a broader and enormously influential, economist-driven policy zeitgeist. Documenting this influence defies summary. Over the past three or more decades, government policy fundamentally has shifted away from distributive policies that required direct intervention in market activities, something we might call "predistribution" (Hacker 2011), such as a federal jobs guarantee, higher minimum wages, protectionism, stricter antitrust enforcement (or stronger regulatory oversight of monopolistic industries), and stronger unions. Instead, an alternative idea came to dominate: Let the untrammeled market work its wealth-creating magic, and to the extent we do not like the distributive outcomes, use the income tax to clean up the mess. As Jacob Hacker pithily put this attitude: "just let the market rip and clean up afterward" (Irwin 2016). The idea is also crystallized in the famous napkin story of the Laffer curve, which purported to show that the government could actually increase tax revenue by *reducing* taxes.[1] Although tax rates may be lowered, the greater economic activity they should generate will

[1] According to lore, at a 1974 dinner meeting with Ford Administration officials Dick Cheney and Donald Rumsfeld, the economist Arthur Laffer drew a curve on the back of a napkin to illustrate how a too-high tax rate could lower tax revenue by undermining economic and entrepreneurial incentives; conversely, lower taxes could stimulate the economy and create more tax revenue. Hence, the "Laffer curve" was born (Appelbaum 2017).

raise tax revenues. The political consequences of this shift have been profound. According to a recent research paper, the Democratic Party's embrace of this new market logic has contributed to the substantial realignment among the electorate, where the Party has hemorrhaged working-class voters and replaced them with more educated and affluent supporters (Kuziemko, Marx, and Naidu 2023). These consequential policy shifts therefore warrant a close reexamination of their intellectual foundations.

This book is hardly the first contribution to respond critically to Kaplow and Shavell's double-distortion argument. A number of brilliant scholars have already done so (see, e.g., Jolls 1998; Sanchirico 2000; Liscow 2014; Fennell and McAdams 2016). However, most of these responses have been conducted on the same abstract terrain on which Kaplow and Shavell first clarified their objection to the use of redistributive legal rules. To illustrate their claims, Kaplow and Shavell used an example from tort law. This was less because tort law is a major tool for redistribution, either in precedent or in policy, and more because it was a simple way to demonstrate a more abstract claim. Indeed, although there certainly are distributive stakes within the narrower realm of products liability, few people first reach for tort law when contemplating the legal levers we can pull for ameliorating income inequality. Nevertheless, critics of Kaplow and Shavell have responded at the same level of abstraction, often deploying modified versions of their tort-law example.

As insightful as these responses have been, I believe that the abstract nature in which the debate has been conducted has been a disservice to the larger conversation about equity in legal rules.[2] For one thing, no one seems to have closely examined the distributive effects of legal rules that activists, advocates, and policy makers actually propose when talking about how to redistribute income. I am thinking of legal rules such as the minimum wage, collective bargaining legislation, antitrust law, intellectual property, and housing regulation, among others. Does the double-distortion argument continue to hold when the redistributive efficiency of such policies is explicitly compared to the optimal tax-and-transfer system?

But perhaps the most unfortunate consequence of this abstract discourse surrounding the double-distortion argument is that it has allowed Kaplow and Shavell's basic claim to remain relatively unscathed. Precisely because the conversation remains abstract, Kaplow and Shavell have been able to describe each objection as an exception – a mere qualification – to their more fundamentally universal insight. For example, in answering Sanchirico's (2000) critique of their (1994) article,

[2] Recently, it has become common in popular discourse to distinguish between equality and equity. Various definitions abound but, in sum, equality may be used to describe more formal, equal treatment while equity is different treatment in the service of some more substantive, goal-oriented standard of equality. As redistribution can be easily conceptualized as falling into the latter category, the way I use "equity" is consistent with this usage. For similar reasons, equality and equity will be treated as interchangeable in this book.

Kaplow and Shavell (2000b) responded by saying that they had already identified the qualification in question and it had "only a tangential bearing on the question whether legal rules should favor the poor."[3] Likewise, they dismissed Ackerman (1971) and Kennedy (1987), who argued that housing codes could improve the material well-being of tenants with no or little economic cost. Kaplow and Shavell (2002) wrote that while Ackerman and Kennedy had "gone to great lengths to show that it is possible – not necessarily likely – that *some* redistribution can be accomplished in particular legal settings … such illustrations do not establish a *general* ability to achieve substantial redistribution in any systematic manner through use of the sorts of legal rules generally analyzed" (33 n.36, emphasis added). Thus, they allowed for rare cases where it might be appropriate to use legal rules to redistribute income. But they painted those as exceptions, too idiosyncratic to be treated with the same degree of presumptive validity possessed by the double-distortion thesis itself.

This book takes a different approach. Rather than trying to provide some general, abstract reason why legal redistribution will never or will always be more efficient than redistributing income through taxation, the book looks at specific areas of law where the distributive stakes actually lie. While it does address the redistributive potential in more general areas of private law – property, contract, and tort – the book's heart examines the minimum wage, collective bargaining legislation, housing regulation, antitrust law, and intellectual property law. This approach challenges the double-distortion argument in a more effective way. By identifying reasons why legal rules can in fact redistribute income more efficiently than taxes at a more concrete level, this case-by-case approach shows that these reasons are not mere exceptions. That is, if the double-distortion argument fails in too many cases where the redistributive stakes of law matter, it is no longer possible to dismiss these cases as exceptional. As we will also see, a case-by-case approach reveals several different reasons why the double-distortion argument fails. Just as there is not a single, "silver bullet" reason why the income tax is always more efficient than legal rules in redistributing income, there is not a single, "silver bullet" reason for the opposite proposition. But these particular reasons do not – cannot – emerge from a general, abstract analysis.

[3] In their response to Sanchirico (2000), Kaplow and Shavell (2000b) repeat several times the claim that Sanchirico's objection is a mere "qualification" without any significant implication. For example, they say that "we believe Sanchirico's claim that our basic argument is subject to certain qualifications is correct but does not go to the heart of whether legal rules should be systematically adjusted to favor the poor and disfavor the rich in order to further distributive objectives" (828). They also write, "Sanchirico's abstract exploration of one of our qualifications does not, unfortunately, illuminate the empirical question and, more important, does not in our opinion provide any basis for modification of our prior conclusion concerning the proper emphasis of normative economic analysis of legal rules" (835). In this last quote, note the way that Kaplow and Shavell describe Sanchirico's exploration as "abstract."

1.1 SOME CLARIFYING REMARKS

It is easy to misconstrue the preceding remarks, and so this section will offer three clarifications. First, I will explain what is meant when we describe the economic analysis of law's *sole* commitment to efficiency, or wealth maximization. Put simply, while law-and-economics scholars have in recent times embraced approaches in welfare economics that expressly encompass distributive concerns, they have not given up the claim that the income tax redistributes more efficiently than legal rules. As long as this latter claim stands, it will continue to encourage a neglect toward distributive concerns, even if this neglect is unintended.

In considering this first question, some may object that my characterization of law and economics as concerned exclusively with efficiency, rather than distribution, is uncharitable or narrow. Are not economists concerned with maximizing social welfare, rather than wealth, a goal that expressly accounts for the distribution of income and not exclusively its total size? For example, Kaplow and Shavell (2002) have recently made clear their commitment to redistributive policy objectives and that these objectives can be fully subsumed within the economic notion of social welfare. In their book, *Fairness and Welfare* , they write, "[T]he economic notion of social welfare is one that is concerned explicitly with the distribution of income" (4) and also, "Our main point is that many basic concerns about the overall distribution of income are encompassed by the welfare economic approach" (29).[4] Nevertheless, in that same book, they never retract the conclusions made in their prior, 1994 *Journal of Legal Studies* article. Just having claimed that welfare economics is fully adequate to address distributive concerns, Kaplow and Shavell then explain why "ignoring distributive effects in legal policy analysis is often the most sensible course even though the distribution of income is generally viewed to be important, as it is under welfare economics" (32). They then briefly provide three familiar reasons for this conclusion. First, it is often useful to ignore distributive concerns for the sake of "analytical convenience"; second, "many legal rules probably have little effect on the distribution of income"; and third, the income tax system can redistribute income more efficiently than legal rules (32–34). Kaplow's commitment to efficient, rather than redistributive, legal rules is also confirmed in his recent work on market power and inequality, where he concludes, "Perhaps surprisingly, the overall result is to leave largely intact some standard competition policy prescriptions that ignore distribution, labor supply distortion, and income taxation …" (Kaplow 2021, 330).

How do we reconcile these seemingly conflicting statements? On the one hand, Kaplow and Shavell defend the economic notion of social welfare as being fully capable of addressing concerns about inequality and income distribution. On the other

[4] Kaplow and Shavell (2002) also write, "[W]e elaborate on how questions about distribution of income fit within the framework of welfare economics, especially because the relevance of income distribution under welfare economics contrasts sharply with the popular view that income distribution is unimportant under normative economic analysis of law." (28–29)

hand, they show no signs of retreating from their earlier claim that legal rules should ignore the distribution of income and be oriented primarily, even exclusively, toward efficiency. In order to make sense of this apparent contradiction, one has to appreciate the intricate "division of labor" that economists have constructed. According to this view, policymakers should clearly separate the government's "efficiency" goals from its "distributive" goals.[5] Thus, by all means, economists should be concerned about the distribution of income; and economic theory, with the concept of social welfare, is able to determine how much wealth is worth sacrificing for the sake of society's, or the government's, distributive tastes. But Kaplow and Shavell's crucial point is that the best way to achieve these distributive goals is through the income tax system, not the legal system. Thus, to claim that the normative analysis of legal rules should be concerned solely with efficiency is not to argue that efficiency is the only goal economists should pursue. Rather it is only a claim about the proper standard for a "subset" of government policy, that subset concerned with the design of legal rules in both private and public law.

So far, we have only mentioned the distribution of *income*, and have ignored other bases for redistribution and other normative concerns about equity, such as equality before the law, or racial, gender, and other group-based forms of discrimination. This brings us to the second question needing clarification: What exactly is being distributed when we debate legal rules that redistribute? Should we redistribute well-being, income, status, or what? Elucidating this issue will allow us to avoid some pertinent, but side-tracking, objections.

This silence may not only cause confusion about what exactly is being distributed, but also raise concerns about whether economists' basis for redistribution is too narrow. However, clarifying this issue also gives us another way to reconcile Kaplow and Shavell's seemingly conflicting commitments to distribution and efficiency. This book, and the debate about using redistributive legal rules, is primarily about the distribution of income – or, more accurately, if less precisely, the distribution of *material goods*.[6]

Excluding redistribution on the bases of non-income factors has indeed been one way of criticizing Kaplow and Shavell's double-distortion argument. When other

5 The historical and theoretical basis for this division of labor is explained in the next chapter.

6 "Income" remains inaccurate because much government redistribution takes place in-kind, or with cash-like vouchers earmarked for specific purposes. Food stamps, medical services, and public education all come to mind as examples of non-cash transfers. As will be shown in Chapter 2, the debate about using legal rules to redistribute income itself began with a non-income, but material form of redistribution: housing codes and the warranty of habitability. Kaplow and Shavell may themselves protest that the optimal or efficiency form of redistribution is solely through cash transfers. Nevertheless, there is little doubt they would disagree that the warranty of habitability, for example, is an example of "income" redistribution to which their double-distortion argument would apply (see, e.g., Kaplow and Shavell 2002, 33 n.36). To avoid confusion, therefore, it will sometimes be useful to say that "income" in this book is shorthand for something like "material goods."

axes of redistribution exist, it is contended, legal rules may be better equipped than the tax-and-transfer system to address them. Blumkin and Margalioth (2005) use the example of race discrimination. In principle, the income tax could be used to undo the effects of earnings inequalities generated by discrimination based on race rather than ability. The income tax could be used to grant a refundable tax credit to members of the racially disfavored group, calculated to fully eliminate race-based earnings differences. Yet, "[t]ransfers based on ethnic origin are not common in practice because of the desire to eliminate the ability of discriminators to purchase their right to discriminate – which seems intrinsically immoral – and for symbolic reasons" (16). To put it simply, income is inadequate to address all forms of inequity, including and especially the intrinsic wrongness of racial discrimination.

However, Kaplow and Shavell may not entirely disagree with this conclusion and, for them, the difference between income and non-income bases of redistribution probably correlates with the economist's distinction between efficient and distributive policy goals. According to them (e.g., Kaplow and Shavell 2000b, 827–32), redistributing goods or values other than income falls outside the concern of their double-distortion argument. For Kaplow and Shavell, using legal rules "to redistribute" means "to redistribute income."[7] Furthermore, they contend, a legal-rule adjustment made on some non-income basis is "qualitatively different from the adjustments that we suspect most legal academics have in mind when they talk about adjusting legal rules to favor the poor" (829–30).[8] To clarify the objectives of this book, it will focus on the distribution of income, rather than non-income forms of inequality, for these reasons and because the debate about redistributive legal rules has focused primarily on the distribution of income. Non-income forms and axes of redistribution are extremely important topics for discussion, but they remain outside the scope of this work.[9]

The third clarification I would like to make is to situate the debate about redistributive legal rules within the universe of normative discourse and clarify my own commitments in this conversation. Participants in the debate for the most part

7 Liscow (2014, 2502) recognizes this: "[Kaplow and Shavell] are not 'wrong' in not considering non-income factors; they are just asking a different question. The Kaplow-Shavell argument is a non sequitur in the context of redistribution for non-income reasons."

8 Lewinsohn-Zamir (2006) makes a more subtle point about the difference between income and other "goods." Using the example of the warranty of habitability, she argues that income is no substitute for a "rat-infested, leaking and broken-down apartment." Such a dwelling "cannot grant the basic security, comfort and means that are essential for advancing self-respect and autonomous action, acquiring knowledge, pursuing long-term goals, or developing deep and meaningful social relationships with other people" (350–51).

9 Finally, proponents of the double-distortion claim will in fact argue that rules that address other forms of inequality – such as anti-discrimination legislation – may actually be efficient and therefore pose no efficiency-equity trade-off. The absence of the trade-off means that the issue falls outside the debate about redistributive legal rules. For a discussion of the efficiency of disparate impact rules, see, e.g., Ayres (2007).

agree on the ultimate end or goal: the maximization of welfare or well-being. Income inequality or the maldistribution of material goods is "bad" because it lowers social welfare. Conversely, social welfare can be raised by redistributing income – that is, by transferring income to those who value an additional dollar more (the poor) from those who value an additional dollar less (the rich). Of course, welfare maximization, coming from the tradition of utilitarianism, is not above criticism and has frequently, even legitimately, been accused of ignoring other fundamental norms and values – justice, rights, or fairness, for example.[10] Nevertheless, this book does not take issue with the ultimate end or normative goal of welfare maximization. Rather, the crux of the debate, and the focus of this book, is on the *means* or method by which this goal is achieved: Can legal rules or income taxes redistribute income, and therefore raise social welfare, more efficiently than the other? Moreover this means invokes a different metric, *wealth* or *efficiency*, which is translatable into welfare but is not always the same thing. To underscore the distinction, the question is which means of increasing *welfare* is the least destructive of the *wealth* we are attempting to transfer? This book is primarily concerned with the "means" question and not with the "ends" question. In fact, with reference to the terms of the debate itself and the perspectives of the participants, there is little controversy over the ultimate end to be pursued. As far as I can tell, no one takes the redistribution of income as an end in itself. (For further discussion of welfare, wealth, and their maximization, see the book's appendix.)

Thus, this book will set aside the "ends" question, which accepts, for the sake of discussion, that the ultimate goal is to maximize social welfare; the question at the heart of this book is whether the income tax or legal rules can best accomplish this objective. This book functions as an "internal" critique of the law and economics of income inequality, one that accepts the basic assumptions of economic reason but attempts to show that those assumptions do not necessarily lead to the accepted conclusions. I will leave to the side, for a possible future discussion, an "external" critique of law and economics and an examination of its basic assumptions that such a critique would entail. I therefore do not want to be mistaken as subscribing to social-welfare maximization as an appropriate and comprehensive normative framework. I have major reservations about the social welfare point of view, primarily about the

[10] In an extensive series of books and articles, Kaplow and Shavell (1999; 2000a; 2001a; 2001b; 2002; 2003) have made the case that when evaluating legal policies, *exclusive* weight should be put on their effects on individuals' well-being, with no *independent* weight accorded to notions of justice or fairness. For some of the responses to Kaplow and Shavell's approach to fairness versus welfare, see, e.g., Dorff (2001), Craswell (2003), Kornhauser (2003), Waldron (2003), and Markovits (2004). In addition, Adler (2012) has made a detailed and sophisticated case for using well-being as a fully-legitimate *moral* framework for policy evaluation. However, for the purposes of the present volume, Kaplow and Shavell's argument that social welfare is an adequate, or even compelling, language for a comprehensive moral philosophy should be kept distinct from their argument that the tax system is most efficient means for redistributing income.

claim that it can or should be measured and maximized. But I reserve that discussion for another place and time.

Despite those misgivings, I hope that those who have not accepted the economists' normative viewpoint will still find value in the book and find the double-distortion argument worthy of serious reflection and discussion. The argument that legal rules should not be used for distributive objectives is primarily associated with law-and-economics scholarship. But the argument is also deeply ingrained within political liberal thought. The position is quite explicitly found in the work of John Rawls (1999, 254), as well as in that of many other political liberals (e.g., Alstott 1999). The position cannot therefore simply be dismissed as a "pro-market" conservative argument. In addition, even those skeptical of welfare maximization as an adequate moral theory should find the double-distortion thesis worthy of attention. Many, if not most, people who would consider the effects of legal rules on rights, justice, or fairness would also consider their effects on individuals' wealth or well-being. That is, a big part of why we care about economic inequality and poverty is because of their consequences for well-being. So if an argument says that using taxes exclusively will improve the well-being of the poor, it is one we should pay attention to, regardless of the abstract normative justification.

1.2 OUTLINE AND ARGUMENT OF THE BOOK

The argument that legal rules should not be used for distributive objectives is primarily associated with law-and-economics scholarship, which as I have noted can proceed on a rarefied plane, far removed from the complex realities of the actual policy. This overly abstract level of debate has permitted the double-distortion argument to retain a privileged position, so it follows that an argument for legal redistribution should interrogate that argument in more specific settings. This is precisely the approach of this book.

After some preliminary Part I material that reviews the existing literature and the foundational terms of the debate, Part II of this book explores how the question of wealth redistribution plays out in several accepted "common law" areas. These include property in Chapter 3, tort in Chapter 4, and contract in Chapter 5. As the most foundational and "general" areas of the law, these common-law domains are the most frequently analyzed by legal scholars, though they may not always be considered likely areas for redistributive legal rules. These areas' centrality in legal scholarship, including in debates about equity-informed legal rules, makes their inclusion in this book essential. Nevertheless, each chapter will show how, even in places where using the law to redistribute income seems less promising, there are simple reasons and circumstances when the common law can redistribute more efficiently than the income tax.

Furthermore, the book will address those areas of law that are more frequently proposed, in "the real world," so to speak, for addressing income inequality.[11] This makes for a somewhat unique, more inductive approach. According to my argument, any claim that one should always use taxes or always use legal rules is wrong. But for precisely that reason, the claim that legal rules should be considered on an equal basis in any situation requires demonstrating that in enough specific cases, both the a priori superiority of taxes fails and the potential for legal rules is compelling. The goal will be to show that the number of exceptions to the double-distortion argument is large enough to swallow the general rule.

With this goal in mind, Part III of the book will analyze areas of law that have more obvious and potent impacts for the distribution of income, areas of regulation and functional, or goal-specific, law. As already emphasized, it is a curious feature of the double-distortion debate that little of it has taken place over legal rules or areas of regulation than may actually matter most for the distribution of income. Part III fills that gap and is the part of the book that will be the most policy-relevant.

Part III begins with Chapter 6, which examines the labor market. The minimum wage and collective bargaining have been contentious matters, upheld as examples where, because of their inefficiency, they "hurt those whom they are intended to help." The minimum wage and collective bargaining legislation may be inefficient, but Chapter 6 explains why they may be less inefficient at redistributing income than the income tax. Chapter 7 then tackles antitrust law. This area of the law has long been known to have redistributive implications, but its primary objective – and legitimacy, for many law-and-economics scholars – has been to increase efficiency in product markets. This chapter explains when and why we may want to use antitrust law for redistributive objectives, even when it might be inefficient to do so, and notwithstanding the existence of the income tax as a redistributive alternative. Next, Chapter 8 explores the topic of intellectual property, whose distributive importance economists have come to recognize. Intellectual property raises similar anticompetitive concerns as antitrust, but offers a different set of legal tools and instruments for addressing income inequality. Finally, Chapter 9 then addresses housing regulation, such as rent control, housing codes, and habitability standards, which have increasing relevance for the distribution of material well-being and have themselves long been subjects about the wisdom of legal redistribution.

The book's conclusion offers some extended, but brief and tentative, remarks on the economic assumptions that have been granted for the sake of argument in this book's "internal" critique of the double-distortion argument. Finally, an extended

[11] Some of these areas of the law are concerned mainly with market failure and efficiency, rather than redistribution. Antitrust, for example, is about regulating market power, a market failure that can lead to inefficiency. However, conceptually neat divisions in the law between "efficiency" areas and "distribution" areas are illusory. We can, for example, easily contemplate an inefficient antitrust policy that benefits the poor, but that is less inefficient than a distribution-equivalent income tax policy.

appendix provides the reader with an overview of the basic principles of welfare economics, including some of the formal and mathematical tools used in economics and in this book. Readers who already have a grasp of welfare economics may skip this appendix, along with readers who would prefer not to get bogged down by definitions and technical minutiae. Others may want to consult specific sections as a resource for further refining concepts that are employed elsewhere in the book.

2

Redistributing Income Efficiently

As mentioned in Chapter 1, the main approach of the book is to descend from the lofty heights of abstraction typically employed in the double-distortion debate and critically examine a range of more specific policy domains at a somewhat more concrete level of analysis. Readers will object: The discussion is theoretical and employs a great deal of formal reasoning. But the objective is to show how an investigation of specific areas of law and policy reveal distinctive – non-general – reasons that make redistribution through legal rules possibly, if not necessarily, less inefficient than the tax system. So, subsequent chapters will evaluate policy fields such as housing, antitrust, and employment law in order to investigate the effects of particular legal rules in their specific economic environments.

Before we can turn to that, however, we need to understand some economics of inequality and redistribution. This opening chapter introduces the terms of the debate about taxation and legal rules, describing how the dispute arose within legal scholarship and explaining the primary role of efficiency as an evaluative standard. Then, I will turn to the double-distortion argument and various criticisms that economists have lodged against it – for example, that it fails to account sufficiently for individual heterogeneity or that it ignores the political costs of changing the tax code.

2.1 TAXATION, LEGAL RULES, AND REDISTRIBUTION

Before we investigate the role of the double-distortion argument in upholding the normative value of efficiency, this section will explore the evolution of the debate within legal scholarship. This story will show how the double-distortion argument arose as a response to other, faltering attempts to make efficiency the primary, if not the exclusive, evaluative principle within law and economics. While reviewing the evolution of this debate, it is important to distinguish three separate claims. First, should the economic analysis of legal rules consider only their consequences for efficiency, or should it be concerned with equity as well? Second, is it even possible for legal rules to redistribute income? And third, if it is possible for legal rules to redistribute income, is taxation superior to legal rules as a tool for redistribution?

We will see how the failure by some economists to address the first two questions led to the double-distortion argument as an answer to the third. Moreover, if the double-distortion argument is a successful, affirmative answer to the third question, then it also supplies an affirmative answer to the first question and makes the second question irrelevant. Much more is at stake then than simply whether taxes or legal rules should be used to redistribute income.

2.1.1 *The Origins of the Debate*

The idea that income taxes should be the exclusive means of redistributing economic resources is deeply entrenched within academic economic thought (as well as in much liberal political thought). We see this notion expressed, for example, in the foundational principles of "welfare economics." Welfare economics can be described as economics' *normative* wing, and is taught as a core part of any economist's microeconomics training in graduate school.[1] According to the so-called first fundamental theorem of welfare economics, a perfectly competitive economy (so defined) will be Pareto efficient: No one can be made better off without making someone worse off. There is a detailed explanation of Pareto efficiency in the book's appendix, but it is enough to know for now that the second fundamental theorem says that *any* Pareto-efficient distribution of resources (and there may be an infinite number) can be achieved with lump-sum transfers.

The practical implication of these two theorems, if there is any, is that the government faces a clean division of labor between its "efficiency" tasks and its "distribution" tasks.[2] More importantly, the government need not interfere with markets in order to achieve a more "desirable" distribution of income.[3] The only problem with this practical advice is that using lump-sum transfers for inequality-reducing objectives is generally thought to be impossible.[4] Lump-sum taxes and transfers mean that the person being taxed cannot alter the amount of tax they

1 See, for example, the treatment given in the standard graduate-level microeconomics textbook, by Mas-Colell, Whinston, and Green (1995). Fennell and McAdams (2016, 1065 n.42) and McCaffery (2005, 817 n.21) also recognize the link between the taxes-versus-legal-rules debate and the fundamental theorems of welfare economics.

2 This philosophy was classically expressed in Musgrave's (1959) "monumental" treatise on public finance. See Boadway (1997) for a summary discussion.

3 I use scare quotes because the standard of Pareto efficiency has no way of ordering Pareto-efficient allocations, either in terms of distribution or by any other criterion. Making distributional judgments within economics requires the use of a "social welfare function," which requires additional and, for some, more controversial assumptions, such as interpersonal comparisons of well-being. These issues are discussed at length in the book's appendix.

4 Stiglitz (1987, 1006) puts this point nicely: "It is sometimes assumed that lump-sum taxes are not feasible. Uniform lump-sum taxes are clearly feasible (provided they are not too large). What is *not* feasible are lump-sum taxes at different rates for individuals of different abilities; this is not

pay by changing their behavior (Hindriks and Myles 2013, 428). Otherwise, the tax will "distort" the taxpayer's incentives and lead us away from a Pareto-efficient allocation of resources. Yet, if anything is true about taxation – income taxes, commodity taxes, estate taxes – it is that people will change their behavior in order to reduce their tax obligations. It would be a different story if the government had the requisite information about people's abilities. Then a person's taxes would depend on her "endowment" or "ability" rather than, say, the amount of income she earned. But, alas, this information is not available to the government.[5] Despite the impracticability of redistributive lump-sum taxation, the accepted wisdom persists that the government's economic role in promoting efficiency should be cleanly separated from its distributive role. It perseveres on the assumption, more or less implicit, that the income tax is the next best instrument, after lump-sum taxes, for redistributing income.

One source for the debate about using legal rules to redistribute income is therefore found within highly abstract theorems of economics. Within legal scholarship, the debate has a more concrete, policy-oriented source, beginning in the 1970s. The *radix* can arguably be designated as Bruce Ackerman's (1971) article "Regulating Slum Housing Markets on Behalf of the Poor." Although he did not identify himself as a law-and-economics scholar, Ackerman's analysis is straightforwardly economic. He demonstrated that under certain conditions, housing code enforcement could redistribute from rich to poor. The article provoked a small firestorm about the efficiency and equity of housing regulation. Several critiques of Ackerman's article appeared (Komesar 1973; Rabin 1983) as did several articles defending or extending Ackerman's analysis (Markovits 1976; Kennedy 1987). Notably, not all of those who disagreed with Ackerman's analysis were opposed to his conclusions (Komesar 1983, 613). Furthermore, all of the participants accepted the basic framework of economic theory, including those who identified with different schools of legal thought (e.g., Kennedy 1987). What we can see emerging within this debate are the three distinct questions that were raised at the beginning of this section.

2.1.2 *First Question: Should Economic Analysis of Law Consider Equity as well as Efficiency?*

The first question the housing-code debate generated was whether equity as well as efficiency should be considered when evaluating any legal rule. The main argument from some law-and-economics scholars was that efficiency is a normatively neutral

feasible because the government does not have the requisite information to implement such a tax."

5 Despite the impracticality of endowment or ability taxation, it has been the subject of a rich debate in the legal literature about its normative justification, even as an "ideal" tax (see, e.g., Stark 2005; Hasen 2006; Zelenak 2006).

concept, while distribution required making value judgments that are beyond the ken of economists. This section traces that argument to its conclusion.

Like its attitude about taxes, economic thought is deeply imbued with the Pareto criterion. One normative justification for Pareto efficiency is that it rests on a principle of *consent* (Posner 1979, 489–90). Because a Pareto improvement is one where at least one person is made better off and no one worse off, no one can really object to such a change (unless unjustifiably spiteful). The criterion tracks the person-to-person exchange of a well-functioning market: No one is forced into an exchange and people only accept exchanges that make them better off. Pareto efficiency is thus considered *neutral*: There are no losers in Pareto efficiency, only winners.

Yet, as legal scholars were quick to point out, few legal rules have such benign effects. Typically, changes in legal rules have winners and losers. For example, international trade liberalization makes winners out of firms whose exports increase and losers out of firms who go bankrupt from new imports. The United Kingdom's 1846 repeal of the Corn Laws' protective tariffs benefited consumers, it has been said, by lowering the prices of cereals while harming landlords by exposing them to import competition (Kaldor 1939, 550). A lot of recent discussion about globalization has focused on the negative impacts of rising imports on workers. Rising imports cause higher unemployment, lower labor force participation, and lower wages in local labor markets with manufacturing industries exposed to import competition (Autor, Dorn, and Hanson 2013). It was hardly unrecognized that such policy changes would produce winners and losers. The question is, were the policies, in some sense, worth it? Recognizing this dilemma, scholars advanced a new definition of efficiency: Kaldor-Hicks efficiency.[6] Under the Kaldor-Hicks test, a legal rule change is efficient if the aggregate benefits exceed the aggregate costs. In other words, if the winners could monetarily compensate the losers, the change is efficient. In the case of international trade, if consumers could be taxed and landlords compensated at an amount that left landlords as well off as before the repeal of the Corn Laws, and consumers better off, the policy would be considered efficient.[7]

When the winners can compensate losers, and still be better off, then everyone can be made better off and no one worse off. However, to satisfy the Kaldor-Hicks criterion, the compensation need not actually be made; compensation is merely hypothetical. That would seem to undermine the practical relevance of Kaldor-Hicks efficiency because the distributive effects remain unaddressed. Nevertheless, some scholars argued that even with winners and losers, everyone would consent "ex ante" to Kaldor-Hicks efficient policy changes (Posner 1979). For example, consider two

6 For a clear and rigorous introduction to and critique of the concepts of Pareto efficiency, Kaldor-Hicks efficiency, and wealth maximization, see Coleman (1980). One can also consult the book's appendix.

7 In fact, the Kaldor-Hicks test was forged using examples like these from international trade (see, e.g., Hicks 1939; Kaldor 1939; De Scitovszky 1941).

legal rules: strict liability, which favors pedestrians, and negligence, which favors automobile drivers. For the sake of argument, also assume that strict liability is inefficient and negligence is efficient. Now, it is clear which rule you would prefer if you knew whether you were a driver or a pedestrian. But, from behind a veil of ignorance, not knowing which you would be, your best bet is to choose the efficient rule – negligence – because this rule minimizes ex ante, expected costs. And, indeed, because many of us are sometimes drivers and sometimes pedestrians, we can say that the winners and losers are the same.[8] Under this argument, Pareto efficiency's "consent" attribute survives under Kaldor-Hicks efficiency.

In response to the alleged neutrality of Kaldor-Hicks efficiency, critics showed that it could give "indeterminate" answers, especially when distribution-related issues – for example, income (or wealth) effects – were included in the analysis (Kelman 1987, 141–50). In a nutshell, quite different distributive outcomes can both be efficient once it is recognized that persons' "willingness to pay" for a good, service, or (legal) entitlement depends on their income or wealth. Suppose a factory has the right to pollute, with the consequence that the pollution not only degrades air quality but also lowers home values in the neighboring community. Because this influences the homeowners' wealth, it also contracts their budget constraints, which affects their demand for goods, including their willingness to "purchase" the factory's entitlement to pollute. In other words, individuals' wealth influences their willingness to pay for a clean environment. Conversely, suppose we give the homeowners the property entitlement to enjoin the factory from polluting. Without pollution, home values are higher, wealth is higher, and they might be willing to pay for a clean environment as well. In this case, the amount the factory has to pay the homeowners for the right to pollute may be higher than what the homeowners were willing to pay to get the factory to stop polluting. If so, homeowners may be willing to pay to stop pollution when they own the entitlement but not so willing when the factory has the entitlement. In this scenario, either allocation of the entitlement is "efficient" and we cannot decide which one is superior on Kaldor-Hicks grounds. Because of that indeterminacy, critics concluded that efficiency alone is insufficient and that any adequate evaluation of legal rules and entitlements had to include distribution as well.[9]

8 To the contrary, the poor are more often pedestrians and therefore are more likely than the rich to suffer traffic-related accidents. Roll and McNeil (2022) find that "pedestrian injury risk is not experienced equally across sociodemographic groups. National data and prior research shows that Black, Indigenous and people of color (BIPOC) and lower-income people bear a disproportionate burden."

9 Posner's (1985, 92) answer to this objection is that Kaldor-Hicks efficiency, or wealth maximization, "can suggest how property rights can be defined in the first place in order to maximize a society's wealth." Though he admits that "wealth maximization provides no guidance to the initial assignment of property rights" in the pollution example just described, he suggests that such cases are "rare" (Posner 1985, 92–93).

The efficiency-only view could also be attacked from other angles within law and economics. Readers familiar with this literature will be aware of the Coase theorem (Coase 1960). Chapter 3 discusses the Coase theorem at length, but the key idea is that in a world of zero transaction costs, the allocation of resources – efficiency – is independent of initial legal entitlements. Less appreciated is what Schwab (1989, 1195) dubs the "distributive corollary" to the Coase theorem. Schwab explains, "With zero transaction costs, initial entitlements cannot be justified on efficiency grounds, and so should be awarded on the basis of need or desert" (1195). Stated slightly differently, the distributive corollary says that although legal entitlements do not affect efficiency, they will affect the distribution of resources,[10] at least in bargaining environments or "thin" markets (where bargaining over surplus takes place) (1178–79)). Therefore, this version of Coase's insight tells us that efficiency has no place in the evaluation of legal rules. An efficient allocation of resources will be obtained, no matter the distribution of entitlements. Therefore, recommending a certain policy or legal rule on the basis of efficiency is meaningless. However, because legal entitlements will still affect the distribution of income, this becomes the only basis of policy advice remaining for the economist.

On this interpretation, the Coase theorem threatens to upend the entire efficiency edifice. With zero transaction costs, the choice of legal rules is irrelevant for efficiency; only distribution matters. This is, of course, the complete opposite of the argument that the economic analysis of law should consider only efficiency and ignore distribution. The rub, of course, is that we do not live in a world of zero transaction costs. With positive transaction costs, we cannot be sure about the consequences of legal rules for either efficiency or distribution.

Yet, even with positive transaction costs, Calabresi (1991) argued that Coase's distributive corollary still could not be ignored. Transaction costs, he argues, no less than existing technology, define what is maximally feasible. "It follows that any given society is always or will immediately arrive at a Pareto optimal point *given* transaction costs" (Calabresi 1991, 1212). Hence, no moves from the status quo are possible without making someone worse off. We are always on the Pareto frontier; distributional issues are inevitable.

Furthermore, Calabresi finds Posner's ex ante consent theory unconvincing. First, we typically *do* know something about winners and losers, and they are often not the same group: "Once we are no longer ignorant, any number of differences may cause us to believe that losses or gains to *some* matter more than losses or gains to *others*" (1223, emphasis in original). Second, "no such [ex ante] social contract was

[10] The corollary has obvious similarities with both older and newer criticisms of both the tax-only view of redistributive policy as well as law and economics more generally. In terms of the older, see Hale (1923, 1943). In terms of the newer, see Kennedy (1991, 1998). Schwab (1989, 1195–96), citing the distributive corollary, concludes that it is "wrong" to rely on the Coase theorem in favor of any particular political position or "ethical view on wealth distribution."

ever made" (1225) and, if there was, who is to say that Kaldor-Hicks would be the standard rather than, say, Rawls's maximin principle?

The conclusion is that the effort to turn principles of efficiency – Pareto or Kaldor-Hicks – into neutral standards for evaluating legal rules did not succeed. It is impossible to ignore equity on these standards alone.

2.1.3 *Second Question: Can Legal Rules Redistribute Income?*

In the preceding debate, the issue was whether the distributive effects of legal rules should be considered in their economic evaluation. No one doubted that legal rules did *have* distributive effects. The embrace of the Kaldor-Hicks criterion – which makes efficiency judgments possible when some are made better off and others worse off – indicated as much. Yet some scholars argued that in important cases the law would *not* have distributive consequences. This exception arises when we attempt to redistribute between parties in a competitive market relationship. When parties are in a competitive exchange relationship, the cost of legal rules can be "passed on," frustrating the redistributive intent of the rule (see, e.g., Polinsky, 1989, 123–24; Schwab, 1989, 1179).[11] This led Polinsky (1989, 122) to conclude that "legal rules often cannot redistribute income in contractual disputes, whereas legal rules always can redistribute income in disputes between strangers."

For example, in an elegant analysis, Hamada (1976) demonstrated that in a competitive market with potentially defective products, liability rules (whether no liability, negligence, or strict liability) make no difference either to the allocation of resources (i.e., efficiency) or to the distribution of income.[12] Whatever the rule, the damages caused by a potential defect are part of either the implicit or the explicit price of the good. In the case of negligence, for instance, the buyer will be responsible for damages (as long as the seller has taken reasonable precautions).[13] This may make for a nominally low explicit price for the good, but the buyer understands that the implicit price, which includes the potential cost of harm, is higher. Conversely, under a strict-liability rule, the seller is liable for product accidents. But because

[11] The existence of a *competitive* market relationship is indeed important. Schwab (1989, 1179) writes: "In competitive markets, price equals cost and cost is the minimum possible cost; if the contract presumption would increase costs, the parties will write around it (assuming low transaction costs), and cost and price remain unchanged. But in markets where price can exceed cost, a favorable contract presumption may increase one's bargaining power. Even if the beneficiary waives the presumption, he may receive a greater share of the surplus for doing so."

[12] This conclusion depends on four assumptions: (1) homogeneous consumers with risk-neutral preferences, (2) perfect (i.e., actuarially fair) insurance markets, (3) perfect foresight about the possibility of damages, and (4) victims are always the purchaser of the product (Hamada 1976, 228, 229–30).

[13] It is typically argued that either negligence or strict liability leads sellers to choose a reasonable or efficient level of precaution. The existence of competitive markets encourages the same under a rule of caveat emptor. Otherwise, a seller who takes an inefficiently low level of precaution will have higher costs than their competitors.

the liability rule changes neither the probability nor the cost of accidents, the expected cost simply becomes part of the (higher) explicit price of the good. Thus, in competitive markets, liability rules make no difference to the distribution of income.[14]

Richard Craswell (1991) responded to the "passing on" objection in a remarkably lucid analysis.[15] The full discussion is saved for Chapter 5, but in a nutshell Craswell says that when, first, consumers are heterogeneous in their willingness to pay for the benefits of the legal rule and, second, when those most willing to pay for the legal rule are also the most willing to pay for the good or service itself, then legal rules can be distributive, even in competitive market conditions.

In sum, legal rules can indeed be redistributive. And not just in disputes between strangers, but within the competitive marketplace as well. Furthermore, Craswell's argument may be only one reason why it is possible for legal rules to redistribute in competitive markets. In Chapter 5, we will encounter other reasons for when and why legal rules can redistribute in market relationships.

2.1.4 *Third Question: Is the Income Tax Superior to Legal Rules in Redistributing Income?*

Fierce resistance thus confronted legal scholars who thought the economic analysis of legal rules should be concerned exclusively with efficiency rather than equity. First, the choice of standard for efficiency, Kaldor-Hicks, could not effectively allay concerns about distribution. Second, the distributive effects of legal rules could not be ignored – even in the case of competitive markets where it was believed that the choice of legal rules was irrelevant to efficiency or distribution.

But if efficiency-only scholars had to concede the first two points, they began to concentrate on the third. That is, even if distribution was a normatively valid concern and even if legal rules have distributive consequences, legal rules are less effective in redistributing income than the income tax. Prevailing on this point would be an answer to the first question as well. If the tax-and-transfer system alone should address society's distributive concerns, then the evaluation of legal rules could focus on efficiency and ignore equity. This in turn would also make the second question

[14] It is sometimes objected that the "bargaining around" argument "is essentially equivalent to the issue of tax incidence" (see, e.g., Blumkin and Margalioth 2005, 4–5). According to this objection, who pays for a tax (or cost of a legal rule) depends on the relative elasticities of supply and demand. Depending on these elasticities either the buyer or the seller may primarily bear the burden of the tax (or cost of the legal rule). Because of this, taxes have no inherent advantage over legal rules. Yet the analogy between the cost of legal rules and tax incidence is inaccurate. As we just showed with Hamada (1976), the cost of the legal rule is not always extrinsic to the product in the way a tax is. Craswell (1991) identifies another difference, a discussion that we pursue further in Chapter 5.

[15] Kennedy (1981) explores a very similar economic analysis.

moot: Even if legal rules can change the distribution of income, you would not want to use them to do so.

There are various supporting arguments for the claim that legal rules redistribute income less efficiently than taxes, but the literature has boiled them down to three. The first can be called the "imprecision" or "haphazardness" argument (Polinsky 1989, 124–27). Redistributive legal rules may favor tenants over landlords, employees over employers, and consumers over producers. But each of these groups only imperfectly overlaps with rich and poor, as defined by income. Some consumers, after all, are quite rich. Redistribution through legal rules therefore depends on "crude averages" (Cooter and Ulen 2016, 8). Income taxation, on the other hand, precisely targets the problem we wish to solve: income inequality.

A second counterargument can be labeled the "bargaining around" (Polinsky 1989, 122–23) or "passing on" objection, which we just reviewed in Section 2.1.3. The important point here is that although legal rules can redistribute, they are not guaranteed to do so effectively and may, in certain instances, pass on a significant amount of the costs to consumers. Broad-based income taxation avoids these kinds of highly specific price effects and is therefore a more effective redistributive tool (Cooter and Ulen 2016, 8).

2.1.5 *The Double-Distortion Argument*

There is also a third counterargument, perhaps the strongest argument for why the income tax is more efficient than legal rules in redistributing income. This is the "double distortion" argument by Kaplow and Shavell (1994).[16] Kaplow and Shavell are quite conscious of the challenge that lack of information about individual abilities poses for the second fundamental theorem of welfare economics. They write:

> [The debate between using legal rules and taxes] would be moot if the income tax system – understood here to include possible transfer payments to the poor – could be used freely to achieve any desired distribution of income. But income taxes and transfer payments distort incentives to work, limiting the degree to which it is socially desirable to employ the income tax system to redistribute income. (667)

They nevertheless are also adamantly clear in claiming, as manifested in their article's title, that "redistribution through legal rules offers no advantage over redistribution through the income tax system and typically is less efficient" (667).[17]

[16] An early version of the argument is found in Shavell (1981). The double-distortion argument has been defended in Kaplow and Shavell (2000b) and elaborated in Kaplow (1996). Kaplow and Shavell frequently cite Hylland and Zeckhauser (1979) in support of their argument.

[17] From other research, it is also clear that Kaplow and Shavell take inspiration from Musgrave's (1959) division of policy tasks between the efficiency and distribution branches of government, which translate welfare economics' two fundamental theorems into their institutional analogs (see, e.g., Kaplow, 1996, 521–23; Kaplow, 2008, 217; Kaplow, 2012).

Their claim follows from the "double distortion" caused by legal rules. Taxation causes a single distortion to labor-supply incentives, alternatively called the labor-leisure decision. Individuals choose both consumption and leisure to maximize their utility. Consumption is obtained with money, which is earned entirely (or mainly) by supplying one's time to the labor market and which comes at the expense of time spent on leisure. Individuals then choose how to allocate their time between labor and leisure in a way that maximizes their overall well-being. Whatever that choice is, an increase in income taxes takes a bite out of wages or salaries and makes labor (and consumption) relatively less worthwhile compared to leisure. Individuals therefore respond to an income-tax increase by "substituting" more leisure for work and reducing their supply of labor to the market. Because the choice of labor and leisure in the presence of the tax is not the one that individuals would choose in its absence, it is said to "distort" their labor-supply decisions, and reduce efficiency. Specific individuals may benefit from policies financed by the income tax, but in the aggregate taxation reduces the amount of wealth in society.[18]

Unlike taxation, a redistributive legal rule not only distorts labor supply, but it "also creates inefficiencies in the activities regulated by the legal rules" (668). On the one hand, if the legal rule redistributes income, then it will function exactly like the income tax and cause people to alter their labor-leisure decisions. On the other hand, legal rules also regulate other kinds of behavior: how cautious individuals behave in risky situations, whether they substantially perform under a contract, or whether a merger of two companies raises profits by creating real economic synergies or merely by enhancing their joint market power. So if, by hypothesis, distribution through legal rule comes at the expense of efficiency, it will also "distort" this second dimension of their behavior, which also leads to a loss of wealth and well-being. This leads to a simple conclusion. Because it is better to have a single rather than a double distortion, replacing the redistributive legal rule with an efficient, non-redistributive legal rule, coupled with a change in the tax schedule, makes everyone better off. A modification of the tax schedule can achieve the same income distribution as the redistributive legal rule, but replacing the redistributive rule with an efficient one will save on resources. In fact, those savings can be used to make the poor better off than they would be under the redistributive legal rule. Of course, there may be distortions

[18] In addition to the "substitution" effect identified in this paragraph, there is also an "income" effect. Because leisure is a normal good, the demand for which increases with income, an income-reducing tax also reduces the demand for leisure, which then causes an increase in labor supply. Thus, tax-induced reduction in income has two, opposing effects: The substitution effect reduces labor supply while the income effect increases it. Generally, the substitution effect is assumed to outweigh the income effect, particularly at very low wages where the value of consumption is much greater than that of leisure. But at very high wages the income effect is sometimes believed to dominate the substitution effect because leisure becomes more valuable once one's consumption goals are satisfied.

and costs other than these two, such as administrative burdens. But because a legal system has administrative costs as well, these are typically ignored in the analysis of the economics of taxation.

We can use Kaplow and Shavell's own example in order to make this claim more concrete. Suppose we have a tax regime where high-income individuals are taxed at a rate of 30 percent. Also suppose that we want to increase redistribution by using a legal rule that benefits the poor at the expense of the rich. In their example, such a legal rule is a damages rule in tort that depends on the wealth of the injurer: "damages [are] higher when the injurer is wealthy and lower when the injurer is poor" (669). This rule is inefficient because it induces the wealthy to take more care and the poor to take less care than is efficient. Assume this legal rule transfers an additional 1 percent of income from high earners to low earners. High-income individuals therefore pay 30 percent of each additional dollar to the tax system and 1 percent to the legal system (so to speak).

Compare this regime to one with an efficient, non-redistributive legal rule. Their choice is strict liability, where an injurer, rich or poor, must pay for all harm caused. This rule is efficient because it internalizes an externality: The social costs caused by harm-inducing activities are now made private when individuals must pay for those harms. Suppose also that in this second regime we raise the tax rate for high earners to 31 percent.

Which regime should we choose? In terms of labor-supply incentives, the two are identical. Thirty-one percent of a high earner's income goes to the tax authorities with the efficient legal rule, and the same percentage is split between the tax and legal systems with the inefficient, redistributive legal rule. What a high earner gets to keep at the end of the day is the same, so the choice of rules makes no difference for labor supply.

However, the choice of behavior regulated by the legal rule will be different. With the income-dependent damages rule, the rich spend too many resources on precaution and the poor too little. In the aggregate, resources are therefore saved with the efficient legal rule and these savings can be used to improve everyone's welfare (making it a Pareto improvement) by increasing transfers to the poor or lowering everyone's taxes. As Kaplow and Shavell (1994) explain, "[B]ecause redistribution is accomplished in the presence of an efficient legal rule, resources would, by definition, be saved. With these savings, all individuals could be made better off (for example, by reducing taxes and increasing payments to the poor)" (668).

Thus, according to Kaplow and Shavell, the fact that legal rules *can* redistribute income and improve the welfare of the poor is not a sufficient reason for using the law for those objectives. This is because the tax system is more efficient at redistributing income than the legal system: Everyone – including the poor – could be made better off by redistributing exclusively through the tax system. This, in turn, becomes an argument for why the economic analysis of legal rules should be concerned primarily with efficiency.

2.2 CRITICISMS OF THE DOUBLE-DISTORTION ARGUMENT

Several important and extremely insightful critiques have been made of the double-distortion argument. Proponents of the double-distortion argument, however, tend to shrug them off as mere "qualifications" to the basic, presumably more general, claim that the income tax redistributes income more efficiently than do legal rules. This section will review some of these criticisms, which will allow us to better situate this book's contribution to the debate.

For example, Sanchirico (2000, 2001) contends that Kaplow and Shavell do not pay enough attention to *heterogeneity* across individuals. Kaplow and Shavell accept that people differ in their "abilities," or income-earning potential, which gives rise to income inequality in the first place. But they also assume the individuals are homogeneous when it comes to their risk-taking and precautionary behaviors. Using their own tort example, Sanchirico instead asks what happens when people differ not just in their income-earning abilities but their precautionary abilities as well. When you do, contrary to Kaplow and Shavell, the damage rule may well want to adjust for the wealth of the injurer. Thus, legal rules should be informed by equity, not just efficiency.[19]

As another example, Jolls (1998) introduces insights from behavioral economics. Her key application is that people will treat certain events (like taxes) differently than uncertain events (like accidents). According to Jolls (1998), "People will tend to underestimate the probability that they will be hit with liability under a redistributive legal rule; therefore, their perceived cost of the rule will be lower" (1662). For example, suppose a high-income person faces a tax bill of \$10,000. Suppose they also face a 0.02 probability of causing an accident that incurs a tort liability of \$500,000. In expected terms, these two costs are the same ($.02 \times \$500,000 = \$10,000$). However, because the accident is uncertain, their perceived tort liability is lower than their tax liability. Accordingly, the tort damages will distort their work incentives less than the taxes. This will make the damages rule in tort a better tool for redistribution than taxes.

More recently, Liscow (2014) has helped revive the debate over the double-distortion argument. Liscow questions whether redistributive rules will always distort behavior more than taxes. In contrast to Kaplow and Shavell, who compare an (efficient) strict-liability rule with an (inefficient) wealth-dependent damages rule, Liscow instead compares strict liability with the negligence rule. His point is that both rules are equally efficient with respect to the activities they regulate. Both strict liability and the negligence rule create incentives to make efficient risk-taking and precautionary decisions. But each rule has distinctly different distributive implications. Strict liability requires defendants to pay for all harm caused, while

[19] Avraham, Fortus, and Logue (2003) also make the heterogeneity critique. The debate between Sanchirico (2000, 2001) and Kaplow and Shavell (2001b) is explored in more detail in Chapter 4.

negligence only requires defendants to pay damages if their behavior was negligent. Wealth is redistributed when accidents happen under strict liability, but not under the negligence rule, which (ideally) encourages individuals to not act negligently. (Accidents still happen under either rule, just an efficient number of accidents.) Thus, Liscow calls strict liability a "zero-distortion legal rule" that allows redistribution to take place without any distortion in the activities regulated by the legal rules, which contradicts Kaplow and Shavell's claim.

When Kaplow and Shavell compare redistributive legal rules to a tax system, the "distribution neutral" tax alternative is (sometimes only implicitly) hypothetical. Indeed, what guarantee do we have that, if an efficient but inequitable legal rule is chosen over an inefficient but equitable one, the tax system will adjust in order to compensate for the greater inequality? In another more recent contribution, Fennell and McAdams (2016) challenge what they describe as Kaplow and Shavell's "distributive-invariance" hypothesis.[20] This hypothesis states that the overall level of redistribution in society is fixed – unique – such that if a court, for example, were to adopt a redistributive legal rule, the legislature (reflecting the current political equilibrium) would offset the distributive change through a tax adjustment.[21] As this hypothesis effectively means that the amount of redistribution in society is fixed, "then it is obvious that one should want to accomplish that redistribution in the most efficient way" (1070). Conversely, if redistribution is not fixed and significant political costs prevent the introduction of a superior tax-and-transfer scheme, implementing redistribution through legal rules can increase welfare. While they successfully rebut the distributive-invariance hypothesis, to my mind (see, Dimick 2019, 571–73) the real issue is what Fennell and McAdams call "political actions cost," "the large and variable costs associated with the political impediments that must be surmounted to achieve welfare-maximizing distributive results" (Fennell and McAdams 2016, 1052–53).[22] If modifying the tax code requires greater political action costs than the redistributive, but admittedly inefficient, legal rule, then the legal rule may still be the more sensible and (overall) efficient choice.

One other contribution ought to be mentioned. The double-distortion argument applies to tax policy itself. Policymakers have a variety of tax instruments to choose

[20] Markovits (2004) also recognizes and criticizes the distributive-invariance hypothesis.

[21] Fennell and McAdams explicitly acknowledge that they do not attribute to Kaplow and Shavell "one single, clearly stated proposition but rather a mostly unacknowledged premise revealed in scattered remarks" (Fennell and McAdams 2016, 1072).

[22] There are obviously a large number of potential forms and amounts of political action costs. Fennell and McAdams describe *search and opportunity-spotting* costs, the costs that proponents of distributive changes must incur to identify them, whether those shifts involve new changes or offsets of undesired changes; *decision-influencing* costs, the costs sustained to bring the proposed distributive change to the attention of a relevant decisionmaking body and convince the decisionmaker to undertake it; and *execution, enforcement, and maintenance* costs, which are those that are required to actually undertake the distributive change and ensure that the efforts are not sidelined or undone by others (Fennell and McAdams 2016, 1082–83).

from: consumption taxes (which include value-added taxes, sales taxes, or excise taxes), wealth taxes, or income taxes (which could be levied on labor income, capital income, or both). One version of the double-distortion argument says that only taxes on labor (or, earned) income should be used. The idea, in brief, is that levying different tax rates on different consumption goods – for example one rate for goods that only the wealthy buy (like a special tax on yachts) another for goods everyone buys (like groceries) – distorts consumption decisions *in addition to* labor-supply decisions. Different tax rates for different goods distort one's consumption choices, while consumption taxes in general increase the overall cost of consumption, which has the same effect as a tax on labor income.[23] Hence, differential consumption taxes create a double distortion, which can be avoided by taxing only earned income.[24] Gamage (2014, 2015) contests this prescription by identifying differences between various kinds of tax inefficiencies (or "distortions"). When analyzing income taxes, most economists focus on a single distortion: the trade-off between labor and leisure. But as Gamage points out, the labor-leisure distortion is hardly the only distortion caused by income taxation. In fact, more important is what Gamage calls "tax gaming" – tax avoidance and tax evasion. Tax gaming is inefficient because it wastes resources on avoiding or evading taxes that could be allocated to more productive uses. Indeed, especially for "high-income taxpayers, for whom distributional considerations are particularly relevant" tax gaming is of primary, and the labor-leisure distortion only of secondary, importance (Gamage 2014, 5). Gamage then shows that tax gaming affects the choice of tax instruments. Tax gaming distortions are "quite idiosyncratic and contingent" (4). Indeed, Gamage argues that "taxpayers' incentives to engage in tax gaming … are a direct function of only the tax rates of the labor income tax. … [E]xcise tax rates should have only secondary effects on incentives to engage in [tax gaming]" (8–9). Therefore, it may indeed be optimal to impose a special yacht tax as mentioned previously. The luxury tax may distort both labor-supply and consumption decisions, but it can also induce savings by lowering the income tax and the tax gaming associated with it.[25]

[23] Thus, differential commodity taxation is inefficient and uniform commodity taxation is useless in the presence of an optimal income tax. This result was first demonstrated in a famous paper by Atkinson and Stiglitz (1976). On similar assumptions, Kaplow (2006) demonstrated that this result holds under any income tax schedule, not just the optimal one. Not surprisingly, legal scholars have contested this application of the double-distortion argument as well. One line follows closely Sanchirico's heterogeneity critique (see, e.g., Saez 2002b; Sanchirico 2010, 2011).

[24] The argument also applies to taxes on capital income. Because a tax on capital income is seen as a tax on savings, and because savings is seen as merely deferred consumption, taxes on capital distort a person's consumption choices across time, an additional distortion on top of the labor-supply distortion.

[25] This is underscored by Gamage's focus on the "marginal cost of public funds." Because the economic costs of a tax instrument increases exponentially in the tax rate, using many tax instruments at relatively moderate rates will be better than one, high rate on income (Gamage 2014, 10–11, 20). This is called the "tax-smoothing" principle (Gamage 2015, 358).

2.3 A SNEAK PEEK OF THE BOOK'S ARGUMENTS

All of these contributions offer enormously important insights into the debate about the comparative wisdom of using taxes and legal rules to redistribute income. Some of them, frankly, are devastating to Kaplow and Shavell's double-distortion thesis. For example, Sanchirico's (2001, 1017) observation that the "double-distortion argument employs a form of 'distortion counting' that was discredited long ago" should arguably have ended the entire debate.[26] As scholars of public economics well recognize, "One lesson that we have learnt from second-best welfare economics is that one cannot evaluate tax systems simply by comparing the *number* of distortions involved: one has to consider the magnitude of the various effects and their interaction … ." (Atkinson and Stiglitz 2015, 471). That insight holds even more strongly for legal and policy analysis generally because of the range of behaviors regulated and the forms of distribution entailed that are not strictly income. Nevertheless, the double-distortion argument lumbers on and Kaplow and Shavell have never expressly backed away from it. Why is this?

As argued in the introduction, one reason the double-distortion argument retains a privileged position is because of the overly abstract level at which the debate has been conducted. By this I mean that no one within the debate has given serious attention to *actual* legal rules, proposed and adopted in policy, for mitigating income inequality. Most of the double-distortion debate has been conducted at a very general level, using arbitrary legal rules as an illustrative example of more universal claims. Most of the time, tort law is used as the example, which is true for Jolls (1998), Liscow (2014), and Sanchirico (2001), as well as for Kaplow and Shavell's (1994) original contribution. Yet none of those interlocutors have evidenced any fervent commitment to actually using tort law to redistribute income. And even though Fennell and McAdams (2016) eschew the tort analysis and introduce many illustrative examples, they too remain on a very abstract level of analysis, concerned mainly with Kaplow and Shavell's "distributive-invariance" hypothesis and the "political action costs" required for *any* redistributive intervention, whether through taxes or legal rules. When thinking more practically about candidates for legal redistribution, what comes to mind are areas of law such as the minimum wage or collective bargaining legislation, intellectual property, antitrust, rent control, or warranties of habitability. But the double-distortion debate rarely, if ever, addresses any of these more specific areas of the law.[27]

[26] "Distortion counting" has been discredited because "distortions may well counteract one another," (Sanchirico 2001, 1009) rather than simply add up as in Kaplow and Shavell's tort example. Sanchirico bases this conclusion on the well-known "theory of the second best," summarized in Lipsey and Lancaster (1956). See the book's appendix for further discussion.

[27] There are of course exceptions to this statement. We have already encountered the early debate on housing regulation – which nevertheless precedes the double-distortion debate. And, within economics, there is a modest literature on the redistributive analysis of minimum-wage legislation, which is addressed in Chapter 6. There is also a great deal of *efficiency* analysis of these areas of law within both economics and the legal literature. But precisely because of this

There are at least a couple of reasons why staying at an overly abstract level of analysis is problematic. One reason is that, given that more general orientation, demonstrated exceptions to the double-distortion argument remain exactly that: exceptions to an otherwise general rule. As exceptions, they do little to dislodge the more general injunction. Another problem with an overly abstract level of analysis is that it obscures precisely those *particular* features of the behaviors regulated by legal rules in more concrete domains that reveal shortcomings of double-distortion thinking. Among the contributions reviewed in Section 2.2, the sole exception to the rarefied mode of analysis is Gamage's work on tax law. And it is precisely Gamage's more concrete intervention that reveals the "quite idiosyncratic and contingent" (Gamage 2014, 4) features of tax law – in his case, "tax gaming" – that make it both plausible and appropriate to depart from the injunctions handed down by more abstract double-distortion reasoning. Had more engagements with the double-distortion argument focused, like Gamage, on concrete legal domains, rather than remaining at a general level with tort law as a kind of toy example, I suspect that more such exceptions would have been discovered. For both of these reasons, the sense persists that the concrete possibilities for legal, as opposed to income tax, redistribution are exceptional.

The approach of this book is therefore to take the opposite tack, and dive below the accustomed level of analysis, in order to interrogate the double-distortion argument in more specific settings. This book will start with the accepted "common law" areas of property, torts, and contract, and emphasize the redistributive particularities in these areas that have been overlooked. Furthermore, the book will address those areas of law that are more frequently proposed, in "the real world," so to speak, for addressing income inequality: employment law, labor law, housing regulation, antitrust, and intellectual property.[28] This makes for a unique, more inductive approach. According to my argument, any claim that one should *always* use taxes or *always* use legal rules is wrong. But for precisely that reason, the claim that legal rules should be considered on an equal basis in any situation requires demonstrating that in *enough* specific cases, *both* the a priori superiority of taxes fails *and* the potential for legal rules is compelling. The goal will be to show that the number of exceptions to the double-distortion argument is large enough to swallow the general rule.

Another implication of rejecting a priori reasoning – whether in favor or against using legal redistribution – is that, ultimately, the choice of law or tax is an empirical matter that should be made on a case-by-case basis. Without a "general theory" of

literature's orientation towards wealth maximization, the redistributive implications, *especially in explicit comparison to the tax system*, have been ignored.

[28] Economists often construe some of these areas as concerned mainly with market failure and efficiency, rather than redistribution. Economists think of antitrust, for example, as about regulating market power, a market failure which can lead to inefficiency. But this stance belies a long tradition of thinking about antitrust in distributive terms, as well as common-sense concerns about the distributive consequences of market power.

legal redistribution to answer the question a priori, we are compelled to investigate the effects of particular legal rules and their specific economic environments. Theory can of course aid in, and even drive, this investigation, but the models considered must be purpose-built, so to speak, for the policy environment that is under consideration. As it turns out, this kind of "applied theory" constitutes the main approach of the book, which is the theoretical analysis of concrete legal and economic environments across a range of policy domains. The objective of this program is to show how the particular circumstances of each area reveal the *possibility*, if not the necessity, that legal rules can redistribute income more efficiently than the tax system. The contrast between a priori and a posteriori I am using can be likened to Judge Calabresi's (2016, 2–5) distinction between "Economic Analysis of Law" and "Law and Economics."

The remaining subsections of this chapter will give a glimpse of the variety of particular and idiosyncratic features of specific areas of law that bolster the case for redistributive legal rules.

2.3.1 *Distributing through Legal Entitlements*

As we noted previously (in Section 2.1.1), Schwab (1989) identified what he called the "distributive corollary" of the Coase (1960) theorem. That corollary says that, in a world with no transaction costs, the initial allocation of entitlements makes no difference for efficiency; therefore, entitlements should be allocated on grounds of distribution (or desert). This suggests a potentially non-distortionary, Pareto optimal form of income redistribution. This discussion arose before the appearance of the double-distortion argument, so its implications – in a "horse race" between taxation and legal entitlements – have never been fully explored (but see Cooter and Ulen 2016, 106–08). Sometimes, the possibility of exploiting this corollary is summarily dismissed on the grounds that transaction costs are not zero.[29] But this objection is too hasty. That is because the transaction costs that exist between potential bargainers may be very different than those facing the tax authorities (e.g., information asymmetries). For example, neighbors may have more relevant information about each other than the Internal Revenue Service has about either of them, which suggests the potential for using property rules to redistribute income more efficiently than the income tax system.

More generally, we know that fractional, or divided, legal entitlements can facilitate Coasean trade (Ayres and Talley 1995) and efficient bargaining (Segal and Whinston 2014) even in the presence of transaction costs. That insight opens the possibility that such entitlements can also embrace an equity concern. If individuals reveal information in legal settings about their preferences that are not revealed in

[29] See, e.g., Fennell and McAdams (2016, 1052 n.2): "If transaction costs were zero, legal rules could be selected based exclusively on distributive concerns – a point Stewart Schwab has dubbed 'The Distributive Corollary of the Coase Theorem'."

their income-earning or labor-supply decisions, courts can adjust damages to favor the poor over the rich. Such adjustments actually reduce labor-supply distortions caused by the income tax system, making these equity-informed legal rules more redistributively efficient than taxes. These kinds of questions are explored in Chapter 3, on property.

2.3.2 *Double, or Offsetting, Distortions?*

The double-distortion argument rests on the assumption that both distortions will be compounding, such that the total distortion is larger than either one alone. But why should this be so? As already pointed out, that sort of reasoning rests on an illegitimate form of "distortion counting" (Sanchirico 2001, 1009, 1017). But that objection is not just a theoretical possibility. In fact, it is easy to think of examples where, even if the legal rules distort incentives, the second – or double – distortion *offsets* rather than compounds the first.

Consider, for example, the minimum wage. A minimum wage redistributes income (from firms to workers) and distorts labor incentives, just as an income tax would. The wage contract also regulates other behaviors: how much effort a worker provides, how much the employer monitors the workers' efforts, whether a worker decides to quit, and so forth. A profit-maximizing employer will choose wages so that marginal benefits (e.g., in worker effort, level of supervision, or turnover) equal the marginal wage cost. If so, private wage-setting decisions will lead to socially efficient outcomes and a minimum wage will be inefficient. Does that mean it is inferior to income taxes? Not necessarily. An increase in the minimum wage will increase worker effort, lower the costs of supervision, or reduce turnover, *offsetting* the cost of the wage increase. In this case, a minimum wage would be less inefficient than simply transferring a dollar of taxes from employers to employees. This case is more fully made in Chapter 6, on labor and employment law. Chapter 9, on housing regulation, also shows how the offsetting effects of legal rules can make them more redistributively efficient than taxes.

2.3.3 *Two, Three … Many Distortions*

Similarly, legal rules may have more than two distortions, and it is not obvious, a priori, what their net effect will be when they are "added" up. Consider the effects legal rules might have in the areas of antitrust or intellectual property law. For example, suppose we reduce the level of patent protection by reducing the length of a patent or its scope of infringement. The consequence will be two distortions. First, lowering patent protection will (tend to) shift surplus from producers to consumers and, in the aggregate, lower income inequality, which will reduce labor supply just like a distribution-equivalent increase in income taxes would. Second, there will also be lower incentives to innovate and create new patentable products and techniques. Because both of these distortions come at the cost of efficiency, it would seem that it would be better to redistribute through income taxes rather than through intellectual property law.

But there is at least a third distortion as well: The patent has inefficient, anticompetitive effects by virtue of the temporary monopoly it confers. When this distortion is included with the other two, it is not obvious that patent rules should be chosen on the basis of efficiency alone. As in Williamson's (1968) classic contribution, "economies" from a merger should be traded off against their anticompetitive effects, which may very well swamp any positive labor supply or investment effects. Suppose additional patent protection will lead to greater innovation and investment but that these wealth gains, in addition to increasing income inequality, are *almost* exactly offset by their anticompetitive effects. Since there is a slight efficiency gain, the prescription to maximize wealth would endorse the greater patent protection. But an equitable approach would disagree whenever the costs of redistribution required to counteract the rise in inequality (under the optimal tax schedule) exceed the small efficiency gain.

The implications of considering "triple" distortions are more fully explored in Chapters 7 and 8, on antitrust law and intellectual property, respectively.

2.3.4 *Imperfect Competition and Search Frictions*

Directly related to the previous scenario is the nature of the competitive environment. Most of the double-distortion literature assumes perfect competition.[30] In the context of imperfect competition, the problematic assumption with double-distortion reasoning is that the labor-supply effects caused by market imperfections are equivalent to the effects of the income tax. If this were true, we could simply offset or reproduce, dollar for dollar, the effects of the competition policy with a tax policy that leaves the distribution of income unchanged, compared to the situation before implementing the policy. Unfortunately, this is often not, and may be rarely, true. Normally, increases in income lead to an increase in labor supply, all else being equal. But in a monopolistic setting, greater market concentration (for example), can lead to an increase in income *but* a decrease in "labor supply" (or, the supply of capital, or the supply of firms). This makes it impossible to use distribution-neutral income tax adjustments, and obviates the simple double-distortion argument.

Some forms of price discrimination, for example, are characterized by surplus transfers from some (poor) buyers to (rich) sellers, perhaps because poorer buyers

[30] Once we introduce market power, and more generally, market failure, the temptation is to divide the policy issue into efficiency and distributive problems, using first-best, or wealth maximizing, principles to address the market failure and the income tax to address the distributional concerns. For an example of this in the area of competition policy or antitrust, see Kaplow (2012) and Kaplow (2021).

lack adequate information or mobility (Salop and Stiglitz 1977; Katz 1984).[31] In an environment of monopolistic competition,[32] the higher profits induced by price discrimination will attract the entry of other firms. On the other hand, the anti-competitive practice itself may restrict total output. The overall efficiency effects are ambiguous, which makes it possible for legal rules to redistribute more efficiently than taxes. For example, one possible function of the unconscionability doctrine is to prohibit forms of price discrimination that disadvantage poor consumers (Klock 2002). Even where price discrimination is more efficient than single pricing, the unconscionability doctrine can redistribute more efficiently than taxes.

Search frictions also make it difficult for the income tax to simply offset the labor-supply effects of otherwise efficient policies. Such markets are "thin" and feature substantial rents and rent sharing. Explicit negotiation and contracting arise, or are potentially available, in order to divide these rents. These are markets for which contract law is particularly germane; in thick markets, market participants are price takers and negotiation over rents is not possible. In such environments, the distributive effects not only influence labor supply but how those rents are divided and how information is shared. Once again, it is not at all obvious that the income tax can simply and identically replicate the labor-supply effects of legal rules and thereby cleanly negate the total distributive consequences in such environments.

These implications of forms of imperfect competition are explored in Chapter 5, on contracts.

2.3.5 *More Questions about Labor Supply*

As just mentioned, a particularly crucial assumption for the double-distortion argument is the symmetry or identity between the labor-supply effects of legal rules and those of distribution-equivalent changes in the tax schedule – the "first" distortion in the double-distortion hypothesis. The assumption that each labor-supply effect is equal guarantees that any other cost the legal rule adds will make it less efficient than taxes. But for that to work, Kaplow has to adopt special assumptions about the "weak separability" between consumption and leisure – an assumption that sounds merely technical but is far from innocuous.[33] Others have

[31] Traditionally, perfect price discrimination has been understood as pure transfers from consumers to producers, without sacrifices to efficiency. In fact, price discrimination can reduce efficiency in fairly general settings (Schmalensee 1981; Varian 1985). In any case, prohibiting price discrimination where it is efficient would appear to be a zero-distortion redistribution.

[32] As distinguished from pure monopoly, where there is only one seller, monopolistic competition is characterized by price-making behavior but with free-entry of firms (Dixit and Stiglitz 1977).

[33] According to Kaplow (2008, 127), weak separability of consumption and leisure "implies that, for a given level of after-income-tax income, individuals will allocate their disposable income among commodities in the same manner regardless of the level of labor effort required to generate that level of income." Kaplow adopts this assumption explicitly in, for example, Kaplow (2004, 2008, 2021).

highlighted the untenable weight this assumption bears, so I do not address it in this book.[34]

Instead, I concentrate on another assumption Kaplow employs to ensure that the distributive effects of taxes and legal rules have identical effects for labor supply. This important case is when income comes from different sources: labor and capital. Kaplow (2021) again adopts simplifying assumptions in order to ensure identical labor-supply effects, namely, the assumptions that all capital income is savings, and not just savings, but merely deferred consumption. Thus capital income just becomes labor income consumed at a later point in time. But in general it would be heroic to believe that identical dollar changes in capital and labor income will have identical labor-supply effects. Labor supply, after all, is primarily a function of labor income, not capital income. For instance, a standard result in labor-supply theory and research is that increases in non-labor income – say, inherited wealth – will reduce labor supply while an income-equivalent increase in labor income will increase labor supply. Changes in capital and labor income therefore tend to have *opposite*, not identical, effects on labor supply.

When less herculean assumptions about labor supply are employed, legal rules will redistribute more efficiently than taxes. For example, a merger between two large companies may raise total surplus but do so by increasing producer surplus (profits) more than it reduces consumer surplus (by raising prices and lowering the purchasing power of wages and salaries). This will translate into an increase in capital income (to the rich) and a loss of labor income to everyone else. That, in turn, will increase income inequality while *lowering* overall labor supply. For example, those earning income from capital can retire early while everyone else also reduces labor supply because the returns to labor income have diminished. But this reduction in labor supply contradicts the double-distortion argument. According to that argument, an increase in inequality should *raise* labor supply because this is equivalent to a reduction in marginal tax rates. Thus, attempts to allow the efficient but inequality-raising merger to proceed, while correcting it with an increase in marginal tax rates, will be inefficient, because they will only further distort labor supply. In that case, it may be more redistributively efficient to block the merger. This reasoning is explored particularly in Chapter 7, on antitrust.

2.3.6 *Uncertainty and Ex Post Inequality*

Any degree of income uncertainty significantly influences the optimal tax problem. Compared to the expected, or ex ante, distribution of income, uncertainty increases

[34] For a particularly intensive examination, see Sanchirico (2010, 940–54). Among a newer generation of economists, the assumption appears to have little credibility. Piketty and Saez (2012, 1 n.1) regard the weak "separability of preferences" as an "unplausibly [*sic*] strong" assumption that "has little relevance for practical policy discussions."

actual, or ex post inequality, which may have significant implications for the optimal tax schedule and in crucial cases raise the costs of income taxation. Legal rules can shift the distribution of uncertainty in ways that reduce ex post inequality, and by so doing reduce the costs of redistributive taxation.[35]

Consider the choice of liability rules – strict liability or negligence – for some accident risk where injurers are richer than average. To fix ideas, one might consider a products liability scenario, with manufacturers richer than the average consumer. As we noted above, Hamada (1976) demonstrated that in a competitive market, the choice of product liability rules makes no difference to either the distribution of income or the allocation of resources. But this conclusion applies only to expected (ex ante) inequality (229–30). As long as the incidence of harm is uncertain (i.e., probabilistic), some individuals will be injured (and lose income) and others will not, which makes actual, ex post inequality higher than ex ante inequality. As a result, a strict liability rule will shift damages and uncertainty to the manufacturers, concentrating the uncertainty onto a smaller and wealthier subset of the population; doing so will lower ex post inequality. And since ex post inequality is lower, the costs of redistribution will be lower. Thus, strict liability can be the optimal (welfare-maximizing) legal rule, even if negligence is the efficient (wealth-maximizing) rule, as long as the savings in the costs of redistribution are large enough.[36] This argument is unpacked and presented in Chapter 4, on tort law.

2.4 CONCLUSION

It would be tempting at this point to generalize and identify two overall reasons for why the double-distortion argument fails in general. The first reason is the problem of "distortion counting" mentioned previously by Sanchirico (2001) and Atkinson and Stiglitz (2015): Distortions do not move in the same direction but rather can be offsetting rather than compounding. The second is that labor-supply effects of taxes and legal rules are not always identical. Each of the more specific mechanisms introduced in subsections 2.3.1 through 2.3.6 can be categorized into one of those two broader labels.

35 For papers that explore, in a somewhat different framework, the role of uncertainty in the optimal tax problem, see Eaton and Rosen (1980), Varian (1980), and Mirrlees (1990). Adler and Sanchirico (2006) explore the importance of uncertainty for the choice of the policy-maker's social welfare function. They do not draw out the implications for the debate about using legal rules to redistribute income.

36 There are two potential objections to this argument. One argument is that an ex post social welfare function will violate the Pareto principle (Kaplow, 1995; Kaplow, 2008, 374–75). However, Adler and Sanchirico (2006) make a case that giving up Pareto superiority for ex post welfare maximization is a sacrifice worth making. The second objection would point out that perfect (public or private) insurance would eliminate the difference between ex ante and ex post inequality. Yet insurance (public or private) is rarely perfect in the real world (Liscow 2014, 2505–06).

However, while that reduction may help clarify the discussion, it already takes us away from the main point I want to make. This point is that these "qualifications" can only be identified by exploring the effects of legal rules in relatively more concrete legal settings. Once that is done, it becomes easy to identify these contradictions to the double-distortion argument. The remainder of the book does exactly this.

PART II

The Common Law

3

Property

The 2005 case *Kelo v. City of New London*,[1] labeled "one of the most controversial decisions in modern Supreme Court history" (Somin 2016, 11) and a "truly horrible … judicial thunderbolt" (Epstein 2015), extended the government's takings power to private economic development projects. At the time of the decision in 2005, over 80 percent of Americans disapproved and voices across the political spectrum denounced it, including conservative talk-show host Rush Limbaugh, anti-corporate activist and presidential candidate Ralph Nader, and the NAACP (Somin 2016, 107, 137). Justice Sandra Day O'Connor expressed similar sentiment in her dissent in *Kelo*, "[T]he fallout from this decision will not be random. The beneficiaries are likely to be those citizens with disproportionate influence and power in the political process, including large corporations and development firms. As for the victims, the government now has license to transfer property from those with fewer resources to those with more."[2] In a separate dissent, Justice Clarence Thomas noted how "suspiciously agreeable to the Pfizer Corporation"[3] the city's arrangement seemed to be and pointed out the history of similar urban-renewal projects as "negro removal."[4]

Evidence from the intervening years suggests that *Kelo* has ineed emboldened local governments to displace more citizens for the purpose of economic development, transferring property from the poor to the wealthy. Attorney Dana Berliner (2006) writes that cities "know that now they rarely need to file condemnation actions because owners largely give in rather than fight what they believe, after *Kelo*, to be a hopeless battle" (2–3).

[1] 545 U.S. 469 (2005).
[2] Kelo v. City of New London, 545 U.S. 469, 505 (O'Connor, J., dissenting).
[3] *Id.* at 506 (Thomas, J., dissenting).
[4] *Id.* at 522. (Thomas, J., dissenting).

The Fifth Amendment Takings Clause prohibits "private property be taken for public use, without just compensation."[5] "Public use" had historically been interpreted to mean use for government-provided goods, such as infrastructure, schools, and military bases.[6] The 1954 Supreme Court decision *Berman v. Parker* redefined "public use," establishing the more expansive "public purpose" test,[7] in order to uphold urban renewal programs of federal, state and local government.[8] In the first few decades of the "public purpose" test, the Supreme Court authorized government-forced private to private transfers for housing redevelopment[9] and land redistribution.[10] The reason *Kelo* alarmed so many was that the decision further expanded "public purpose" to legalize government takings for private economic development projects. Justice O'Connor, who had written the majority opinion authorizing eminent domain to redistribute land in the 1984 decision *Hawaii Housing Authority v. Midkiff*, dissented in *Kelo*, noting how tenuous the relationship between "public purpose" and "public use" had become.[11] The "despotic power" that the Supreme Court once excoriated[12] became a sanctioned economic development tool for the government and developers.

Writing for the *Kelo* majority, Justice Stevens explained, "There is ... no principled way of distinguishing economic development from the other public purposes that we

5 U.S. CONST. amend. V, cl. 4. The Fourteenth Amendment Due Process Clause applies the Takings Clause to state and local governments. *See Chicago, B. & Q.R. Co. v. City of Chicago*, 166 U.S. 226 (1897).

6 *See, e.g.*, Clark v. Nash, 198 U.S. 361, 369 (1905) ("[W]e do not ... approv[e] of the broad proposition that private property may be taken in all cases where the taking may promote the public interest and tend to develop the natural resources of the State"); United States v. Gettysburg Elec. R. Co., 160 U.S. 668, 680 (1896) ("[W]here the land is taken by the government itself, there is not much ground to fear any abuse of the power. The responsibility of congress to the people will generally, if not always, result in a most conservative exercise of the right. It is quite a different view of the question which courts will take when this power is delegated to a private corporation").

7 "Public purpose" appeared in decisions as early as the late nineteenth century. However, in those cases the term was used to distinguish the concept of "public use" that would allow the public to use the land from one in which the government could take the land to provide for the public. *See, e.g.*, Fallbrook Irrigation Dist. v. Bradley, 164 U.S. 112, 113 (1896) ("The irrigation of really arid lands is a public purpose, and the water thus used is put to a public use, and the statutes providing for such irrigation are valid exercises of legislative power").

8 Berman v. Parker, 348 U.S. 26 (1954).

9 *Id.* (Transferring blighted properties to private developers for housing redevelopment in Washington D.C.).

10 Hawaii Housing Authority v. Midkiff, 467 U.S. 229 (1984) (Taking land held in trust by descendants of the Hawaiian monarchy and selling to private landowners).

11 *Kelo*, 545 U.S. at 501 (O'Connor, J., dissenting) ("[T]he Court today significantly expands the meaning of public use. It holds that the sovereign may take private property currently put to ordinary private use, and give it over for new, ordinary private use, so long as the new use is predicted to generate some secondary benefit for the public – such as increased tax revenue, more jobs, maybe even esthetic [*sic*] pleasure").

12 Vanhorne's Lessee v. Dorrance, 2 U.S. 304, 310–11 (1795).

have recognized"[13] and "there is no basis for exempting economic development from our traditionally broad understanding of public purpose."[14] Some economists would disagree, pointing to economic theory's distinction between public versus private goods.[15] Because private markets do not appropriately price public goods, government intervention is justified. In the case of private goods, however, governments should refrain from providing private goods, and leave them to the market to work its putative magic. Therefore, when the government condemns land and turns it over to private companies, one can argue that it is not only unconstitutional, but inefficient as well.

The outcomes of the economic-development takings in *Kelo* and state court decisions such as *Poletown*[16] show just how unfortunate the results can be. As one reporter noted of the New London economic-development project eight years after the *Kelo* decision,

> Weeds, glass, bricks, pieces of pipe and shingle splinters have replaced the knot of aging homes at the site of the nation's most notorious eminent domain project. There are a few signs of life: Feral cats glare at visitors from a miniature jungle of Queen Anne's lace, thistle and goldenrod. Gulls swoop between the lot's towering trees and the adjacent sewage treatment plant. But what of the promised building boom that was supposed to come wrapped and ribboned with up to 3,169 new jobs and $1.2 million a year in tax revenues? They are noticeably missing. (Nelson 2009)

Instead of a big shiny new project with Pfizer as a lead tenant in a $350 million research facility and a $60 million Coast Guard museum, nothing happened, besides the condemnation and demolition of people's homes. The 2008 financial crisis doomed the project. As John Brooks, executive director of the New London Development Corp. said, "we are victims of the economic cycle, and there is nothing we can do about that" (Nelson 2009).

This inefficiency argument has been the stock-in-trade for many condemnations for *Kelo*'s defense of economic development takings. And, to be sure, the argument that economic-development takings will tend to be inefficient is convincing. But should we presume that *every* taking will be inefficient? When evaluating the redistributive efficiency of legal rules – or in the case of takings, government action and policy more generally – a more interesting question is whether even efficient economic-development takings, however unlikely, should be endorsed, especially when they raise income inequality. Indeed, if economic-development takings are prone to be inefficient, they are even more prone (even when they are efficient) to be inequitable because, without the government's taking, the developer would

[13] *Kelo*, 545 U.S. at 484.

[14] *Id.* at 485.

[15] Rolnick and Davies (2006) note that there are two primary differences between the two: Private goods are (1) rival (one person's consumption of the good reduces that of another's) and (2) excludable (the good can be limited to paying customers), whereas public goods are neither.

[16] Poletown Neighborhood Council v. City of Detroit, 304 N.W.2d 455 (Mich. 1981).

probably have had to pay a higher price to the expropriated property owners. Therefore, eminent domain results in a net gain for the developer and a net loss for the landowner, transferring resources up the income ladder. It is thus clear that economic development takings have distributive implications.

Evidence for eminent domain's other inegalitarian repercussions exist. The owners of condemned properties are not random. Research shows that they are poorer, less educated, and disproportionately people of color compared to surrounding communities.[17] This fact is not lost on the public. After *Kelo*, property-rights advocates attempted to condemn Supreme Court Justice David Souter's home in rural New Hampshire in order to build a hotel (Burke 2006, 666). Unsurprisingly, this attempt was not successful. Also unsurprising is the fact that the people who benefit from such economic development takings are disproportionately private developers and large corporations, such as Pfizer in New London and GM in Detroit. To make matters worse, these projects often receive tax breaks and public incentives. The inclusion of economic development as a "public purpose" to satisfy the "public use" requirement of the Fifth Amendment has underwritten a great deal of – upwards – redistribution.

* * *

Takings jurisprudence represents one, particularly dramatic, way that property rules and rights affect the distribution of income. But it is certainly not the only way. In fact, what Schwab (1989) has called the "distributive corollary of the Coase theorem" says that when there are no transactions costs, property entitlements are irrelevant for efficiency – they are relevant *only* for distribution. This is the exact opposite of Kaplow and Shavell's double-distortion claim, which is that the law should be used only for efficiency and never for distribution. How is it possible for two of the best-known claims in law and economics to arrive at opposite conclusions? The answer is to recognize that transaction costs – the costs of searching for, bargaining for, and enforcing an agreement – are rarely zero. In that case, the choice of legal rules becomes relevant for efficiency. In fact, most scholars concede that when transaction costs are positive or significant, the distributive implications of the Coase theorem no longer have any purchase.

This chapter aims to rehabilitate the distributive corollary of the Coase theorem and show how property entitlements can be used to redistribute income more efficiently than taxes. Section 3.1 begins with a brief overview and illustration of the Coase theorem itself. Section 3.2 then discusses the general relevance of the Coase

[17] Carpenter and Ross (2007) provide some evidence on the demographic consequences of economic development takings. They find that "in project areas in which eminent domain has been threatened or used for private development," "58% of the population includes minority residents, compared to only 45% in the surrounding communities"; that "the median income is less than $19,000 per year, compared to more than $23,000 in surrounding communities"; that "25% live at or below poverty, compared to only 16% in surrounding communities"; and that "a greater percentage of residents have less than a high school diploma and smaller percentages have various levels of college education compared to surrounding communities" (2).

theorem for distributive concerns, and why scholars have dismissed its relevance because of transaction costs. Section 3.3 then turns to the central issue and shows how property entitlements can be used to redistribute income more efficiently than taxes. This section begins by summarizing the research of Ayres and Talley (1995), who show how legal rules can facilitate Coasean exchange even in the presence of transaction costs. However, the section demonstrates that if legal rules can facilitate more efficient trade then, in contrast to Ayres and Talley, legal rules can also facilitate more efficient redistribution. Section 3.4 concludes by returning to the topic introduced here and shows how distribution-informed thinking should influence takings jurisprudence.

3.1 THE COASE THEOREM

The Coase theorem (1960) has a privileged place within law and economics. It can be summarized in two statements. First when transaction costs are zero, an efficient use of resources results from private bargaining, regardless of the legal assignment of property entitlements. Second, when transaction costs are high enough to prevent bargaining, the efficient use of resources will depend on how property rights are assigned. These are two ways of expressing the same theorem, but with different implications depending on the level of transaction costs.

We can illustrate the Coase theorem with a well-known example, taken from Cooter and Ulen (2016). Consider a rancher and a farmer, who engage in their economic pursuits on adjoining parcels of land. Initially, the boundary separating their land is unfenced. This creates a problem, because the rancher's cattle sometimes like to wander onto the farmer's land and, in the process, destroy the farmer's corn crops. There might be a number of possible responses to this dilemma, each of which is costly. For instance, the rancher could spend all of his time supervising the cattle or the farmer could grow less corn and confine her growing area to a far corner of her property. Alternatively, and more naturally, a fence could be built to prevent the cattle from wandering onto the farmer's land. Most importantly, the farmer and the rancher are always free to bargain, and make enforceable agreements, about how to manage their entangled affairs.

Legal rules also mediate the rancher and farmer's relationship. Should the rancher be liable for the damage his cattle cause to the farmer's crop? In this scenario there are two possible rules a court could adopt. The first would make the farmer responsible for protecting her own land and crops. Under this rule, which we will call the "open-range" rule, the rancher is allowed to let his cattle roam freely.[18] This means that

[18] In his investigation of the Coase theorem, Ellickson (1991) studied the variety of disputes arising from the damage caused by escaped cattle in Shasta County, California. His conclusion was that informal social norms, rather than the law, played a larger role in resolving disputes among ranchers than generally thought.

the farmer has no legal cause against the rancher if and when the cattle wander and destroy her crops. If the farmer wants to avoid the destruction to her crops, she must build a fence or reduce the amount of crops grown. The second rule would make the rancher responsible for the damage that his cattle cause. Under this rule, which we can call the "closed-range" rule, the rancher would be liable to the farmer for any damage that his cattle cause. This naturally implies that if the rancher wants to avoid paying damages to the farmer, he must erect a fence or continually watch his cattle.

We can say a little more about the costs involved. Suppose that crop destruction caused by the cattle amounts to $100. The farmer can also build a fence around her cornfields for $50, while the rancher could build a fence around his cattle range for $75, the area of land required to raise cattle being larger than that required to grow corn.

Which rule should the court adopt, the open-range rule or the closed-range rule? Part of Coase's answer is that this is not a fully formed question. To understand this, let us first establish what the *efficient* outcome is. We can do this by thinking of the farm and ranch as a joint enterprise, owned by a single entity. Or, as Cooter and Ulen (2016, 83) put it, suppose that the farmer and the rancher got married. What would be the efficient, wealth-maximizing choice to prevent the cattle from destroying the corn? Certainly, we want to avoid corn destruction, which costs $100 and loses more money than either of the fencing options. Among the fencing options, building a fence around the cornfields is a clear winner, because it saves $25 over building a fence around the range. The efficient solution to the problem, one that maximizes the wealth of the joint enterprise, is to erect a fence around the cornfields.

We have established the efficient benchmark. Now let us see what happens when the farm and ranch, as originally conceived, operate as separate legal entities. Under the open-range rule, the farmer has no legal recourse against the rancher, and it would cost only $50 to build a fence, compared to losing $100 in crops. The farmer's choice is therefore an easy one: to erect a fence around her cornfields which, as we just established, is the efficient outcome. Under the closed-range rule, the rancher is liable for the crop destruction, which will put him $100 in debt should he allow his cattle to wander. The rancher could also build a fence around his range for $75, which saves more money than paying the farmer, and that *seems* like what the outcome would be under the closed-range rule. And because building the fence around the cattle range is more costly than building a fence around the cornfields, that in turn *might* lead us to conclude that the open-range rule is actually the better one, if we are judging rules on the basis of their efficiency consequences.

But we have not yet considered the possibility of bargaining between the rancher and the farmer. Under the closed-range rule, building a fence around the cornfields is still cheaper than building a fence around the range. Knowing this, the rancher has every incentive to approach the farmer and offer to pay her $50 to build a fence around her cornfield, rather than spend $75 to fence the ranch. But the farmer is indifferent. If she rejects the deal, the rancher will fence his range, and the farmer is no worse off for it. Furthermore, if she takes the deal, the rancher only incurs costs of $50 rather than $75, leaving the rancher with all of the surplus from the bargain. The farmer might therefore counter by mentioning this fact to the rancher, and proposing that they split the $25 savings the rancher will receive if the farmer fences her cornfield. The farmer's counteroffer would therefore have the rancher pay the farmer $62.50 to build a fence around the cornfields, making them both $12.50 richer than in the event of no deal.

If the farmer and rancher can bargain, then under the closed-range rule, the outcome is again the efficient outcome: building a fence around the cornfields. That leads to Coase's conclusion that, with no transactions costs, it does not matter for efficiency which rule the court adopts – or, more generally, to whom the court assigns the legal entitlement. Thus, the tempting conclusion that the open-range rule is the more efficient rule was incorrect: Either rule leads to the same, efficient outcome. Put another way, this demonstrates the first version of the Coase theorem: When transaction costs are zero, an efficient use of resources results from private bargaining, regardless of the legal assignment of property rights. It also shows why the question of which legal rule is "better" or "more efficient" is not a fully formed one: The question assumes that one rule is better than the other. As Coase shows, when transaction costs are zero, they are equally good.

The catch is that condition, "when transaction costs are zero." In our example, there is no additional cost to the time or other resources it takes to actually negotiate a deal between the farmer and the rancher. In general, transaction costs are typically broken down into three, more specific kinds of costs: (1) search costs, the time and resources spent in looking for an exchange partner; (2) bargaining costs, the time and resources spent in negotiating, drafting, recording, and reviewing an agreement; and (3) enforcement costs, the time and resources spent in monitoring performance and sanctioning or punishing violations of the agreement (Cooter and Ulen 2016, 88–91).

All exchanges have some transaction costs, but in some cases these may be negligible, so that Coase's insight about the irrelevance of legal rules for efficiency carries through. What happens, however, when transaction costs are large and prohibitive? Suppose that in our farmer-rancher example it costs $35 hire an attorney to draft and review the agreement. Because this $35 eats up the entire surplus from a deal between the rancher and farmer under the closed-range rule ($25), neither has an incentive to bargain. Even if the rancher promises to pay all of the attorney's fees in exchange for giving the farmer $50 to fence the cornfield, this would not make the farmer any better off than no deal, and it would make the rancher worse off than simply fencing the range. Any other distribution of the costs of the attorney would only make both worse off.

Positive, and significant, transaction costs then lead us to the second version of the Coase theorem, that when transaction costs are high enough to prevent bargaining, the efficient use of resources will depend on how property rights are assigned. Under the closed-range rule, where transaction costs are high and there is no incentive for the parties to bargain, the outcome will be the rancher fencing the range, which is inefficient relative to the open-range rule. Under the open-range rule, the outcome will be the farmer fencing the cornfields, whether transaction costs are high or low, and is the efficient outcome relative to the closed-range rule.

It is now apparent that the choice of legal rules does matter for efficiency. Thus, when transactions were small or zero, it didn't matter (for efficiency) which legal rule the court adopted. Now, with significant transaction costs, the choice does matter and, in order to maximize wealth, the court should adopt the open-range rule.

3.2 THE DISTRIBUTIVE COROLLARY TO THE COASE THEOREM

Usually, discussions of the Coase theorem end with the insight that, when transaction costs are zero, the choice of legal rules doesn't matter for efficiency. Legal scholars draw various policy prescriptions from this conclusion. That, for example, because transaction costs are positive, legal rules should be chosen to promote efficiency or to minimize transaction costs. However, the Coase theorem does have more to say, in particular, about the distribution of economic resources. Other writes have recognized the "distributive corollary of the Coase theorem," but assume that it is only relevant when transaction costs are zero (Schwab 1989; Liscow 2014; Fennell and McAdams 2016). This, too, is not a completely accurate statement of the relevance of Coase's insight into distribution. As we will see, legal entitlements influence the distribution of income, with or without the presence of transaction costs.

Cooter and Ulen (2016) write, "It follows that law is unnecessary and undesirable where bargaining succeeds, and that law is necessary and desirable where bargaining fails," (p. 81). This assertion conveys a common sentiment within law and economics, one that is implied more often than expressed. The assertion suggests that the only function of legal rules is to promote efficiency. But it is the law itself that assigns the property entitlements that are the foundation of the economic system, and this is true whether or not transaction costs are negligible or prohibitive, and whether or not the farmer and rancher strike a bargain. Because of this, legal entitlements, and therefore the law, very often have distributive consequences.

We can see this distributive import of legal rules at work in our farmer-rancher example. Let us first consider the case of zero transaction costs. Under the open-range rule, the rancher is not responsible for damage caused by his cattle. The farmer faces a choice of allowing the cattle to trample her cornfield, at a loss of $100, or erecting a fence, at a cost of $50. The private, and social, maximum, is to build the fence. In this situation, recall, the rancher has no incentive to bargain even when transaction costs are zero. So the cost of building the fence is borne entirely by the farmer, even though building it on her own also saves her $50. Under the closed-range rule, as we know, the outcome is different. The rancher now has an incentive to bargain with the farmer about the efficient choice of building a fence around the cornfield – rather than a more expensive one around the range. Because transaction costs are negligible, they make a deal, and the rancher pays the farmer $62.50 to build a fence around the cornfield.

As far as efficiency is concerned, these outcomes are irrelevant. However, the distributional contrast between the legal rules is significant. Under the open-range rule, the well-being of the farmer and the rancher, which we can denote as v_F and v_R respectively, are whatever they enjoy from the use of the land (which could be the monetary returns from market activities, e.g., selling corn or cattle) minus $50 for the farmer and nothing for the rancher: $v_F - \$50$ and v_R. Under the closed-range rule, by contrast, the farmer gets her valuation of the land *plus* $62.50 minus $50 to build the fence, while the rancher is out $62.50: $v_F + \$12.50$ and $v_R - \$62.50$. The farmer is therefore $62.50 wealthier under the closed-range rule than under the open-range rule, and the rancher is poorer by the same amount. The adoption of the closed range rule has the same effects as a $62.50 transfer from the rancher to the farmer. If the farmer is poorer, in terms of market income, than the rancher, then the adoption of the closed-range rule will increase social welfare, under any social welfare function.

Here we see that the choice of legal rules may be irrelevant for efficiency, but it matters quite a bit for welfare and distribution. This observation is what Stewart Schwab (1989) has called the "distributive corollary of the Coase theorem." He puts the corollary this way: "With zero transaction costs, initial entitlements cannot be justified on efficiency grounds, and so should be awarded on the basis of need or desert" (1195). This corollary applies perfectly to the farmer-rancher scenario. Because transaction costs are zero, there is no reason for choosing between the open-range or closed-range rules on the basis of efficiency. However, under the closed-range rule income inequality is lower, and therefore social welfare higher, than under the open-range rule. Distributive considerations – "need or desert" – direct us to adopt the closed-range rule. This distributive insight into the Coase theorem has also been recognized more recently by Zachary Liscow (2014), who writes, "With costless bargaining, injunctive remedies or damages at any level will not cause distortions. … Thus, with costless bargaining, the scope for equity-informed legal rules expands significantly" (2500).

Both Schwab and Liscow appear to agree that Coase's distributive corollary applies only, or primarily, to the case of "zero transaction costs" or "costless bargaining." Schwab (1989, 1196) remarks, "The Distributive Corollary applies only when transaction costs are low." This conclusion has some consensus, as Fennell and McAdams (2016, 1052 n.2) concur, citing firstly Schwab, and then Liscow and others, for the proposition that "[i]f transaction costs were zero, legal rules could be selected based exclusively on distributive concerns." This implies that when transaction costs are positive or at least nonnegligible, the distributive implications of the Coase theorem are irrelevant.

Is this consensus true? Does the distributive corollary of the Coase theorem lose all force when bargaining is costly? It is not obvious that it is. If we assume, as before, that the transaction costs of bargaining between the rancher and the farmer amount to \$35, then any deal will not be worthwhile. The *efficiency* principle of the Coase theorem then becomes relevant, telling us that an open-range rule leads us to an outcome that maximizes social wealth. But the distributive implications do not thereby go away. Under the open-range rule, the distributive outcomes are the same as when transaction costs were zero: $v_F - \$50$ for the farmer and v_R for the rancher. Under the closed-range rule, without bargaining, the farmer gets her market income without any loss of income – either because the rancher is obligated to pay for damages or, more likely, decides to fence his range to prevent crop destruction. If the rancher does make the (privately) cost-minimizing choice, and fences his range, the rancher is \$75 poorer. Under the closed-range rule, the incomes are v_F and $v_R - \$75$. Adopting the closed-range rule therefore results in a transfer of \$50 from the rancher to the farmer, in addition to a loss of \$25, borne entirely by the rancher.

There is therefore no question that the closed-range rule changes the distribution of income, even when transactions costs make bargaining prohibitively costly. By reducing inequality, the closed-range rule may even increase social welfare. The central issue is not the problem of transaction costs, but rather the one raised by the double-distortion claim: Is the loss of \$25 in social wealth greater than that induced by the income-tax used to respond to the higher inequality of the open-range rule? Remember that the \$25 is *not* the transaction cost. The transaction cost is the \$35 required to hire a lawyer. That cost does prevent the parties from privately benefiting from the efficient option, but is not directly related to it. Suppose for example that fencing the ranch costs \$60 instead of \$75. Now it is even harder to justify the transaction costs in order to get an agreement between rancher and farmer. But, conversely, the redistributive case for the closed-range rule is stronger. Not only does it improve farmer welfare by \$50 (and reduces the rancher's by \$60), but there is also a smaller loss in efficiency compared to the previous case. Transaction costs are only tangentially related to the relevance of the distributive corollary.

We can make another point about the applicability of the double-distortion claim. Assume again that fencing the ranch costs \$75. If we endorse the closed-range rule on distributive grounds, Kaplow and Shavell would respond that, in addition to the \$25 loss in wealth from choosing the more costly fencing option, the closed-range rule would also cause labor-supply distortions (equivalent to a change in the income tax used to achieve the same level of distribution as the closed-range rule). Hence, a double distortion, which would make a change in the tax code more sensible than adopting the closed-range rule. However, it is fair to ask, at least within the confines of this simple example, whether the closed-range rule would have any negative labor-supply effects. Building a fence sounds like a fixed cost, and would not make any difference to the amount of labor that ranchers supply or how many cattle they produce. In that case, if the costs of taxation exceeded \$25 it might indeed be better to adopt the closed-range rule.

By this point we have exhausted what we can say about the double-distortion debate within the confines of this simple farmer-rancher problem. We can summarize the discussion with two concluding observations. First, although the existence of transaction costs may make efficiency relevant to the evaluation of legal rules, they do not eliminate their distributive effects. The validity of the distributive corollary therefore does not depend on the level of transaction costs – as Schwab, Liscow, and Fennel and McAdams assume – but on whether the costs of redistributive legal rules, which are different from and may be *less* than the transaction costs, are more than the costs of redistributive taxation. In other words, the issue is not transaction costs, but the double-distortion claim. Second, there is no a priori relationship between the allocation of legal entitlements and labor-supply decisions, nor is there any a priori relationship between the costs of legal rules and their distributive effects. Once any of those assumptions are relaxed, the force of Kaplow and Shavell's argument against using legal rules to redistribute income loses much of its power.

3.3 DIVIDED ENTITLEMENTS AND LEGAL REDISTRIBUTION

Ayres and Talley (1995) have advanced the argument that divided property entitlements can facilitate efficient bargaining and Coasean trade. This section argues that divided property entitlements can also redistribute income more efficiently than taxes. The previous section's farmer-rancher problem suggested that property rules can change the distribution of income, but without decisively reaching that starker conclusion. Using Ayres and Talley's theory of "Solomonic" bargaining supplies that decisiveness. In the end, we will see that property rules can redistribute income more efficiently than taxes, that transaction costs are not necessarily a barrier to the distributive corollary of the Coase theorem, and that Ayres and Talley's theory of divided entitlements can not only support efficiency goals but redistributive objectives as well.

3.3.1 *Using Divided Entitlements to Facilitate Trade*

To understand the redistributive implications of divided entitlements, we first need to recapitulate Ayres and Talley's (1995) argument, in which they consider two different "axes" of divided property rights.[19] The first refers to the "degree of protection" given to an entitlement, while the second describes the "structure of ownership" itself.[20]

Liability rules are a kind of divided entitlement, according to Ayres and Talley, because they give the "nonowner" of the entitlement the option of appropriating

[19] For other work on property rights and efficiency bargaining, see Segal and Whinston (2014) and Segal and Whinston (2016).

[20] The first axis owes its genesis to Calabresi and Melamed's (1972) celebrated article, and their distinction between liability rules and property rules.

the entitlement nonconsensually, as long as they are willing to pay the damages associated with doing so. Property rules, by contrast, represent undivided entitlements, because they absolutely prohibit nonowners from taking legal entitlements without the consent of the owner. The second axis of divided property entitlements refers to the division of entitlements accordingly by use, space, or time. For example, ownership in land might be "fractionally" divided such that Smith owns Greenacre in fee simple subject to an executory interest owned by Jones that becomes possessory should Smith ever use the property for some impermissible purpose.

Under either axis, divided property entitlements facilitate Coasean bargaining by serving an "information-forcing" function (Ayres and Talley 1995, 1032).[21] Let us focus on the liability-versus-property-rules axis, because this is the simplest and most policy-relevant application, in my opinion. Ayres and Talley's argument rests on the problem of private information. In all of our preceding examples, we have assumed that each party's valuation of the entitlement in question (e.g., the value of unpolluted water, or the value attached to undisturbed land) is both fixed and commonly known. In reality, this is seldom the case, and negotiating partners do not know how the other values the entitlement. Some have a high value for the entitlement, others a low value. Uncertainty about the other party's valuations is a chief source of transaction costs and may cause some exchanges never to take place. For example, Smith may think that Jones values Greenacre highly, because he has lived there a long time. In fact, Jones is ready for a move, and would take a relatively low offer for Greenacre to avoid the time and expense of placing it formally on the market. Private information about heterogeneous entitlement values makes bargaining more time consuming and expensive. Acquiring this information is costly and difficult. Moreover, parties may act strategically in order to disguise their own or discover the other party's valuation, which further consumes resources.

Ayres and Talley argue that liability rules, but not property rules, give entitlement owners an incentive to reveal how much they value the entitlement to potential buyers. Liability rules arguably provide less protection to an entitlement owner. But that insecurity actually encourages owners to reveal to other interested parties how much they are willing to pay in order to hold on to the entitlement. The threat of a taking encourages high-value owners – owners who value the entitlement more than the damages amount – to pay other parties' not to appropriate the entitlement. Owners who value the entitlement less than the damages amount may be willing to trade the entitlement away for less than that amount, particularly because the threat of taking is itself uncertain.

Thus, liability rules, but not property rules, create incentives for entitlement owners to distinguish themselves, offer information to a person interested in acquiring the entitlement and, by so doing, facilitate trade. As Ayres and Talley demonstrate,

21 Ayres and Talley (1995, 1034) also write: "Once again, the Solomonic division can make it more difficult for either side to offer a price that diverges from her private valuation."

parties are on average better off under a liability rule than under a property rule. This conclusion contrasts sharply with the thinking at the time about liability rules, property rules, and transaction costs. Prior to their "Solomonic Bargaining" article, the standard intuition was that in the presence of transaction costs, a property rule was superior to a liability rule, because it would force parties who desired an entitlement to bargain with the owning party instead of engaging in potentially costly strategic behavior.

To illustrate the Ayres-and-Talley insight, let us construct a slightly different version of the farmer-rancher entitlement problem. To simplify, let us remove the fence-building issues and focus on the underlying entitlement at hand: the choice between closed-range or open-range rule. As in Ayres and Talley, we can introduce transaction costs by supposing that the valuations that the rancher and farmer attach to this entitlement are private information. To make our problem as similar as possible to Ayres and Talley, say that the farmer values her undisturbed tract of land in the amount v_F, which can vary anywhere between $0 and $100. Let us assume that these values are uniformly distributed so that, from the rancher's perspective, the farmer's expected valuation is $50. For instance, instead of cattle overrunning the farmer's cornfields causing a fixed amount of damage, let us instead say that the rancher does not know which use the farmer has for her land. As he sees it, there could be many possible uses, each with a different valuation; at least some of the uses would depend on the farmer's own subjective preferences, skill sets, experience, and so forth. Likewise, let us suppose that ranchers differ in the value they attach to the open-range rule. Some value highly the ability to have their cattle graze wherever they wish, others less so. For example, some may prefer to use specific kinds of feed rather than let them graze.

Following Ayres and Talley, let us designate the value of the entitlement to the rancher as v_R, which can take one of either two values, $60 or $40, with equal probability. Thus, the rancher's expected valuation, from the farmer's perspective, is also $50.

The problem now is that transaction costs, in the form of imperfect information, may prevent mutually beneficial exchanges from taking place. Because some ranchers highly value the ability to let their cattle roam freely ($60) and some farmers value lowly the enjoyment of undisturbed land (on average only $50) there are potential gains from trade. When the farmer values the entitlement less than the rancher, she is willing to give up the right to undisturbed land in exchange for cash, and will allow the rancher to let his cattle roam freely. On the other hand, some ranchers value the free-range option more modestly ($40). If the farmer values the closed-range option more highly than the rancher does, it would be better (from an efficiency perspective) that no exchange take place. First-best efficiency could be achieved if all of this information was common knowledge – that is, if every individual's private and idiosyncratic valuation were publicly known – and courts could deter inefficient transactions with damages that perfectly matched the valuations of the defendants.

With perfect information and enforcement, whenever the valuation of the rancher exceeded that of the farmer, $v_R \geq v_F$, exchange would take place and both parties would be better off. Likewise, whenever the valuation of the farmer exceeded that of the rancher, $v_R < v_F$, no rancher would violate the farmer's entitlement because, taken to court, the rancher would have to pay in damages to the farmer more than the rancher valued the entitlement. In these circumstances, resources end up with their most highly valued users, and efficiency is achieved.

When information is private, circumstances are not so propitious. When the rancher and farmer do not know each other's valuation, they consume time and resources trying to elicit that information. More seriously, parties have an incentive to act strategically in order to extract a greater part of the surplus, and this may increase bargaining costs or derail wealth-enhancing exchanges. Nevertheless, not all is lost, and Ayres and Talley contend that liability rules, rather than property rules, can help facilitate exchanges when information is imperfect.

The inherent qualities of property rules limit their ability to facilitate trade. A property rule absolutely prohibits a nonconsensual taking of a defendant's entitlement. Especially in light of Calabresi and Melamed's (1972) famous paper, we think of property rules in terms of the availability of equitable relief, which orders the defendant to stop the behavior that is interfering with the plaintiff's property right, or return the property that is taken. Liability rules, in contrast, are thought of in terms of damages, where the plaintiff's relief is a monetary sum ordered to be paid as compensation for interfering with the entitlement or for its nonconsensual taking. Under a liability rule, courts try to set damages to fit with the plaintiff's valuation of the entitlement. But this is obviously difficult to do, because it may be impossible to verify the plaintiff's subjectively honest valuation.

For instance, if the rancher "takes" the farmer's entitlement – allowing his cattle onto the farmer's land – the event is easily enough proved in court (in fact, let us assume it is costless to do so). However, the plaintiff's valuation of the entitlement is difficult, if not impossible to verify. Even if market value is readily determinable, for example, this will not necessarily equal the plaintiff's actual valuation. The problem is illustrated in the classic contracts case, *Jacob & Youngs v. Kent*, where the court awarded the (de minimus) diminution in market value, rather than the much more exorbitant costs of repair. In cases like these, plaintiffs have a strong strategic incentive to overstate their true valuations.[22] In our problem, therefore, if a rancher "takes"

[22] In *Jacob & Youngs v. Kent* the plaintiff wanted the builders to install a very specific kind of pipe into his home. The builder installed a type of pipe of equivalent quality, but not the exact brand for which the plaintiff had specifically contracted. A monetary damages award equal to the cost of repair would have been very high, because repair would require tearing out walls in order to replace the pipe with the desired brand. With the pipe already installed, the plaintiff had an incentive ex post to claim that his valuation for the specific kind of pipe was very high, when in fact he could have been entirely indifferent between the equal-quality brands. If the plaintiff's brand-insistence was actually insincere, simply pocketing the cost-of-repair award would have essentially allowed him rewrite the contract after the fact and to pay substantially less than

the farmer's entitlement, the court, under a liability rule, will award some specified amount of damages which may depart from the farmer's subjective valuation.

Ayres and Talley show that one interesting way of seeing the relationship between the two kinds of rules is by thinking about property rules as a limit case of liability rules. Suppose, for example, that the court sets damages at $100 for an entitlement taking. Because $60 is the most that any potential rancher values the entitlement in our hypothetical, this effectively raises an absolute prohibition on nonconsesual takings. A liability rule, however, gives the rancher a "call option," an option to buy the farmer's entitlement in the amount specified by the damages. This, somewhat paradoxically, gives the rancher something to "sell" to the farmer, who otherwise holds the entitlement. Hence, in this sense, the entitlement to the land is divided. This is not the case under a property rule. Because the property rule absolutely prohibits any taking, it deprives the rancher of his call option. If the rancher wants to bargain with the farmer about acquiring her entitlement, he must do so purely as a buyer. For Ayres and Talley, liability rules illustrate one way of dividing an entitlement, which gives both farmer and rancher something to sell.

When the farmer's entitlement is protected by a liability rule, two different kinds of transactions are made possible. In the first, which Ayres and Tally call Coasean Bargain number 1, the farmer bribes the rancher not to take her entitlement. In this transaction the farmer buys the rancher's call option, casting the farmer in the role of buyer and the rancher in the role of seller. In the second kind of transaction, Coasean Bargain number 2, the rancher buys the farmer's entitlement, and each party assumes their more traditional roles.

We can illustrate the first Coasean bargain, where the farmer buys the rancher's "call option," by using a simple example. Suppose the farmer values her undisturbed land at $90 and the rancher values the ability to let his cattle roam free at $60. Also suppose the court sets damages at $50 for taking the entitlement under this liability rule. Under these conditions, the farmer would be willing to pay the rancher $15 for the latter's call option. That is, in this bargain the farmer pays the rancher $15 not to take her entitlement by running his cattle over the farmer's land. If there is no bargain, the rancher would find it worthwhile to let his cattle run freely and pay the damages – in fact, $50 is less than the $60 the rancher would be willing to pay. If the rancher does this, the farmer receives $50 and the rancher has a net gain valued at $10. (The farmer does not get to enjoy her land undisturbed, which deprives her of the value of the entitlement, but she receives the $50 in damages awarded by the court; meanwhile, the rancher obtains the entitlement of letting his cattle roam free minus the damages paid, or $60 – $50 = $10.) However, if the farmer buys the rancher's

the contracted-for price. Realizing this potential hold-up problem, the court awarded damages equal only to the diminution in market value which, because of the essentially equivalent pipe, was nominal. Examples such as these, give us good reasons for believing that court-awarded damages under a liability rule will not be perfectly tailored to the plaintiff's own valuation.

call option, both are better off. If the farmer pays the rancher \$15 not to take her entitlement, the farmer gets \$75 (the value of the entitlement less the contract price of the call option, or \$90 – \$15 = \$75) while the rancher gets \$15 (no entitlement but the price for selling the option).

In the second kind of Coasean bargain, the farmer sells her entitlement to the rancher. To illustrate this kind of transaction, suppose the farmer values undisturbed land at nothing more than \$10, while the rancher values the ability to let his cattle run free at \$40. With this allocation of preferences, the rancher would be willing to pay the farmer \$25 for the right to let his cattle roam free on her land. Likewise, the farmer would accept such an offer, because she values the \$25 more than the right to undisturbed land. Without such an agreement, the rancher would not find it worthwhile to let his cattle range freely, because doing so would cost him \$50, ten dollars more than his valuation of the entitlement. Without an agreement, the farmer has \$10 and the rancher \$0. With an agreement, each is better off: The farmer has \$25 (no entitlement but \$25 in cash) and the rancher has \$15 (the value of the entitlement to the rancher less the contract price: \$40 – \$25 = \$15).

While the possibility of entering into two different bargains generally does not constrain the rancher's incentives to misrepresent his valuations, it does constrain the farmer's. Only high-value farmers, who value the entitlement more than the damages award, are willing to pay to purchase the rancher's call option (i.e., a Coasean bargain number 1). A farmer who values the entitlement less than the damages award has no reason to pay the rancher anything. Indeed, if the rancher takes the entitlement, the low-value farmer is in a position to make a windfall. Likewise, only low-value farmers have an incentive to sell their entitlement (a Coasean bargain number 2). A farmer who values the entitlement more than the damages amount would never sell the entitlement for less than that amount (\$50) and, moreover, would never be able to sell it for more than that – because a low-value rancher would not pay that much and because a high-value rancher could simply take the entitlement nonconsensually for that amount.

The result is that a liability rule reliably partitions the farmers into one of two groups: When damages are set at \$50, high-value farmers will never offer to sell their entitlement for less than that amount, while low-value farmers will never be willing to pay for the rancher's call option. This is a case of self-selection: Farmers' own private incentives induce them to identify whether they are, relative to the damages amount, low- or high-value farmers. Ranchers can identify which kind of farmer they are negotiating with simply by asking the farmer which kind of transaction she prefers. This feature of liability rules gives them an "information-forcing" feature that is not shared by property rules (Ayres and Talley 1995). With a property rule – say, damages set at \$100 – it is not possible for farmers to select themselves into either kind of Coasean bargain, because every farmer's valuation lies below the damages amount. Some farmers are interested in purchasing the rancher's call option precisely because they value the entitlement more highly than the damages; likewise, some are willing to sell their entitlement precisely because some farmers value the entitlement below \$50. The consequence is that liability rules do a better job at eliciting reliable information from farmers, and this, in turn, facilitates exchange. Exchanges are still possible under the property rule, but social welfare is not as high as under a liability rule.

We can report here some of the conclusions from Ayres and Talley's numerical model. As already indicated, any level of damages set above \$60 or below \$40 fails to elicit any self-selecting information from farmers. No rancher has an effective call option with damages greater than \$60; and every rancher has an effective call option with damages below \$40. Above or below this range, the expected welfare of the parties turns out to be the same: \$59.75. Only damages in the intermediate range below \$60 or above \$40 facilitate trade. In fact, Ayres and Talley show that damages set at \$50 maximize the social surplus. Perhaps not surprisingly, this amount corresponds to the expected, or average, valuation of the farmers. The consequence is an expected social welfare of \$59.875, higher than the \$59.75 than in either of the extreme damages scenarios.

The numerical results of Ayres and Talley's model are displayed in Figure 3.1. The figure illustrates that as damages are increased (on the horizontal axis), the total welfare (farmer welfare plus rancher welfare) at first increases, and then decreases, in a single-peaked fashion. Total social welfare is maximized when damages reach \$50. Any damages above \$60 effectively act as a property rule. Thus, liability rules are more efficient than property rules.

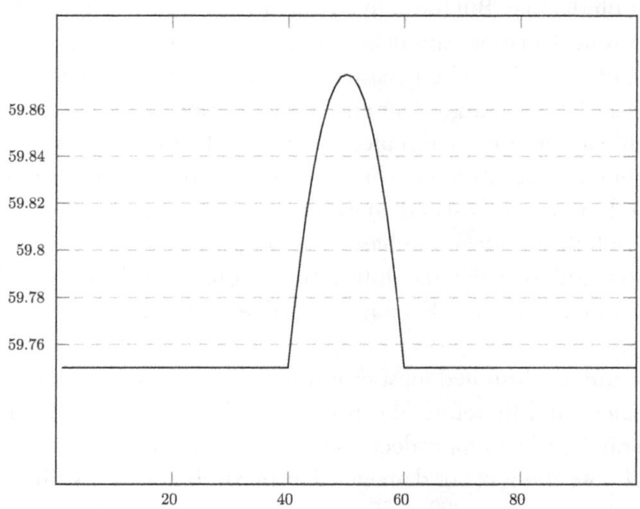

FIGURE 3.1 The efficiency liability rules over property rules

This figure displays graphically the results of Ayres and Talley's (1995) numerical illustration of their model. The horizontal axis displays the damages level, ranging from \$0 to \$100. The vertical access displays total social welfare, the sum of the well-being of, in our version, the farmer and the rancher.

3.3.2 *Using Divided Entitlements to Redistribute Income*

Ayres and Talley show that liability rules, in place of property rules, can be adopted in order to facilitate trade. However, their objective is a wealth-maximizing one: efficiency. This section will show how liability rules can be used to further a different objective: income redistribution. Rather than showing that liability rules are more efficient than property rules in the context of transaction costs, because they facilitate trade, I will argue that courts can adjust damages away from the efficient level in order to strengthen the bargaining power of poorer parties. As we will see, some departure from efficiency can enhance welfare and promote a more equitable distribution of income.

To explore this claim, we will add a few more details to our farmer-rancher hypothetical. To begin, suppose that the ranchers are richer than the farmers. Let us also assume that the group of ranchers we are considering all earn the same amount of income; likewise, all farmers earn the same amount of income. These assumptions do two things. First, the income *differences* between farmers and ranchers ensure that we are dealing with a legitimately distributive concern. Second, the income *identities* among ranchers and farmers ensure that the government has no better information about the farmers and ranchers than either has about the other. Thus, ranchers, farmers, and the government each have the *same* information available to them: Only income is common knowledge, and not each person's private valuation of the entitlement.

Of course, the notion that all farmers and ranchers have, as a group, the same income is counterfactual. But the core observation this assumption captures – that an individual's private valuation cannot be determined by merely observing that person's income – is entirely valid. The persistence of private information is a key feature, both in Ayres and Talley's argument and in the distributive claim I will be making. As pointed out earlier, it is an accepted conclusion that the distributive corollary of the Coase theorem loses its force when transaction costs are positive or significant. And, because transaction costs are always present, the distributive corollary would appear to have little practical purchase. The purpose of this section is to challenge this conclusion, and show that the distributive corollary is valid even in the presence of significant transaction costs. Even here, legal redistributions can be more efficient than taxation.

This claim can be illustrated most simply if, for now, we assume that changing the liability damages (and therefore also prices in either type of Coasean transaction) has no effect on the labor-supply decisions of the ranchers or farmers. In this case we can simply choose the level of damages that maximizes (the distribution-sensitive) social welfare for a given social welfare function. (For more background on social welfare functions, see the discussion in the book's appendix on welfare economics.) In the presence of inequality, with farmers poorer than ranchers, this social-welfare maximizing liability amount will in general be higher than the efficient level. Recall that when damages are at their "extreme" levels, less than or equal to $40 or greater than $60, expected social welfare is identical, at $59.75. That identity of outcomes at the social level, however, masks some significant distributive differences between farmers and ranchers. For instance, when the liability amount is set at $40, the farmer's expected welfare is $46.25 while the rancher's is $13.50. Conversely, when the liability amount is set at $60, the farmer's expected welfare is $56.25 and the rancher's is $3.50. Whether damages are set at $40 or $60, the sum of the expected welfare of the farmer and rancher is $59.75. But when the well-being of the farmer and rancher are taken separately, the difference in damages makes a significant difference in well-being.

In fact, in Ayres and Talley's numerical example, the distribution effects are far more dramatic than the efficiency effects. The amount that efficiency adds to total social welfare is twelve-and-a-half cents. By contrast, increasing damages can add $10.00 to the farmer's well-being and reduce the rancher's well-being also by $10.00, as shown in Figure 3.2. This is displayed graphically in Figure 3.3 where aggregate welfare is displayed alongside the farmer's and the rancher's expected welfare. The strong, parabolic shape of the efficiency effect in Figure 3.1 barely appears when compared to the changes in the farmer's and rancher's well-being in 3.3: The graph of the efficiency effects is closer to a straight line. Of course, no strong quantitative conclusions can be drawn from Ayres and Talley's arbitrarily chosen numerical illustration. But it does demonstrate the qualitative possibility that the distributional effects of legal rules can be more significant than their efficiency effects.

Clearly, a higher liability amount increases the farmer's expected welfare – at the expense of the rancher's and regardless of transaction costs. The reason is obvious: Higher liability amounts increase the farmer's bargaining power in either type of Coasean transaction. For damages in the intermediate range, farmers, knowing they are guaranteed the damages amount, can be more selective in accepting offers,

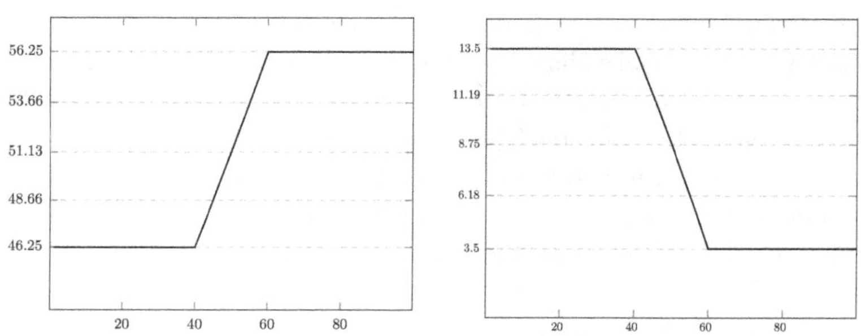

(a) Farmer's Well-being (b) Rancher's Well-being

FIGURE 3.2 Distribution effects of liability rules

This figure illustrates the way that liability rules affect the distribution of income. The horizontal displays the level of damages, which ranges from $0 to $100. The vertical axis is the welfare of the farmer or rancher, respectively.

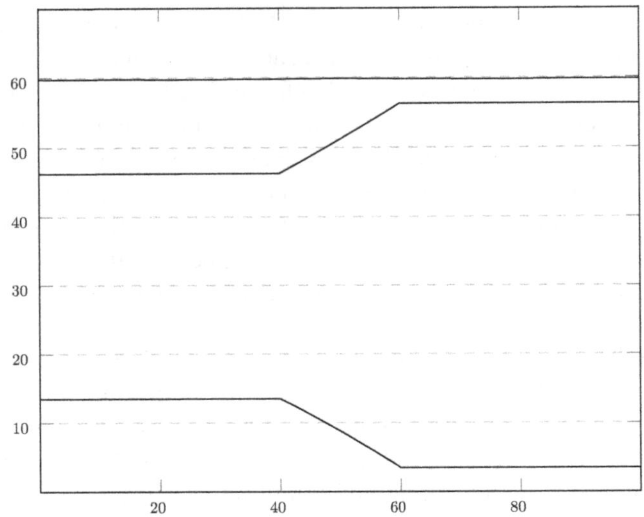

FIGURE 3.3 Comparison of distribution and efficiency

This figure compares the distributional and efficiency effects of liability rules that were displayed separately in Figures 3.1, 3.2a, and 3.2b. The horizontal axis again displays the damages level, ranging from \$0 to \$100. The vertical access displays welfare, separating total social welfare (the top line) from farmer welfare (the middle line) and rancher welfare (the bottom line).

requiring ranchers to increase their bids as damages increase. Farmers also know that the benefits that high-value ranchers get from taking diminish as damages increase, meaning that farmers have to pay less for the rancher to sell his "take" option. Indeed, in our stylized model, it is easy to show that the rancher's optimal "buy" offer is increasing in the liability amount, while his optimal "sell" offer is decreasing in the liability amount, as intuition suggests.

In sum, the distributive corollary of the Coase theorem applies even in the presence of transaction costs. When changes in liability damages do not affect labor supply and when the social welfare function is sensitive to the distribution of income, liability damages should be set at the amount that maximizes social welfare, not efficiency. Because there are no labor supply effects, entitlement-based, Coasean redistribution is necessarily more efficient than the tax system in redistributing income. Put another way, it is not necessary for transaction costs to be zero for the distributive corollary of the Coase theorem to be valid.

3.3.3 *Including Labor-Supply Effects*

A more significant challenge is to show that the distributive corollary of the Coase theorem extends to the case where changes in liability damages also affect labor-supply decisions. Bringing labor-supply effects into the model also allows us to engage directly with the double-distortion argument. This section will show that the distributive corollary to the Coase remains valid in this context, even when labor-supply effects are considered.

In accordance with Kaplow and Shavell (1994) and Kaplow (2008), we assume that the expected value of the entitlement has identical effects on labor supply as an equivalent amount of income. This means that changing the level of damages, for example, will have identical effects on labor supply as increasing taxes by the same expected dollar amount. For instance, we showed previously that raising liability damages from \$40 to \$60 reduces ranchers' expected utility by \$10 and increases farmers' by the same amount. The assumption is that this change has the identical economic response as would increasing the income tax on ranchers by \$10 (likewise, the same response as would lowering taxes on, or increasing subsidies to, farmers by \$10). Finding cattle raising less profitable, for example, will cause ranchers to spend less time engaged in earning income – that is, all of the activities associated with raising and selling cattle – and more time pursuing leisure. Likewise, farmers will respond to income changes by increasing or decreasing the time spent in growing crops.

Despite labor-supply effects, equity-adjusted liability rules redistribute income more efficiently (less inefficiently) than income taxes. The fundamental reason for this follows from the self-selection mechanism that was discussed earlier. Liability rules take advantage of ranchers' and farmers' heterogeneous valuations – their "willingness to pay" so to speak – in a way that taxes cannot. Only high-value ranchers are willing either to exercise their call option or to pay for the farmers' entitlement; low-value ranchers are not. The distributive burden of the legal redistribution is, in this sense, carried by those ranchers "most willing to pay" for the redistribution. Ranchers' labor-supply is therefore higher, on average, than if the same amount of revenue was collected from an income-tax increase whose incidence was uniform across all ranchers. The same sort of reasoning applies to farmers because the liability rule also discriminates between high- and low-value farmers.

These differences in labor-supply responses *should* dictate correspondingly different tax rates *among* ranchers and farmers, not just between them. But the tax authority, which sets taxes based on observed differences in income, does not have the relevant information about the various valuations among ranchers and farmers. It can only distinguish between ranchers and farmers – that is, by income – and not among ranchers or farmers – that is, by non-income factors. The legal system, in contrast, can exploit this unobserved information by eliciting inframarginal differences in individuals' valuations for the entitlement. The legal system receives information about individuals' differing valuations through the "signals" farmers send with their buy or sell offers and ranchers' "taking" behaviors. The legal system, therefore, can adjust damages, with redistributive objectives in mind, taking advantage of both observed taking behavior and incomes. By doing so, it shifts the identity of the marginal farmer, the one who is just indifferent between sending a "buy" signal

(Coasean bargain number 1) and a "sell" signal (Coasean bargain number 2). Raising damages makes more farmers send sell signals but, more fundamentally, shifts bargaining power to farmers.

If the government had better information about ranchers' valuations, an optimal tax schedule would adjust tax rates for each type of rancher, setting higher rates on high-value ranchers. It could also do the same for farmers who send buy-versus-sell signals. However, with access only to information about income differences, and not entitlement valuations, this option is essentially foreclosed. Without that information, the tax authorities set a uniform tax on ranchers (more specifically, on that level of income) in a way that taxes high-value ranchers too little, causing them to supply too much labor (relative to the social-welfare optimum), and taxes low-value ranchers too much, causing them to supply too little labor. For the legal system, on the other hand, farmers' transaction signals and defendants' takings actions reveal information about their type, and this can be used to adjust damages and exploit marginal differences among ranchers and farmers to redistribute income more efficiently than taxes.

We can summarize this conclusion by putting it in double-distortion terms. On the one hand, redistribution through the tax system has one form of economic cost: the distortion of labor-supply incentives that accompanies the change in the distribution of income. On the other hand, redistribution through legal rules, by adjusting damages in a pro-plaintiff direction (or pro-farmer direction, in this example) has two forms of economic costs, rather than one. The first distortion is the economic loss that comes from moving the damages away from Ayres and Talley's efficient level. In their example, damages set at \$50 maximizes efficiency. So, any increase from that level will cause a loss of total wealth. The second distortion is, just as with taxes, a distortion in labor-supply incentives that comes with changing the distribution of income. However, there is a crucial difference in this second, tax-like distortion. Because the increase in liability damages is better tailored to defendants' (ranchers') valuations of the entitlement, the labor-supply distortion is less than in the case of taxes for the same amount of redistribution. The double-distortion claim rests on these two labor-supply distortions being the same. When they are, we can automatically conclude that any second economic cost associated with the legal rule will make the total redistributive cost of the legal rule greater than taxes. But when, as in this case, the legal rule has a smaller labor-supply distortion than taxes, we cannot make that conclusion. Both redistributive costs of damages may be less than the single redistributive cost of taxation.

Finally, a numerical example, reported in Table 3.1, will illustrate the conclusion a little more concretely. In this example, imagine a population that is divided into three groups, ranchers (*R*), farmers (*F*), and the "unemployed" or society's least well off (0), who subsist on transfers from the government. For simplicity, labor supply is captured on the extensive margin; that is, both farmers and ranchers decide whether to work in each of those occupations or stay unemployed. The cost of work variable,

TABLE 3.1 *Efficiency of legal rule redistribution*

	$D = \$50$	$D = \$55$	$D = \$50 + \hat{T}$
u_R	148.7500	146.1875	146.1875
u_F	59.1250	61.6563	61.6563
u_O	5.0000	5.0000	5.0000
$h_R \cdot u_R$	68.3777	67.1495	67.1501
$h_F \cdot u_F$	25.8946	27.0755	27.0745
$h_O \cdot u_O$	0.5185	0.5139	0.5138
W	94.7908	94.7389	94.7383

Notes: D = liability damages; u_i = expected utility for ranchers (R), farmers (F), and unemployed (O); $h_i \cdot u_i$ = group-specific per capita utility, for $\sum h_i = 1$; $\hat{T}$ = distribution-neutral income tax adjustment; W = wealth, or efficiency.

θ_i, is assumed to follow a Pareto distribution.[23] Utility is a function of income, y_i, taxes or transfers, T_i, and the results of the Ayres-and-Talley Coasean bargaining problem. This value is a complicated function of the players' buy offers, sell offers, individual valuations of the entitlement, and damages (if the rancher takes the entitlement) all weighted by the probabilities of each decision node of the game. (The reader is referred to Section 3.5 and Ayres and Talley (1995) for further details.) To ensure that the problem is genuinely redistributive, I assume that ranchers' earned income is \$200, farmers' is \$10, and the unemployed is \$0. Taxes rates are arbitrarily set at 30 percent for ranchers, 20 percent for farmers, and the unemployed receive a transfer of \$5.

The first column of numbers gives the results when damages are set at their efficient level, as established by Ayres and Talley, $D = \$50$. The first three rows give group-specific, expected (or average) utility of high- and low-value ranchers, farmers, and the unemployed. The second three rows give per-capita utility, which is group-level utility weighted by population shares *inclusive* of labor-supply effects. Finally, the bottom row is a sum of the per-capita utilities of the second three rows, and gives total (per-capita) wealth, i.e., without regard to the distribution of welfare, which then becomes a measure of efficiency. The second column gives the same results for a redistributive damage rule, which is higher than its efficient level, set at $D = \$55$, and redistributes income from ranchers to farmers. As expected, this change is both inefficient and redistributive. As reported in the bottom row, overall efficiency is higher with the efficient damages rule than with the redistributive one

[23] Specifically, the cumulative distribution function of θ_i for $i \in \{1, 2\}$ is $1 - (1/\theta_i)^{(1/2)}$. Because type-1 and -2 individuals choose to work when $c_i - \theta_i \geq c_O$, the type-i individual who is just indifferent between work and unemployment is $\bar{\theta}_i = c_i - c_O$. Hence labor supply for group i is given by $1 - (1/(c_i - c_O))^{(1/2)}$.

(94.7908 > 94.7389). And, as can be seen in the top three rows, the redistributive damages rule lowers ranchers' expected utility (from 148.7500 to 146.1875) and raises farmers' expected utility (from 59.1250 to 61.6563).

Can legal rules redistribute more efficiently than taxes? The third number column reports the results when damages are kept at their efficient level, but an adjustment is made to the tax schedule, labeled $\hat{T}$, that gives the same distribution of utility as the redistributive legal rule. Comparing the second and third columns, we see that the utilities are identical between each group. However, as can be seen in the second three rows in the last two columns the damages rule and the tax adjustment each affect labor supply differently. The tax adjustment increases the labor-supplied utility of ranchers and decreases the labor-supplied utility of farmers. But, the net effect, as seen in the bottom row and last column reduces total wealth-measured well-being (which leaves the unemployed slightly worse off, as well). The reason for this is as explained before. The redistributive legal rule better discriminates between the different types of ranchers and farmers than taxes, yielding an overall less distorted labor-supply effect. Thus, the legal rule redistributes income more efficiently than taxes.

3.3.4 *Responses to Objections*

The remainder of this section will anticipate and address some challenges to the argument for entitlement-based, Coasean redistribution. There are at least three possible objections. The first objection is that the main claim is not new; specifically, the way legal rules exploit differences in valuation among individuals essentially boils down to the same argument that authors have already advanced in terms of "heterogeneity" (e.g., Sanchirico 2000, 2001; Avraham, Fortus, and Logue 2003). A second objection is that, as such, the argument is vulnerable to Kaplow and Shavell's objections to the heterogeneity claim. A final objection is that the income tax system can exploit the information revealed by the legal system to overcome its inability to distinguish between individuals' heterogeneous valuations. I will address each objection in turn.

With respect to the first objection, despite the similarity to the "heterogeneity" argument, there are subtle yet significant differences. Sanchirico (2000, 2001) advanced the original heterogeneity argument in terms of tort law, and its success depends on the correct correlation between income-earning ability and what we might call "precautionary ability," that is, aptitude in reducing risky activities and avoiding harm. For instance, we might not want to raise damages on rich yacht owners who also happen to be "klutzy" compared to poor, well-coordinated fishing-boat owners. In fact, we would want to reverse the redistributive presumption and favor rich, klutzy yacht owners at the expense of the poor but deft fishing-boat owners. As Gamage (2014, 14, emphasis in original) puts it, "[A]lthough Sanchirico's framework prescribes that overall distortionary costs could be reduced by *either positively taxing or subsidizing* various luxury commodities (such as yachts), Sanchirico's framework does not prescribe whether yachts or other luxury commodities should be positively taxed or subsidized in order to reduce overall distortionary costs." In Sanchirico's framework, only if the correlation between precautionary ability and income-earning ability were reversed (so that we'd have adroit yacht owners and klutzy fisherman) would we want to adjust damages to favor the poor. As Kaplow and Shavell (2000b) also pointed out, the role of heterogeneity in Sanchirico's elaboration is therefore ambiguous.

The entitlement-based, Coasean approach to legal distribution presented in this chapter avoids Kaplow and Shavell's ambiguity objection because it works through parties' deliberate transactions and not the random coincidence of accidents. What is crucial is how liability rules, with distributive objectives, facilitate trade by revealing information when potential transactions exist between high-value ranchers and farmers, on the one hand, and low-value ranchers and farmers, on the other. It is therefore not essential to the results that ranchers' or farmers' valuations of the entitlement correlate in any particular direction with income-earning ability. All of the results obtain if entitlement valuations and income-earning ability are assumed to be independent of each other. Furthermore, nothing important hinges on assuming that farmers are poor and ranchers are rich. Assume instead the opposite, that farmers are rich and ranchers poor. The prescription would now be to lower, rather than raise, damages to favor the poor ranchers, but for precisely the same reasoning as before: Lowering the liability amount shifts bargaining power in favor of poorer ranchers. Once again, legal rules would be adjusted to favor the poor, in the conventional sense. Of course (returning to the case of poor farmers and rich ranchers), if farmers' valuations were systematically high and ranchers' systematically low, liability rules would be of no value. But this is because there is simply no gains from trade, which would take the problem not only out of the realm of redistributive interest, but outside of any economic interest whatsoever. There is therefore no ambiguity, as in the Sanchirico case, about whether damages should be adjusted to favor the poor: They should. Heterogeneity plays a different role than in Sanchirico's argument and, for that reason, Kaplow and Shavell's objections to Sanchirico's argument do not apply to the case of Coasean redistribution.

Kaplow has another objection to the heterogeneity point, based on discussions about the value of differential commmodity taxation, that may also potentially relate to this chapter's claim. Double-distortion thinkers often object to heterogeneity arguments for using differential commodity taxation (on top of the income tax) as not "conventionally redistributive, that is, from rich to the poor" (Kaplow 2008, 141). Kaplow explains that using differential commodity taxation does not really redistribute from rich to poor but is actually a form of redistribution within income groups, because it is in fact the income tax system that handles redistribution from rich to poor (140–41). By exploiting the heterogeneity of tastes within particular income groups, commodity taxes and subsidies "allow the income tax to increase the extent of distribution by lowering the distortions from progressivity" (Weisbach 2015,

172). A similar objection might be raised in the present context: Adjusting liability rules, upwards or downwards, exploits differences within the groups of ranchers (and likewise farmers) in a way that reduces the distortions of progressive taxation. To be sure, in our divided entitlements argument, increasing damages on high-value ranchers does allow an *effective* lower rate on the low-value ranchers when the income tax is set optimally (although both high- and low-value ranchers still pay the same "statutory" income tax rate). Nevertheless, it is still higher damages on the rich, and paid to the poor, that is the principle mechanism of redistribution. Indeed, when the income tax is set optimally, the damages adjustment *decreases* the amount of redistribution that takes place through the income tax system. Thus, entitlement-based redistribution is not merely a disguised form of income-tax redistribution. After all, entitlement-based redistribution can take place even in the absence of an income-tax system.

One final objection to entitlement-based redistribution is that, with damages set at their Ayres-and-Talley efficient level, the tax authorities could use the information revealed by the legal system (farmers' "buy" and "sell" signals, and ranchers' taking behaviors) to adjust the income tax system optimally, and thereby distinguish between high- and low-value ranchers and farmers. This indeed would restore the superiority of the tax system as a more efficient redistributive instrument. Several responses to this specific objection can be made. First, the best response to this objection is to point out, once again, how totally it depends on the assumption of *identical* labor-supply responses to distributive changes regardless of the form. There are strong reasons to be skeptical of that assumption and how it hinges on Kaplow's controversial supposition of a weak separability between consumption and leisure. For example, perhaps the rancher also likes letting his horses (rather than his cattle) roam freely over the farmer's land, because this enhances his value for leisure. In that case, the value from taking the entitlement would not increase labor supply but decrease it. Second, one should recall that I have assumed for the sake of argument that individuals, the legal authorities, and the tax authorities all have, ex ante, the same information available to them. But, as also pointed out, it seems plausible that individuals have better information available to them than either, in which case even information elicited by the legal system and collected by the tax authorities may not be sufficient to give taxes a redistributive advantage. Third, and even more fundamentally, as also mentioned earlier, the distributive corollary of the Coase theorem that I have presented does not hinge on labor-supply effects at all, and indeed the case for it is strengthened when one drops the strong assumption that labor-supply responses are identical across taxes and legal rules.

3.4 TAKINGS

A distribution-sensitive approach to the evaluation of legal rules can also provide insights into the controversies in takings jurisprudence that started this chapter.

According to double-distortion reasoning, legal decisions should be concerned exclusively with efficiency, and ignore their distributive consequences. On that reasoning, takings should be endorsed when they raise total wealth (even if they raise income inequality) and inefficient takings should be rejected (even if they reduce income inequality). As we will see in this section, however, we should reject some efficient takings and accept some inefficient takings in the interest of reducing income inequality.

Critics of decisions such as *Kelo v. City of New London* have made spirited arguments against the use of the takings power for the purposes of economic development (Somin 2007). The economic-development rationale can be used to justify just about any taking that would benefit a commercial enterprise (191–92). In addition, the usual absence of binding obligations on the private developers who benefit from the taking invites public authorities to rely on exaggerated claims of possible economic benefits (192–97). Moreover, economic development takings do not consider the full costs of the condemnation, ignoring the subjective values of the owners of the condemned properties (197–201). Finally, "the nearly limitless applicability of the economic development rationale; severe limits on electoral accountability caused by low transparency; and time horizon problems" make economic-development takings "especially vulnerable" to the danger of rent-seeking and interest group "capture" (Somin 2007, 201, 201–03)

Whatever their incisiveness, these objections essentially sidestep the central question at the heart of this chapter. What if a particular taking is upwardly redistributive, benefiting primarily the wealthy, but is also *unambiguously* efficient? Despite the very palpable dangers that Somin illustrates, this is hardly an impossibility. In addition, although an efficient, inequality-increasing exercise of eminent domain would presumably be more likely with an economic development taking, an increase in inequality through a more legitimate "public use" taking also seems a possible, depending on who benefits from the public good. In any case, the primary point is that there is nothing impossible about an efficient, but inequality-increasing, exercise of public domain. The question is whether they are to be recommended or not.

According to double-distortion reasoning, an efficient economic-development taking, even one that raises income inequality, poses no problem and should indeed be encouraged. The income tax system can be used to compensate those burdened or harmed by the taking. By contrast, an egalitarian but inefficient taking would have tax-like distribution affects but presumably other distortions as well. But the source of these other distortions is murky. Indeed, and to the contrary, the very possibility of efficient and inefficient takings presumes the existence of wealth-neutral takings.

For example, suppose public authorities are considering an economic development taking that will harm the poor residents of an economically deprived neighborhood and enrich the developers who are backing the proposal. As in *Poletown* or *Kelo*, the project will destroy neighborhood businesses and jobs, and the fair market value the government offers in compensation is below what many residents would be willing to accept for their homes. For their part, developers will turn a tidy profit from their contemplated commercial and residential real-estate investment. Also suppose that, holding the tax system constant, the gains to the developers equal the losses to the residents. These gains and losses are also inclusive of labor-supply responses, in accordance with Kaplow and Shavell's (1994) assumptions.

Should the economic development taking be approved? From an efficiency perspective, we should be indifferent. Whether the government approves or rejects the taking results in the same total level of wealth. However, if we take a social-welfare perspective, and use the tax system to change the distribution of income, the conclusion is an unambiguous rejection of the taking. Because the economic-development taking would increase inequality, the optimal tax response will require more redistribution and an increase in marginal tax rates, compared to the status quo ante. But higher marginal tax rates imply an increase in labor-supply distortions and a loss of wealth (again, compared to the status quo ante). Furthermore, even with the optimal tax response, post-tax inequality will remain higher after the economic-development taking has occurred than it was before. As a result, both total wealth and income equality are lower after the taking, with the optimal tax response, than before. Any social welfare function would reject the taking.

This kind of reasoning will also apply to some strictly *efficient*, but inequitable, takings. Assuming, as we just did, that wealth is the same before and after the taking makes it clear that any optimal tax response will have *strictly* positive costs. But that, in turn, makes it clear that any efficiency-raising taking would not *necessarily* generate a social welfare improvement. This is because not just any increase in efficiency will outweigh the strictly positive loss in wealth that results from the optimal income-tax response. For example, if the taking raises inequality significantly but raises efficiency only marginally, this gain in wealth may still be smaller than the loss in wealth that would be required to optimally adjust tax rates following the taking's increase in inequality. If that is the case, we should reject an *efficient*, wealth-maximizing taking. Rejecting the taking is, in effect, a more efficient way to keep income inequality low than it would be to approve the taking and use the tax system to attempt to correct for the rise in inequality. This contravenes double-distortion reasoning, which would be to apply standard "first-best" reasoning and endorse any efficient taking, regardless of its effect on income distribution. Sometimes, an efficient legal action should be rejected in favor of a more equitable outcome.

Labor-supply effects play an important, but inessential role in this conclusion. If we followed Kaplow (2008) and used a distribution-neutral income tax adjustment, one that exactly negated labor-supply effects, we might find that blocking the takings is efficient and permitting it actually inefficient. In other words, Kaplow may agree in our conclusion but, because absent labor-supply effects, it is efficient to do so. As I explore in the book's appendix, distribution-neutral income tax adjustments are a somewhat arbitrary way to judge efficiency; they also effectively undermine the double-distortion claim, which requires including labor-supply effects when comparing legal and tax redistributions. More critically, the taking may have no labor-supply effects at all. In that case, a social welfare function would favor blocking an efficient, inequality-increasing taking, provided that gain in wealth is not dramatically large.

3.5 APPENDIX

The formal claims for this property chapter are found in the online appendix. The property section of the online appendix provides a detailed presentation of the mathematical elements of the Ayres and Talley (1995) game, along with a reproduction of their results. Next, the online appendix uses optimal tax theory to show how damages can redistribute more efficiently than the tax system, by eliciting informative differences among both ranchers and farmers that are not available to the income tax system. Finally, the online appendix shows why some efficient takings should be sacrificed for distributive reasons (reasons that increase social welfare).

4

Torts

The tort-reform movement has led to significant changes in the American civil justice system over the past fifty years (Hubbard 2006, 468). Headlines about spilled coffee generating multi-million-dollar verdicts (Enghagen and Gilardi 2002) and excessive litigation running rampant in the country's courts (Gabuthy and Lambert 2018, 571) have popularized the issue. The movement has proven successful, as nearly all states have adopted some aspect of the tort reform agenda, while many have enacted comprehensive tort reform legislation (Thompson, 1997, 65; Congressional Budget Office, 2004).

The tort reform movement has been, at least in part, a reaction to prior legal changes. Legal and procedural developments during the post-war years tended to favor plaintiffs. These included: relaxed pleading standards,[1] increases in damages for pain and suffering (Belli, 1951; Merkel, 2006, 545), the adoption of strict products liability,[2] and the creation of the modern opt-out class action lawsuit, which empowered plaintiffs to band together to fight large-scale injustices.[3] After these changes, courts were opened for newly empowered plaintiffs.

In the midst of these legal changes, tort costs as a percentage of GDP increased from 0.62 percent in 1950 to 2.33 percent in 1987 (Towers Watson 2011) – a $366 billion increase in 2019 dollars. Arguably, these legal changes were not distributively neutral. Plaintiffs tended to be individuals while defendants were large corporations owned by the wealthy. It is likewise not difficult to interpret the tort reform movement as being similarly animated by distributive stakes. Hence, the "tort reform" movement was born.

Tort reform encompasses many different policy objectives and legal doctrines, several of which are a direct response to the aforementioned post-war legal developments. Most reform legislation was enacted in the areas of medical

[1] Conley v. Gibson, 357 U.S. 41 (1951).

[2] Greenman v. Yuba Power Products, 59 Cal.2d 57 (1963); RESTATEMENT (SECOND) OF TORTS § 402A (AM. LAW INST. 1965).

[3] Fed. R. Civ. P. 23(b)(3).

malpractice and products liability. Smith (2004, 1221–22) identified six key areas of reform, including:

> (1) reducing the time period of the statute of limitations for filing claims; (2) regulating attorneys' fee structures; (3) modifying the collateral source rule; (4) putting monetary caps on noneconomic, economic, and punitive damages; (5) adjusting the requirements for expert testimony; and (6) modifying the standard of care in professional malpractice cases.

The tort reform movement has led to changes at the state and federal level through both legislation and judicial opinions. While all states have enacted some tort reform legislation,[4] several, including Alaska, Florida, Mississippi, Texas, Alabama, Tennessee, Wisconsin, South Carolina, and Oklahoma, have passed comprehensive tort reform legislation.[5] In 2005, Congress passed the Class Action Fairness Act, allowing defendants to remove claims with limited diversity to federal court while also limiting class action attorney fees.[6] Beginning in the 1990s, the Supreme Court issued a series of decisions curbing punitive damage awards,[7] strengthening standards of admissibility for expert witness testimony,[8] limiting jurisdiction over defendants,[9] and altering the pleading standard to one requiring "plausible" claims.[10] Tort reform has affected all levels of the American legal system. These legal changes had economic consequences as tort costs as a percentage of GDP declined from the aforementioned high of 2.33 percent in 1987 to 1.74 percent in 2009 (Towers Watson 2011). The goal of the tort reform movement – change laws to save money – has arguably prevailed.

4 Even states friendly to the trial attorney bar have passed tort reform legislation. For example, in New York State, the rule of joint and several liability was amended to exclude defendants from absolute liability that were found to be less than 50 percent at fault. *See* N.Y. C.P.L.R. § 1601 (McKinney 2014).

5 For a broad overview and summary of state-legal changes as of 2004 as well as a review of the literature on the effects of tort reform, see the report by the Congressional Budget Office (Congressional Budget Office 2004).

6 The central feature of the Class Action Fairness Act intended to reduce plaintiffs from forum shopping in friendly state courts by making it easier to remove cases to federal courts (Lee and Willging 2008). The Class Action Fairness Act also sought greater scrutiny of class-action settlements and attorney's fees (Vance 2005), a response to notorious cases such as *Kamilewicz v Bank of Boston Corp.*, 100 F.3d 1348, 1349 (7th Cir. 1996), where one class-action member received a net debit by paying more in attorney's fees than receiving in the award's share (1620, 1634). Overall, the Act is a good example of how even procedural legal doctrine has substantive – social, political, and distributive – stakes.

7 Pacific Mut. Life Ins. Co. v. Haslip, 499 U.S. 1, 18 (1991); Honda Motor Co., Ltd. v. Oberg, 512 U.S. 415 (1994) (requiring judicial review of punitive damage awards); State Farm Mut. Auto. Ins. Co. v. Campbell, 538 U.S. 408 (2003) (requiring greater proportionality between actual harm and punitive damages); Philip Morris USA v. Williams, 549 U.S. 346 (2007) (preventing punishment for harm to nonparties).

8 Daubert v. Merrell Dow Pharms., Inc., 509 U.S. 579 (1993).

9 Bristol-Myers Squibb Co. v. Superior. Ct. of Cal., 582 U.S. __, 137 S. Ct. 1773 (2017).

10 Bell Atlantic v. Twombly, 550 U.S. 554 (2007); Ashcroft v. Iqbal, 556 U.S. 662 (2009).

However, the intentions behind tort reform cannot be plausibly described as disinterested or concerned solely with efficiency, however they are publicly portrayed. It is commonly argued that high tort costs drive excessive liability insurance premiums, reduce wages and employment, undermine corporate profits, decrease productivity growth, discourage research and development, and reduce corporate risk-taking, all to the detriment of society at large (Chimerine and Eisenbrey 2005, 1). In fact, American liability costs as a percentage of GDP in 2011 were 2.6 times higher than the Eurozone average (U.S. Chamber Institute for Legal Reform 2013, 2).[11] However, such international comparisons do not take into account the different welfare systems between the various countries. What may count as liability costs in the U.S., such as medical bills or lost wages, is paid for in Europe through national health insurance or generous unemployment systems. Not counting Europe's welfare state artificially inflates the cost of the U.S. tort system (Chimerine and Eisenbrey 2005, 12). Whatever consequences tort reform has for efficiency, important distributive implications also underlie it.

* * *

Tort law has been absolutely central to the debate about using redistributive legal rules. As with most of economic analysis, the law of torts is often scrutinized in terms of efficiency, shunting aside distributive perspectives (Polinsky and Shavell, 2010, 1440; Hylton, 2013, 2457–58). But as the preceding brief history of the the tort-reform movement has demonstrated, tort law has significant distributive ramifications, even in this well-trodden domain of efficiency evaluations. Moreover, Kaplow and Shavell's (1994) landmark contribution appears to have been motivated, at least in part, by Arlen's (1992, 414–15) claim that in the optimal tort system,"in principle, wealth differences generally should be taken into account in setting both the level of due care and the amount of compensatory damages." Against Arlen's claim, Kaplow and Shavell contend, as the reader should by now be familiar, that the tort system should ignore wealth differences, not be used to redistribute income, and be concerned only with efficiency.

Section 4.1 of this chapter takes a closer look at Kaplow and Shavell's argument against redistributive legal rules by considering in more detail their specifically tort-related illustration of this claim. Section 4.2 looks at two of the most sustained responses to the double-distortion argument, which have also utilized tort law: Sanchirico's (2000; 2001) heterogeneity critique and Liscow's (2014) argument for zero-distortion legal rules. In Section 4.3, the chapter then introduces a new argument for using tort rules to redistribute income by defining the difference between ex ante and ex post evaluations of social welfare in cases of risk and uncertainty – the

[11] It is worth noting that the publisher of this information, the Institute for Legal Reform, was founded in the 1990 by the U.S. Chamber of Commerce, not a disinterested organization when it comes to distributive politics.

domain of tort law. Ex ante refers to the evaluation of social welfare before a given risk or uncertainty is realized, and ex post refers to the social-welfare evaluation after the realization. Section 4.4 then illustrates how and when tort law might redistibute income more efficiently than taxes once that distinction is taken into account. The basic insight is that Kaplow and Shavell only consider individuals' welfare ex ante, before we know, for example, who has and has not been injured in an accident. In the real world, however, when people get hurt, we know their identities, and not accounting for these ex post outcomes fails to maximize social welfare. Specifically, when ex post outcomes are included in the optimal tax appraisals, the costs of redistributive taxation increase. Tort law, which can change the distribution of risk and uncertainty, may then be able to redistribute income more efficiently by avoiding these additional costs.

Certainly, it is debatable whether American tort law provides adequate compensation for injury victims or whether the common law of torts provides coverage as commensurate as government run social programs. Perhaps not. But this chapter will show that it is at least possible that tort law may be a more efficient way of redistributing income, especially where some of these alternatives have other administrative costs. More generally, by highlighting the hidden inequality of ex ante measures of social welfare, the law, even if not tort law, can compensate for ex post inequality in unique ways.

4.1 TORTS IN THE DOUBLE-DISTORTION ARGUMENT

In Kaplow and Shavell's (1994) tort-law example, they ask us to consider a situation where increasing redistribution to the poor would be desirable. A tax-and-transfer system is already in place, where the rich pay taxes (the starting point in their article is that the rich pay a 30 percent income tax rate). However, another way to increase redistribution is by adopting a legal rule that benefits the poor at the expense of the rich. Specifically, they ask us to consider a strict liability tort rule that makes damages depend on the wealth of the injurer. For simplicity, say any accident caused by any injurer (rich or poor) causes harm of amount $\mathcal{H}$. If the rich person causes an accident to a poor person, they pay more than the actual harm caused, $D_R > \mathcal{H}$; while, if a poor person causes an accident to a rich person, they pay less than the actual harm caused, $D_P < \mathcal{H}$. If a person causes an injury to someone of the same income level, they need only pay for actual harm caused, $D = \mathcal{H}$.

Individuals can take precautions to avoid accidents. The amount of precaution reduces the chances of causing an accident. We can say that precautions cost, in dollar amounts, x, while the probability of an accident π is a function of the level of precaution: $\pi(x)$. The probability of an accident is decreasing in precaution, but at a decreasing rate as we approach a zero percent chance of an accident; it is therefore prohibitively costly to reduce the probability of an accident to zero. There is thus an efficient, cost-minimizing level of precaution one can take. This level of care minimizes both the costs of precautions, x, as well as the expected harm, $\pi(x)\mathcal{H}$, caused.[12] Let us denote this efficient level of care by adding an asterisk: x^*.

It is critical to Kaplow and Shavell's argument to note what happens at this stage. Under a strict liability rule, where one pays for actual harm caused, any potential injurer will be led to take the efficient level of precaution. If damages are equal to actual harm caused, the potential injurers will want to minimize the sum of costs of precaution and probability of harm – which requires choosing the efficient, cost-minimizing, level of care. On the other hand, when damages are *not* equal to actual harm, potential injurers will be led away from the efficient level of precaution. In fact, because rich defendants have to pay damages higher than actual harm they spend too much on precaution; while poor defendants spend too little, because damages they pay are less than actual harm caused. Put another way, the level of precaution the rich take is not *total* cost-minimizing because the amount they spend on precaution is not worth the lower probability of harm that level of precaution induces. The probability of harm is lower with a higher-than-efficient level of precaution, but the costs of precaution are higher than their efficient level. Put together, total costs are higher than the cost-minimizing level of care. Similarly, the level of precaution the poor take does not cost less because, while the costs spent on precaution are lower than the efficient level, the probability of harm is greater. Again, in the aggregate, the total of these two costs is higher than when an efficient level of care is chosen.

Although the wealth-dependent damages rule is inefficient, it also redistributes income in favor of the poor. While the damages that rich and poor pay, when set to levels other than actual harm, increase the *social* costs of precaution, this is not necessarily how each individual experiences this alteration privately. In fact, the private costs to a rich person increase, while the private costs to a poor person decrease. In other words, the adjustment in damages to reflect differences in wealth is redistributive. In addition to expending more on precaution, a rich individual also (1) must pay higher damages than actually caused if they injure a poor person and (2) is not fully compensated for actual harm if injured by a poor person. This leaves a rich person worse off than under an efficient damages rule. On the other hand, while they spend less on precaution than otherwise, a poor person (1) pays lower damages than actually caused if they injure a rich person and (2) is more than compensated for actual harm if injured by a rich person. These changes leave the poor person better off compared to a legal rule that makes any injurer liable for actual harm caused. To be sure, the greater social costs of the wealth-dependent damages rule are borne by someone. In this case, the greater social costs are borne by the rich, in the form of higher precautionary costs and in uncompensated injuries. Nevertheless,

[12] In mathematical terms, the optimal level of care is reached once the final, marginal dollar spent on precaution is equal to the marginal benefit of reducing the probability of harm: $1 = -\pi'(x)\mathcal{H}$. See Section 4.5 for further discussion.

by improving the welfare and income of the poor person, at the expense of the rich person, the legal rule change does accomplish its redistributive objective.

We can now turn to the crucial question: Should we endorse the redistributive damages rule? Kaplow and Shavell (1994) say we should not. They argue this by conceiving of a distribution-neutral income tax adjustment.[13] Instead of the wealth-dependent damages rule, suppose instead that we adopt the more efficient damages rule that makes each injurer pay for actual harm caused. In addition, suppose that we increase taxes on the rich and transfers to the poor by exactly the amounts that the wealth-dependent damages rule does. When those tax adjustments are adopted, the distribution of income and welfare is exactly the same as with the redistributive legal rule. The alternative policy – an efficient damages rule plus increased taxes and transfers – does just as well, distributively speaking, as the wealth-dependent damages rule. But because the efficient damages rule has lower social cost, it beats the wealth-dependent damages rule in terms of efficiency. That efficiency shows up in a budget surplus in the revenue that the government collects. A surplus exists because the social costs of the inefficient, wealth-dependent legal rule is borne by the rich. The difference between the higher costs carried by the rich and caused by the more redistributive legal rule, and the lower costs of the efficient legal rule, gets reflected by the higher taxes levied on the rich, which are necessary to make the income of the rich identical under either rule.

The choice for Kaplow and Shavell is then obvious. Because the adoption of the alternative policy (the change in the tax schedule coupled with the strict liability rule) achieves as much redistribution as the wealth-dependent damages rule, but at lower social cost, they view it as superior to the wealth-dependent legal rule. Instead, the alternative policy should be implemented and, because it generates a budget surplus, those gains can be used to increase transfers to the poor – raising the income and well-being of the poor above that which is achieved by the wealth-dependent damages rule. Alternatively, the budget surplus can be used to increase transfers to the poor *and* reduce taxes on the rich, improving everyone's welfare. The use of a social welfare function can determine which option, or combination of options, should be chosen. But because we have a Pareto improvement, Kaplow and Shavell's recommendation holds regardless of the social welfare function chosen.

This example illustrates, for Kaplow and Shavell, a general feature – and a deficiency – that comes with using legal rules to redistribute. By changing the distribution of income, the wealth-dependent legal rules act like a distribution-equivalent change in the tax schedule. This will be accompanied by distortionary (efficiency-reducing) labor-supply responses by both the rich and the poor. This labor-supply response

[13] Kaplow had not invented the term "distribution-neutral income tax adjustment" when he and Shavell published their 1994 article. Strictly speaking, they also use the distribution-neutral income tax adjustment differently than how Kaplow (2008) later explicitly conceived of the method. See the book's appendix for further discussion.

counts as one distortion. The wealth-dependent damages rule also changes the way rich and poor take precautions against causing accidents. Because these responses are wasteful compared to the less redistributive but more efficient rule, the precautionary response constitutes a second distortion. Finally, because a distribution-equivalent change in the tax schedule could replace the wealth-dependent damages rule, and make everyone better off, the tax system is more efficient than legal rules in redistributing income. Although they illustrate this argument with the use of a tort rule, Kaplow and Shavell claim that the insight they glean goes well beyond the realm of torts. Legal rules distort not just in a "tax" way, by changing each individuals' disposable income; they also distort the behavior regulated by the legal rule, unlike taxes. Because one distortion is better than two, it follows that the tax system is a better tool for redistributing income than legal rules.

For readers wanting a more formal treatment of Kaplow and Shavell's (1994) argument, see Section 4.5.

4.2 USING TORTS TO REDISTRIBUTE INCOME EFFICIENTLY?

4.2.1 *Heterogeneity*

Sanchirico (2000) presents perhaps the most sophisticated critique to-date of the double-distortion argument. Sanchirico contends that "even in the presence of an optimally redistributive tax, any concern for 'equity' dictates that legal rules should deviate from efficient standards in a manner that redistributes toward the less well-off" (797). According to Sanchirico, the missing element in Kaplow and Shavell (1994) is sufficient *heterogeneity* in individuals' characteristics.[14] For example, while Kaplow and Shavell assume in their formal model that persons are different in their ability to earn income, they also assume that people are *identical* (i.e., homogeneous) in their ability to take precautions against accidents. Because of this identical status, the income-dependent damages rule affects everyone similarly, leading only to a loss of efficiency. However, as Sanchirico argues, if individuals also differed in their precaution-taking abilities, an income-dependent damages rule will actually increase welfare.

Kaplow and Shavell quickly responded to the heterogeneity critique, writing, "we believe Sanchirico's claim that our basic argument is subject to certain qualifications is correct but does not go to the heart of whether legal rules should be systematically adjusted to favor the poor and disfavor the rich in order to further distributive objectives" (Kaplow and Shavell 2000b, 828). Suppose that rich yacht owners are prone to accidents ("klutzy") and that their victims are poor fishing boat owners. Should damages be raised to redistribute from the rich yacht owners to poor fishermen? Kaplow and Shavell say, "No." In fact, the legal rule should be adjusted to favor

[14] Avraham, Fortus, and Logue (2003) also make the heterogeneity critique.

rich yacht owners and disfavor poor fishing boat owners because a pro-defendant adjustment helps klutzier yacht owners, who are less well-off than their rich, non-klutzy peers. What about the poor? Kaplow and Shavell contend that an adjustment to the income tax could compensate fishing boat owners for lower damage payments. Thus, redistribution between rich and poor is kept the same while helping klutzes within the group of rich yacht owners. The bottom line: Sanchirico is technically correct, but "optimal adjustments to legal rules have no general, a priori relationship to the notion that legal rules should favor the poor in order to further redistributive objectives" (832). Furthermore, rules that favor the well-being of the rich-but-klutzy yacht owners increase overall well-being, in part by increasing the efficiency of the tax system, but do not redistribute *income* in the conventional sense (826).

Sanchirico mounted a rejoinder. He observed that neither were Kaplow and Shavell targeting income per se, but rather, like Sanchirico, were attempting to reduce inequality in overall well-being. In terms of Kaplow and Shavell's example (critiquing Sanchirico), "if the rich yacht owners are better-off overall [than poor fisherman], then Kaplow and Shavell have it backwards. ...[T]he equity adjustment to the tort system should favor the poor fishing-boat owners, and not the rich yacht owners" (Sanchirico 2001, 1035–36). Nevertheless, Sanchirico's (2000; 2001) own models show that whether legal rules should favor the rich or the poor depends on the correlation (or covariance) between income-earning ability and care-taking ability. Kaplow and Shavell therefore seem at least technically correct that optimal (i.e., social-welfare maximizing) adjustments to legal rules should not *always* be used to favor the income poor.[15] However, we will return later to the significance of this conclusion.

4.2.2 *Zero-Distortion Legal Rules*

More recently, Liscow (2014) has helped revive the debate over the double-distortion argument. Liscow argues that some legal rules may be less inefficient than taxes in redistributing income – in fact, some may reduce income inequality with *zero* economic distortion. Liscow builds his argument around a simple yet insightful hypothetical case. In this case, a legislature is deciding which liability rule to adopt for all polluting factories in a jurisdiction. The choice is between a rule in which factory owners would only be liable for negligently caused harm or a strict liability rule in which owners would be liable for all harm caused. Liscow also assumes for the sake of argument that factory owners are, on average, substantially wealthier than those residents near the factory harmed by pollution.

Which liability rule should the legislators adopt? As is well known (Cooter and Ulen 2016, 201–04), both strict liability and negligence lead the potential injurers (the factory owners) to take the appropriate level of care – for example, how much the

[15] Gamage (2014, 14) draws a similar conclusion.

owners should spend on abatement efforts. But as Liscow points out, the distributive effects of these two legal rules are very different. Under a negligence rule, a factory owner must only pay for negligently caused harm; some pollution, and therefore some harm, will continue to be felt by the local residents. In contrast, under a strict liability rule, a factory owner must pay for all harm caused. A strict liability rule therefore increases the income of the residents and decreases the income of the factory owners compared to the negligence rule. And because both rules are equally efficient, this redistribution is carried out with zero economic loss; the legal rule is more efficient than taxation in redistributing income.

Strict liability can therefore redistribute income without any economic distortion. But does this make liability rules better than income taxes? It would seem so, because the liability rule has zero economic distortion, compared to the positive tax distortion. But is the zero-distortion assumption justified? On this point, we do not have quite enough information to give a persuasive answer to this question. In Liscow's case, factory owners are presumably allowed to vary the amount of pollution and the number of factories is fixed in the short run (Liscow 2014, 2486–87). But he does not specify whether factory owners have a margin of decision regarding how much, of whatever it is, they produce (for which pollution is the negative externality). The "activity level" is how the literature describes this margin of decision (Shavell 1980). Such a margin of decision would necessarily be related to both the amount of pollution and the income of the polluter. If so, it is quite possible that a negligence rule, combined with an adjustment to the income tax, could deliver the same levels of efficiency and distribution as the strict liability rule.

These questions leave open at least three distinct issues. To fully determine whether strict liability has a "zero-distortion" distributive advantage over negligence, we need to know if that advantage exists: (1) when factory owners are allowed to leave the jurisdiction in the long run, or (2) when factory owners are allowed to vary the output – the "activity level" that is associated with the social harm, and in either case (3) when an income tax intervention is combined with the negligence rule. Each open question will be addressed in that order.

The first issue to examine is the long run. In the long run, Liscow is more explicit about economic distortions, as factories have time to enter and leave the jurisdiction (Liscow 2014, 2494–97). However, he does not appear to recognize the problem this poses for equity-informed legal rules. In the long run, the negligence and strict liability rules are no longer neutral with respect to efficiency. Because the negligence rule gives factory owners higher profits or income compared to the strict liability rule, in the long run the negligence rule induces an excess supply of factories in the jurisdiction. More specifically, under a negligence rule, the market price of the factory's output does not reflect its full cost because a nonnegligent factory owner does not pay for any of the harm the factory's production causes. This generates a negative externality, and leads to an excessive number of factories in the jurisdiction (if we were to ignore or hold constant the effects of the tax system on individuals' choices – analyzing the choice of *i-efficient* legal rules, as Liscow (2014, 2483) calls them). By contrast, under strict liability, factories must pay for all harm caused, which leads to both an efficient choice of care and an efficient number of factories. Strict liability forces factories to internalize the externality. So, not only is strict liability more equitable, it is also more efficient than the negligence rule. Most critically, this conclusion weakens the case for equity-informed legal rules. Because strict liability poses no equity-efficiency trade-off, Kaplow and Shavell would endorse it on efficiency grounds alone. Strict liability may also be more equitable, but this is merely incidental, according to double-distortion reasoning, in light of its superior efficiency.

The long-run issue poses another problem for the case for redistributive legal rules. Liscow (2014, 2494–97) introduces factory mobility when discussing the timing of distributional benefits and behavioral responses. He suggests that legal rules work well when "the good parts of the rule change (redistribution) …happen quickly, and the bad parts (distortions to behavior) …accumulate with time as individuals have time to respond." But it is not clear why legal rules have an advantage in this respect. Taxes would also have immediate redistributive impact and a slow behavioral response (as factories leave the jurisdiction), giving legal rules no clear advantage. Adopting strict liability would lower the profits to factory owners, causing them to leave the jurisdiction, just as increasing the income tax would. Indeed, adopting a negligence rule, along with an increase in income taxes set to the amount of harm caused would cause (in the long run) *exactly the same* amount of redistribution and economic distortion (through factories leaving the jurisdiction) as would a strict liability rule. Thus, introducing the long-run margin of decision does not make any difference to the choice between legal rules and income taxes, and yields no advantage for the former over the latter.

Precisely the same sort of analysis applies to the second issue, the factory's choice of "activity level." The activity level refers to allowing individual factories to vary whatever it is they produce that also generates the social harm. For example, the activity level could refer to how much a person uses their lawn mower, with the externality being the risk of an accident (e.g., caused by projectiles ejected from the mower's spinning blades) whose frequency will depend obviously on the activity level itself. In our case, factories can burn coal to produce electricity; the more coal is burned, the more pollutants are also produced. The key point is that different legal rules will change the activity level. Under a negligence rule, for example, factories will not be liable for all harm caused, and therefore will not factor in the (marginal) cost of harm with the (marginal) value of output. On the other hand, a strict liability rule will compel factory owners to internalize the full (marginal, social) cost of their output and restore efficiency. The implication, once again, is that strict liability should be adopted but because it is efficient, not because it is more equitable. That it is more equitable is merely incidental to this double-distortion endorsement.[16]

Finally, does strict liability have any distributive advantage over the negligence rule when the latter can be coupled with an income tax intervention? As already indicated, if the income tax is raised on factory owners, equal to the amount of harm caused by the pollution, and distributed to the victims, this would have an effect fully equivalent to the strict liability rule. A tentative answer to that question therefore comes in the negative. However, one question arises. Would the income tax also fall on non-polluting individuals in the same income bracket? If so, the tax-cum-negligence policy would not perfectly duplicate to the strict liability policy because the incidence of the tax would also fall on non-polluters. Compared to a strict liability rule, which would narrowly target polluters, an income tax increase would create additional, unnecessary distortions on non-polluters. Given this fact, does strict liability have a distributive advantage after all?

As an answer to this, double-distortion reasoning would ask, Why *not* a narrowly tailored tax intervention? Policy already has available an instrument for addressing externalities, including pollution. This policy option is a corrective or Pigouvian tax, which would be targeted only at polluters at an amount equal to the marginal social cost of the harm. As Kaplow (2008) indicates elsewhere, a corrective-tax intervention would involve nothing more than cost-benefit, efficiency analysis, and need not be concerned with distributive complications. That is, the corrective, Pigouvian tax should be set at its efficient level and ignore its distributive effects. To be sure, the Pigouvian tax *would* have distributive consequences because it would fall on primarily wealthy factory owners but benefit society as whole. But because these distributive effects are merely incidental to the efficiency problem, no independent distributive-analysis or corrective is required. Instead, double-distortion reasoning yields the anticipated conclusion: Its prescription would direct us to choose corrective taxes with only efficiency in mind and let the income tax handle the distributive problems. This prescription would conclude, once again, that strict liability has no advantage over the negligence rule coupled with a Pigouvian tax on pollution. Despite Liscow's (2014, 2485 n.15) laudable desire to separate corrective taxes from income taxes, it does not seem possible to do so in this case because the equity issue and the externality (inefficiency) are inextricably linked.

The conclusion drawn from these three complicating factors is that strict liability has no distributive advantage over the negligence rule. If strict liability does have any advantage over negligence, it is an efficiency advantage, not a distributive one. Consequently, it is not at all clear that strict liability is a good candidate for validating the claim for redistributive legal rules. Even setting aside the difficulties of this

[16] The recognition that strict liability is more efficient than negligence, once endogenous activity levels have been introduced, can be found in classic analyses of liability rules such as Polinsky (1989, 91–96) and Shavell (1980).

example, another drawback with Liscow's analysis is that it is hard to know how general the insight is. Are there other rules that have zero economic distortion? Liscow is silent on this question. In fact, the distributive consequences of choosing between negligence and strict liability is well-trod territory and its discussion predates Kaplow and Shavell's double-distortion argument.[17] Presumably, Kaplow and Shavell believed that the distributive superiority of strict liability over negligence was merely an isolated exception to their general insight. Furthermore, arguments in the older discussion about liability rules were much less conclusive than Liscow's analysis might suggest. For example, when harm is probabilistic rather than deterministic (as in Liscow's example) and insurance is available, negligence may be more efficient than strict liability, making the equity-informed case for strict liability even more difficult (Polinsky 1989, 67–74, 123–24). In any case, Liscow's focus on the tort case, which is merely illustrative, underscores how the abstract nature surrounding the double-distortion argument has played in favor of Kaplow and Shavell's (1994) initial conclusion.

4.3 EX ANTE VERSUS EX POST SOCIAL WELFARE

The distinction between deterministic and probabilistic harms brings up another interesting avenue for thinking about the possible advantages of redistributing income with legal rules. When harm is probabilistic it raises the problem of uncertainty.

Uncertainty is important in the law and pervasive in social life, especially in areas governed by torts, liability rules, and other forms of regulation. When it comes to the choice of legal rules, uncertainty is critical because income inequality will be *larger* after (ex post) the risk or uncertainty is realized than it will before (ex ante).[18] This difference requires the legal analyst to choose one of these normative standards (ex ante or ex post) when evaluating legal rules. However, in previous research this choice is typically avoided by assuming risk neutral agents, the availability of actuarially fair insurance, or by invoking arguments for why the standard should always be to maximize ex ante social welfare.

If we take seriously the role of uncertainty and the choice between ex ante and ex post welfare then, as this chapter shows, different legal rules can shift uncertainty from poorer to richer individuals and reduce ex post income inequality, without changing incentives or labor supply choices, which are made ex ante. By lowering ex post inequality, legal rules can therefore avoid the costs of redistributive taxation, making legal rules a more efficient method of redistributing income. This does not

[17] See, for instance, Posner (1979), and Polinsky (1989, 123–24).

[18] *Larger* by any measure of income inequality – Lorenz dominance, Gini coefficient, second-order stochastic dominance – but perhaps most intuitively in this case as a mean-preserving spread (Rothschild and Stiglitz 1970).

mean that every redistributive legal rule is more efficient than taxation and should be adopted. Nevertheless, uncertainty is legally and socially pervasive, so it would not be surprising if legal rules could often be more efficient than taxes in redistributing income.

4.3.1 *Concave Social Welfare Functions*

The ex ante versus ex post distinction matters because it changes the way we measure social welfare. In simple terms, the ex ante perspective measures *expected* welfare (or income) outcomes while the ex post perspective measures *actual* outcomes. A person's expected outcome is, in a sense, *identical*, despite many different possible outcomes. Once those different possibilities are realized, however, that individual could occupy many *non-identical* situations. Furthermore, those realized differences increase the variation in outcomes, compared to the ex ante situation and before those differences are realized; and greater variation is simply another way of saying greater inequality. An ex ante perspective therefore hides a lot of yet-to-be-realized inequality.

For example, say a person earns an income of y but faces some probability π that they will suffer a loss D. Let us suppose policymakers measure welfare with the concave function $G(\cdot)$. If we judge this person's welfare from an ex ante perspective, we weigh the well-being of the person's expected income, as follows: $W_{EA} = G(\pi(y - D) + (1 - \pi)y)$. By contrast, if we judge this person's welfare from an ex post perspective, we will weigh the actual outcomes, as follows: $W_{EP} = \pi G(y - D) + (1 - \pi)G(y)$. The two measures will not be equal, and this inequality derives from the *concavity* of the social welfare function $G(\cdot)$, which means that with every additional increase in income, Δy, its social value, as measured by $\Delta G(y)$, gets smaller. When social welfare measures expected income, every dollar has equal value, so changing distributions between "states of the world," injured or uninjured, will not change social welfare. On the other hand, when social welfare measures actual outcomes, each dollar does not have equal value: The final, or marginal dollar in state y will have less value than the marginal dollar in state $y - D$, given that y is more than $y - D$ *and that* $G(\cdot)$ *is concave*.

"Concavity" is another way of expressing "diminishing marginal value," and so the reason that an ex ante measure reports less inequality than an ex post measure is the same reason that any social welfare function reports lower social welfare whenever income inequality is higher for a fixed amount of total wealth. The presumption of a social welfare function is that the marginal dollar of a rich person is valued less than the marginal dollar of a poor person. If, instead of applying the social welfare function to each individual's income, we first added up all individuals' income and *then* applied the social welfare function, the resulting value would not reflect any differences in income. It would not reflect any inequality at all. The same thing happens when we measure expected outcomes, or incomes, compared to actual, realized incomes. In the first case, there are differences of welfare between individuals and, in the second case, differences of welfare among similarly situated individuals at different times. That symmetry makes it hard to ignore differences in ex post welfare among individuals of the same ex ante income once we accept the differences of income between individuals are relevant for social welfare.[19]

To illustrate the relevance of the ex ante versus ex post social welfare distinction, consider the following stylized example. Suppose that in a given geographic area there are two groups, the rich and the poor. The rich earn after-tax income of $300,000 a year and make up 25 percent of the population. The poor earn $5,000 a year after taxes and transfers and make up the remaining 75 percent of the population. Suppose the rich own factories whose production emits a pollutant that poses a 50 percent chance of causing harm to the poor. The pollutant has monetary costs of $5,000; these losses could be medical expenses, time spent out of work, or perhaps permanent damage from the illness causes a loss of future earnings. As in Liscow's problem, a court whose jurisdiction includes this area must decide whether to adopt a negligence or strict liability rule. The court measures social welfare as the square root of every person's income. Which liability rule should it choose?

4.3.2 *Social Welfare from an Ex Ante Perspective*

If we take an ex ante perspective, the answer is that the choice of rules doesn't matter. Under the strict liability rule, the rich will be liable for all damage caused. Therefore, the rich will have to pay damages of $5,000 in 50 percent of cases. The expected income of the rich is therefore $297, 500.[20] From an ex ante perspective, we measure the welfare of *expected*, rather than actual, outcomes. In terms of welfare, as the square root of expected income, the well-being of the rich becomes 545 "welfare units." The poor are not liable for damages in the case of strict liability, and are fully compensated for their injuries, and so their expected income is $5, 000 in either case, injured or uninjured.[21] In welfare terms, this amounts to the well-being of the poor being measured at 71. If we weight each welfare outcome by the population share of each group, total social welfare is calculated to be 189 under the strict liability rule.[22]

Now, compare those results with the negligence rule. Under the negligence rule, the rich will not be liable for damages, as long as they take reasonable care. Thus, their expected income remains the same at $300,000. The poor will be liable, making their expected income $2,500.[23] Notice that the negligence rule makes the poor poorer and the rich richer in expected terms. This difference therefore presents itself

[19] For discussions on the choice of ex ante versus ex post social welfare functions, see Adler and Sanchirico (2006).

[20] Specifically, $0.50(\$300,000 - \$5,000) + 0.50(\$300,000) = \$297,500$

[21] $0.50(\$5,000 - \$5,000 + \$5,000) + 0.50(\$5,000) = \$5,000$

[22] $0.25(\sqrt{\$297,500}) + 0.75(\sqrt{\$5,000}) = 189$

[23] $0.50(\$5,000 - \$5,000) + 0.50(\$5,000) = \$2,500$

as an invitation to select the strict liability rule on distributive grounds. However, if we simply increase taxes on the rich and reduce taxes (or increase transfers) on the poor by \$2,500, the expected amount of damages,[24] we can achieve the identical outcomes as under the strict liability rule – and without any loss of efficiency because incomes, and therefore labor supply incentives, will be identical. For example, with the transfer, the expected income of the poor will be restored to \$5,000. Because expected incomes and therefore expected welfare will be the same, social welfare will therefore be *identical* under either rule: 189. The takeaway point is that with the existence of an income tax system and an ex ante perspective on social welfare, it does not matter which legal rule we choose.

4.3.3 *Social Welfare from an Ex Post Perspective*

What if we take an ex post perspective? Then the choice of rules does matter. We now measure social welfare with actual outcomes. Expected incomes will be identical under either welfare measure, but expected welfare changes. For example, under strict liability this will be 545 for the rich and 71 for the poor. Because the poor are fully compensated for their injuries under strict liability, and so get the same income in either state, their welfare is the same under either perspective, ex ante or ex post. For the rich, their welfare also looks the same as under ex ante welfare, but this is only because of rounding. That is, the welfare of the rich *is* lower in the ex post perspective, compared to the ex ante.[25] But because the high incomes of the rich put them out a long way down the social welfare curve, so to speak, the (relatively) small loss that comes with having to compensate an injured poor person makes little difference to their social welfare. In other words, because the rich value an additional dollar less than the poor do, burdening them with the risk of harm has little effect on overall social welfare. Consequently, when we weight the welfare of each group by population shares, we get 189, which again is similar because of rounding, but nevertheless very close to the ex ante case.

However, under the negligence rule, and using the same tax adjustment as in the ex ante case, we have an expected welfare of 545 for the rich and 68 for the poor. In this case, the welfare of the rich is the same in ex ante and ex post cases because, not being responsible for damages, their income is the same whether they suffer an injury or not. For the poor, however, we have a different story. Because the poor have little income, an accident makes a big difference in their welfare. Therefore, when the poor are saddled with the costs of accidents, their welfare is significantly lower under the negligence rule than under the strict liability rule.

To put it a slightly different way, the strict liability rule places the uncertainty of the costs of accidents on the rich; the negligence rule consigns that uncertainty

[24] $0.50 \times \$5,000 = \$2,500$

[25] More precisely, strict liability gives the rich a welfare measure of 545.4356 under the ex ante perspective and 545.4308 under the ex post.

to the poor. From an ex ante perspective, this makes no difference because dollar differences in actual outcomes *within* income groups do not translate into social welfare differences. From an ex post perspective, however, this variation matters. Shifting the uncertainty of the costs of accidents with the negligence rule essentially makes the poor poorer – more than the strict liability makes the rich poorer, in social welfare terms. Thus, weighted by population shares, social welfare then becomes 187 under the negligence rule, which is *less* than social welfare under the strict liability rule. Unlike the ex ante case, social welfare in the ex post case expresses a clear preference. In the ex post case, the choice of legal rules does matter, and the rule that maximizes social welfare is the strict liability rule.

These outcomes are displayed in Table 4.1. To summarize to this point, once our social welfare function accounts for ex post outcomes – including their greater variability, which raises inequality and reduces social welfare – legal rules can make a difference for social welfare compared to when our social welfare function considers only expected outcomes. The strict liability shifts the responsibility for the uncertain

TABLE 4.1 *Liability rules and social welfare*

Legal Rule	Welfare: Ex Ante
Strict Liability	$U_R = \sqrt{0.50(\$300,000 - \$5,000) + 0.50(\$300,000)} = 545$ $U_P = \sqrt{0.50(\$5,000 - \$5,000 + \$5,000) + 0.50(\$5,000)} = 71$ $W = 0.25(545) + 0.75(71) = 189$
Negligence	$U_R = \sqrt{0.50(\$300,000 - \$2,500) + 0.50(\$300,000 - \$2,500)} = 545$ $U_P = \sqrt{0.50(\$5,000 - \$5,000 + \$2500) + 0.50(\$5,000 + \$2500)} = 71$ $W = 0.25(545) + 0.75(71) = 189$

Legal Rule	Welfare: Ex Post
Strict Liability	$U_R = 0.50\sqrt{\$300,000 - \$5,000} + 0.50\sqrt{\$300,000} = 545$ $U_P = 0.50\sqrt{\$5,000 - \$5,000 + \$5,000} + 0.50\sqrt{\$5,000} = 71$ $W = 0.25(545) + 0.75(71) = 189$
Negligence	$U_R = 0.50\sqrt{\$300,000 - \$2500} + 0.50\sqrt{\$300,000 - \$2500} = 545$ $U_P = 0.50\sqrt{\$5000 - \$5000 + \$2500} + 0.50\sqrt{\$5,000 + \$2500} = 68$ $W = 0.25(545) + 0.75(68) = 187$

Notes: U_R is the utility of rich and U_P the utility of the poor. W is total social welfare, with outcomes indicated in bold text. There is no difference in social welfare in the ex ante case (both 189). In the ex post case, social welfare is strictly higher under the strict liability rule (189) than under the negligence rule (187).

costs of accidents from the poor, who have a high social marginal welfare weight, to the rich, who have a low one. Moreover, shifting this variation only matters because we take an ex post approach. Otherwise, from an ex ante perspective, this variation is only considered part of an individual's expected income, and makes no difference in the social-welfare evaluation.

To summarize, once we take an ex post perspective, social welfare is higher under strict liability than under negligence. But that raises the next question: Does that make legal rules a more *efficient* way to redistribute income? All we have shown thus far is that legal rules can matter distributively depending on whether one takes an ex ante or ex post perspectives. The tax system has played only a limited role. If we were to explicitly compare and evaluate the income tax system, will negligence be more redistributively efficient than strict liability, even ex post? As Section 4.4 will argue in more detail, legal rules still have an advantage over income taxes in the ex post perspective.

4.4 RISK, UNCERTAINTY, AND LEGAL REDISTRIBUTION

It is now necessary to explore in closer detail the problem of uncertainty, both in light of the availability of insurance and, from an ex post perspective, one that measures the social welfare of actual outcomes, rather than expected outcomes. The goal will be to demonstrate that an inefficient, redistributive legal rule can redistribute more efficiently than an efficient, non-redistributive legal rule because the latter legal rule generates greater ex post income inequality, and therefore greater costs of redistribution.

We return to our three-category model of inequality that we have employed throughout the book, with three basic social classes. (For a basic introduction, see the book's appendix.) The essential addition is to include a probabilistic, harm-generating activity. As in Liscow's (2014) example, only the rich engage in this harm-causing activity (e.g., factory owners polluting). Everyone, however – poor, middle class, and rich – can suffer harm. This harm is probabilistic, and therefore uncertain. In our simple model with three groups of individuals, wealthy entrepreneurs produce the good that also creates some chance of harm to the entire population – including the wealthy. From an ex ante perspective, each income level has an equal chance of being harmed, which allows us to calculate an expected level of income – the average of the incomes if harmed or unharmed.

4.4.1 *No Insurance: Ex Ante and Ex Post*

To clarify the argument that legal rules may be able to redistribute more efficiently, we will first concentrate on the case where insurance is not available.[26] Setting aside

[26] One simple way of motivating this lack-of-insurance case is to assume that utility is linear in income. There is therefore no risk aversion, and no demand for insurance.

insurance will allow us to show how rules that are otherwise similarly efficient from an ex ante perspective can lead to different social-welfare judgments ex post. Rules that lower ex post social welfare raise the costs of redistribution, and make the alternative, equally efficient legal rule preferable on redistributive grounds.

Again comparing the strict-liability and negligence rules, we will begin by replicating the standard ex ante result, and show that in this case there is no efficiency-equity trade-off with respect to legal rules. That is, the negligence and strict-liability rules are *equally* equitable and efficient. This changes when we consider the ex post case. At the risk of overemphasis, the basic point again is that the ex post distribution of incomes (under either legal rule) is more unequal than the ex ante distribution. However, the ex post distribution of income is *even more* unequal under the negligence rule than under the strict liability rule. This makes the strict liability rule the welfare maximizing rule under an ex post social welfare function.

The Ex Ante Case

Let us get out of the way, first, the entrepreneur's choice of care. According to standard results, a risk-neutral entrepreneur will exercise an efficient level of care under either legal standard. In the strict liability case, this is because the entrepreneur is liable for all the harm they cause. The entrepreneur then chooses the level of care so that the marginal benefit in reducing the chances of harm equal the marginal costs of care – the very definition of optimal, efficient behavior. Under the negligence rule, an entrepreneur will only be liable if the care they take falls below some specified standard of care. This produces incentives to take exactly this level of care and no more, because they will only be liable for damages if the care they take falls below that level. They have no incentive to take more care, because doing so will not change her liability and only increases their costs of care. Because the reasonable level of care, according to the Learned Hand rule, is the level of care that minimizes the sum of accident costs and care, an entrepreneur also takes an efficient level of care under the negligence rule.

Although each legal rule induces efficient, precautionary behavior, they produce different distributions of harm, and therefore different expected incomes. How does the choice of legal rule affect the distribution of these expected incomes? First, because entrepreneurs, who take a reasonable level of care, will not be liable for the harm they nevertheless cause, this increases profits to the firm. Likewise, the rest of the population, who must bear these costs, are poorer.[27] For the opposite reasons, entrepreneurs are poorer and the population richer under strict liability.

A second effect of legal rules is that there will be excessive – inefficient – firm entry under the negligence rule. Higher profits encourage greater firm entry, but a larger number of firms also increases the amount of the externality and therefore the

[27] Although the wealthy can also be harmed, they are, on net, richer, because they enjoy all of the gains of no liability while the expected costs of harm are spread among the entire population.

chances of being harmed. As long as each firm generates a roughly equal chance of harm, more firms means a greater number of expected – and actual – accidents. This is inefficient because entrepreneurs, who are not liable for harms caused, do not take this cost into account when creating a firm. Nevertheless, this inefficiency can be corrected through taxation. Raising taxes on entrepreneurs equal to the expected harm leads to the efficient level of firm activity. Under strict liability, firms already bear this cost because of the strict liability rule. This leads to the conclusion that the income distribution is identical under the two rules; and because incomes are identical, so will be the levels of labor supply and welfare. Thus, welfare is identical under the strict liability and negligence rules.

The Ex Post Case

Let us now turn to the ex post case. The first thing to observe is that, under either rule, income inequality is higher under an ex post social welfare function than under an ex ante one. Under the negligence rule, for instance, we are no longer dealing with three groups, each with identical *expected* income, but with effectively six groups. That is because at each income level some are injured and some are not. Not only does this increase the variance of the income outcomes, but the wealthiest person, ex post, is richer than the wealthiest person, ex ante, and the poorest ex post is poorer than the poorest ex ante. For example, in the ex post case, the wealthiest person is an unharmed entrepreneur; in the ex ante case, the wealthiest person has an average income of harmed and unharmed entrepreneurs. Likewise, in the ex post case, the poorest person is an injured, unemployed individual; and so forth.

Again, the key point is that overall inequality is higher under the ex post, compared to the ex ante, perspective. This point implies that because a social welfare function embodies a preference for equality, the welfare gains from redistribution will be larger under an ex post than under an ex ante approach. Furthermore, because the gains from redistribution will be higher, marginal tax rates will also be higher in the ex post case. And larger marginal tax rates also immediately imply greater tax-induced distortions in labor supply. Thus, when an ex post perspective is taken, the negligence rules generate greater redistributive costs in the tax system, something that gets ignored in the ex ante perspective.

Let us illustrate this point in more detail. In the ex post case, realized income inequality increases under either legal rule. That is because we have adopted an ex post perspective. However and importantly, with a strict liability rule, the rich bear more of that uncertainty than society does. Under the negligence rule, the wealthy take efficient precaution and are therefore never liable for the harm they cause. The risk of harm under negligence is consequently spread throughout society – including, importantly, the poor. Compare this outcome with the strict-liability rule, which makes entrepreneurs compensate those who are harmed. The risk of accidents therefore shifts from society as a whole to the entrepreneurs themselves. Because entrepreneurs are only one group, the uncertainty is more concentrated under the

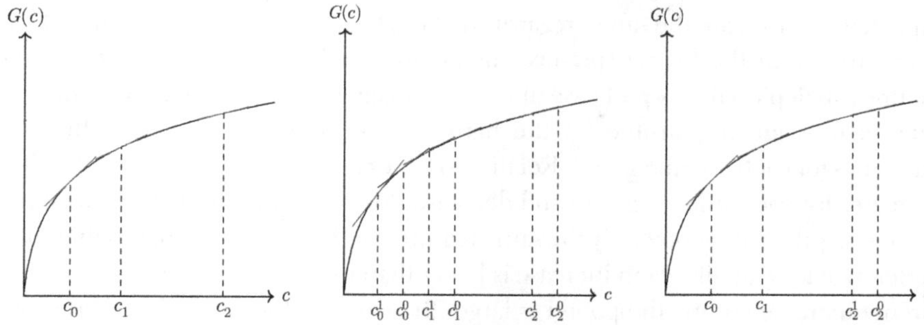

(a) Ex ante (b) Ex post (negligence) (c) Ex post (strict liability)

FIGURE 4.1 Ex ante versus ex post social welfare functions

Each subfigure depicts social welfare (G(·), on the *y*-axis) as a function of disposable income (*c*, on the *x*-axis). Marginal social welfare is higher for lower income individuals, as indicted by the lines tangent to the G(*c*) curve at each point *c*. Figure 4.1a shows that, since each group has the same expected income, there is no difference in the distribution of income between the negligence and strict liability rules. Considered ex post, income inequality increases under the negligence rule, as shown in Figure 4.1b: The increase in the slope of the tangent line for injured members of each income groups is larger the decrease in the slope for uninjured members. Finally, as Figure 4.1c shows, income inequality under strict liability is also larger ex post, but smaller compared to the negligence rule.

strict-liability rule. Moreover it is concentrated on the richest group – the group of least redistributive concern as judged by a social welfare function.

The upshot from this is that strict liability delivers lower income inequality ex post (higher social welfare) than negligence. Not only is income inequality lower, but *because* income inequality is lower, tax distortions will be lower as well. The implication is central: Because negligence generates greater tax distortions than strict liability, strict liability redistributes income more efficiently than taxes.

Figure 4.1 can help illustrate these conclusions. Each subfigure depicts the mapping of disposable income, *c*, into a social welfare function, G(*c*). Social welfare is increasing in disposable income, but at a decreasing weight. In other words, *marginal* social welfare is decreasing in disposable income. The line tangent to the curve at each point $(c_i, G(c_i))$ gives the marginal social welfare at each income level. At lower levels of disposable income, marginal social welfare is larger – i.e., the curve of the social welfare function is steeper, as indicated by the tangent lines. These marginal social welfare weights describe the value of redistribution. For example, because the marginal social welfare for a person with disposable income c_0 is larger than for a person with c_2, social welfare can be increased by transferring a dollar from the richer person to the poorer person.

Each subfigure in Figure 4.1 depicts the interaction between the choice of social welfare function, ex ante or ex post, and the liability rule, negligence or strict liability. Figure 4.1a depicts the ex ante case. Because the expected income is the same for each income group, there are only three different groups. Moreover, these expected incomes are the same, regardless of the legal rule: The tax system perfectly compensates for the higher (pre-tax) inequality generated by the negligence rule. Figure 4.1b depicts the ex post case under the negligence rule. Under the negligence rule, victims are responsible for the harm they experience. There are thus two outcomes for each income group. Relative to the ex ante case, marginal social welfare increases for each injured group and decreases for each uninjured group, as shown in Figure 4.1b. But for precisely the same reason that the social welfare function has a preference for equality, each increase is larger than the corresponding decrease, and the net increase among the poorer is larger than among the rich. Finally, as shown in Figure 4.1c, income inequality also increases under the strict liability rule, when considered ex post, but because this increase occurs only among the rich, it is smaller than the increase under the negligence rule.

To summarize, strict liability can redistribute more efficiently than taxes. Not only does strict liability redistribute from rich to poor in the conventional sense – by making the rich pay for the harm their pollution causes – but it also reallocates the distributive effects of risk, by shifting accident-driven income variability from society as a whole to the harm causers, the rich. This second effect only appears in an ex post social welfare perspective. And it also makes the negligence rule more costly to administer. Under the negligence rule, taxes not only have to redistribute in the conventional sense, but they also have to mop up the additional inequality created by the risks of harm borne by society.

These results differ from Kaplow and Shavell (1994) for primarily two reasons. First, because I analyze a different legal rule, there is no double distortion in this case. Kaplow and Shavell essentially compare two versions of the strict liability rule. In their analysis, fault is irrelevant; one rule simply requires the injurer to pay for harm caused, while the other makes the amount of damages an injurer pays depend on her income. Because this rule is income-dependent it has a redistributive effect; but it also distorts the incentive to take care, since damages do not depend on harm actually caused. This produces a double distortion. In contrast, the two rules compared in my example are strict liability and negligence. Each rule has different distributive consequences, but both result in efficient levels of care, so there is no double distortion. This is why strict liability and negligence are equivalent in the ex ante case. The second reason has to do with the difference between the ex ante and ex post distributions of income. In the ex post case, one could say that negligence creates a double – really, a second *tax* – distortion. Because ex post inequality is higher under negligence, marginal tax rates are also higher, and so are the tax distortions. To put this additional tax distortion in the larger context of the book, the labor-supply responses between legal rules are not equivalent, contrary to Kaplow and Shavell's (1994) hypothesis.

It is also instructive to compare these results with Cooter and Ulen's (2016) "targeting" argument against the use of redistributive legal rules. According to their argument, legal rules rely on "crude averages" to redistribute income, unlike the income tax, which targets the problem of income inequality precisely. To capture precisely this aspect of "crudeness," I have constructed the model so that all income groups – not just the poorest – are potentially harmed. Yet, even in the ex ante model, this does not prevent strict liability from being just as efficiently redistributive as the tax system under the negligence rule. The reason, to put it simply, is that redistributive precision matters less than whether the marginal value of inequality reduction exceeds its marginal cost.

4.4.2 *Insurance Case*

The previous analysis assumed insurance was unavailable in order to clarify how otherwise efficient legal rules have different social-welfare implications when considered from an ex post perspective. Insurance allows a person to shift – we could even say "redistribute" – money between the "good" states of the world (in our case, uninjured states) to the "bad" states of the world (injured states). Economists sometimes call this function of insurance "consumption smoothing," because it "smooths" consumption across different states of the world for the person who has insurance. Insurance is crucial in this discussion because when it is available – and priced at "actuarially fair" rates – a person will purchase complete coverage, which will fully insure them against losses, and give them the same income even if they are in an injured state. But this set of circumstances also eliminates the difference between ex ante and ex post distributions of income. Because of the consumption smoothing function of insurance, every person within each income group not only has the same expected income, but the same realized or actual income as well.

We now broaden the analysis to include the possibility of purchasing insurance. I assume that insurance is available to both the potentially injured (first-party insurance) and to potential injurers (third-party or liability insurance). In terms of form and pricing, both types of insurance will be treated the same, but we will see that their behavioral effects are different – and important. An insurance contract is such that the insurer offers insurance at a premium, b, with a fixed cost, z. This fixed cost can be interpreted as the cost of administering the plan, or it could reflect the insurer's own risk preferences. The insured chooses a level of coverage, χ. The premium is paid in either state of the world, while in the injured state the insured will receive a payment equal to the contractually agreed-upon coverage.

Who purchases insurance, and what are its effects? Let us start with the case under the negligence rule. Under the negligence rule, potential victims are liable for harm and, if risk averse, will be interested in purchasing first-party insurance. If the administrative cost of insurance is zero, $z = 0$, then everyone in each income group will purchase full coverage. Full coverage obtains because when the administrative cost of insurance is zero, insurance simply allows a person to transfer (costlessly) income from an uninjured to an injured state. The utility maximizing choice of coverage is the one that gives the person the same income in either state.

What if the administrative cost of insurance is positive, $z > 0$? It is then possible that (under a negligence rule) the poor will not purchase insurance, while everyone else will purchase full coverage. If, for example, the administrative cost exceeds a poor person's disposable income, $z > c_0$, they will be unable to afford it. Or they may not be willing to pay for it because of a limited budget. In either case, they will be worse off with insurance than without it. Suppose there exists a certain level of the administrative cost such that if a person's income is below that threshold, they will not purchase full coverage. (For a full demonstration of this model of insurance choice, see Section 4.5.)

Who purchases insurance under a strict liability rule? Because the strict-liability rule itself provides full insurance, potential victims will be uninterested in obtaining it. However, with liability now placed on potential injurers, risk averse entrepreneurs will desire insurance (as harm causers rather than harm recipients). We assume that entrepreneurs are wealthy enough to afford insurance. But the problem is that there is moral hazard: For any level of positive coverage, χ, the entrepreneur will reduce the level of care, x, she exercises. The outcome, as Shavell (1979) shows, is that the entrepreneur will only purchase partial, incomplete coverage. The seriousness of the moral hazard problem depends on the cost of care. Intuitively, as the cost of care diminishes, the extent of moral hazard declines and the level of coverage approaches full coverage. It is also worth pointing out that choice-of-care incentives are not distorted under the negligence rule (when entrepreneurs do not purchase insurance) even with concave (risk averse) utility functions. (See Section 4.5 for further details on both of these conclusions).

To sum up, under the negligence rule, all potential victims purchase first-party insurance when its administrative costs are low enough; when administrative costs are high, the poor will be unable to afford insurance. Under the strict liability rule, no one purchases first-party insurance, but entrepreneurs purchase third-party, liability insurance. The catch under strict liability is that liability insurance induces moral hazard by distorting care-taking incentives, and this increases the rate of accidents.

What are the ultimate welfare effects for each legal rule and their associated insurance decisions? Consider the two possible cases, first, where everyone is able to purchase full, first-party insurance coverage and, second, where the poor cannot afford first-party insurance.

If everyone can afford full, first-party insurance coverage, then the negligence rule wins over strict liability in the efficient-redistribution contest. Under the negligence rule, first-party insurance eliminates the difference between ex ante and ex post welfare. This removes any additional costs of redistributive taxation considered under an ex post social welfare function. Under the strict liability rule, by contrast, third-party liability insurance purchased by entrepreneurs will induce moral hazard. Moral hazard causes the rate of accidents to increase, which reduces efficiency and, by extension, social welfare. Unlike the risk-neutral case, negligence and strict liability are no longer equally efficient. Negligence is more efficient and maximizes (ex ante or ex post) social welfare. In other words, when everyone can afford full, first-party insurance, the strict liability rule generates a double distortion, and Kaplow and Shavell's argument is validated.

In the second case, the poor cannot afford insurance. In this case, strict liability may be the social welfare-maximizing rule, notwithstanding the moral hazard it creates. Because the poor cannot afford insurance, the ex post costs of redistribution again differ between the negligence and strict liability rules. Under the negligence rule, the poor will be liable for harm caused to them, creating an ex post welfare difference between injured and uninjured poor persons. Under strict liability, the poor are not liable for harm, and are effectively "insured" by the rule, eliminating any difference between ex ante and ex post welfare. This difference makes the cost of redistribution higher under the negligence rule than under strict liability. Moreover, although partial insurance coverage implies income uncertainty for the rich, any coverage will reduce that variance compared to no coverage. Thus, if the additional ex post costs of redistribution under negligence are greater than the inefficiency of moral hazard under strict liability, strict liability wins the efficient redistribution contest.

One possible answer to the case where the poor cannot afford insurance is to have the government provide social insurance. This would turn the second case into the first and make negligence more desirable because of the strict liability's second, moral-hazard distortion. But social insurance also has its own costs. As a government-funded program, some might say it would be less efficient than private insurance. So if the costs of social insurance, administrative or otherwise, exceed the moral-hazard costs of strict liability, then strict liability would again prevail.

Note that the presence of insurance actually *enhances* the social-welfare value of the strict liability rule when the poor cannot afford insurance. This is a paradox, because we would expect insurance to mute the differences between strict liability and negligence from an ex post perspective. How is it that insurance actually makes strict liability more desirable, all else equal? To put it most simply, without insurance we face a choice between the negligence rule, where the uncertain costs of accidents is spread out among *all* income groups, and the strict liability rule, where the uncertain costs of accidents rest only with the wealthy. On the other hand, with costly insurance, we face a choice between the negligence rule, where only the poor bear the uncertain costs of accidents (because they can't afford insurance), and the strict liability rule, where the reduced uncertainty of the costs of accidents (because of partial insurance) again rests with the wealthy.

The costly insurance case therefore increases the social-welfare value of strict liability for two reasons. First, without insurance, the uncertainty of harm is "spread out" among both rich and poor, effectively muting the value of redistribution. After all, the negligence rule also decreases the social welfare of the rich and the middle class, and the social welfare function takes this into account. However, with costly insurance, all of the uncertainty is essentially placed on the poor, for whom the marginal social welfare value is highest. Second, although strict liability shifts the uncertainty to the rich, with or without insurance, that uncertainty is reduced with costly insurance because partial coverage is better than no coverage. In other words, the introduction of insurance increases inequality by concentrating income uncertainty among the poor and reducing it among the rich.

We can translate the costly-insurance case into double-distortion terms. As mentioned, strict liability does indeed generate a double distortion. The first distortion is the economic costs of changing labor-supply incentives by reducing income inequality, which we can say equals amount T'. The second distortion is the moral hazard problem that accompanies partial, third-party liability insurance. Say that this distortion causes a loss of wealth of Δ. Compare this to the negligence rule, with a distribution-neutral tax adjustment. Under the negligence rule, there are only the economic costs of taxation, which reduce income inequality and distort labor-supply incentives, and which we can say amount to T. Normally, when taxes and, in this case, strict liability change the distribution of income by the same amount, we should expect labor-supply distortions to be the same under either legal rule. This would mean $T' = T$, and that inequality would make the negligence rule necessarily more efficient, redistributively. For, as long as the moral hazard cost is more than zero, strict liability's double distortion will be more than negligence's single distortion. Let Δ represent the amount of economic waste caused by moral hazard. Then the total costs of strict liability are greater than negligence, and $\Delta + T' > T$ is necessarily satisfied as long as $T' = T$. But that equality only holds in the ex ante case. In the ex post case, with costly insurance, realized inequality among the poor is higher with the negligence rule, making the redistributive cost of taxation higher: $T > T'$. With that difference, it is not obvious a priori that negligence is preferred to strict liability. Despite strict-liability's double distortion, the comparison of costs could very well be $\Delta + T' < T$, in which case strict liability can redistribute more efficiently than taxes plus the negligence rule.

To summarize, does the double distortion induced by the strict liability rule make the negligence rule superior? Not necessarily. The answer depends on whether the poor can afford insurance and whether the double distortion induced by moral hazard creates a welfare loss that is smaller or larger than additional, ex post costs of redistribution induced by the poor's lack of insurance.

These results can again be illustrated with the help of the following Figure 4.2. Figure 4.2a illustrates the case where first-party insurance is too expensive for members of the poorest income group, 0. Ex post, welfare-weighed income inequality is higher under the negligence rule than without insurance (compared to Figure 4.1b) because the increased inequality is confined to society's poorest members. And because inequality with insurance is higher than without, inequality with insurance is also higher compared to the ex ante case (Figure 4.1a).

Under strict liability, the moral hazard problem prevents entrepreneurs from purchasing complete coverage, so a difference between expected and ex post incomes

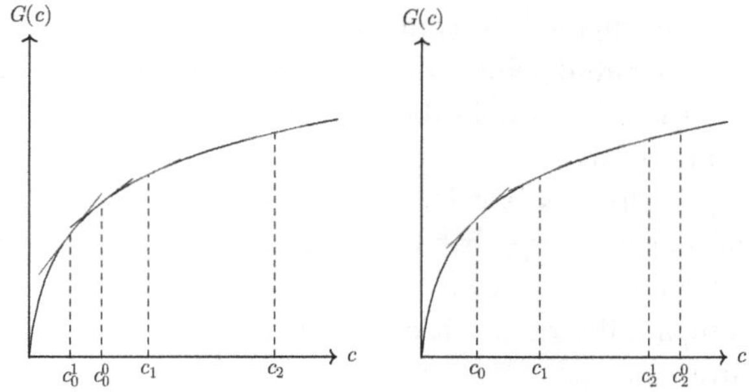

(a) Negligence (b) Strict liability

FIGURE 4.2 Social welfare with costly insurance

Each subfigure depicts social welfare ($G(\cdot)$, on the *y*-axis) as a function of disposable income (c, on the *x*-axis). Marginal social welfare is higher for lower income individuals, as indicted by the lines tangent to the $G(c)$ curve at each point c.

remains, as shown in Figure 4.2b. But this increase in inequality is small compared to the increase under the negligence rule, confined as it is, to the top of the income distribution. And as long as the cost of care is small enough, the welfare loss from moral hazard will be smaller than the welfare loss from the greater redistributive cost under the negligence rule.

4.5 APPENDIX

The full, formal arguments for this chapter are found in the online appendix. The torts section of the online appendix has two main parts. The first part reconstructs a formal version Kaplow and Shavell's (1994) argument for why a *wealth-dependent* damages rule redistributes income less efficiently than an equally redistributive change to the income tax schedule. The second part establishes formally this chapter's main claim that legal rules can redistribute more efficiently than the income tax when an ex post social welfare perspective is taken. This second part first uses optimal tax theory to show how legal rules have different implications for the cost of redistribution ex post, even though they have identical implications ex ante. The basic model is elaborated and then the case without risk aversion is analyzed, where the ex ante and ex post cases are compared. Then, the more elaborate case of risk aversion and insurance is evaluated. Model elements are added to capture the role of insurance, including first- and third-party (liability) insurance, and the choice of care under the negligence rule with liability insurance. The online appendix concludes with a simple extension to show how the optimal tax schedule with risk aversion can be derived.

The following appendix presents only the online appendix's risk aversion model, which uses a distribution-neutral income tax adjustment (see the book's appendix for a discussion of this method) to compare and contrast the cases of costless and costly insurance. The central point of this contrast is to demonstrate that the double-distortion argument is valid only in the case of perfect, costless insurance, a case unlikely to be met in practice.

This chapter appendix proceeds in the following steps. Section 4.5.1 presents a basic model of accidents with probabilistic harm, liability rules, and agent payoffs. Section 4.5.1 then presents the key results, using a distribution-neutral income tax adjustment to compare the risk aversion and insurance model with, first, costless and then costly insurance.

4.5.1 *Model*

The following model describes all of the essential elements of a model of optimal taxation with accidents and liability rules.

Accidents and Liability

Firms produce a good or service that causes monetary damages, D, with some probability, $\pi(x)$, per unit of the good. Firms can take some level of costly care, x, also measured in monetary units, which reduces the probability of an accident. Specifically, a higher level of care reduces the probability of an accident, but the reduction becomes smaller as the level of care gets larger. Formally, $\pi: \mathbf{R}_+ \rightarrow (0, 1)$ and $\pi'(x) < 0$ and $\pi''(x) > 0$.

Who pays for these damages depends on the liability rule. To capture this, let $\mathbb{L}$ be an indicator function that takes on the values of 0 or 1 depending on the liability rule, R. I consider three possible liability rules: no liability (i.e., caveat emptor), L; strict liability, S; and negligence, N. Formally, $\mathbb{L}(R)$, for $R \in \{L, S, N\}$.

With no liability, the victim bears all of the accident costs. Under strict liability, the injurer (the firm) bears all of the costs. Under a negligence rule, injurers bear all of the costs if the level of care they exercise falls below a certain standard, labeled $\tilde{x}$. Otherwise, if the level of care meets or exceeds that standard, then victims bear all of the accident costs.

These different liability rules can be captured formally in the following fashion:

$$\mathbb{L}(R) = \begin{cases} 1 & \text{no liability, } L, \\ 0 & \text{strict liability, } S, \\ \begin{cases} 1 & \text{if} \quad x \geq \tilde{x} \\ 0 & \text{if} \quad x < \tilde{x} \end{cases} & \text{negligence, } N. \end{cases} \tag{4.1}$$

Under the negligence rule, it is often argued that the standard of care is equivalent to the efficient, cost-minimizing level, x^*. The reasoning for this is based on the "Learned Hand rule," which can be interpreted as requiring that the standard of care minimize the sum of the costs of taking care and expected accident loses. Hence, $\tilde{x} = x^*$.

Putting this all together, the per unit potential harm to victims can be written as: $\mathbb{L}(R)\pi(x)D$. Similarly, the expected cost to firms is: $[1 - \mathbb{L}(R)]\pi(x)D + x$. The incidence of harm also depends on the activity level, denoted q. In the benchmark model, q is the level of output or quantity of the good sold by the firms. For simplicity, I will assume that each firm produces one unit of output. As we will see, output can be measured relative to the population, so it can be thought of as a share variable and as a probability.

Income and Labor Supply

As throughout the book, individuals have the choice of working in three different occupations: $i \in \{0, 1, 2\}$. In this model, I assume that occupation 2 is being a firm owner or entrepreneur. This assumption collapses the issue of firm ownership – essentially capital income – and earned income which is the primary determinant of an individual's labor supply. (For another way to bridge the gap between firm ownership and labor supply, see Chapter 7, on antitrust, as well as the model in Kaplow (2021).)

The tax authorities establish a tax schedule prior to individual's labor supply decisions. As is normally assumed, the government can observe incomes, but not the individual costs of work or consumption decisions. I also assume without loss of generality that the government conditions taxes and transfers on observable *earnings* outcomes, y_i, rather than distinguishing between injured and uninjured states. This choice is made for simplicity and does not bias the main results. Distinguishing between injured and uninjured states would simply introduce additional moral hazard into the problem and therefore increase the costs of taxation, which would favor my claim that legal rules can, in important cases, redistribute more efficiently than taxes. In any case, the distinction between injured and uninjured states is nonsensical in the case of an ex ante social welfare function. Since there are three earnings outcomes, let T_i denote the tax (or if $T_i < 0$, the transfer) associated with each earnings outcome i.

To add further precision, we denote the injury state, $s \in \{0, 1\}$, with 0 referring to the uninjured state and 1 to the injured. Therefore, an uninjured individual in occupation i earns $y_i^0 = y_i$, while an injured individual earns $y_i^1 = y_i - D$ for $i \in \{0, 1\}$, respectively $y_i^0 = y_i - x$ and $y_i^1 = y_i - D - x$ for type-3 individuals. Realized disposable incomes in the injured and uninjured states are thus written as:

$$c_i^0 = y_i^0 - T_i \tag{4.2}$$

in the uninjured state, and

$$c_i^1 = y_i^1 - T_i \tag{4.3}$$

in the injured state.

The probability of liability for harm to a bystander depends on the per unit probability of harm, $\pi(x)$, the liability rule, $\mathbb{L}(R)$, and the activity rate, q. We denote the probability of harm as $p_i = \mathbb{L}(R)\pi(x)q$ for $i \in \{0, 1\}$. Because firm owners, occupation 2, are also potential causers of harm (as well as potential victims), we need to write $p_2 = \pi(x)(1 - \mathbb{L}(R)(1 - q))$.[28] Because the context will make it clear, I will normally suppress the subscripts, but it should be remembered that $p_0 = p_1 \neq p_2$.

Finally, in the insurance model, there is risk aversion and a desire for insurance. Individuals therefore have an increasing and concave utility function over disposable income, $u(c_i)$ with $u'(c_i) > 0$ and $u''(c_i) < 0$.

Results of the Insurance Model

As previously mentioned, the online appendix has details on the modeling of insurance, including first-party insurance, third-party (liability) insurance, and occupation 2's choice of care under the negligence rule. The following subsection gives a brief overview of modeling insurance and the key results from doing so. The next two sections then report results for costless and costly insurance, respectively.

Modeling Insurance

An insurance contract is such that the insurer offers insurance at a premium, b, with a fixed cost, z. This fixed cost can be interpreted as the cost of administering the plan, or it could reflect the insurer's own risk preferences. The insured chooses a level of coverage, χ. The premium is paid in either state of the world, while in the injured state the insured will receive a payment equal to the contractually agreed-upon coverage. Thus, utility is $u(c_i^0 - b)$ in the uninjured state and $u(c_i^1 - b + \chi)$ in the injured state. In addition (for potential victims under first-party insurance contract), the insurer's expected costs are $p\chi$. The expected return on the insurance contract is therefore $b - p\chi - z$. Assuming a competitive insurance market, an insurance company's break-even point is: $b - p\chi - z = 0$, so the premium is determined by $b = p\chi + z$.

Under the negligence rule, potential victims are liable for harm and, if risk averse, will be interested in purchasing first-party insurance. The utility maximizing choice of coverage is the one that gives the person the same income in either state. This condition requires $c_i - D - b + \chi = c_i - b$, which reduces immediately to $\chi = D$: The amount of coverage chosen exactly covers the damage caused.

A key result in this case is that there exists a level of cost of insurance administration, defined as $\bar{z} > 0$, such that for income below some threshold, defined as

[28] For example, under strict liability type-2 individuals will not be liable to harm caused to them while they will be liable for harm they cause, with probability $\pi(x)$. Under the negligence rule and taking reasonable care, type-2 individuals will not be liable for harm they cause to others but will be liable to harm caused to them, the probability of harm being identical to that of non-entrepreneurs: $\pi(x)q$.

$\tilde{y}$, those with income below $\tilde{y}$ do not purchase insurance. If the administrative cost of insurance is zero, $z = 0$, then everyone in each income group will purchase full coverage. Full coverage obtains because when the administrative cost of insurance is zero, insurance simply allows a person to transfer (costlessly) income from an uninjured to an injured state.

By contrast, under strict liability, potential injurers are liable for harm and will be interested in purchasing third-party, liability insurance. A key result in this case is that, because it covers the cost of harms caused by potential injurers, liability insurance induces moral hazard. Shavell (1979) shows that when care is not observed by the insurer, (1) the optimal insurance policy under moral hazard always offers positive coverage – moral hazard alone cannot eliminate possibilities for insurance. However, (2) the optimal insurance policy offers partial rather than full coverage if the cost of taking care is sufficiently low, but the level of coverage approaches full coverage as the cost of taking care tends to zero. For the proof of this proposition, see Shavell (1979). Partial insurance coverage implies $\chi < D$. How partial that coverage is depends on the costs of taking care, r, and degree of risk aversion. As one might expect, the lower the costs of care, the greater the contracted-for insurance coverage, so that as the costs of care go to zero, $r \to 0$, coverage becomes complete, $\chi \to D$, and the choice of care becomes efficient, $x_S \to x^*$.

(It may also be worth noting that the entrepreneur's choice of care is not distorted by first-party insurance under the negligence rule.)

With the basic elements of the insurance model established, we can turn to an analysis of the results for efficiency and welfare. I first consider the case of costless insurance, where the poor can afford it, and then analyze the case of costly insurance, where they cannot.

Costless Insurance

This subsection will demonstrate the following claim. Suppose that everyone purchases full (first-party insurance) coverage. (Formally, suppose $z = 0$ and therefore $y_0 > \tilde{y}$.) Then, because of the moral hazard problem induced by liability insurance under the strict liability rule, the income tax system along with an efficient legal rule (negligence) redistributes more efficiently for any positive level of the cost of care, r.

It will be easiest to demonstrate this claim by using the method of distribution-neutral tax adjustments as employed by Kaplow and Shavell (1994) and, more extensively, Kaplow (2008). (See the book appendix for further discussion of this method.)

Under the negligence rule, when administrative costs of insurance are zero, $z = 0$, everyone purchases full coverage, first-party insurance. Moreover, negligence does not distort entrepreneurs' choice of care. Utility can be written as

$$pu(c_i^1 - b + \bar{\chi}) + (1 - p)u(c_i^0 - b) - \theta_i$$

for $i \in \{0, 1, 2\}$, where $b = p\bar{\chi}$, $\bar{\chi} = D$, and $p = \mathbb{L}(N)\pi(x^*)q = \pi(x^*)q$. With full coverage, utility is the same in either injured or uninjured states. Therefore, utility under the negligence rule simplifies to: $u(y_i - T_{i,N} - \pi(x^*)Dq) - \theta_i$. Under the strict liability rule, victims are not liable for harm. Therefore utility for type-0 and -1 individuals is simply: $u(y_i - T_{i,S}) - \theta_i$ for $i \in \{0, 1\}$. Now we want to choose $T_{1,N}$ and $T_{0,N}$ to equalize utility under the negligence and strict liability rules: $u(y_i - T_{i,N} - \pi(x^*)Dq) - \theta_i = u(y_i - T_{i,S}) - \theta_i$. This gives:

$$T_{1,N} = T_{1,S} - \pi(x^*)Dq \quad \text{and} \quad T_{0,N} = T_{0,S} - \pi(x^*)Dq.$$

Under strict liability, entrepreneurs purchase liability insurance, but this induces moral hazard and therefore they obtain only partial coverage. This generates utility of:

$$pu(c_2^1 - b + \chi_S) + (1 - p)u(c_2^0 - b) - \theta_2$$

where $b = p\chi_S$, $p = \pi(x_S)(1 - \mathbb{L}(S)(1 - q)) = \pi(x_S)$, $\chi_S < D$, $x_S < x^*$, and $\pi(x_S) > \pi(x^*)$. Let:

$$pu(c_2^1 - b + \chi_S) + (1 - p)u(c_2^0 - b) = u(y_2 - x_S - T_{2,S} - \pi(x_S)D - \hat{T})$$

where $\hat{T}$ measures the loss of utility as a result of risk aversion. Now, we can choose $T_{2,N}$ such that $u(y_2 - x_S - T_{2,S} - \pi(x_S)D - \hat{T}) - \theta_2 = u(y_2 - x^* - T_{2,N} - \pi(x^*)Dq) - \theta_2$. This gives us:

$$T_{2,N} = T_{2,S} + \hat{T} + \pi(x_S)D - \pi(x^*)Dq - (x^* - x_S).$$

Summing additional revenue and expenditures, we obtain

$$\begin{aligned}\sum h_i T_i = \sum h_i (T_{i,N} - T_{i,S}) &= = h_2(\hat{T} + \pi(x_S)D - (x^* - x_S)) - (h_2 + h_1 + h_0)\pi(x^*)Dq \\ &= q(\hat{T} + \pi(x_S)D - (x^* - x_S)) - \pi(x^*)Dq \\ &= q(\hat{T} + \pi(x_S)D + x_S - (\pi(x^*)D + x^*)) > 0\end{aligned}$$

which follows because x^* minimizes $\pi(x^*)D + x^*$. Hence, there exists a set of taxes and transfers under the negligence rule that yields the same level of utility for each individual as under the strict liability rule, while at the same time generating a budget surplus. This surplus can be used to adjust taxes and transfers to make everyone better off. In other words, in the case of costless insurance, the double-distortion argument is validated.

Costly Insurance

We now see if the double-distortion argument necessarily holds true in the case of costly insurance. In fact, we will demonstrate the following claim. Suppose that everyone except the poor purchases full (first-party insurance) coverage. (Formally, suppose that $z > 0$ and therefore that $y_1 > \tilde{y} > y_0$.) Then for a cost of care below a critical threshold, r^*, the inefficient strict liability rule redistributes more efficiently than the negligence rule.

For type-0 individuals, choose $T_{0,N}$ so that:

$$pu(-T_{0,N} - D) + (1 - p)u(-T_{0,N}) = u(-T_{0,S})$$

To do this, let:

$$pu(-T_{0,N} - D) + (1 - p)u(-T_{0,N}) = u(-T_{0,N} - \pi(x^*)Dq - \hat{T}_0)$$

where $\hat{T}_0$ equalizes the loss of utility as a consequence of risk aversion. Then choose $T_{0,N}$ so that $u(-T_{0,N} - \pi(x^*)Dq - \hat{T}_0) = u(-T_{0,S})$. This gives:

$$T_{0,N} = T_{0,S} - \hat{T}_0 - \pi(x^*)Dq.$$

Under the negligence rule, type-1 individuals purchase full coverage, first-party insurance, giving utility $u(c_1 - b)$, where $b = p\bar{\chi} + z$, $\bar{\chi} = D$, and $p = \mathbb{L}(N)\pi(x^*)q = \pi(x^*)q$. Therefore, $u(c_1 - b) = u(y_1 - T_{1,N} - \pi(x^*)Dq - z)$. For type-1 individuals, choose $T_{1,N}$ so that:

$$u(y_1 - T_{1,N} - \pi(x^*)Dq - z) - \theta_1 = u(y_1 - T_{1,S}) - \theta_1.$$

This gives:

$$T_{1,N} = T_{1,S} - \pi(x^*)Dq - z.$$

For type-2 individuals, choose $T_{2,N}$ so that:

$$u(y_2 - x_S - T_{2,S} - \pi(x_S)D - z - \hat{T}_2) - \theta_2 = u(y_2 - x^* - T_{2,N} - \pi(x^*)Dq - z) - \theta_2,$$

the only difference from the costless-insurance condition being the addition of administrative costs (which in any case, cancel out). This gives:

$$T_{2,N} = T_{2,S} + \hat{T}_2 + \pi(x_S)D - \pi(x^*)Dq - (x^* - x_S).$$

Summing additional revenue and expenditures, we obtain

$$\begin{aligned}\sum h_i T_i = \sum h_i(T_{i,N} - T_{i,S}) &= h_2(\hat{T}_2 + \pi(x_S)D - (x^* - x_S)) \\ &\quad - h_1 z - h_0\hat{T}_0 - (h_2 + h_1 + h_0)\pi(x^*)Dq \\ &= h_2\hat{T}_2 - h_1 z - h_0\hat{T}_0 + q(\pi(x_S)D + x_S - (\pi(x^*)D + x^*))\end{aligned}$$

This gives the condition that whenever it is true that

$$h_1 z + h_0\hat{T}_0 > h_2\hat{T}_2 + q(\pi(x_S)D + x_S - (\pi(x^*)D + x^*))$$

then strict liability redistributes more efficiently than taxes and the efficient, negligence rule. Both $\hat{T}_2$ and $\pi(x_S)D + x_S - (\pi(x^*)D + x^*)$ go to zero as the cost of care, r, goes to zero; the first because the welfare of the rich becomes the same under either rule when the choice of the care is the same, and the second because the choice of care becomes efficient, $x_S \to x^*$, as the cost of care falls to zero. Thus, there exists some r^* (corresponding to the condition holding at equality) such that for all $r < r^*$, negligence yields the same utility for each individual but yields a budget deficit, which indicates that strict liability redistributes more efficiently.

5

Contracts

In February 2002, Vincent and Liza Concepcion entered into an agreement for cellular phone service, including phone, at a Cingular retail outlet in Carlsbad, California. According to the terms of the contract of sale, the Concepcions were not charged for the phone. However, Cingular – later, AT&T Mobility – charged the Concepcions a total of $30.22 in sales tax, based on the full retail value of the phone.[1] The Concepcions believed that charging full sales tax on a free phone was unfair and deceptive, so they brought a claim in federal court against the cellphone company.

However, the contract also contained an agreement to arbitrate disputes arising under the contract, and AT&T Mobility moved to compel arbitration. Along with other members of a class-action lawsuit, the Concepcions resisted this motion. Like many other Americans, the Concepcions were probably unaware that they had waived their right to a court trial when agreeing to the contract.[2] Furthermore, though "merely" a different procedure for resolving claims, arbitration often differs meaningfully from legal adjudication. There are no clear rules of evidence, no jury or independent fact-finder, no option to appeal, and the defendant often has influence over which arbitrator hears the dispute (Silver-Greenberg and Corkery 2015).

Over the last thirty years, the Supreme Court has issued a series of decisions that favor and expand the scope of mandatory arbitration agreements. The Court's 1991 decision in *Gilmer*,[3] enforced a standard "form" agreement to arbitrate between

[1] Laster v. T-Mobile USA, Inc., No. 05cv1167 DMS (AJB), 2008 WL 5216255 at *1 (S.D. Cal.).

[2] Colvin (2017, 2, emphasis in original) finds that "Among private-sector nonunion *employees*, 56.2 percent are subject to mandatory employment arbitration procedures. Extrapolating to the overall workforce, this means that 60.1 million American workers no longer have access to the courts to protect their legal employment rights and instead must go to arbitration."

[3] Gilmer v. Interstate/Johnson Lane Corp., 500 U.S. 20 (1991). In this decision, the Court dismissed an age discrimination claim under the Age Discrimination in Employment Act (ADEA) because the employee had signed an employment contract with a binding arbitration agreement.

an employer and employee, endorsing the enforcement not just of negotiated agreements between sophisticated business entities, but of standardized contracts for consumers, employees, borrowers, credit-card holders, patients and other "unsophisticated" legal parties (Sternlight 2001, 670). In 2011, *AT&T Mobility LLC v. Concepcion*,[4] the facts of which began this chapter, upheld the legality of mandatory arbitration agreements that waive an individual's right to class or collective action. In 2013, *American Express v. Italian Colors Restaurant*[5] severely curtailed the standard of "effective vindication" of rights under the law,[6] upholding arbitration agreements unless they "actually block[ed] access to the forum" or "explicitly den[ied] substantive rights" (Estlund 2018, 705).

These decisions have had a palpable effect on plaintiffs' access to the courts and justice. Commentators describe *Concepcion* and *Italian Colors* as unleashing a "tsunami" (Sternlight 2011, 705) that created a "black hole of mandatory arbitration" (Estlund 2018, 705). In 1992, roughly 2 percent of private-sector workers were covered by mandatory arbitration agreements (Colvin 2017). This number increased to around 20 percent in 2007 and jumped to 55 percent in 2017 (Colvin 2017). Looking at 2016 data, professor Cynthia Estlund estimates that there were roughly 9,600 to 28,400 fewer arbitration filings for employment claims than would be expected from federal court filings and between 315,000 and 727,000 "missing" arbitration claims per year if state law claims and individual claims contained in class action lawsuits are included (Estlund 2018, 692, 696).

Not only are there substantially fewer claims when employees, consumers, and other "little guys" are forced into arbitration, but the results for claimants are also worse. In a study of American Arbitration Association (AAA) employment arbitrations from 2003 to 2013, employees won something 19.1 percent of the time (Colvin and Gough, 2015, 1019; Estlund, 2018, 688). "That compares to the findings of other scholars that plaintiffs won something in 29.7% of federal employment discrimination cases, 57% of state non-civil rights employment cases, and 59% of California state wrongful discharge cases."[7] Furthermore, the damages recovered were much less. "The median award was $36,500 in arbitration versus $176,426 in federal discrimination cases, $85,560 in state non-civil rights employment cases, and $355,843 in California wrongful discharge cases."[8] Synthesizing the data reveals that mandatory arbitration has transferred billions of dollars from consumers and employees to the balance sheets of corporations and their shareholders.

* * *

4 563 U.S. 333 (2011).
5 570 U.S. 228 (2013).
6 *Id.* at 234–37.
7 Estlund (2018, 688) citing Eisenberg (2015, 28) and Oppenheimer (2003, 535).
8 Estlund (2018, 688) citing Colvin (2014, 80).

The substantive and distributive effects of these procedural changes in the law, from court adjudication to informal arbitration, raises the question of whether contract might be an avenue for reducing income inequality. For many reasons, contract law initially appears as the area of law least hospitable to the goal of legal redistribution. To recall our discussion in the chapter on property, the distributive implications of the Coase theorem were thought to hinge on the level of transaction costs. They were also believed to extend only so far as contractual relations are "thin." As Schwab (1989) explains,

> Waivable contract rights (or contract presumptions) may, in some situations, increase the wealth of the nominal beneficiary. The basic line is probably between thick, competitive markets and thin markets where individual bargaining over surplus occurs. In competitive markets, price equals cost and cost is the minimum possible cost; if the contract presumption would increase costs, the parties will write around it (assuming low transaction costs), *and cost and price remain unchanged.* But in markets where price can exceed cost, a favorable contract presumption may increase one's bargaining power. Even if the beneficiary waives the presumption, he may receive a greater share of the surplus for doing so. (1179, emphasis added)

In other words, it is often thought that there is no possibility of redistributing income or welfare in truly competitive, or "thick," markets. Thus far, our discussion has been about whether legal rules were able to redistribute more efficiently than taxes. No one in the debate has doubted whether legal rules *can* redistribute income. But when parties are engaged in competitive exchange, the idea is that legal rules have no redistributive effects whatsoever. In that view, the question of the law's redistributive efficacy is moot. If all costs are ultimately born by the consumer, then any attempt to shift those costs are simply "passed on" to the consumer.[9]

However, procedural conflicts over mandatory arbitration provisions reveal that more than simply costs are at stake. Certainly, large corporations include mandatory arbitration provisions in their contracts in order to reduce costs. But as profit maximizers they are indifferent to whether such cost reductions are efficient (and lower total social costs) or distributive (merely shift costs to consumers). The cost to the consumer of reading the contract allows firms to exploit information asymmetries, which creates a difference in the actual costs and the customer's perceived costs. It does not bode well for the efficiency of arbitration that plaintiffs are much less likely to bring suits under such provisions. If arbitration reduced costs for everyone, we should see more arbitration than litigation, not less.

This chapter shows when and how legal rules can redistribute income more efficiently than taxes even in the unlikeliest of legal domains. Section 5.1 begins by describing in more detail the claim that legal rules merely "pass on" the costs of redistribution when parties are engaged with each other through the competitive marketplace. In this view, redistribution through legal rules is not only inefficient

9 In addition to Schwab (1989), Polinsky (1989, 123–24) also expresses this insight.

but *impossible*. This section of the chapter also addresses a similar claim, which is that the costs of legal rules are not simply passed on, but are born inversely by the relative elasticities of supply and demand, just like the incidence of a sales tax. As we will see, Craswell (1991) offers an elegant response to both claims. The costs of legal rules are not like taxes, nor are they merely passed on to consumers. The passing-on argument, Craswell shows, assumes counterfactually that consumers are homogeneous. This discussion leads directly into Section 5.2, where I recount Craswell's argument that when consumers are heterogeneous, legal rules may redistribute income more efficiently than taxes, even when the parties exchange with one another in a competitive marketplace.

The chapter's third and final section, Section 5.3, considers two other, previously unconsidered, bases for efficient redistribution in contractual relationships. The first is price discrimination. Because the efficiency effects of price discrimination are ambiguous, rules that limit the practice, such as the unconscionability doctrine, can potentially redistribute more efficiently than taxes. The second is default rules, which we will explore in the context of markets with matching frictions. Markets with matching frictions generate rents, which means that default rules may not only reduce transaction costs or perform "information forcing" functions, but can also shift bargaining power – and rents – to the poorer side of the transaction.

5.1 COMPETITIVE MARKETS AND "PASSING ON" THE COSTS OF LEGAL RULES

Before we can explain how contract law can redistribute more efficiently than taxes, we need to address the long-time presumption that legal rules cannot redistribute at all when individuals engage in competitive market relationships. This is the "passing on" argument, the idea that any attempt to shift the legal burdens from, say, poor consumers to wealthy producers will simply be passed back on to the consumer in the form of higher prices.

5.1.1 *"Passing On" the Costs of Legal Rules*

Hamada (1976) presents an excellent example of the "passing on" argument. Suppose that firms produce products that may be defective and cause harm. Should the government impose a mandatory warranty in every contract of sale? Hamada's article demonstrated that in a competitive market with potentially defective products, whatever liability rule the government imposes (whether no liability, negligence, or strict liability) makes no difference either to the allocation of resources (i.e., efficiency) or to the distribution of income. Whatever the rule, the damages caused by a potential defect are either part of the implicit or explicit price of the good. In the case of negligence, for instance, the buyer will be responsible for damages as long as the seller has taken reasonable precautions. This may make for a nominally low explicit price for the good, but the buyer understands that the implicit price, which includes the potential cost of harm, is higher. Conversely, under a strict-liability rule the seller is liable for product accidents. But because the probability of accidents or their costs do not change with the liability rule, they will simply become part of the (higher) explicit price of the good. The same sort of reasoning applies to the caveat-emptor rule. Thus, in competitive markets, the choice of strict liability versus negligence makes no difference to the distribution of income.

Adapting an example from Polinsky (1989), we can explore this intuition a little more concretely. Taking our cue from the (in)famous exploding bottle case,[10] let us consider the market for carbonated beverages. A firm has two production methods to choose from. The first method has a per unit production cost of 40 cents, but there is a probability that a soda bottle will explode once with every 100,000 bottles and cause \$10,000 of damage to the buyer. The second method is more costly, with a per unit production cost of 43 cents. However, the risk of explosion is only once in every 200,000 bottles, and the damage from the explosion is less, only \$4,000. In expected terms, the first method is more costly than the second because $1/100,000 \times \$10,000 = \$0.10 > 1/200,000 \times \$4,000 = \$0.02$. This makes the *total* per unit production cost of the second method cheaper than the first. Including the expected cost of harm, the first method comes out to be $\$0.40 + \$0.10 = \$0.50$ and the second comes out to be $\$0.43 + \$0.02 = \$0.45$.

Should courts intervene and impose a particular legal rule to regulate these harms? It is easy to see that choosing negligence or strict liability will not affect the efficiency of the outcome. Suppose the court adopts a strict liability rule. The producer now knows that it will have to pay not just for the production costs, but for any damages an exploding bottle causes. Naturally, a profit-maximizing producer will choose the most cost-effective method, and this will of course be the second method, where the combined costs are 45 cents. Bringing the product to market under strict liability, the price tag will also read 45 cents.

Compare this to the negligence rule. If a court declares that the second production method is reasonable and the first unreasonable, negligence will require the producer to select the second or pay the damages if a bottle explodes. However, when choosing the second method, the producer sells its product with a price tag that reads 43 cents, two cents cheaper than under strict liability because consumers are liable for the costs of accidents. That difference will lead a distributively minded person to object. "Producers should bear the costs of accidents!" this person might say. But the answer is that under strict liability the consumer already pays for the costs of accidents with the higher price tag. In fact, in both cases the effective or implicit price is the same. Under strict liability, the consumer pays the explicit sticker price of the bottle at 45 cents, which includes the damages the producer must pay but "passes on."

[10] Escola v. Coca-Cola Bottling Co., 24 Cal.2d 453, 150 P.2d 436 (1944).

Under negligence, the price tag reads 43 cents but that consumer knows, that with each bottle purchased, there is an extra 2 cent expected cost. Either way, the consumer pays 45 cents and the producer enjoys the same profit. Ultimately it is the consumer that pays for the accident costs, so the choice of legal rules has no distributive effects. (An important caveat: Recalling the lesson of the Chapter 4, this formal identity of consumers across legal rules is true only ex ante or only with perfect insurance. Ex post, under strict liability, a consumer who is actually injured pays only 45 cents. Under negligence, an uninsured and injured consumer pays $4,000.43.)

This logic even applies to the case of caveat emptor. Under that rule, suppose that the beverage maker chooses the first method, thinking that because the production costs (40 cents) are cheaper, it can beat its method-two competitors in the market, whose production costs (43 cents) are higher. However, when comparing goods in the market, consumers know that method-one beverage has a higher, implicit price. The price tag may say 40 cents, but consumers know that an accident is more likely and more damaging, so the effective price is 50 cents. This will lead consumers to choose from method-two producers, where the effective price of a bottle of soda is 45 cents, even if the price tag says 43 cents. Because this competitive pressure threatens to put the method-one producer out of business – it's offering a more expensive product after all – it will switch to the second method. Thus, no matter the legal rule – strict liability, negligence, or caveat emptor – competition in the market place ensures that outcomes are the same. Both efficiency (the choice of production method) and distribution (the implicit, total price of the product) remains the same.

Hamada thus showed that Coase's main insight held within the context of a competitive market; namely, that the choice of legal rules made no difference to the efficient allocation of resources. However, and more importantly for our purposes, he also showed that Coase's distributive corollary does *not* necessarily survive when exchange is mediated by the price mechanism. This led Polinsky (1989, 122) to conclude that "legal rules often cannot redistribute income in contractual disputes, whereas legal rules always can redistribute income in disputes between strangers."

5.1.2 *Responses to the "Passing On" Argument*

There are a number of ways to respond to the "passing on" argument. First of all, we can be more explicit about the assumptions under which the Hamada-type argument holds. These assumptions are not trivial. The first one is that consumers are homogeneous and that each consumers' willingness to pay for the product (or, more precisely, for the legal rule associated with the product) is the same. The implications of this assumption will be more critically examined below, when we address heterogeneous consumers. A second assumption is that consumers are risk-neutral. This means that risk aversion has no independent effect on consumer demand, separate from the probability and costs of accidents. This is also a counterfactual assumption. A third assumption is that there are perfect – that is, actuarially fair – insurance markets.

Perfect insurance compensates consumers for accidents or injuries, and makes them indifferent between the "accident state" and the "non-accident state." By making consumers indifferent between the accident occurring or not, perfect insurance markets dispose of the issue of risk aversion. It also means that we can approach social welfare in purely ex ante, expected terms. A fourth assumption is that consumers have perfect foresight about the possibility of damages – that their subjective assessments of accident probabilities are identical to the actual, objective accident probabilities. A fifth, and final, assumption is that victims are always purchasers of the product. Without this assumption, the price mechanism is unable to mediate the expectation of harm. (Hamada 1976, 228, 229–30).

Based on the absence of some of these conditions, scholars have offered a variety of arguments for why the government should mandate specific terms in contracts. A favorite target is the fourth assumption: how accurately consumers are able to predict the likelihood of accidents. In the presence of subjective errors or consumer irrationalty in product markets, such as consumer misperceptions about the likelihood of accidents (Spence 1977; Polinsky and Rogerson 1983), mandated terms can improve efficiency. Wickelgren (2006) argues that even with rational consumers, if consumers cannot accurately observe the safety characteristics of products, producers will inefficiently underinvest in product safety. Hua and Spier (2020) analyze product safety in an imperfectly competitive market, where firms have market power and consumers are heterogeneous.

It is important to note that in each of these contributions, mandated contract terms can improve the efficiency of the market mechanism. But just for that reason, it does not follow that because government intervention is justified in the name of efficiency, that legal rules can be chosen for their distributive effects. In most of these cases, for example, mandated terms *do* benefit consumers – but they benefit producers as well. Thus, these arguments show that mandated contract terms can make a difference to the efficient allocation of resources. They have not shown that legal rules can redistribute income more efficiently than taxes. To demonstrate that, we need to examine Craswell's (1991) argument and consider other bases of redistribution through contract law.

5.1.3 *Legal Incidence as Tax Incidence?*

Before exploring Craswell's (1991) answer to the "passing on" objection, we need to address another possible response to that contention. It is sometimes objected that the "passing on" argument "is essentially equivalent to the issue of tax incidence" (see, e.g., Blumkin and Margalioth 2005, 4–5). According to this objection, who pays for a tax (or cost of a legal rule) depends on the relative elasticities of supply and demand. Depending on these elasticities, either the buyer or the seller may primarily bear the burden of the tax (or cost of the legal rule). Because of this, according to the objection, taxes have no inherent advantage over legal rules.

Yet the analogy between the cost of legal rules and tax incidence is faulty. As we just showed with Hamada (1976), the cost of the legal rule is not always extrinsic to the product in the way a tax is. In the product liability example, the expected cost of an accident associated with the purchase of a good is an intrinsic part of the product. Whether as part of the explicit price of the good, or an implicit component of its total cost, the consumer *always* pays for it. In this case, the legal rule is not an "additional" cost, like a tax, but merely determines whether the expected accident costs are part of the explicit or implicit price of the good. To put it another way, in the product liability example, cost and total (implicit and explicit) price are still equal. In the case of a tax, price and cost are not equal; the tax drives a wedge between cost and price.

Craswell (1991, 366–68) identifies another difference between taxes and the costs of legal rules. A tax merely increases the cost of a product or service. In contrast, a legal rule increases the cost but *also* provides some benefit to the consumer (e.g., a warranty), and therefore changes her willingness to pay for it. Put a different way, the addition of a tax changes only product price and therefore quantity. A legal rule, in contrast, often affects product quality. Thus, in general one cannot treat the effects of legal rules like taxes. Craswell's line of thinking will be more fully unpacked in Section 5.2.

5.2 HOMOGENEOUS VERSUS HETEROGENEOUS CONSUMERS

Richard Craswell (1991) responded to the "passing on" argument in a remarkably lucid analysis.[11] Craswell says that whether legal rules can redistribute between parties in a competitive market depends on two conditions. First, consumers must be heterogeneous in their willingness to pay for the legal rule. Second, those most willing to pay for the benefit of the legal rule must also be those most willing to pay for the product or service itself. Under these conditions, legal rules can indeed be redistributive, even in competitive market conditions.[12]

Consider whether a court should read an implied warranty into every contract for a sale of a product. Craswell starts with the case of homogeneous consumers, observing that this implies that each consumer would pay exactly the same amount for the warranty.[13] Craswell also assumes that social welfare is measured solely by reference to consumers' own tastes and preferences, and that there are no externalities – all costs and benefits are borne by buyers and sellers. Under these assumptions, Craswell

[11] Kennedy (1981) explores a very similar economic analysis.

[12] Craswell also demonstrates that Ackerman (1971) is a special case of his argument (see Craswell 1991, 380–83).

[13] He also notes that consumers may have different valuations for the good *itself* – the homogeneity applies only to the warranty: "consumers may differ in their tastes regarding the product itself, but they have identical preferences concerning the presence or absence of a warranty (Craswell 1991, 368).

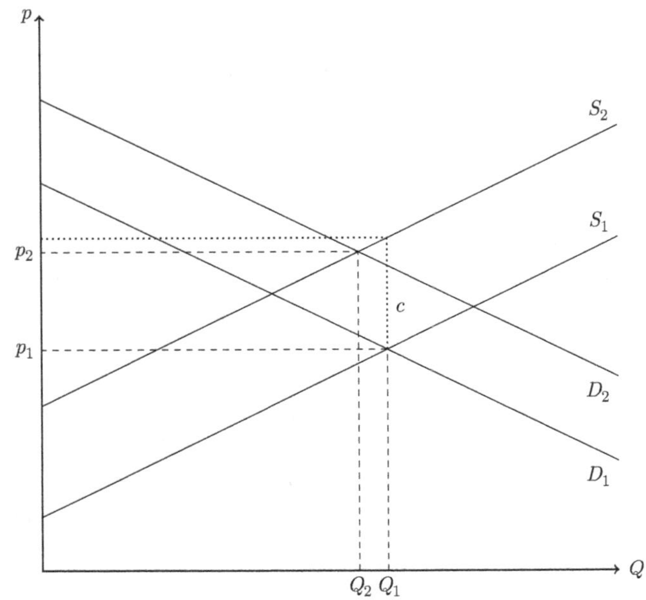

FIGURE 5.1 Homogeneous consumers: Inefficient warranty

This figure illustrates the equilibrium effects of an inefficient warranty with homogeneous consumers.

shows that consumers can only benefit from the addition of the warranty if their willingness to pay for it exceeds the cost of its addition to sellers. "If the value of the warranty to consumers exceeds its cost to sellers, the demand curve will rise by more than the supply curve; if not, then demand will rise by less than supply" (Craswell 1991, 369). This amounts to saying that consumers cannot gain, as a group, relative to producers, if the warranty is inefficient. Distribution and efficiency work in tandem in this case.

To see this, consider the following figures. Figure 5.1 illustrates the case where homogeneous consumers do not value the warranty as highly as its cost. Because of this, demand does not rise, from D_1 to D_2, as much as supply, from S_1 to S_2. The price of the good rises, but not by as much as the cost of the warranty: The increase from the initial price, p_1, to the warranty-inclusive price, p_2, is smaller than the cost of the warranty, c, as indicated by the dotted lines. Thus, the full cost of the warranty is not passed on to consumers. Furthermore, the equilibrium quantity declines, from Q_1 to Q_2. However, at the same time, consumers are made worse off. Clearly, the marginal consumer, for whom the value of the good is equal to its cost, and who values the warranty less than its cost just like all other consumers, will no longer purchase the good. But even consumers who continue to purchase the good, because they value it more than the marginal consumer does, are made worse off. This is demonstrated by

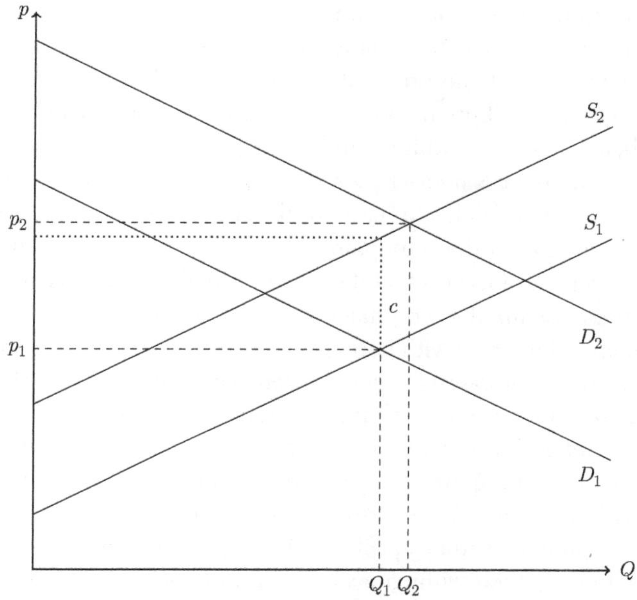

FIGURE 5.2 Homogeneous consumers: Efficient warranty

This figure illustrates the equilibrium effects of an efficient warranty with homogeneous consumers.

the fact that the increase in demand (which captures the value of the warranty) is less than the increase in the price. Even continuing consumers are therefore receiving less satisfaction from the good with the warranty than they were before. Interestingly, consumers do *not* gain as a group even though producers do *not* pass on all of the costs of the legal rules. This just underscores, in a surprising way, that the incidence of legal rules cannot be analogized to the incidence of taxes.

Figure 5.2 illustrates the case where homogeneous consumers do value the warranty more than its cost. Now that consumers value the warranty more than its cost, the increase in demand (D_1 to D_2) will outstrip the increase in supply (S_1 to S_2). Total quantity produced with the warranty exceeds the quantity produced without it and increases from Q_1 to Q_2. To meet this increased demand, producers have to increase their production costs. The consequence is that the eventual price increase exceeds the cost of the warranty. As illustrated in Figure 5.2, the price increase, p_2, is larger than the warranty's cost, indicated by *c* and the dotted line. More significantly, the *entire* cost of the warranty has now been "passed on" to consumers. Nevertheless, consumers still benefit from the warranty because their valuation of the product, made manifest by the increase in the equilibrium quantity, exceeds the price increase. It is in fact precisely because of the greater valuation that the increased demand results in a price that exceeds the cost of the warranty. The surprising result of the efficient warranty is that consumer welfare has increased as a group, even though producers have been able to pass the entire cost onto them.

Craswell draws two conclusions at this stage of the analysis. First, with homogeneous consumers, distribution and efficiency are congruent. Homogeneous consumers will benefit from a warranty (and, perhaps, a legal rule) if and only if the warranty is efficient in the Kaldor-Hicks sense. Second, and more counterintuitively, the significance of sellers' ability to "pass on" the costs of the legal rule is the opposite of what is presumed from the standpoint of the incidence of taxes. It is when the warranty passes on *less* of its cost that it does not benefit consumers, and only when the warranty passes on *all* of its cost that consumers are better off.

We have analyzed the case with homogeneous consumers. What about the more common and important case of heterogeneous consumers? Craswell considers a market where consumers value a warranty differently. Producers also charge the same price to all relevant consumers; they cannot price discriminate. The analysis is more subtle in this case, and requires analyzing the effects on both the "marginal" and "infra-marginal" heterogeneous consumers. Marginal consumers are those whose valuations of the product-warranty package place them just on the "margin" between buying or not buying; their willingness to pay is just equal to the product's cost, so they are indifferent between buying or not. Marginal consumers are critical because, given that their valuations are close to the price of the product, they will stop buying the package if the price rises. It is therefore the behavior of marginal consumers that will determine how high the price of the combined package will increase. Infra-marginal consumers are those who value the product-warranty package more highly than the marginal consumers, and at least somewhat significantly more than its cost. For that reason, they will continue to buy the product even when its price rises.

The economic behavior of *marginal* consumers – not necessarily infra-marginal consumers – largely tracks the analysis of the homogeneous consumer. If marginal consumers, on average, value the addition of the warranty more than its cost, demand will increase and price will rise higher than the cost of the warranty; marginal consumers are then better off. If, on the other hand, marginal consumers value the warranty less than its cost, demand will decrease, and the price increase will be less than the cost of the warranty; marginal consumers will be worse off in this case. It is more difficult to determine whether the *infra-marginal* consumers gain or lose from the introduction of a warranty. The easiest scenario to analyze is when the marginal consumer values the warranty exactly equal to its cost. In that case, the price increase, determined by the behavior of the marginal consumer, will also equal precisely the cost of the warranty. As a result, infra-marginal consumers who value the addition of the warranty more than marginal consumers will benefit more than the price increase, and be net winners. Conversely, infra-marginal consumers who value the warranty less than marginal consumers, will get benefits less than the price increase and will be net losers.

When the marginal consumers' valuation of the warranty differs both from its cost and from that of infra-marginal, consumers, the analysis becomes more complicated, both in terms of determining whether consumers benefit *as a class* as well as what *constitutes* that class. Stated most simply, however, Craswell concludes that the relationship between efficiency and (pro-consumer) distribution in markets with heterogeneous consumers "depends on how consumers' willingness to pay for the addition of a warranty is correlated with their willingness to pay for the underlying product without the warranty" (Craswell 1991, 377). If those consumers who are most willing to pay for the warranty are also most willing to pay for the product alone, then most consumers will benefit even if the warranty fails the Kaldor-Hicks efficiency test. Alternatively, if the willingness to pay for the warranty is inversely correlated with willingness to pay for the product, consumers will be worse off as a class, even if the warranty is efficient. If there is no correlation, either positive or negative, between valuation of the product and the warranty, the distributional and efficiency concerns will tend to converge.

These outcomes can be illustrated with the aid of Figures 5.3 and 5.4. In Figure 5.3, the steeper slope in the upward shift of the demand curve illustrates that infra-marginal consumers are willing to pay more for the combined warranty-product

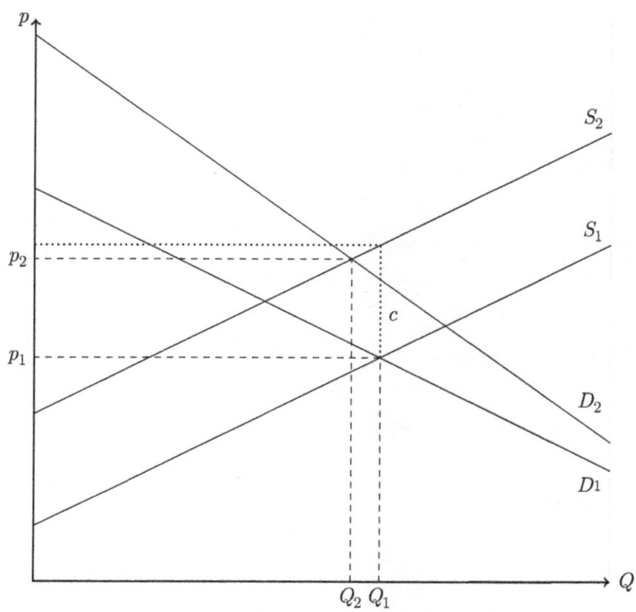

FIGURE 5.3 Heterogeneous consumers: High-valuing marginal consumers

This figure illustrates the equilibrium effects of the addition of a warranty that is valued less than its cost by the marginal consumer, but more than its cost by infra-marginal consumers.

package than are the marginal consumers. The *marginal* consumer values the warranty less than its cost. As a result, the quantity demanded falls with the addition of the warranty, and price increases less than the cost of the warranty, just as in the analysis of homogeneous consumers. However, because *infra-marginal* consumers value both the product and the warranty highly, most consumers are left better off with the addition of the warranty despite the price increase. Thus, in Figure 5.3, the vertical shift in the demand curve exceeds the price increase for most consumers, and consumers may benefit as a class even though the warranty is inefficient. The only consumers who are worse off are those whose demand increases by less than the price increase, who are located between the quantity decrease, between Q_1 and Q_2.

In Figure 5.4, by contrast, the correlation is reversed and those most willing to pay for the product are least willing to pay for the warranty. Now the valuations of the infra-marginal consumers change less, rather than more, following the introduction of the warranty. This is indicated by the flatter slope that comes with the increase in the demand curve. Once again, the marginal consumer values the warranty less than its price. Therefore, demand falls, and the price rises by less than cost. But welfare gains are lowest for the infra-marginal consumers, so the demand curve rises least on the left-side of the graph. Because these consumers will value the warranty less than the price increase, they are made worse off by its addition.

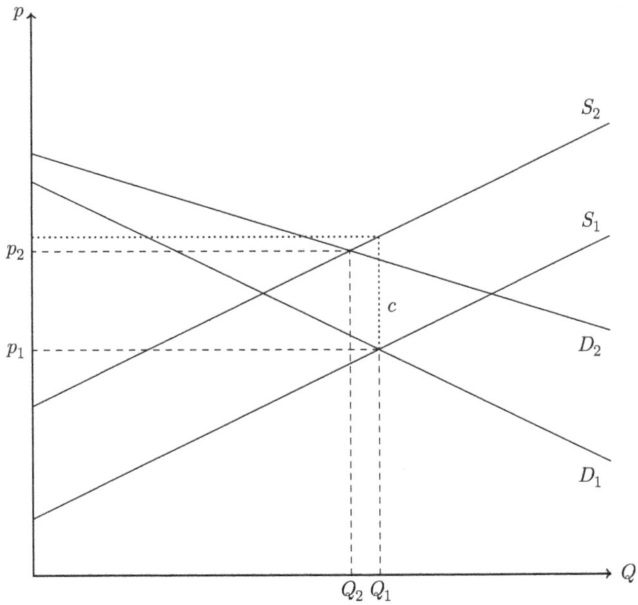

FIGURE 5.4 Heterogeneous consumers: Low-valuing marginal consumers

This figure illustrates the equilibrium effects of a warranty that is valued less than its cost by marginal consumers and even less so by infra-marginal consumers.

The case that demands our attention the most is represented in Figure 5.3. This case represents the possibility of a legitimately redistributive legal rule, one where consumers benefit as a class even though the rule is inefficient. "The important point," as Craswell summarizes, "is that such a warranty might be regarded as good … for consumers as a class *even if it were inefficient under an overall Kaldor-Hicks standard*" (Craswell 1991, 380, emphasis in original). When the marginal consumers place a low value on the warranty, this will limit the price increase induced by the addition of the warranty, even if the warranty is very costly for the producers. The increase in cost might even be large enough to make the addition of the warranty inefficient from the standpoint of total social wealth, particularly when the increase in consumer welfare is modest. However, what is critical is that the infra-marginal consumers gain from the warranty more than the price increase it induces, not more than the cost of the warranty. Thus, when those who value the warranty the most are also those who value the product the most (and those who value the warranty the least also value the product the least), "it may be possible for a pro-consumer or distributional analysis to endorse a warranty that an efficiency analysis would condemn" (380).

One question Craswell does not address, because his article appeared a few years before Kaplow and Shavell's paper, is whether an equity-improving but inefficient warranty should be adopted in light of the presence of the income tax system. The double-distortion argument hinges on the claim that legal rules cause two distortions, rather than a single distortion, like taxes. The first distortion is the behavior regulated by the legal rule, while the second is the labor-supply decisions affected by the rule's impact on the distribution of income. Craswell's analysis focuses solely on the first distortion – consumer behavior – but does not consider how the rule's distributive effects influence the supply of labor. But it would not be hard to incorporate labor-supply effects into Craswell's analysis. Nor would it be difficult to show that a redistributive but inefficient warranty (inclusive of labor-supply effects) could still redistribute income more efficiently than taxes.

For example, suppose that (1) producers are wealthier than consumers, (2) the warranty benefits consumers relative to producers, but also that (3) the warranty is just as efficient as the no-warranty allocation, inclusive of labor-supply effects. Nothing in Craswell's analysis preempts this possibility. Because the warranty may increase or decrease efficiency, it is also possible for it to be neutral with respect to efficiency. Thus, under our assumptions (1)–(3) an efficiency judgment is indifferent to the adoption of the warranty. That fact, combined with the more equitable distribution that comes with the warranty makes the warranty the unambiguous winner in a social-welfare judgment.

5.3 OTHER BASES OF REDISTRIBUTION THROUGH CONTRACT LAW

The remainder of the chapter will go beyond the warranty analysis, and explore other potentially redistributive contract rules. The first is a conspicuous candidate: the unconscionabilty doctrine, which addresses contracts that are formed unfairly or feature unduly harsh or one-sided terms. The second will look at the role of default rules in the context of markets with matching frictions and use the foreseeability rule in contract damages as an example.

5.3.1 *Unconscionability and Price Discrimination*

The unconscionability doctrine makes a common appearance in first-year contracts classes (Spence 1993). Students are frequently introduced to the doctrine through *Williams v. Walker-Thomas Furniture Co.*[14] According to Spence (1993, 91–92), "The plaintiffs [in *Walker*] were customers who were largely dependent for their ability to make major consumer purchases on the willingness of certain merchants to sell in low-income urban areas." A clause in the contract secured the debt through which the plaintiffs acquired the goods by giving the merchant the right to repossess all of the items previously purchased, not just the good that was the subject of the immediate transaction. In the case, the plaintiff had defaulted on payment for a stereo with a stated value of $524.95. The plaintiff owed a balance of $164 on all prior purchases, and total payments amounted to $1,400. The value of all purchases over the years came to $1,800.[15] The defendant then sought to replevy all of the items the plaintiff had purchased. In court, the plaintiff's "principal contention" was that the contract was "unconscionable and, hence, not enforceable."[16]

Within the law-and-economics literature, the unconscionability doctrine has earned, at best, a grudging respect. Whenever courts refuse to enforce contracts under the doctrine, they prima facie undo agreements that people voluntarily enter into. Refusing to enforce such contracts may make one party better off ex post, but that risk presumably makes them both worse off ex ante. The unfavorable terms low-income people face in consumer transactions reflect the greater risks merchants undertake when selling to these consumers. Refusing to enforce such agreements simply worsens the terms for low-income consumers or makes merchants unwilling to transact with them at all. Both Posner (1998, 129) and Epstein (1975) essentially endorse this position. Although Epstein concedes a narrow role for procedural unconscionabilty – alongside fraud, duress, and incapacity – he is skeptical about the doctrine's substantive application: "Yet when the doctrine of unconscionability is used in its substantive dimension, be it in a commercial or consumer context, it serves only to undercut the private right of contract in a manner that is apt to do more social harm than good" (315).

However, other law-and-economics scholars have been more sympathetic to the unconscionability doctrine. Posner (1995) discusses it explicitly within a redistributive

[14] 350 F.2d 445 (D.C. Cir. 1965).
[15] *Williams v. Walker-Thomas Furniture Co.*, 350 F.2d 445, 447 n.1.
[16] *Id.* at 447.

context, fully cognizant of the limitations of redistributive legal rules highlighted by Kaplow and Shavell (1994). Acknowledging these limitations, Posner argues, "The provision of welfare in a free market produces perverse incentives to take credit risks, which both drive up the cost of the welfare system and undermine its goal of poverty reduction." Nevertheless, restrictive contract doctrines, like unconscionability, "are appropriate means for deterring this socially costly behavior." Posner's basic intuition is that the guaranteed support of the welfare state induces more risky borrowing by "cushioning" the downside of the risk. In other words, with the backstop of a social safety net to catch them, individuals will be less responsible in their spending habits, risking indebtedness over frugality. Refusing to enforce one-sided terms, through the unconscionability doctrine, is a way to preempt such excessive riskiness, albeit a heavy-handed and rather paternalistic one.

While finding "a great deal of intellectual merit" in Posner's argument, Klock (2002) nevertheless takes an entirely different approach. Klock's defense of the unconscionability doctrine centers on the phenomenon of price discrimination, or the practice of selling the same or very similar goods or services at different prices to different markets or customers. There are several different kinds of price discrimination. First-degree price discrimination is selling a unit of the good in question at a price equal to the customer's (idiosyncratic) maximum willingness to pay. Second-degree price discrimination, also called nonlinear pricing, entails selling goods at different prices depending on the number of units purchased. For example, this might entail giving a large-quantity purchaser a "bulk" discount. Because each customer faces the same price schedule, second-degree price discrimination does not formally discriminate across consumers. Finally, third-degree price discrimination is the mirror image of second-degree discrimination, which means that different customers pay the same amount for each unit they purchase, no matter how many units they buy, but are charged different prices based on demographic or other group-based distinctions. Examples of third-degree price discrimination are student discounts, senior discounts, or charging higher prices for later booking on flights or hotels (Varian 1989, 600). It is important to acknowledge these different degrees of price discrimination because they have different implications for efficiency, a point to which we will return shortly.

Price discrimination is quite common as a practice[17] and can arise for a variety of reasons. Firms may price discriminate because of differences among consumers in the costs of acquiring information (Salop 1977; Salop and Stiglitz 1977) or the distance required to travel to purchase goods (Salop 1979). Thus, at the expense of low-income consumers like those in *Williams*, merchants may exploit either or both informational or spatial barriers to extract higher prices or demand less-favorable terms from consumers who face such obstacles.

[17] Varian (1989) states that "[p]rice discrimination is one of the most prevalent forms of marketing practices" (598) and that among the forms of price discrimination, third-degree price discrimination "is perhaps the most common form" (600).

Poor consumers, such as those in *Williams v. Walker-Thomas*, face unfavorable price or contract terms, not necessarily because of their poverty itself, but because of the closely related informational and spatial barriers they confront in the market. Poor consumers may not have as much access to information about goods, prices, or contract terms as rich ones do. They are excluded from the social networks in which better information about products and services circulates. The poor are often not the intended targets of advertising campaigns that aim to convey such information. If poor consumers spend more hours working, they will have less time to research and compare different products and services. The poor may not be able to afford the products or services that provide information about prices and quality of commodities. And the poor have more limited transportation options, which restrains the choice and frequency of retailers they patronize. When it comes to poverty, there is more than just being "unsophisticated" about contracts and exchanges. All of these barriers allow sellers to price discriminate and thereby exploit different segments of the market.

In fact, one ethnographer described the Walker-Thomas Furniture Company in precisely these terms (Greenberg 1980). Taking advantage of consumer's limited mobility, the Walker-Thomas employed around thirty "traveling" sales representatives who worked door-to-door in order to make itself "the only accessible merchant of credit" in the neighborhood (382). These salespeople engaged their customers "in personal as well as commercial relationships" (Greenberg 1980, 382) and actively required them to purchase on credit (381). The representatives kept large amounts of cash on hand and scheduled collections on days when clients' welfare checks would arrive (382). Walker-Thomas not only exploited customers' information deficits, but cultivated them as well. The company deliberately disguised information about "total cost and financing charges, product quality, and collection requirements" (384). Through such practices, Walker-Thomas "buil[t] consumer dependency" and "fashion[ed] a quasi monopoly hold over their purchasing power" (381).

According to Klock, the unconscionability doctrine is a way for disadvantaged consumers to combat price-discrimination. What is interesting about using unconscionability to achieve this objective is that it acquires a distinctive doctrinal rationale. In other words, with price discrimination as its target, the unconscionability doctrine cannot be adequately subsumed under fraud, duress, or breach of fiduciary obligation, as Richard Epstein might have it. Used to combat that practice, unconscionability is no longer just a "voguish term" for those contract wrongs.

However, Klock's primary concern with price discrimination is its potential inefficiency. Although price discrimination has inequality-increasing effects, Klock explains in a familiar double-distortion tone why the primary concern should be with efficiency: "A wealthy society has the economic capability of minimizing the problems of poverty whereas an impoverished society can only dream of minimizing these problems" (Klock 2002, 346). Klock therefore does not answer the question with which we are preoccupied: Can the unconscionability doctrine reduce income inequality more efficiently than the tax system?

I argue that the answer is yes. There is a valid distributive argument for the unconscionability doctrine. First, we should make clear the distributive implications of price discrimination. Firms price discriminate because doing so increases profits – they would not engage in the practice if it did not. These extra profits must come from somewhere, and the source is consumer surplus. Hence, as long as firms, or firm owners, are wealthier than average, price discrimination will increase income inequality.

Second, whether price discrimination is efficient or not is ambiguous. It is well known that first-degree price discrimination results in a Pareto efficient allocation of resources (Varian 1989, 602). Depending on a variety of circumstances, however, other forms of price discrimination can be efficient or inefficient relative to an otherwise similar market with uniform pricing. For example, Schmalensee (1981) shows in a formal model that a necessary condition for third-degree price discrimination to improve welfare is that it increases output.[18] In a model of price discrimination with monopolistic competition, Katz (1984) shows that uniform pricing is more efficient than price discrimination when the purchases made by uninformed consumers, who are discriminated against, constitute a small proportion of the total purchases. Naturally, the opposite is the case when uninformed consumers are a larger proportion of the market. Most generally, when firms price discriminate there is no necessary reason why the equilibrium quantity for the higher-priced consumers should fall less than the quantity should rise for the low-priced consumers. In other words, the effects of price discrimination for efficiency are ambiguous: Price discrimination may increase or decrease total output compared to uniform pricing.

When distributive and efficiency characteristics of price discrimination are combined, it is fairly easy to see why applying the unconscionability doctrine to exploitative agreements may accomplish redistribution more efficiently than taxation. First, note that if eliminating price discrimination increases efficiency, including those effects, then unconscionability is both efficient and egalitarian. In this case, there is no equity-efficiency trade-off, and the double-distortion argument has no objection. The test occurs when unconscionability is inefficient. The question then becomes which policy is less inefficient: taxes or the unconscionability doctrine.

A useful benchmark is to again imagine an efficiency-neutral application of the unconscionability doctrine (similar to the thought experiment at the end of Section 5.2). I will assume that any efficiency judgments include the labor-supply effects of the legal rules.[19] Suppose unconscionability is neutral with respect to efficiency;

[18] Schmalensee (1981) established this result with independent demand functions and constant marginal costs; Varian (1985) demonstrates the same result in a more general model.

[19] The issue of labor-supply effects arises acutely in the antitrust case but is just as relevant here. For further discussion, see the antitrust chapter.

changes in consumer surplus and profits, and their add-on labor-supply effects, exactly offset one another when the unconscionability rule prohibits differentiated pricing. In that case, the unconscionability doctrine is necessarily more efficient than taxation at redistributing income because the costs of redistribution are necessarily higher owing to the higher income inequality with price discrimination. This makes it clear that unconscionability will still beat taxes even if it is marginally inefficient. If the inefficiency of unconscionability is lower than the inefficiency of redistribution taxation – which is possible with a choice of legal rules that are neutral with respect to efficiency – then unconscionability is better than taxation for redistributive purposes.

To be clear, of course, the unconscionability doctrine is not guaranteed to be more redistributively efficient than the income tax. This issue, as emphasized previously, is an empirical one. For example, if the price-discriminating monopolist abandons the practice by ending its sales in low-income neighborhoods, cutting those consumers off entirely, the unconscionability doctrine may indeed do more harm than good. This is a legitimate possibility. However, if, anticipating adverse judgments based on the unconscionabilty doctrine, merchants abandon price discrimination and adopt a uniform-pricing strategy in all of their outlets, even at the expense of some inefficiency (say, because the increased demand from low-income consumers does not make up for the decreased demand from high-income consumers), redistribution will occur at less cost than taxation.

5.3.2 *Damages and Default Rules*

The irony of contract law is that contracts are needed most where the practice of exchange – buying and selling – differs most from its textbook presentation. The economists' ideal exchange is the spot contract – the sale, for example, of a cup of coffee. Because information is readily available and performance is simultaneous, the spot contract is scarcely a contract. As Cooter and Ulen (2016) explain, "Many exchanges occur instantly and simultaneously, as when a shopper pays cash for goods in the grocery store. In a simultaneous, instantaneous exchange, there is little reason to promise anything. The making of promises, however, typically concerns *deferred exchanges* – that is, transactions that involve the passage of time for their completion" (Cooter and Ulen 2016, 283, emphasis in original). Parties will give money now in exchange for a promise to deliver goods or services in the future, which Cooter and Ulen call a "payment for a promise" (283). Parties will also deliver goods or services now in exchange for a promise to pay in the future ("goods for a promise") (283). And, of course, parties can promise to pay in the future for services performed or goods delivered in the future ("promise for a promise") (283).

Contracts are valuable because they address the shortcomings of the inevitable, nonideal exchange. As Cooter and Ulen (2016) also observe, "The passage of time between the exchange of promises and their performance creates uncertainties and risks" (283). Contract law, in their argument, serves to address these risks and uncertainties. That a promise can be enforced by a court – or at least make the breaching party liable for damages – gives the parties some certainty that the other party's promise means something.

For our discussion, what is interesting about the uncertainties and risks of exchange – whether or not they arise from deferred performance – is that they also produce rents, which in economics simply means a difference of price over cost, a pure transfer. A large literature in economics has explored the effects of matching frictions on exchange and efficiency.[20] In a market with matching frictions, buyers and sellers meet one another probabilistically, and are not guaranteed to find a trading partner in a given period. In a free-entry equilibrium, these frictions will not be consistent with the marginal-price-equals-marginal-cost assumption of perfect competition. Price and cost will diverge – generating rents – to cover sellers or buyers for risk and uncertainty that the exchange will fail.

Critically, the existence of rents influences the exchange parties' incentives, including bargaining and investments in performance. In that context, the default rules of contract shape the bargaining power of parties and, as a result, the distribution of income. As an example, we will consider the celebrated case of *Hadley v. Baxendale*.[21] *Hadley* stands for the proposition that a defendant is liable, in breach of contract, only for losses that are *foreseeable* at the time of the contract's formation.[22] For law-and-economics scholars, the natural interpretation of the foreseeability doctrine is an efficiency one. According to Bebchuk and Shavell (1991), for instance, limited liability for losses encourages buyers – in a pay-for-promise situation – to communicate, or signal, how much they value the seller's performance. This theory of *Hadley* and the foreseeability doctrine can be seen as a special case of Ayres and Gertner's (1989) more general theory of contract default rules. According to that theory, default rules should be chosen, not necessarily to minimize bargaining costs, as in the traditional Coasean interpretation of default rules, but rather to encourage parties to reveal information. Indeed, "*Hadley* illustrates a 'penalty' default rule: a rule which 'forces' the revelation of information which the revealing party might generally wish not to reveal" (Johnston 1990, 616).[23]

[20] For some of the key contributions to this literature, see Diamond (1982), Mortensen (1982), Hosios (1990), Moen (1997), and Pissarides (2000). An overview of the literature can be found in Mortensen and Pissarides (1999).

[21] 9 Exch. 341, 156 Eng. Rep. 145 (1854).

[22] For a more recent statement of the foreseeability doctrine in contracts, see *Sunnyland Farms, Inc. v. Central New Mexico Electric Cooperative, Inc.*, 301 P.3d 387 (N.M. 2013). See also the Restatement (Second) of Contracts §351, "Unforeseeability and Related Limitations on Damages."

[23] For an alternative perspective both on *Hadley v. Baxendale* and the economic theory of default rules, see Johnston (1990). Johnston argues that parties' *strategic* bargaining interests typically counter the information-revealing actions parties are assumed to make under the information-forcing theory of default rules. Johnston instead offers an "expansive" theory of default rules, in which default rules remove the strategic impediments to bargaining around them.

To study the relative efficiency of the foreseeability doctrine, Bebchuk and Shavell (1991) present a stylized model with buyers and sellers, which I will adopt and augment in this section. A seller can reduce the likelihood of breach by taking precautions, but extra precautions will naturally entail additional expense or effort. Buyers come in two varieties: A minority of buyers place a high value on performance, while the majority place a lower or "normal" value on it. The buyers' valuation of performance, however, is not readily observable to sellers. Notwithstanding that, buyers may choose to identify themselves, and indicate to sellers whether they place a high or a low value on performance. These communications, or signals, can then be reflected in the terms of contract, which determine how much liability the seller will be responsible for in case of a breach and whether that includes all damages or only those that are ordinarily foreseeable. For example, we might say, following the *Hadley* case, that most mill owners have a backup crankshaft when one breaks, but a minority do not. This minority places a high value on getting a broken crankshaft repaired promptly and adequately; a failure or delay in repair will result in further delays, and losses, at the mill. However, because a repair shop cannot tell the difference between the two kinds of mill owners, the more desperate owner may need to communicate this and specify the consequences in the contract. Finally, in the model, these communications involve transaction costs for both buyers and sellers, which Bebchuk and Shavell (1991, 285) refer to as "communication costs." Accordingly, the model incorporates two types of decision: buyers' decisions about communicating their valuations; and sellers' decisions about the level of precautions they must take to reduce the likelihood of breach. Bebchuk and Shavell use the model to identify which decisions are efficient and then compare how the decisions induced by the limited and unlimited liability rules measure against that benchmark.

Bebchuk and Shavell (1991) derive several key insights from their model. The first important derivation is that as long as communication is efficient, only high-value buyers, but not low-value buyers, should communicate their preferences about performance. Buyers who communicate that they place a high value on performance allows sellers to infer (costlessly) that buyers who do not communicate are low-value buyers. This way of transferring information minimizes transaction costs; all other possible ways of communicating buyer types are socially inefficient because they entail greater communication costs.[24] The second insight is that the unlimited liability rule is inefficient. "Under the unlimited liability rule, high valuation buyers will have no reason to identify themselves (indeed, doing so would be costly, as it would result in sellers' raising the contract price)" (286). This leads either to no communication, in which case sellers cannot determine buyer types and take

[24] Specifically, having all buyers communicate their preferences is more costly than only a subset engaging in costly communication; and because low-value buyers are a majority, having only low-value buyers identify themselves is more costly than having only high-value buyers identify themselves.

inadequate precautions; or to only communication from low-value buyers, which fails to minimize communication costs. The third insight is that *Hadley*'s limited liability rule induces socially optimal behavior, where only high-value buyers identify themselves. Even though high-value buyers will have to pay a higher contract price, the additional cost of identifying themselves is worth the fuller protection they are able to secure against breach by negotiating around a default rule that provides only limited liability.

At first blush, the foreseeability doctrine might appear to have distributive implications, in addition to efficiency ones. By insulating sellers from the full (if unforeseeable) consequences of the breach of their performance, it appears to be pro-seller. However, whether the rule has these distributive effects depends on the circumstances, especially because we are talking about contracts and exchange, where the "passing on" of costs looms large. In fact, as Bebchuk and Shavell (1991, 297–98) describe their model, "The market is assumed to be in a state of (Nash) equilibrium and to be perfectly competitive. Thus, sellers make expected profits of zero." In this environment, we do not even reach the question about whether an alternative to the foreseeability doctrine – some form of unlimited liability rule – might be less inefficient than taxation at redistributing income. Instead, with perfect competition, sellers will pass on all of their costs to the buyer. In Bebchuk and Shavell's model, not only do buyers bear their costs of communication, they also bear all of the sellers' costs. Thus, under the perfect-competition assumptions of Bebchuk and Shavell's model, *Hadley*'s limited liability rule has no distributive consequences. In other words, the cost of legal rules are entirely "passed on."

In order to study the distributive effects of default rules, we need to contemplate a more general setting. Matching models of exchange fulfill just this need. In a matching model, one is not guaranteed to find a trading partner and, hence, the chance of concluding an exchange (in a given time period) is probabilistic. The probability that a seller finds a buyer depends on the ratio of buyers to sellers in the market; the more buyers there are relative to sellers, the better the chances a seller will find a buyer. (The inverse applies to buyers' chances of finding a seller.) These matching "frictions" drive a wedge between marginal cost and marginal price. If price is equal to (certain) costs, but some sellers find no buyers, those sellers will be forced to leave the market. In a free-entry equilibrium with matching frictions, therefore, the probability of finding a trading partner is included in the seller's ex ante entry decision. This implies prices above marginal cost and, more importantly, the existence of rents. Ex post, after a seller and buyer have been matched, they will bargain over the division of this surplus. We have, in effect, a model of a "thin" market, as described by Schwab (1989).

One virtue of a matching model of the market is that it can treat the extent of the search frictions as a parameter. Suppose, for example, that q is the ratio of sellers to buyers, or the "queue" length. We can then say that the probability that a seller finds a buyer is $\mu(q)$. Thus, the larger (or longer) q is, the more sellers there are relative to buyers (which ratio may vary between zero and infinity), and the smaller the chances the seller will find a buyer. Likewise, $\eta(q) = q\mu(q)$ can be used to represent the probability that a buyer will find a seller, given the queue length, q.[25] Naturally, the inverse relationship holds: The longer is q (the more sellers there are relative to buyers), the *greater* the probability that a buyer will find a seller. As a limit on this matching process, we can think of a "frictionless" market where the shorter side of the market is fully employed: $\eta^F(q) = \min\{1, q\}$ and $\mu^F(q) = \min\{1/q, 1\}$. In this version of the matching process, the chances of finding a trading partner depend less on the queue length and more on the absence of friction in the market. As the probability of finding a trading partner approaches one, there will be smaller rents, and less for the parties to bargain over. Thus, one could say that Bebchuk and Shavell's (1991) assumption of perfect competition is a special, limiting case of a general model of matching "technology."

To underscore how default rules matter in the context of rent sharing, we will add one more feature to the Bebchuk and Shavell model. We will assume that the buyer, in addition to paying money up front, makes an ex ante investment in their enterprise, whatever it may be, that increases the value of any transaction. Otherwise, the model is identical to Bebchuk and Shavell (1991). Thus, there are two types of buyers (although for simplicity we will assume that the type is revealed to the buyer only after they make their investment). After the buyer makes their investment, and the buyer learns her type, the buyer can communicate that type – high- or low-value of the seller's performance – to the seller at a cost to both. As in Bebchuk and Shavell's model, under the limited liability rule of *Hadley* a buyer is only entitled to the low-value performance in the case of a breach. Under an unlimited liability rule, the buyer gets that value of performance associated with their type.

Can legal rules redistribute income in an environment with market frictions? And if they can, will they do so less inefficiently than taxes? The remainder of this section argues that they can. The crucial feature is rent sharing, which, as was indicated by Schwab (1989) previously, takes us out of a "thick" market and into a "thin" one where producers do not necessarily pass on all of their costs, and bargaining over the surplus affects the distribution of income. As we will also see, the division of rents influences the behavior of the parties. Changing that division in a more equitable direction not only changes the income distribution, but may also produce an *offsetting* rather than a compounding double distortion. In other words, it may produce distortions that go in the opposite direction, which makes it impossible to say that legal rules will be less efficient than taxes in redistributing income.

To get to this conclusion, we need to further unpack the implications of rent sharing. In the context of matching frictions, efficiency requires an appropriate

[25] By employing the expression $\eta(q) = q\mu(q)$ or, equivalently, $\mu(q) = \eta(q)/q$ we are implicitly defining the matching function as having constant returns to scale, which is a standard assumption. See Pissarides (2000, 6).

division of the rents between buyer and seller (Hosios 1990). If the buyer gets all of the surplus, too few sellers will enter the market place. If the seller gets all of the surplus, the buyer's investment incentives will be distorted. There is, however, a particular division of the rents that will maximize the joint gains of the trading partners. Rent sharing also implicates the distribution of income. Each party's relative bargaining power will determine the distribution of the surplus. Most importantly, default rules will influence each party's relative bargaining power. For example, compared to the limited liability rule, an unlimited liability rule strengthens the buyer's bargaining position. Both parties know that, in the case of a seller's breach, the buyer is entitled to the (ex post, demonstrable) value of the entitled performance, regardless of whether this value was communicated to the seller or not. The damages rule creates a kind of "outside option," a floor if you will, on what the buyer can minimally expect from that contract. The better that outside option – the higher the floor – the stronger the buyer's bargaining power. Thus, an unlimited liability rule places the buyer in a position to demand more of the surplus, and therefore shifts the distribution of income in the buyer's favor.

This shift, of course, depends on the existence of rents. In a frictionless market, there will be no rents and therefore the choice of rules will affect only total wealth, and not its distribution. Nevertheless, this is the point I want to make: The fact that there are no distributive effects of legal rules in the case of a frictionless market shows precisely why search frictions are important.

Let us say, for whatever reason, that the sharing rule optimizes the matching of buyers and sellers (including the buyer's investment) under the limited liability rule, which itself ensures the efficient level of the seller's performance, as demonstrated in Bebchuk and Shavell's (1991) analysis. (Many models rationalize this possibility by showing that if parties are able to make firm, ex ante commitments, competitive conditions in an otherwise frictional market will induce one party to offer an efficient division of the rents (see, e.g., Montgomery 1991; Moen 1997; Acemoglu and Shimer 1999).) The efficient sharing rule, combined with the foreseeability rule therefore gives us an efficient allocation of resources.

Now consider the adoption of an unlimited liability rule, under which income is redistributed from sellers to buyers by strengthening the buyer's bargaining position in negotiations over the friction-generated surplus. In addition, buyers no longer communicate their performance valuations, which means consequently that sellers do not make efficient precautions against breach. This creates a double distortion: The change in the income distribution distorts labor supply while the choice of an inefficient legal rule distorts sellers' precautionary incentives.

However, adopting the unlimited liability rule has another effect as well. Rent sharing creates a hold-up problem with respect to the buyer's ex ante investment – a nevertheless necessary one given the requirement that sellers require some of the surplus in order for the matching of buyers and sellers to be constrained efficient. However, because more of the surplus goes to the buyer, the buyer will be induced to make a larger up-front, value-improving investment in the contract. From a wealth-maximization perspective, this is an *over*investment with respect to the constrained-efficient conditions of the market with matching frictions. However, because that response increases the buyer's investment, and therefore the value of the transaction, it moves in the opposite direction as the other two distortions. Put another way, because we started from an efficient allocation of resources under the limited liabilty rule, this overinvestment will by definition not be efficient. Nevertheless, if the overinvestment offsets the loss of wealth caused by the seller's change in precautionary behavior, it will be less inefficient than a distribution-equivalent adjustment to the tax schedule. In other words, using a pro-buyer liability can redistribute income more efficiently than the income tax system.

In summary, under the assumptions of perfect competition, legal rules may not redistribute income and, more importantly, may do nothing more than generate inefficiencies. By contrast, in a market with matching frictions, legal rules may not only redistribute income but do so more efficiently than the income tax. Frictions produce rents, which make bargaining over income, and its redistribution, possible. Shifting bargaining power also changes investment decisions, which have offsetting effects. These offsets mean that the double-distortion is not compounding – a necessary assumption for why taxes should be more efficient than legal rules. We have asked, more generally, whether contract rules have any use in perfectly competitive markets. Our exploration of the foreseeability rule in the context of matching frictions, gives us one more reason for thinking that contract rules are made for a world of imperfect, rather than perfect, competition and that one of their functions is to influence the distribution of income.

5.4 APPENDIX

The following appendix provides formal proofs for the distributive effects of the foreseeability rule. The model generalizes Bebchuk and Shavell's (1991) model of limited and unlimited liability rules by embedding it in a market with matching frictions. The online appendix reproduces the foreseeability model as well as presents the formal model of the unconscionability doctrine.

The foreseeability rule demonstrates the redistributive value of default rules. Section 5.4.1 builds the basic model by incorporating Bebchuk and Shavell's (1991) model of the foreseeability rule into a market with matching frictions. Section 5.4.2 specifies the equilibrium conditions of the basic model. Section 5.4.3 shows how changing the default rule determines the actors' outside options and buyers' ex ante investment incentives. Section 5.4.4 derives the basic result and shows that adopting the inefficient, unlimited liability rule can redistribute income more efficiently than taxes. Finally, Section 5.4.5 clarifies why market frictions are crucial for the results. As in the standard Hamada-type analysis (Hamada 1976), the costs of legal rules are "passed on" in perfectly competitive, frictionless markets.

5.4.1 *Model*

As in Bebchuk and Shavell (1991), we examine two different liability rules: an unlimited liability rule, where the breaching party pays full expectation damages to the injured party, and a limited liability rule, where the breaching party pays expectation damages, but only for those that are foreseeable. Denote the limited liability rule as $\mathcal{L}$ and the unlimited rule as $\mathcal{U}$.

The buyer's valuation of performance is at one of two levels, $v \in \{H, L\}$. Let L be the value of performance to a low valuation buyer, with $L > 0$, and let H be the value of performance to a high valuation buyer, with $H > L$. At all times, we assume that the fraction of high-value buyers is less than half: $\alpha < 0.5$. Let the cost of communication be $\kappa = \kappa_B + \kappa_S$, where κ_B is the cost of communication to the buyer and κ_S is the cost of communication to the seller.

Sellers can enhance the probability of performance by taking costly measures on precaution. Let x be the seller's expenditures on precautions and let $\pi(x)$ be the probability of contract performance. More specifically, $\pi : \mathbf{R}_+ \to [0, 1]$ with $\pi'(\cdot) > 0$ and $\pi''(\cdot) < 0$. If sellers breach – fail to substantially perform – they are liable for the value of performance to buyers. As in Bebchuk and Shavell, this means that under a rule that limits damages to those that are foreseeable, sellers are liable only to the extent of L. High-vale buyers must inform sellers that they value performance at H in order for sellers to be liable for that amount. Under the rule that eliminates foreseeability as a ceiling for damages, sellers are liable for the buyer's value of performance, regardless of buyer's communications. Because sellers seek to maximize their returns to the transaction, they choose the level of precaution to do so. Letting x^* denote the optimal expenditure on precautions, then the total cost c to a seller who is transacting with a known, low-value buyer is $c_L = x_L^* + (1 - \pi(x_L^*))L$; when transacting with a known, high-value buyer, the total cost is $c_H = x_H^* + (1 - \pi(x_H^*))H$; when the seller does not know the buyer type (e.g., an unlimited liability rule when the buyer does not communicate their type), total cost is $c_{LH} = x_{LH}^* + (1 - \pi(x_{LH}^*))((1 - \alpha)L + \alpha H)$.

As explained in the text, sellers and buyers are matched probabilistically which means that neither is guaranteed to find a trading partner in a given period. These matching frictions generate rents. Rents are bargained over. Therefore, once a seller and buyer are matched they bargain over a price. We use the Nash bargaining solution to determine this price. Write the buyer's payoff as:

$$V = v - p - \kappa_B$$

which is the value of performance, $v \in \{H, L\}$, minus the contract price, p, and the cost of communication (if there is any), κ_B. We also assume that the buyer's outside option is $\bar{V}$, which critically depends on the liability rule, hence we will write $\bar{V}_{\mathcal{L}}$ or $\bar{V}_{\mathcal{H}}$ when it is necessary to be more precise.

Similarly, the seller's payoff is

$$U = p - c - \kappa_S$$

which is the contract price, minus the cost of precaution, $c \in \{c_L, c_H, c_{LH}\}$, and the cost of communication, κ_S (again, if there is any). We can write the seller's outside option as $\bar{U}$, but for simplicity we assume the seller's outside option is zero, $\bar{U} = 0$.

Setting up the Nash bargaining problem, we can write:

$$(V - \bar{V})^{\beta}(U - \bar{U})^{1-\beta}$$

which can also be written as

$$\beta \ln(v - p - \kappa_B - \bar{V}) + (1 - \beta) \ln(p - c - \kappa_S).$$

Maximizing this expression with respect to p, we obtain the first-order condition and set it equal to zero:

$$-\frac{\beta}{v - p - \kappa_B - \bar{V}} + \frac{1 - \beta}{p - c - \kappa_S} = 0.$$

Solving for p, we get:

$$p = (1 - \beta)(v - \kappa_B - \bar{V}) + \beta(c + \kappa_S). \tag{5.1}$$

Intuitively, the price is a weighted average of the buyer's surplus and the seller's costs. When $\beta = 1$, all of the bargaining advantage belongs with the buyer, and price is minimized at the seller's costs. Alternatively, when $\beta = 0$, all of the bargaining advantage shifts to the seller, and seller appropriates the entire surplus. According to Hosios (1990), there exists a certain division of the bargaining advantage, and thus the rents, which is constrained efficient, that is, efficient subject to the market frictions which always entail a loss of efficiency relative to perfect competition. Define this division of the bargaining advantage as $\beta = \hat{\beta}$ and for the remainder of the analysis we assume this condition obtains. This will make the limited liability rule the globally efficient rule, inclusive of buyers' ex ante investments as well sellers' choice of precaution.

Using the expression for the contract price given in equation (5.1), we can now write the buyer's payoff as:

$$V = \bar{V} + \beta(v - c - \kappa - \bar{V}). \tag{5.2}$$

Notice that the buyer's payoff is increasing in the outside option: $V'(\bar{V}) = 1 - \beta \geq 0$. The seller's payoff in turn is:

$$U = (1 - \beta)(v - c - \kappa - \bar{V}) \tag{5.3}$$

and also notice that the seller's payoff is decreasing in the buyer's outside option: $U'(\bar{V}) = -(1 - \beta) \leq 0$.

5.4.2 *Equilibrium Conditions*

This subsection reviews the conditions that Bebchuk and Shavell (1991)) assume, and which I adopt in this model, in order to ensure that the limited liability is more efficient than the unlimited liability rule.

The central assumption is that the cost of high-value buyers communicating their performance preferences is less than the social value of information. Bebchuk and Shavell express this condition as:

$$\alpha\kappa < I$$

where I is the social value of information (295), which we will define in a moment. Notice that once high-value buyers communicate their performance preferences, sellers can implicitly identify low-value buyers without them having to communicate such information. Sellers would also be able to identify buyer types if all buyers communicate their preferences or if only low-value buyers communicate (implicitly identifying high-value types). However, it is more efficient for only high-value buyers to communicate their preferences because they are a minority of the population. Hence having only high-value buyers communicate minimizes the costs of communication: $\alpha\kappa$ is less than either of the alternatives, $\alpha\kappa < \kappa$ or $\alpha\kappa < (1-\alpha)\kappa$.

The social value of information is given by:

$$I = (1-\alpha)[(\pi(x_L^*)L - x_L^*) - (\pi(x_{LH}^*)L - x_{LH}^*)] + \alpha[(\pi(x_H^*)H - x_H^*) - (\pi(x_{LH}^*)H - x_{LH}^*)]$$

and represents the increase in social welfare (exclusive of communication costs) when sellers choose different effort levels x_L^* and x_H^* for the two types of buyers, rather than the intermediate, common level x_{LH}^*. Hence, when the social value of information is greater than the (minimized) costs of communication, $I > \alpha\kappa$, communication is efficient.

Two more assumptions are required to ensure that in equilibrium the unlimited liability rule and communication by high-value buyers is efficient. The first is that, under a limited liability, high-value buyers must be able to improve their payoff by communicating their preferences to sellers. The payoff to so communicating is $\bar{V} + \beta(H - c_H - \kappa - \bar{V})$. If high-value buyers do not communicate, then they can expect to obtain $\bar{V} + \beta(\pi(x_L^*)H + (1-\pi(x_L^*))L - c_L - \bar{V})$. The condition for high-value buyers to communicate is therefore $\bar{V} + \beta(H - c_H - \kappa - \bar{V}) > \bar{V} + \beta(\pi(x_L^*)H + (1-\pi(x_L^*))L - c_L - \bar{V})$. This condition simplifies to $H - c_H - \kappa > \pi(x_L^*)H + (1-\pi(x_L^*))L - c_L$. From here, it is easy to see that this condition is identical to the condition specified in equation (14) in Bebchuk and Shavell (1991, 298):

$$\begin{aligned} \kappa &< (H - c_H) - [\pi(x_L^*)H + (1-\pi(x_L^*))L - c_L] \\ &= (\pi(x_H^*)H - x_H^*) - (\pi(x_L^*)H - x_L^*) \end{aligned}$$

If this condition holds, then there is a unique equilibrium where high-value buyers identify themselves, low-value buyers do not, and sellers choose the appropriate level of precaution for each buyer. If this condition does not hold, then there is a unique equilibrium where no buyers identify themselves and sellers choose the lower level of precaution for all buyers. Because we are interested in the former equilibrium, we assume the condition holds.

Finally, under an unlimited liability rule, there is another equilibrium condition. Under an unlimited liability rule, low-value buyers may have an interest in communicating their preferences, in order to lower the cost of the transaction. If the low-value buyer communicates this preference, they receive $\bar{V} + \beta(L - c_L - \kappa - \bar{V})$; if they do not communicate, they receive $\bar{V} + \beta(L - c_{LH} - \bar{V})$. (Note that, under the unlimited liability rule, the buyer receives in either case their value of the performance or its equivalent in a liability payment.) The condition for communication is therefore $\bar{V} + \beta(L - c_L - \kappa - \bar{V}) > \bar{V} + \beta(L - c_{LH} - \bar{V})$. This condition reduces to

$$c_{LH} - c_L > \kappa,$$

which is identical to the condition given in equation (17) by Bebchuk and Shavell (1991, 300). If this condition is satisfied, there is a unique equilibrium where only low-value buyers identify themselves, and sellers incur the appropriate level of precautions for each type of buyer (with high-value buyers identifying themselves by *not* communicating their preferences). If this condition is not satisfied, there is a unique equilibrium in which no buyers identify themselves and sellers choose the intermediate level of precaution. To keep matters simple, we will assume that this condition is not satisfied, and so that low-value buyers do not distinguish themselves under the unlimited liability rule.

5.4.3 *Outside Options and Buyer Investments*

This subsection will illustrate two points: (1) how liability rules change the buyer's outside option (which in turn affect buyer and seller payoffs) and (2) how changes in buyer payoffs influence their ex ante investments. The first point is probably the most critical feature of the bargaining model presented in this chapter.

First, how does an unlimited liability rule improve the buyer's outside option (and therefore their bargaining power and payoff)? Once we assume a bargaining scenario, where parties explicitly negotiate an agreement, the foreseeability rule has clear bargaining and distributive implications. An unlimited liability rule certainly favors, in this case, the buyer. The buyer need not contemplate or communicate special needs, requirements, or expectations about performance or what should happen if there is a breach. Of course, an unlimited liability rule imposes additional costs on the seller relative to a limited liability rule. But with both rents and unlimited liability as the default rule, the seller will have to give something up in order to negotiate a higher price or a term that limits its liability. Conversely, the opposite holds when a limited liability rule is the default. In that case, it is the buyer who must give something up if it wants to lower the price or negotiate an unlimited liability term.

There are many ways one could model this bargaining scenario. In this section, I assume a "second-hand," competitive market that buyers can turn to if negotiations break down. In this second-hand market, there are no negotiations nor communications. Thus, under a limited liability rule, high-value buyers can expect to receive in value $\pi(x_L^*)H + (1 - \pi(x_L^*))L$. Sellers choose the lower level of precautions, and because this second-hand market is competitive, price (denoted p_L) equals cost, which includes c_L and other costs, such as taxes and labor effort (or other investments) which we assume constant for the purposes of the distribution-neutral analysis. On the other hand, the value of performance is guaranteed to buyers under an unlimited liability rule, so they can expect to receive H with certainty. Sellers, not knowing which type they are contracting with, will choose the intermediate level of precautions, which entails price p_H and cost c_{LH}. Price is higher under unlimited liability, $p_H > p_L$, and the difference is equal to the difference in costs: $p_H - p_L = c_{LH} - c_L$. However, because costs are lower than when the seller contracts with a high-value buyer with certainty, $c_{LH} < c_H$, buyer effectively gets a bargain. Furthermore, low-value buyers will now pay an increased price and this may make them worse off (under either rule, they are entitled to L). However, because the intermediate cost, c_{LH}, entailed by the unlimited liability rule minimizes the expected losses over both buyers, it means that buyers are better off in the aggregate (despite the loss of efficiency from not "tailoring" precautions to each buyer type). Ultimately, the unlimited liability rule favors buyers in the aggregate, as argued intuitively in the previous paragraph. Finally we should assume that the values of performance, and correlatively the costs, are appropriately discounted in this second-hand market by some amount $\delta \in (0, 1)$. It is not terribly important how large this discount is, except to the extent that payoffs in the second-hand market do not exceed those in the primary market.

Thus, the expected outside options for a high-value buyer can be written as $\bar{V}_{H,\mathcal{U}} = H - p_H$ in the case of the unlimited liability rule and $\bar{V}_{H,\mathcal{L}} = \pi(x_L^*)H + (1 - \pi(x_L^*))L - p_L$ in the case of the limited liability rule. Likewise, the outside options of the low-value buyer are, respectively for each rule, $\bar{V}_{L,\mathcal{U}} = L - p_H$ and $\bar{V}_{L,\mathcal{L}} = L - p_L$. Clearly, these equations imply that the outside option of high-value buyers improves with the unlimited liability rule. Moreover, note that the outside option of low-value buyers gets worse with the unlimited liability rule. (Nevertheless, as already pointed out, because limited liability only partially covers buyers' losses and because c_{LH} minimizes buyers' losses in the aggregate, we also know that the unlimited liability rule improves the outside options of buyers as a group.) We can therefore conclude that:

$$\bar{V}_{H,\mathcal{U}} > \bar{V}_{H,\mathcal{L}} \quad \text{and} \quad \bar{V}_{L,\mathcal{U}} < \bar{V}_{L,\mathcal{L}}. \tag{5.4}$$

We next want to show that changes in the outside options also affect buyers' payoffs. As was shown with the buyer's payoff function, given in equation (5.2), the buyer's payoff is directly related to the outside option. If the outside option improves, the buyer's payoff improves; and if the outside option worsens, so does the buyer's payoff. Hence, we have the following result:

$$\bar{V}_{H,\mathcal{U}} > \bar{V}_{H,\mathcal{L}} \Rightarrow V_{H,\mathcal{U}} > V_{H,\mathcal{L}} \quad \text{and} \quad \bar{V}_{L,\mathcal{U}} < \bar{V}_{L,\mathcal{L}} \Rightarrow V_{L,\mathcal{U}} < V_{L,\mathcal{L}}. \tag{5.5}$$

The second issue to address is buyer investments. We have assumed that buyers initially do not know whether they are high- or low-value buyers. As already explained, buyers are high- or low-value buyers according to probability α. Hence, buyer's expected valuations are $\mu(q)[\alpha V_H+(1-\alpha)V_L]+(1-\mu(q))[\alpha\bar{V}_H+(1-\alpha)\bar{V}_L]$. We can think of buyers' investments as a cost undertaken to improve the chances of being a high-value buyer. Suppose the cost is $C(\alpha)$ which is increasing and convex, $C'(\alpha) > 0$, $C''(\alpha) > 0$, and approaches infinity as $\alpha \to 0.5$, $\lim_{\alpha\to 0.5} C(\alpha) = \infty$. Thus buyers make their initial investments by maximizing

$$\mu(q)[\alpha V_H + (1-\alpha)V_L] + (1-\mu(q))[\alpha\bar{V}_H + (1-\alpha)\bar{V}_L] - C(\alpha).$$

We can find the optimal probability α by differentiating this equation with respect to α and setting it equal to zero. This gives:

$$\mu(q)(V_H - V_L) + (1-\mu(q))(\bar{V}_H - \bar{V}_L) = C'(\alpha). \tag{5.6}$$

The next step is to show how changing outside options and, consequently, payoffs influence the buyer's optimizing choice of investment. Looking at the left hand side of the first-order equation, we know from equation (5.4) that for the outside options that $\bar{V}_{H,\mathcal{U}} - \bar{V}_{L,\mathcal{U}} > \bar{V}_{H,\mathcal{L}} - \bar{V}_{L,\mathcal{L}}$. Accordingly, from the fact that a high-value buyer's outside option improves with the unlimited liability rule and a low-value buyer's gets worse, as concluded in equation (5.5), it is easy to see that the difference between high- and low-value buyers' payoffs also increase with the unlimited liability rule. Hence, $V_{H,\mathcal{U}} - V_{L,\mathcal{U}} > V_{H,\mathcal{L}} - V_{L,\mathcal{L}}$. Thus the left-hand side of the previous equation will be greater under the unlimited liability rule compared to the limited liability rule. This immediately implies that on the right-hand side $C'(\alpha)$, and hence α, will have to increase to satisfy the equality. Hence, the proportion of high-value buyers is greater under the unlimited liability rule compared to the limited liability rule. That is, we have

$$\alpha_{\mathcal{U}} > \alpha_{\mathcal{L}}. \tag{5.7}$$

as claimed in the text.

5.4.4 *Results*

We can now identify the conditions under which an unlimited liability rule will redistribute income more efficiently than the income tax. As explained in the text, buyers and sellers are matched in the market probabilistically. In the text, we assumed that with probability $\mu(q)$ sellers find a buyer, and with probability $\eta(q) = q\mu(q)$, buyers are matched with a seller where $q = h_2/h_1$ is the queue length measuring the ratio of sellers seeking buyers. To simplify, I assume that each seller and buyer engages in a large enough number of transactions, normalized to one, so that we can treat the matching probability as a share. We can then define the expected payoffs of buyers and sellers to reflect labor-market choices as follows. If sellers are matched they receive U and if not they receive zero. To ensure that sellers are wealthier than buyers we also assume that sellers have a constant source of income, $y_2 \gg y_1$. Therefore sellers can expect to receive:

$$y_2 + \mu(q)U - T_2 - \theta_2.$$

Similarly, for buyers we assume:

$$y_1 + \eta(q)V + (1 - \eta(q))\bar{V} - C(\alpha) - T_1 - \theta_1.$$

At this level of abstraction, buyers do not know if they are high- or low-value, and similarly sellers do not know whether they are involved in transactions with high- or low-value buyers. The payoffs U and V therefore reflect the distribution (i.e., α) of types.

To test the redistributive efficiency of the unlimited liability rule we implement a distribution-neutral tax policy. For sellers this looks like:

$$y_2 + \mu(q)U_{\mathcal{L}} - T_2 - \hat{T}_2 - \theta_2 = y_2 + \mu(q)U_{\mathcal{U}} - T_2 - \theta_2$$

which simplifies to:

$$\hat{T}_2 = \mu(q)(U_{\mathcal{L}} - U_{\mathcal{U}}).$$

Because the tax adjustment induces the same labor-supply behavior it also generates the same rates in the matching function. Furthermore, because sellers are better off under the limited liability rule than the unlimited liability rule, which follows from equations (5.3) and (5.4), the tax adjustment is positive, i.e., an increase in taxes, $\hat{T}_2 > 0$.

For buyers the distribution neutral tax policy is as follows:

$$\begin{aligned} &y_1 + \eta(q)V_{\mathcal{L}} + (1 - \eta(q))\bar{V}_{\mathcal{L}} - C(\alpha_{\mathcal{L}}) - T_1 - \hat{T}_1 - \theta_1 \\ &= y_1 + \eta(q)V_{\mathcal{U}} + (1 - \eta(q))\bar{V}_{\mathcal{U}} - C(\alpha_{\mathcal{U}}) - T_1 - \theta_1. \end{aligned}$$

Because at this stage the only role of the outside options is as a condition that the surplus in the bargaining scenario be larger, it will greatly simplify the analysis to drop the outside options. This does not change any of the qualitative results. Hence, simplifying the distribution-neutral adjustment for buyers, we get:

$$-\hat{T}_1 = \eta(q)(V_{\mathcal{U}} - V_{\mathcal{L}}) - (C(\alpha_{\mathcal{U}}) - C(\alpha_{\mathcal{L}})).$$

Note that because buyers are better off under the unlimited liability rule as opposed to the limited liability rule ($\mathcal{L} < \mathcal{U}$), the tax adjustment is negative, i.e., a decrease in taxes or an increase in a transfer or subsidy, $\hat{T}_1 < 0$.

The condition for the legal-rule redistribution to be more efficient than the income tax is for there to be a budget deficit, that is, that the distribution-neutral tax adjustment, which reproduces the same distribution of income as the unlimited liability rule, yields lower revenues than it does expenditures. Formally, this condition is $h_2\hat{T}_2 - h_1\hat{T}_1 < 0$. Using the fact that $h_2/h_1 = q$ we can multiply this epxression by $1/h_1$ and rewrite it as $q\hat{T}_2 - \hat{T}_1 < 0$. We can next write the condition as:

$$q\mu(q)(U_{\mathcal{L}} - U_{\mathcal{U}}) - \eta(q)(V_{\mathcal{U}} - V_{\mathcal{L}}) + (C(\alpha_{\mathcal{U}}) - C(\alpha_{\mathcal{L}})) < 0.$$

Recalling that $\eta(q) = q\mu(q)$ and rearranging $(C(\alpha_{\mathcal{U}}) - C(\alpha_{\mathcal{L}}))$ as $\eta(q)(C(\alpha_{\mathcal{U}}) - C(\alpha_{\mathcal{L}})) + (1 - \eta(q))(C(\alpha_{\mathcal{U}}) - C(\alpha_{\mathcal{L}}))$, we can again rewrite the condition as:

$$\eta(q)[(U_{\mathcal{L}}-U_{\mathcal{U}})-(V_{\mathcal{U}}-V_{\mathcal{L}})+(C(\alpha_{\mathcal{U}})-C(\alpha_{\mathcal{L}}))]+(1-\eta(q))(C(\alpha_{\mathcal{U}})-C(\alpha_{\mathcal{L}})) < 0. \quad (5.8)$$

For now, focus only on the expression $(U_{\mathcal{L}} - U_{\mathcal{U}}) - (V_{\mathcal{U}} - V_{\mathcal{L}})$ in the condition (5.8). Using the payoff expressions in equations (5.2) and (5.3), write this previous expression as:

$$\begin{aligned}
&(U_{\mathcal{L}} - U_{\mathcal{U}}) - (V_{\mathcal{U}} - V_{\mathcal{L}}) \\
&\quad = [(1-\beta)(v_{\mathcal{L}} - c_{\mathcal{L}} - \kappa_{\mathcal{L}} - \bar{V}_{\mathcal{L}}) - (1-\beta)(v_{\mathcal{U}} - c_{\mathcal{U}} - \kappa_{\mathcal{U}} - \bar{V}_{\mathcal{U}})] \\
&\qquad - [\bar{V}_{\mathcal{U}} + \beta(v_{\mathcal{U}} - c_{\mathcal{U}} - \kappa_{\mathcal{U}} - \bar{V}_{\mathcal{U}}) - (\bar{V}_{\mathcal{L}} + \beta(v_{\mathcal{L}} - c_{\mathcal{L}} - \kappa_{\mathcal{L}} - \bar{V}_{\mathcal{L}}))]
\end{aligned}$$

The right-hand side of the equation simplifies to:

$$(v_{\mathcal{L}} - c_{\mathcal{L}} - \kappa_{\mathcal{L}}) - (v_{\mathcal{U}} - c_{\mathcal{U}} - \kappa_{\mathcal{U}}).$$

This expression can also be written as:

$$\alpha_{\mathcal{L}}(H - c_H - \kappa) + (1 - \alpha_{\mathcal{L}})(L - c_L) - (\alpha_H H + (1 - \alpha)L - c_{LH}).$$

Because this expression is equal to $(U_{\mathcal{L}} - U_{\mathcal{U}}) - (V_{\mathcal{U}} - V_{\mathcal{L}})$, we can add $(C(\alpha_{\mathcal{U}}) - C(\alpha_{\mathcal{L}}))$ to it, to equal the expression in brackets in condition 5.8. We can then decompose the rearranged expression in brackets into two effects. Doing this, we get:

$$-[(\alpha_{\mathcal{U}}-\alpha_{\mathcal{L}})(H-L)-(C(\alpha_{\mathcal{U}})-C(\alpha_{\mathcal{L}}))]+[c_{LH}-\alpha_{\mathcal{L}}(c_H+\kappa)-(1-\alpha_{\mathcal{L}}c_L)]. \quad (5.9)$$

First, the expression in the first pair of brackets, $-(\alpha_{\mathcal{U}} - \alpha_{\mathcal{L}})(H - L) - (C(\alpha_{\mathcal{U}}) - C(\alpha_{\mathcal{L}}))$ (with, recall, $\alpha_{\mathcal{U}} > \alpha_{\mathcal{L}}$ and $H > L$), represents the efficiency gain due to the greater initial investments by buyers. Second, the expression in the second pair of brackets, $c_{LH} - \alpha_{\mathcal{L}}(c_H + \kappa) - (1 - \alpha_{\mathcal{L}})c_L > 0$, represents the efficiency loss due to unspecific seller precautions in moving from a limited to an unlimited liability rule.

The condition for a budget deficit in (5.8) can then be rewritten as:

$$\begin{aligned}
&\eta(q)\{[c_{LH} - \alpha_{\mathcal{L}}(c_H + \kappa) - (1 - \alpha_{\mathcal{L}})c_L] - [(\alpha_{\mathcal{U}} - \alpha_{\mathcal{L}})(H - L) - (C(\alpha_{\mathcal{U}}) - C(\alpha_{\mathcal{L}}))]\} \\
&\quad + (1 - \eta(q))(C(\alpha_{\mathcal{U}}) - C(\alpha_{\mathcal{L}})) < 0. \qquad (5.10)
\end{aligned}$$

We can then see that when expression (5.9) is negative, the first bracketed expression within braces in (5.10) is sufficiently small, the second bracketed expression within braces is sufficiently large, and $\eta(q)$ sufficiently large, the condition will be satisfied. This means that adopting the inefficient, unlimited liability rule can redistribute income more efficiently than taxes.

5.4.5 *Frictionless Markets*

I conclude by showing that the possibility of efficiently redistributive legal rules does not hold in the absence of market frictions. This is reassuring from my argument's standpoint: Market frictions are essential for my conclusions.

First, it is clear that in the absence of frictions and with free-entry competition, sellers will be forced to price at cost. This eliminates rent-sharing and bargaining between seller and buyer. As a result, the buyer retains all of the buyer's surplus. Moreover, this also means that the increased costs of an inefficient liability rule will be entirely passed on to the buyer.

Second, in the absence of frictions the buyer's ex ante investment incentives are maximized. Examining the buyer's first-order condition in equation (5.6), we see that the benefit of the investment is a weighted average of the returns to the primary market and secondary market. By assumption, the secondary market never pays as well as the primary, which means for any positive level of market frictions, where $\mu(q) < 1$, investment will be suboptimal. Hence when frictions are absent, and finding a trading partner in the primary market is guaranteed, the buyer's choice of α is optimal from a social point of view. Label this efficient choice of investment as α^*. From a social standpoint, therefore, choices that increase the buyer's investment but that are lower than the efficient level will improve social wealth, as assumed in the previous section. Investment choices greater than the efficient level, however, will lower social wealth.

In summary, it is only with market frictions that the buyer's ex ante investments and rent-sharing with sellers are offsetting. In the absence of frictions there are, as in Kaplow and Shavell's classic illustration, compounding. Moreover, in the absence of frictions, all of the costs of the inefficient legal rule are passed on to the buyer. We can state this claim more capaciously. With frictions, there is a trade-off between sellers' market participation and buyers' investments. On the one hand, frictions require rent-sharing in order to induce sufficient sellers to enter the market. On the other hand, frictions make buyers' ex ante investments suboptimal. In this environment, shifting rents by changing the liability rule then has two, counteracting effects. While it discourages sellers' entry into the market it also encourages a larger investment by the buyer. This larger investment improves efficiency, because, as just shown, investments are suboptimal with frictions. Moreover, because we have assumed that the limited liability rule achieves efficiency across the board, these two effects are net inefficient. But because they are offsetting effects, rather than compounding, they falsify the double-distortion argument. By contrast, in the absence of frictions shifting surplus by changing the liability rule not only discourages seller entry into the market, but it also makes buyer's investment inefficient because, in the absence of frictions, they are already optimal.

PART III

Regulation and Functional Law

6

Labor and Employment Law

After a period of slow but steady decline reaching back to the 1950s, labor unions are once again notching victories and making headlines. As of May, 2023, the Starbucks Workers United union has prevailed in over 300 union-representation elections across thirty-six states and covering around 7,600 workers (Bruenig 2023). Meanwhile, the Amazon Labor Union – led by Chris Smalls, an Amazon warehouse worker fired for leading a protest against pandemic working conditions – prevailed in a representation election at the company's Staten Island, NY, warehouse, making it Amazon's first unionized workplace in the United States (Kantor and Weise 2022). In April, 2024, workers at a Volkswagen plant in Chattanooga, Tennessee, voted overwhelmingly to be represented by the United Auto Workers, a breakthrough in a region known for its anti-union sentiment (Boudette 2024). These union victories reflect a broader increase in labor activity across the country. According to the Cornell-ILR Labor Action Tracker Annual Report, in 2022 there were 424 work stoppages involving approximately 224,000 workers. This represents an increase from the previous year of around 52 percent in the number of work stoppages (279 to 424) and of around 60 percent in the number of workers involved (approximately 140,000 to 224,000).[1]

Historically, collective bargaining between firms and unions and union-supported policies such as the minimum wage have made a significant impact on the distribution of income. Several studies conclude that the decline in the share of workers

[1] Over a third of work stoppages came from the accommodation and food services industry and about 91 percent of these stoppages were led by either Starbucks workers organizing with the Starbucks Workers United campaign or fast-food workers organizing with the Fight for $15 campaign. However, accommodation and food services industry stoppages accounted for only about 3 percent of the total workers involved in 2022. The majority of all workers involved in work stoppages came from the educational services industry (approximately 60 percent). It is notable that about 32 percent of strikes in 2022 were undertaken by workers not affiliated with any official union, although these stoppages were considerably smaller than the work stoppages led by unionized workers.

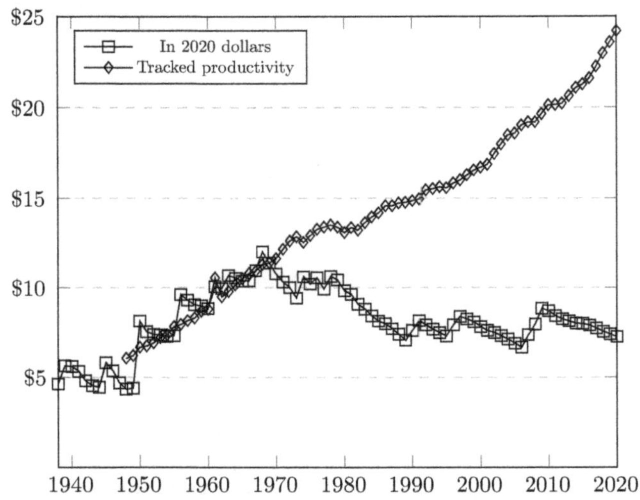

FIGURE 6.1 Trends in the minimum wage

The graph displays the minimum wage both in 2020 dollars and if it had kept pace with productivity starting in 1968, for the years 1938–2020. This calculation uses a productivity growth figure that is economy-wide, is based on net output, and adjusts for differences between the NDP deflator and the consumer price index. *Source*: Baker (2020b)

who are union members explains between 15 to 30 percent of the increase of wage inequality over the same period.[2] The decline in the real value of the minimum wage is associated with similar magnitudes in the rise of wage inequality. In the years 1938–1968, the real minimum wage kept pace with productivity (Baker 2020b). Since then, it has fallen off a cliff, as Figure 6.1 illustrates. The federal minimum wage did not increase at all between 1981 and 1990, during which time its real value decreased 30 percent (Autor, Manning, and Smith 2016, 58). It remained stagnant again in the years 1997–2007 and has not been lifted since 2009 (U.S. Department of Labor, Wage and Hour Division n.d.). It currently rests at $7.25, a far cry from the $24 that it would be if matched with productivity gains over the period (Baker 2020a). Because less than ten percent of working hours are compensated at state or federal minimum wages (Autor, Manning, and Smith 2016, 61), this implies that the minimum wage

[2] Freeman (1980) and Freeman and Medoff (1981) first introduced evidence that unions' inequality-reducing effects outweighed their inequality-increasing effects. DiNardo, Fortin, and Lemieux (1996) estimate that the fall in union membership accounts for up to one-quarter of the rise in male wage dispersion over the 1980s. Card (2001) finds that the fall in union membership compared in the years 1973–74 and 1993 accounts for between 15–20 percent of the rise in male wage inequality. Western and Rosenfeld (2011) report that from 1973 to 2007 private sector union membership in the United States declined from 34 to 8 percent for men and from 16 to 6 percent for women and that during this period, inequality in hourly wages increased by over 40 percent. They conclude that the decline of organized labor explains a fifth to a third of the growth in wage inequality.

has significant spillover effects to higher-wage workers. These spillovers are most pronounced for those in the lower half of the wage distribution (61), yet in some studies they also reach into the eightieth percentile.[3] While there is compelling evidence that the minimum wage's decline in real value has contributed to income inequality, the question is how much.[4] Evidence also supports the view that the minimum wage reduces income, not just wage, inequality, even at the bottom of the wage distribution and despite the widespread stigmatization of the minimum wage as a "job killer."[5]

* * *

Labor and employment law clearly has important distributive stakes. But do collective bargaining and minimum wages redistribute income more efficiently than taxes? This chapter addresses that issue. The chapter begins with a brief review of the fairly extensive normative and theoretical literature on the minimum wage in economics. This review is necessary in order to recognize a crucial distinction. Most normative justifications for the minimum wage are made on grounds of efficiency; fewer contributions are made in terms of redistribution and fewer still explicitly

3 Autor, Manning, and Smith (2016, 62–64) add that although spillover is a plausible explanation for the minimum wage's distributive effect, they cannot rule out that this effect is a product of measurement error. On spillover effects, see also Engbom and Moser (2022, 3805, 3818), who, in a study of the minimum wage in Brazil between 1996 and 2018, "consistently find that spillovers reach up to or above the seventy-fifth percentile of the earnings distribution," althougth "the wage gain is a relatively modest 6 percent at the fiftieth percentile and 2 percent at the seventy-fifth percentile."

4 See, e.g., Autor, Manning, and Smith (2016, 61) ("In most specifications, we conclude that the decline in the real value of the minimum wage explains 30 to 40 percent of the rise in lower tail wage inequality in the 1980s"); Lee (1999) (finding that "almost all of the growth in the wage gap between the tenth and fiftieth percentiles is attributable to the erosion of the real value of the federal minimum during" the 1980s); DiNardo, Fortin, and Lemieux (1996) (finding that between 1979–1988, 40–65 percent of the growth in the wage gap between the tenth and fiftieth percentiles was due to the minimum wage).

5 With respect to income inequality, Dube (2019) studies the effects of the minimum wage on family income, accounting for lob losses and changes in government tax credits and noncash transfers. Dube finds that "higher minimum wages lead to increases in incomes at the bottom of the family income distribution" and specifically that a ten-percent increase in the minimum wage reduces the non-elderly poverty rate by between 2.2 and 4.59 percent (269). Despite the traditional economic expectation of the minimum wage as a "job killer," new research finds that the effects on employment are less than previously thought. Dube, Lester, and Reich (2016, 664) find that "the impact of minimum wage increases on the employment stock is small: for both teens and restaurant workers, our estimated employment elasticities are small in magnitude and are not statistically distinguishable from zero." In fact, research indicates that a higher minimum wage substantially increases employee retention, providing positive employment effects for those at the bottom of the income distribution. According to Dube, Lester, and Reich (2016, 664): "We find striking evidence that separations, hires, and turnover rates for teens and restaurant workers fall substantially following a minimum wage increase – with most of the reductions coming within the first 3 quarters of the higher minimum. For a 10% minimum wage increase, turnover rates decline by around 2.0% for teens and 2.1% for the restaurant workforce."

contemplate the "horse race" between the minimum wage and taxes. After this review, we will turn to the smaller literature on redistributive justifications for the minimum wage, focusing in particular on the articles of Shaviro (1997) and Lee and Saez (2012). After reviewing these contributions, we turn to the central question of the chapter: Can the minimum wage redistribute income more efficiently than the income tax? In addition to explaining why it can, this part of the chapter demonstrates how the minimum wage shows why Kaplow's (2008) method of distribution-neutral income tax adjustments can give misleading answers about the redistributive value of legal rules. Finally, we will explore how the argument in favor of the minimum wage can be extended to address the case of collective wage bargaining between firms and unions.

To preview the argument that follows, the minimum wage can indeed be said to generate two distortions, as Kaplow and Shavell (1994) allege. Like taxes (the first distortion), higher wages redistribute income and distort labor supply. As for the second distortion, wages can also be said to "regulate" the employment relationship in a number of ways, for example, shaping decisions like how much effort a worker gives on the job, when and whether a worker decides to quit, or how much training an employer provides. If the market is functioning competitively, workers and firms will arrive at an efficient labor contract: one that equalizes the marginal benefits of wage increases (in, say, higher productivity or lower turnover) with their marginal costs. Under such conditions, the introduction of the minimum wage will indeed both reduce efficiency and generate a double distortion. However – and this is the critical point – these distortions will be *offsetting* rather than compounding. For instance, the minimum wage may increase worker effort – too much from an efficiency point of view – but this increased effort will nevertheless reduce the cost of the wage increase to the firm. And because the two distortions are offsetting, the net inefficiency is smaller than a distribution-equivalent change to the tax schedule.

As I hope will become clear by the end of the chapter, my argument for redistributive value of the minimum wage differs from previous contributions. First, this chapter's justification for the minimum wage is not efficiency: The minimum wage does not exclusively address a market imperfection or a problem of market power. Efficiency justifications for the minimum wage pose no equity-efficiency trade-off and therefore do not contradict or refute the double-distortion argument. In contrast to the efficiency justification for the minimum wage, the minimum wage in this chapter *does* pose a trade-off between efficiency and equity. Redistribution comes at a cost to wealth maximization.

Second, while this chapter advances a redistributive justification for the minimum wage, most redistributive evaluations typically conclude, in spirit of the double-distortion argument, that the minimum wage does more harm than good. A notable exception is the article by Lee and Saez (2012). In a nutshell, they agree that the minimum wage has redistributive value, but only as a tool to be used in conjunction with a wage subsidy (such as the Earned Income Tax Credit). In this context, the minimum wage should be set at the labor market's *efficient* level, to prevent the wage subsidy from causing wages to fall below that level. Moreover, this combined minimum-wage-subsidy policy is justified only if the social welfare function gives some weight to those other than the worst off – that is, only if the social welfare function is not Rawlsian. In contrast, the argument for the minimum wage developed in this chapter shows that (1) the minimum wage can be more redistributively efficient than the income tax, (2) the optimal, redistributive minimum wage lies above its market-clearing level, and (3) the minimum wage is still justified even under a Rawlsian social welfare function.

6.1 BACKGROUND: THE EFFICIENT VERSUS REDISTRIBUTIVE MINIMUM WAGE

Before exploring the really essential question – the *redistributive* value of the minimum wage – we first need to distinguish, and get out of the way, a line of literature that examines the *efficiency* of the minimum wage when labor markets are imperfectly competitive, or monopsonistic. A quick review is necessary to avoid confusion and clarify how this chapter's argument for the minimum wage differs from the "efficiency" defense of minimum wages. This line of literature is not directly relevant to the double-distortion argument, because it does not contradict it. When the minimum wage can restore efficiency to the labor market, wealth is maximized, which is consistent with Kaplow and Shavell's (1994) central dictate, namely, that because the income tax redistributes more efficiently than legal rules, legal rules should be evaluated on the basis of efficiency rather than distribution. According to this perspective, that the minimum wage in such cases may also reduce income inequality is merely incidental. Thus, an efficient minimum wage does not demonstrate the superiority of legal rules for redistributing income.

The extensiveness of the efficient minimum-wage literature also warrants the digression. The policy motivation for an efficient minimum wage arises when markets are imperfect or employers have market (monopsony) power. Just as *monopoly* refers to a situation of "one seller," monopsony refers to a single buyer. (We can also use "oligopsony" to refer to a few buyers, but more than one.) When there are few buyers of labor in the market, employers have wage-setting power, giving employers some ability to determine the wage they pay. Being profit maximizers, they will naturally want to pay wages lower than would obtain in more competitive conditions. On the standard assumption that labor supply increases with its price – higher wages, more labor supplied – a wage set lower than its competitive level will result in less labor supplied. Consequently, a monopsony wage lowers labor supplied, labor employed, and therefore entails a loss of output and efficiency. In this context, a minimum wage can restore efficiency in the labor market. By setting the minimum wage at its competitive level, this will increase labor supply and output, and maximize wealth.[6]

For a long time it was thought impossible that labor markets could be uncompetitive, except in the outlying case of the small, rural, single-employer town. Scholarly sentiment appears to be shifting, however, and research in labor market theory has articulated a host of reasons why employers may have wage-setting power, beyond simply the number of employers in the labor market.[7] One reason is that jobs are heterogeneous; they involve far more than just a wage. Even when a worker's marginal productivity is the same in two or more different jobs, they may have a preference for one over the other based on the working environment, particular colleagues, distance from home, and so forth (see, e.g., Bhaskar and To 1999; Bhaskar, Manning, and To 2002). Under these conditions, not all employers are alike, and labor mobility will be de facto limited. Employers can exploit this limited mobility to reduce wages below their competitive level. As another example, the simple fact that it takes time to find a job can confer wage-setting power on employers (Burdett and Mortensen 1998). In fact, the sources of possible labor market imperfections are endless. Scholars have considered adverse selection (Drazen 1986), bargaining models (Cahuc, Saint-Martin, and Zylberberg 2001), monopsonistic competition (Robinson 1969; Manning 2004; Cahuc and Laroque 2014), moral hazard (efficiency wages) (Jones 1987; Rebitzer and Taylor 1995), search models (Swinnerton 1996; Acemoglu 2001; Flinn 2006; Hungerbühler and Lehmann 2009), and signaling models (Lang 1987; Blumkin and Sadka 2005).

Finally, this literature is also important for our discussion because, while focused on the efficiency role of the minimum wage, these models also often reveal sources of productivity gains that help offset the costs of a (strictly speaking) inefficient, but redistributive, minimum wage. Indeed, in this chapter's model and in the appendix, I use the moral hazard, or efficiency wage, model of the labor market to show how the minimum wage can redistribute more efficiently than the income tax. Before addressing that argument, we now turn to the strand of the literature that expressly conceives the minimum wage as a redistributive tool.

6.2 REDISTRIBUTIVE MINIMUM WAGE

A much smaller part of the minimum-wage literature has explicitly explored its redistributive desirability with the assumption of competitive labor markets (see, e.g., Allen 1987; Guesnerie and Roberts 1987; Shaviro 1997). This literature typically concludes that the redistributive value of the minimum wage is useless or even

6 For an introduction to the basic concepts of monopsony in labor markets, see Boal and Ransom (1997).

7 For a recent review, see Manning (2021). In the legal literature, monopsony has surfaced as a concern in the antitrust literature. See, for example, Naidu, Posner, and Weyl (2018) and Marinescu and Hovenkamp (2019).

harmful, except under special conditions. For example, Boadway and Cuff (2001) show that the minimum wage can reveal useful information to the government about the abilities of low-wage workers. But this result obtains on the rather demanding requirement that non-working welfare recipients are forced to look for and accept job offers.

The crucial feature of the *redistributive* minimum wage, of course, is that it does not serve to restore efficiency. Rather, it involves paying a wage *greater* than the efficient one and entails some cost in output or efficiency. The question then becomes whether this redistributive trade-off – higher income for low-wage workers versus the loss of efficiency – is worth it when compared to the income tax.

Figure 6.2 illustrates graphically how the redistributive minimum wage differs from the efficient minimum wage. When a firm has market power in the labor market, the monopsony wage, w_M, is lower than the competitive wage, w^*. In this case, an employer's profit-maximizing choice is to employ the amount of labor where its demand curve and marginal cost curve intersect. This lowers the amount of labor employed below its efficient level, from q^* to q_M. When firms have market power, an efficiency argument for the minimum wage favors raising it to its competitive level, w^*, which will restore efficiency by moving labor employed back to q^*. However, a

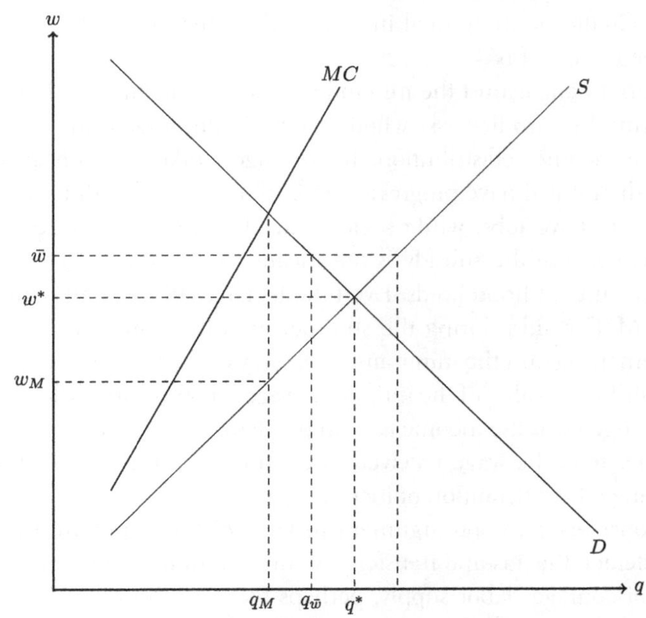

FIGURE 6.2 Efficiency of the minimum wage

The horizontal axis measures the quantity of labor, q, and the vertical axis measures the wage, w. S labels the labor-supply curve, D labels the labor-demand curve, and MC label's the employer's marginal cost curve.

redistributive minimum wage will raise the wage above the competitive level, to $\bar{w}$, which is also inefficient and lowers labor employed, from q^* to $q_{\bar{w}}$. Thus, efficiency arguments for a minimum wage are different than redistributive arguments.

The remainder of this section will review Shaviro's (1997) and Lee and Saez's (2012) contributions to the redistributive minimum wage debate. Both of these articles move the discussion in novel and interesting ways. Shaviro (1997) gives a detailed and insightful comparison of the minimum wage, wage subsidies, and tax systems as alternative redistributive policy tools. Lee and Saez (2012) also pay particularly close attention to the the minimum wage and (tax-financed) wage subsidies as both policy substitutes and complements.

6.2.1 *The Minimum Wage or Redistributive Taxation?*

Shaviro (1997) offers perhaps the most extensive evaluation of the minimum wage made explicitly within a tax-policy framework. His key argument fits well within the double-distortion line of reasoning, although he does not explicitly acknowledge this connection. Accordingly, he is very skeptical about the redistributive value of the minimum wage. His line of reasoning is familiar: To the extent that the minimum wage is redistributive, it creates additional distortions, which would be avoided by using alternative policy instruments, such as wage subsidies (e.g., the Earned Income Tax Credit) or an optimal income tax scheme (which Shaviro refers to as the "Negative Income Tax").

Shaviro's argument against the minimum wage is easily translatable into double-distortion terms. Shaviro first asks whether a minimum wage is justified as a means of progressive income redistribution. If low-wage workers are on average poorer than others, then it will have progressive redistributive effects. But the subsidy only helps those who have jobs, while society's neediest may in fact be unemployed. Furthermore, because the subsidy is not means tested, some of its recipients will be from more affluent households. Even the teenager from an affluent household, working for McDonald's during the summer, gets the minimum wage. This is a familiar argument against the minimum wage. In welfare-economics terms, it means that the redistributive value of the minimum wage is comparatively low, because it is not as finely targeted as the income tax can be. Being assessed directly on household income, rather than the wage received in employment, the income tax can more precisely change the distribution of income.

Shaviro considers a second argument in favor of the minimum wage: whether it can counteract the tax-and-transfer system's discouragement of work.[8] If the income tax discourages labor supply, perhaps the minmium wage can counteract this effect by making work more renumeratively rewarding? Shaviro is unpersuaded by the "work encouragement" argument in favor of the minimum wage. Shaviro

[8] In the then-current, actually existing tax-and-transfer system.

argues that the main sources of work deterrence in the tax-and-transfer system are the means-tested social welfare programs, including TANF (Temporary Assistance for Needy Families, or Aid to Families with Dependent Children (AFDC) at the time of Shaviro's writing), Supplemental Security Income (SSI), the Supplemental Nutrition Assistance Program (SNAP, or "food stamps"), and Medicaid. As Shaviro says, "The phaseout of these benefits as an employee's wages or wealth increase is equivalent to imposing high marginal tax rates on market work by program beneficiaries" (Shaviro 1997, 421). In other words, these means-tested programs create a dilemma because earning even a little more income could cause the total loss of benefits, making the choice of work unattractive.

Despite the disincentives posed by welfare programs, Shaviro is skeptical that the minimum wage can do anything to counteract them. Shaviro computes marginal rates for a single individual, in different states, with and without two children. He finds that the overall marginal rate structure "bounces up and down" in a "bizarre" manner that is impossible to rationalize. In addition, poor households face "astoundingly high marginal rates, at times approaching or even exceeding 100 percent" (426). In this context, a minimum wage – which depends neither on household income nor family size, and applies regardless of anyone's marginal rate – is unlikely to have much of an effect on encouraging work. Shaviro writes, "The efficiency case for responding to the faulty rate structure by layering a low-wage subsidy on top of it, rather than by changing it explicitly and directly, is wholly faute de mieux" (427). In double-distortion terms, the minimum wage may encourage labor-supply for workers at the bottom of the income distribution. But insofar as the minimum wage is redistributive, it raises the effective, if not actual, marginal tax rate and, overall, discourages labor supply for higher-income workers and for all workers in the aggregate. (For instance, minimum-wage workers may have less incentive to pursue higher-paying occupations, all else equal.) Shaviro adds the additional point that the minimum wage also does nothing to counteract the labor-supply distortions induced by the tax system, and may worsen them. We will return to this particular argument when Shaviro considers alternatives to the minimum wage, including the Earned Income Tax Credit (EITC).

Shaviro then considers a third, familiar problem of the minimum wage: its negative effect on labor demand. Viewed as a redistributive policy, the minimum wage's most perplexing feature is why one would want to tax *employment* when this is what proponents of the minimum wage claim they want to encourage. To answer this, Shaviro primarily engages with Card and Krueger's (2015) famous study of the minimum wage, detailed in their book *Myth and Measurement*.[9] Card and Krueger

9 For some of the initial research and ensuing debate, see Card and Krueger (1994), Card and Krueger (2000), and Neumark and Wascher (2000). Card and Krueger's "flagship" study focused on New Jersey's 80-cent increase of its minimum wage, from $4.25 to $5.05 per hour, on April 1, 1992. The study helped popularize the current rage for experimental and quasi-experimental social science research by comparing the employment effects of the increase in New Jersey – the

came to the then highly controversial conclusion that the minimum-wage increase under study had not reduced employment and may have actually raised it. The results challenged the prevailing competitive model of the labor market and pointed to the possibility of employer monopsony power to explain the counterintuitive result.

Shaviro's extended critique of Card and Krueger's research shows just how alarming their empirical and theoretical claims were at the time. Based on others' reactions, Shaviro concludes that Card and Krueger's empirical claims are "unpersuasive" and their theoretical arguments "weak" (457). Shaviro hews to the traditional argument that the minimum wage is disemploying. If that is true, then "the minimum wage clearly is inferior to alternative low-wage subsidies" (457), policy alternatives that we will discuss further in a moment. Putting this in double-distortion language, the minimum wage's "second" distortion – on top of its "tax"-like labor-supply distortions – also negatively affects the *demand* for labor.

To summarize, for our purposes Shaviro identifies three problems with the redistributive minimum wage. First, the redistributive value of the minimum wage is comparatively low, because it is imprecise: It does nothing to help the unemployed (who are worse off than low-wage workers) and may help those higher in the income distribution scale (low-wage workers from wealthy households). Second, the redistributive effect of the minimum wage, limited as it is, distorts labor-supply decisions; in addition, it does nothing to counteract the labor-supply distortions caused by means-tested welfare benefits, and may worsen them. Third, the minimum wage, by effectively "taxing" low-wage jobs, distorts the demand for low-wage labor.

In light of these alleged shortcomings, Shaviro discusses two redistribtuive alternatives. The first is a wage-subsidy policy, such as the Earned Income Tax Credit (EITC). The EITC is a federal refundable tax credit for low- to moderate-income working couples or individuals, whose amount depends on household income and number of children. The EITC phases in as income increases – one has to earn at least some income in order to get the credit. There is then a range of household income over which the credit plateaus before phasing out as income further increases. The EITC's phase-in range generates *negative* marginal tax rates while the phase-out range induces high, positive marginal rates.

That the EITC is conditioned on household income gives it a clear advantage over the minimum wage, as Shaviro acknowledges, which does not depend on household income (the rich teenager working at McDonald's, remember?). Still, the EITC fails to do anything for those who earn no income who, again, may be among society's neediest individuals. In other words, like the minimum wage, the EITC has an imprecision problem. Moreover, the EITC's impact on the problem of the marginal rate structure is "decidedly mixed," says Shaviro (1997, 462). While the phase-in

treatment group – with contiguous eastern Pennsylvania – the control group – which had not changed its minimum wage.

range of the EITC helps offset the high marginal tax rates imposed by other social programs, the phaseout range increases the high positive rates. Ensuring that the rate structure created by different programs functions in a coherent or harmonious way is "inherently difficult" (462). Shaviro finds standard justifications for program phase-outs unpersuasive, while acknowledging that the objections to phase-outs apply to all social welfare programs. Indeed, for our purposes, it will be convenient to lump this problem in with Shaviro's second objection to the minimum wage: its failure to counteract the negative labor-supply effect of means-tested welfare problems. Call this phase-in-plateau-phase-out problem the marginal tax rate EITC "bubble" problem. This feature of both the minimum wage and the EITC is an important issue for other arguments in favor of the redistributive mininum wage, including this chapter's.

Shaviro concludes with his own preferred low-income policy proposal. In this he follows in the footsteps of Mirrlees (1971) (discussed in the book's appendix on welfare economics) and Bankman and Griffith (1987) (the legal scholar version, one could say). According to this line of thinking, the ideal tax-and-transfer policy is a "negative income tax" or NIT. The NIT provides every household (rich or poor) with a lump-sum payment or credit, called a guaranteed income (a basic income is slightly different), and then applies a single tax rate to all earned income. The virtue of this policy is that "one thereby makes conscious and explicit the marginal tax rates that are actually applying as income increases, and one can therefore make explicit, deliberate, and (one hopes) sensible choices" (Shaviro 1997, 470). As income increases, taxes paid eventually exceed the credit, so that net positive tax liability is incurred by the wealthiest households. But structuring the program in this way guarantees a minimal level of income to the poorest, who will have net negative and possibly no tax liability, without the negative substitution effects of positive marginal tax rates. Indeed, the universal lump-sum payment combined with the single-rate schedule means that marginal tax rates are zero in this scheme.

The NIT thus avoids all of the drawbacks of either the minimum wage or the EITC. It avoids the imprecision problem of both the minimum wage and EITC in two ways: first, by dispensing with the requirement that one be employed in order to get the transfer (or subsidy), so that the unemployed, who may be worse off, are compensated; and second, by setting a guaranteed minimum, so that the poorest are assured a benefit. By installing a single, linear tax rate, the NIT also avoids the high, and the "up and down" bouncing of, marginal tax rates that are a result of different program structures, and which are only complicated, in Shaviro's estimation, by the minimum wage and the EITC "bubble." Third, and finally, by levying the tax on income, rather than low-wage jobs, the NIT avoids the minimum wage's labor-demand distortion.

In sum, what Shaviro delivers is a version of the double-distortion argument, one simply more attuned to the thicker complex of policy details involved in transfering income to the poor. Nevertheless, the basic conclusion is the same. Both the minimum wage and the EITC induce additional distortions or complications that can be avoided with the use of the income tax as the sole and exclusive redistributive tool.

6.2.2 *The Extensive Margin Strikes Back*

One reason Shaviro rejects the minimum wage and the EITC is because of their distorting effects on labor supply – the EITC "bubble," which the minimum wage probably compounds. But Shaviro's analysis is grounded in an approach to optimal income taxation that focuses exclusively on the intensive margin of labor supply and ignores entirely the extensive margin of labor supply. In an insightful study, Saez (2002a) showed that once one includes both the intensive and extensive margins of labor supply then a wage-subsidy "bubble" – of the kind generated by the EITC, and criticized by Shaviro (1997) – may actually be a part of an *optimal* income transfer policy. This subsection will explore Saez's (2002a) rationale for this counter-intuitive conclusion.

The extensive margin of labor supply captures the decision to work or not to work (in any particular occupation, whether low- or high-wage), while the intensive margin captures the decision about how much to work. To put this a bit more concretely, contrast the decision to apply for a job with the decision to vary how many hours to work (e.g., full-time or part-time). The former captures the extensive margin of labor supply, the latter the intensive margin. For those reasons, we also call the extensive margin the participation margin and the intensive margin the earnings margin. Intuitively, the extensive margin is quite important in practical life. Many workers have more control over the decision to work or not than they do over how much they work (Diamond 1980). Rothstein (2010) acknowledges "mounting evidence that labor market participation is far more elastic with respect to the wage than are hours among participants ..." (177). The extensive margin has been shown to be particularly important at the lower end of the income distribution (Blundell and MaCurdy 1999; Lee and Saez 2012).

Clearly, in the real world, both margins of labor supply apply. Can an EITC bubble be rationalized when both the extensive and intensive margins are taken into account? Saez (2002a) says yes, and that this depends on the relative weight of the participation (extensive margin) and earnings (intensive margin) elasticities. If the participation elasticity is large relative to the earnings elasticity, the optimal tax schedule will have an EITC structure with larger transfers to the working poor than the unemployed. Conversely, if the earnings elasticity is large relative to the participation elasticity, the optimal tax schedule will have a NIT structure, with nonnegative rates everywhere, and larger transfers to the unemployed than to the working poor (1055). More concretely, if Joe, a low-wage worker, is more likely to drop out of the workforce entirely rather than simply reduce his hours of work in response to a small increase in his marginal tax rate, it would be better to adopt an

EITC rather than a NIT. Conversely, if Joe is more likely to respond by working shorter hours rather than quitting work altogether, the NIT is the better policy.

We can elaborate on this reasoning. Let us begin by focusing first on *only* the extensive margin, and ignore, for the time being, the intensive margin. That is, we are assuming that workers only make the discrete decision to either remain unemployed or work in a distinct occupation that pays a given wage. Different workers have different occupations, which we order by market income from smallest (say, zero, because unemployed) to highest: $0, 1, 2, \ldots, I$. Also suppose the government has redistributive tastes, so that the social marginal welfare weights are strictly decreasing in income: $g_0 > g_1 > g_2 \ldots > g_I$. In this scenario, the government may want to provide a *higher* transfer to low-skilled workers than to the unemployed, even though the social marginal utility of consumption is higher for the latter. The government achieves this by combining a lump-sum guaranteed income (say, $-T_0$) with a negative marginal tax rate at the bottom – just as in the Earned Income Tax Credit.

Starting from a "classical" NIT arrangement, there are three different effects that, when combined, make an EITC an optimal improvement to the tax schedule. First, transferring an additional dollar to the "working poor" costs the government one dollar in revenue. Second, and however, the redistributive value of the transfer is larger than its cost. In particular, this will be the case when the working poor (say, group 1) still have a relatively high social marginal welfare weight, perhaps smaller than for the unemployed (group 0) but larger than for the wealthy, and more importantly larger than on average, which we can normalize to one: $g_0 > g_1 > 1$. Hence, the social welfare value of the transfer, given the social marginal welfare weight, is larger than a dollar: $g_1 >$ \$1. Third, and finally, because the extra transfer to the working poor encourages some of the unemployed to join the labor force, this saves on tax revenue that would otherwise be transferred to the unemployed. Under these circumstances, "it is unambiguously good to increase at the margin the transfer to low income workers" (Saez 2002a, 1050).[10]

This rationale becomes more complicated when we consider both intensive and extensive margins, but the fundamental implication of the extensive margin's inclusion remains. When considering only the extensive margin, decreasing taxes on the working poor unambiguously increases labor supply, which, as just shown, has a government-revenue savings effect. However, when the intensive margin is considered, decreasing taxes on the working poor not only encourages the unemployed to

[10] Saez (2002a) also notes that when the extensive margin of labor supply is considered alone, excluding the intensive margin, this result is obviously strengthened if the welfare of the working poor is valued more highly than the non-working poor, i.e., $g_1 > g_0$, but that condition is not necessary to justify an EITC bubble. A high value on the welfare of the working poor will only vanish in this scenario (i.e., no intensive margin) when the welfare weights approach the extreme Rawlsian case, where all of the welfare concern is placed on the non-working poor. (More obviously, there will also be no rationale for an EITC bubble when the government has no redistributive tastes.)

work, but will also reduce the labor supply of higher-paid workers. This decrease in labor supply is exactly the kind of tax "distortion" that reduces government revenue, as well as overall efficiency. Therefore, a government contemplating an EITC has to weigh the positive effect on extensive labor supply and the negative effect on intensive labor supply. It can do this by comparing the relative participation (extensive) and earnings (intensive) elasticities, just as we did with worker Joe in our earlier example. Hence, where the participation elasticity is large relative to the earnings elasticity, the optimal tax schedule will feature an EITC bubble with larger transfers for low-income workers than for the unemployed. The takeaway from this is that an EITC bubble – the "up and down" switching from negative to positive marginal tax rates criticized by Shaviro – can be rationalized when the extensive margin of labor supply is given its due weight within the optimal tax analysis. Despite Shaviro's antipathy to the EITC bubble, the switch from negative to positive marginal tax rates can, under the right circumstances, be part of an optimal tax policy.

6.2.3 *The Minimum Wage and EITC as Policy Complements*

Saez's (2002a) findings about the choice of NIT and EITC are directly relevant to debates over the minimum wage. Indeed, Saez makes an assumption that is made in almost all optimal tax models, including Kaplow and Shavell's (1994) double-distortion claim. This assumption is that wages are fixed and only the supply of labor is varied. But in a more general demand-and-supply model of the labor market, we know that anything that increases labor supply will cause wages to fall. In such circumstances, the EITC's incidence does not all fall on the workers, as is the textbook case of any other subsidy. Because at any given wage the EITC adds a subsidy, this makes working more attractive, and workers substitute more work for less leisure. But that increase in labor supply causes a fall in the level of the competitive market wage. Indeed, Rothstein (2010) finds that $1 of EITC spending raises after-tax incomes by only $0.73. This undermines the efficacy of the EITC, as employers capture part of the wage subsidy intended for the working poor. (Rothstein (2010) also finds that $1 spent on the NIT yields $1.39 in after-tax income to the poor. This is because the NIT, by *reducing* labor supply, increases wages.)

But this is precisely where the minimum wage becomes relevant. As Lee and Saez (2012) show, the minimum wage emerges as the ideal antidote to the problematic incidence effects of the EITC. By setting the minimum wage at its competitive level, a combined minimum-wage-EITC policy can ensure that employees receive every dollar of the wage subsidy. Thus, the EITC and the minimum wage are ideal complements in a redsitributive policy that favors the working poor. This is a powerful conclusion. In addition to overturning received wisdom about both the EITC and the minimum wage, which are typically treated separately, it is the strongest argument to date for a genuinely redistributive minimum wage.

However, there are limitations to Lee and Saez's (2012) defense of the redistributive minimum wage. For one, the minimum wage's redistributive role is muted. The purpose of the minimum wage is to prevent the EITC's incidence effect from pushing the wage below its *competitive* level. All the redistributive heavy lifting, so to speak, is done by the EITC itself, rather than the minimum wage. Further, Lee and Saez's defense rests on some delicate assumptions. One key assumption of theirs is that the government has "intermediate" redistributive tastes. This assumption is simply an application of Saez's (2002a) earlier insight about the EITC "bubble." In order for wage subsidies, supported by the minimum wage, to be a part of the optimal tax schedule, the government has to value redistribution to low-wage workers, who, in this framework, are assumed to be better off than the unemployed. Conversely, if the social welfare function is Rawlsian, "no minimum wage is desirable to supplement optimal tax policy" (744).[11]

Both of these limitations mark an important difference with this chapter's argument in favor of the minimum wage, which claims both that the redistributive minimum wage should be set *above* the competitive market level and that the justification for doing so is independent of any particular social welfare function; thus, the minimum wage is justified even when the government's redistributive tastes are Rawlsian.

To summarize the previous discussion, what Shaviro (1997) finds to be an irrational "up and down" marginal-tax-rate mess created by the EITC "bubble" turns out to be, according to Saez (2002a), part of the optimal tax schedule when we factor in the extensive margin of labor supply, which is empirically important, especially for low-wage workers. Nevertheless, Lee and Saez (2012) identify a different problem with the EITC. When the demand for labor is included in the analysis, wage subsidies have an incidence effect that allows employers to capture part of the subsidy, intended for low-wage workers, in the form of lower wages. Lee and Saez then demonstrate that a minimum wage, which prevents the EITC from causing a fall in wages, is a complementary low-wage redistributive policy. Where most studies conclude that the redistributive minimum wage is useless or harmful, Lee and Saez provide the strongest case in favor of using the minimum wage to redistribute income.

6.3 THE OPTIMAL, INEFFICIENT MINIMUM WAGE

Let us now explore a different argument for the minimum wage, one that directly addresses the double-distortion argument. Recall that the double-distortion argument says that redistribution through legal rules will always be less efficient than

[11] Slightly more formally, when low-wage workers have social marginal welfare weights above average – that is, greater than one, $g_1 > 1$ – the government favors redistribution to low-wage workers. By contrast, when the government's redistributive preferences are Rawlsian, this implies that the social marginal welfare weight of low-wage workers is zero, $g_1 = 0 < 1$.

redistribution through the income tax because, in addition to the tax-equivalent distortions in labor supply, the legal rule will also create distortions in the behavior regulated by the legal rules. Whatever distribution of income is generated by the legal rule can be replicated by the income tax and, because it will have identical labor-supply distortions, without any additional distortions, it will always be more efficient than the legal rule.

The minimum wage can indeed be said to generate two (or more) distortions. First, the minimum wage has tax-like income and labor-supply effects. As shown more formally in the appendix, income increases to low-wage workers due to the minimum wage are compensated by income reductions to high-wage workers. Like a redistributive adjustment to the income tax, this change distorts labor-supply incentives. Second, wages can be said to "regulate" the employment relationship in several dimensions. For example, the minimum wage shapes decisions like how much effort a worker gives on the job, when and whether a worker decides to quit, or how much training an employer provides. Establishing a minimum wage that diverges from the market-determined wage will have effects on both dimensions and will therefore produce a second distortion. Third, and finally, the minimum wage also has its own specific, and more familiar, distortions, as discussed already by Lee and Saez (2012) and Shaviro (1997). With the introduction of a demand side to the employment equation, the minimum wage reduces employment by "taxing" low-wage jobs with wages above the market-clearing level. Hence, we can say that the minimum wage generates three distinct distortions.

But what is the character of this double, or triple, distortion? Kaplow and Shavell (1994) essentially assume that legal-rule distortions will be additive, having effects that move in the same direction. But why should they (Lipsey and Lancaster 1956)? In the argument developed in the remaining part of this chapter, the minimum-wage distortions are not compounding but instead are offsetting. When two (or more) distortions are additive, the legal rule is necessarily more costly than the income tax. This is Kaplow and Shavell's key point. However, by the same token, when they are offsetting, the legal rule is not necessarily more costly than the income tax.

Let us explore this claim with a standard model of minimum-wage redistribution first devised by Stiglitz (1982) and employed by others, including Allen (1987), Guesnerie and Roberts (1987), and Lee and Saez (2012). The model is explored more formally in the appendix. Unlike most optimal taxation models, which focus only on labor supply, this model also includes labor demand. This is done by contemplating an "aggregate," or economy-wide, production function that features imperfect substitution between higher-paid, high-skilled workers and lower-paid, low-skilled workers. (As in the rest of the book, the appendix model also includes a third category: "poor," unemployed individuals.) In addition to allowing for labor demand, the production function also entails that minimum wages are redistributive. The idea is that competition limits firms to obtaining the "normal," going rate of profit (which is zero, according to economists, after labor and capital have been paid). Increases in low-skilled workers' wages then trigger a change in demand for low-skilled labor as well as a reduction in high-skilled workers' wages, in order to maintain the prevailing profit rate. Hence, the minimum wage redistributes from high-skilled workers to low-skilled workers.

To model the productivity effect of wages, I add another dimension to this redistributive minimum-wage model. This feature is an "efficiency wage" model. Efficiency-wage models capture wage effects in the labor market when the worker's on-the-job level of effort is only imperfectly observed, and the employer decides how intensively it wants to monitor the worker's efforts. Also for simplicity, I assume that firms only monitor low-wage workers (perhaps high-wage work is intrinsically rewarding). The low-wage worker chooses an effort level, either "high" or "low," with high effort being personally more costly to the worker (in terms of utility, nevertheless measured in dollars). This is just one way of capturing workplace-specific productivity effects of wages. Borrowing from the list of efficient minimum-wage models mentioned earlier, one could model productivity effects based on adverse selection, bargaining, search, turnover, training, or other factors.

Naturally, a high level of effort increases the employer's output. If the employee is caught exerting a low level of effort, they are dismissed. The chances of being detected are probabilistic, but the employer can spend money to increase this probability – for example, by installing video surveillance equipment or hiring more supervisors. Given a level of supervision, the employer pays a wage that is just sufficient to ensure the employee's high level of effort.

Another important feature of this model is that it imposes a trade-off between wages and monitoring. By increasing the level of monitoring, and hence the probability of detection, the employer can lower the wage necessary to ensure high effort, but at an increased cost of supervision. Conversely, the employer can increase the wage, making employment to the employee more desirable relative to unemployment, and secure high effort while lowering the costs of monitoring. Higher wages or more supervision – each option is costly, so the employer must choose a combination of wages and supervision that minimizes these costs and maximizes profit. That choice implies that wages above this profit-maximizing choice will increase productivity (or, more specifically, reduces supervision costs), but will nevertheless be inefficient – a key point to which we will return.

Before tackling the central, but more technical, question – whether the minimum wage in this model can redistribute more efficiently than taxes – it will help to illustrate how the minimum wage in this model differs from the standard model of the minimum wage.

How does the efficiency-wage model differ from standard models of the minimum wage? Let us suppose that the minimum wage raises the worker's wages by $1. This will also increase the employer's wage costs by the same amount. So far this is roughly equivalent to a subsidy to the worker's wages and a tax on employment of \$1.[12] But there is another effect. With the wage increase, employment is an even better alternative to unemployment for the worker than before. This means that the employer needs to spend less on supervision than it did previously. Suppose that the minimum wage saves monitoring costs of 70 cents. Thus, the effects of the minimum wage are offsetting. The wage increase raises the costs of employment to the employer, but they also lower the level of supervision costs. The net cost of the minimum wage is 30 cents: $-\$1.00 + \$0.70 = -\$0.30$.

Given our assumptions, these offsetting costs will not be efficient. The net effect is still a cost, not a gain. Prior to the minimum wage intervention, the employer was already making a profit-maximizing trade-off between wages and supervisory costs. As long as that combination of wages and supervision is unique, any divergence from that choice will be inefficient and result in a loss of total social wealth. This means that the savings from lower supervision costs will be less than \$1 (70 cents by our assumption) and the net effect on social resources is negative (a loss of 30 cents). In the aggregate, this will show up in an increase in unemployment, and in the form of excess labor supply. Wages will be higher, which will increase the supply of labor, but because the costs of operating a firm employing low-wage workers has increased on net, demand for labor will be unable to meet that supply. This is the standard result for a price-floor like the minimum wage.

However, there is one crucial difference from the standard minimum-wage analysis, which is that the net loss of wealth is smaller than would be the case in a typical minimum-wage analysis, which ignores the offsetting effect of lower supervision costs. This offsetting effect means that the fall in labor demand will be less than in a textbook minimum-wage analysis. There is still an inefficiency. Demand for labor falls, but this fall is *partially* offset by the reduction in monitoring costs that are accompanied by the minimum-wage hike.

Figure 6.3 illustrates the two different models of the minimum wages, the standard model and (this chapter's version of) the efficiency-wage model. In an unregulated labor market, demand and supply intersect at point a to give equilibrium wages, w^*, and employment, q^*. In a standard model of the minimum wage, the minimum increases the wage from w to $\bar{w}$, reducing labor demand from q^* to q_1 and yielding a new wage-employment equilibrium illustrated by point c. However, in the efficiency-wage model, the fall in labor demand is muted by the minimum wage's productivity effect, which is the savings in monitoring costs. In this case, the minimum wage again raises wages from w to $\bar{w}$, but the savings on monitoring costs shift the demand curve outward, from D to D'. Now, labor demand falls only from q^* to q_2, and the new

[12] I say "roughly," because as previously pointed out, the minimum wage is more than simply a subsidy. A subsidy, like the EITC, would have incidence effects that encourage greater labor supply and drive down the market-determined wage. A true "tax" version of the minimum wage would employ a "knife edge" tax schedule at the bottom of the wage distribution, which would guarantee $\bar{w}$ for all wages below that level, $0 < w < \bar{w}$.

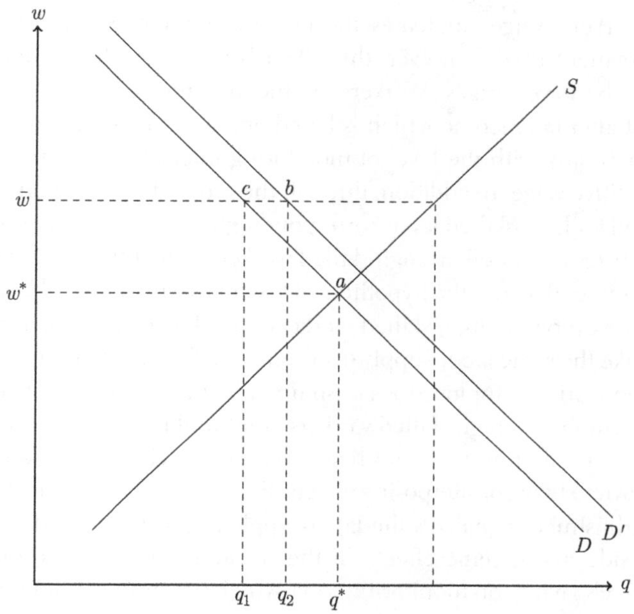

FIGURE 6.3 Standard and efficiency-wage models of the minimum wage

The horizontal axis, labeled q, measures the quantity of labor. The vertical axis represents the wage. S labels the labor-supply curve and D (and D') represent the labor-demand curve.

equilibrium is represented by point b. In sum, the same minimum wage is achieved, but with a smaller loss in employment – that is, a smaller loss in efficiency.

We can now turn to the central question: Can the minimum wage redistribute income more efficiently than the tax system? It will be most straightforward to answer this question using Kaplow and Shavell's (1994) tool for evaluating redistributive legal rules, a distribution-neutral income tax adjustment. This method replicates, through a hypothetical change in the tax system, the distributive effects of a given redistributive legal policy – in this case, the minimum wage. By predicting whether the proposed tax alternative would yield a budget deficit or a budget surplus, we can determine which policy is the most redistributively efficient.[13]

Replicating the redistributive minimum wage with the tax system has the following effects. The minimum wage is lowered to its competitive level, while low-skilled workers get a reduction in taxes (or a subsidy increase) so that they receive the same after-tax, disposable income as with the original, minimum-wage policy. Lowering

[13] I am using terms loosely. The method described here is the one Kaplow and Shavell (1994) use in their original contribution. Later, Kaplow (2008) explicitly uses the phrase "distribution-neutral income tax adjustment" for a subtly different method. The distinction is ultimately not relevant. For further details on distribution-neutral tax adjustments, see the book's appendix.

low-skilled workers' wages increases the demand for low-skilled labor, and low-skilled employment rises. However, this effect is muted by the higher monitoring costs entailed by lower wages. Workers' on-the-job effort decision is motivated by the wage, not after-tax income which is based on, say, annual earnings. Employer's therefore responding with the level of monitoring intensity that corresponds to the lower, competitive wage. In addition, through the production function's substitution effect, demand for high-skilled labor correspondingly falls while their wages increase. Accordingly, taxes are raised on high-skilled workers so that their after-tax income is the same as before. Because the hypothetical tax change maintains the same income distribution for everyone, high-skilled workers, low-skilled workers, and the unemployed all make the same labor-supply decisions as before. And, because the number of high-skilled workers employed is constrained by their supply (unlike low-skilled workers), the amount of high-skilled workers employed remains the same as before.

Whether the minimum wage can redistribute more efficiently than the income tax comes down to two, counterposing effects. Because the hypothetical distribution-neutral tax adjustment equalizes the labor-supply effects between the two policies, we can set aside that specific effect. Of the remaining two effects, the first is the minimum wage's savings on monitoring costs, which lowers the minimum wage's cost of redistribution. The second is the minimum wage's negative employment effect. Because the minimum wage reduces employment, the government's total transfers to the unemployed increase. Hence, if the savings in lower monitoring costs outweighs the extra expenditures on transfers to those made unemployed by the minimum wage, the minimum wage will redistribute more efficiently than the income tax.

Notice that the productivity (monitoring costs) and unemployment effects are linked but move in opposite directions. By our assumption that the employer's wage-monitoring decision is uniquely efficient prior to introducing the minimum wage, savings in monitoring costs can never exceed increases in the minimum wage. Otherwise, the minimum wage would be efficient. Nevertheless, the larger the savings in monitoring costs, the smaller the minimum wage's negative employment impact. For example, if the minimum wage raised wages by \$1 and saved firms \$0.99 in monitoring costs, negative employment effects would be close to zero. The minimum wage would *almost* pay for itself: The savings in monitoring costs would be large and the increase in government expenditures would be minuscule. The minimum wage would redistribute more efficiently than taxes. Conversely, if a \$1 increase in wages only lowered monitoring costs by \$0.01, the negative employment effects would be more palpable.

There is actually a fourth possible effect as well. We have assumed until now that the minimum wage is only lowered, but not eliminated. If the minimum wage is removed, the government must also address the incidence effects of the lower taxes (or increased subsidies) on the wage – the same drawback of the tax system analyzed by Lee and Saez (2012). This incidence effect requires the government to spend additional money, compared to the previous scenario, just to ensure that low-wage workers get the same after-tax income as they did with the minimum wage. Because eliminating the minimum wage requires additional spending, without any improvement to welfare compared to the previous case, this worsens the inefficiency of the tax system. Ultimately, the incidence effect of the tax system makes it more likely that the hypothetical tax alternative will yield a budget deficit, and more likely that minimum wage can reduce income inequality more efficiently.

6.3.1 *Concluding Considerations*

To round out the discussion, I want to address briefly three final issues. The first is whether the tax system can replicate the productivity effect of the minimum wage without the cost of increased unemployment. The second is how this chapter's argument lends stronger policy support for the minimum wage than that of Lee and Saez (2012). Finally, I discuss how the redistributive minimum wage illustrates the limitations in Kaplow's (2008) distribution-neutral tax adjustment analysis.

The idea that the tax system can replicate the benefits of the minimum wage, without the costs, is attractive. But it does not seem possible to do so. As already mentioned, eliminating the minimum wage entirely has an incidence effect that reduces the efficiency of the tax system. Furthermore, as some formal analysis can show, even more precisely targeted wage subsidies (rather than broader household income subsidies, which the EITC effectively is) have their own incidence effects. Wage subsidies will incentivize workers to provide a high level of effort for a lower level of monitoring, but this will prompt employers to *lower* wages in order to restore the profit-maximizing combination of (net) wages and supervision. Higher wage costs for the employer are therefore essential for the productivity effect that comes with higher wages for the employee. Finally, one could use a "knife edge" tax schedule at the bottom of the wage distribution, which would guarantee $\bar{w}$ for all wages below that level, $0 < w < \bar{w}$. Such a schedule would generate the same productivity effect as the minimum wage – as well as all of its other effects. But for that reason, as Lee and Saez (2012, 743 n.11) point out, an intricate policy that replicates the minimum wage in all its particulars is a "tax" policy in name only; there is no substantive difference between that and a minimum wage.

My argument for the minimum wage should also be distinguished from Lee and Saez's (2012). In their analysis, the role of the minimum wage is only to forestall the incidence effect of the income subsidy from lowering wages. In this guise, the minimum wage merely prevents wages from falling below their competitive, efficient level. Consequently, the income subsidy does all of the distributive heavy-lifting. In this chapter, the minimum wage has an additional role to play. If the minimum wage also has a productivity effect, then the combined subsidy-wage floor policy in Lee and Saez can be replicated at lower cost by a minimum wage that is set above the efficient level. In my version, the minimum wage both prevents an incidence effect of taxes and reduces the costs of redistribution.

Further recall that for Lee and Saez (2012), the minimum wage only has redistributive value with an "intermediate" social welfare function, one that does not give exclusive weight to the welfare of the unemployed (or, more generally, the least well off), such as a Rawlsian social welfare function. A Rawlsian social welfare function says that our redistributive concerns should be directed solely to the least well off – typically, the unemployed – and not to anyone better off than them, including the working poor. By contrast, according to my argument, a minimum wage can reproduce the same income distribution generated by a Rawlsian social welfare function while also yielding a budget surplus, which can be used to increase transfers to the unemployed. In other words, my argument for the minimum wage does not depend on the type of social welfare function the policy analyst uses, as it does for Lee and Saez. Even under a Rawlsian social welfare function, the tax savings from the minimum wage can be used to increase the transfers to the least well off, the unemployed (as long as the minimum wage's productivity effect is large enough).

Finally, my analysis illustrates the limitations of Kaplow's (2008) distribution-neutral tax-adjustment analyses. The hypothetical tax adjustment we have used in analysis is the same as in Kaplow and Shavell (1994), and tests the comparative, redistributive efficiency of a given legal rule and the income tax. Kaplow (2008) uses distribution-neutral income tax adjustments to evaluate whether regulatory policies or public-goods provisions satisfy a simple efficiency, or cost-benefit, test. But the differences between the two methods are merely formal. Both affirm the adoption of the minimum wage, as long as the stated condition obtains (i.e., the savings in monitoring costs exceed the additional costs of unemployment): under the first method, because the minimum wage redistributes more efficiently than the income tax; under the second, because the minimum wage satisfies a cost-benefit test. It is hard to accept the second interpretation, because under the standard measures of efficiency, a redistributive minimum wage fails to increase total wealth, for all of the familiar reasons: By increasing wages above the competitive, market level, the minimum wage reduces employment and causes a loss of resources. This conclusion is familiar to anyone with knowledge of the minimum wage's economic impacts, which only underscores how odd Kaplow's opposite conclusion, drawn from a distribution-neutral analysis, is. Put slightly differently, my analysis agrees with Kaplow (2008) about when the minimum-wage should be adopted: The minimum wage should be used whenever, controlling for labor-supply effects, it saves more money than the tax system. But in this case a distribution-neutral tax adjustment analysis merely shows why taxes do *not* always redistribute income more efficiently than legal rules, consistent with the method in Kaplow and Shavell (1994) but contrary to its double-distortion thesis. No one thinks a redistributive minimum wage is a first-best policy solution.[14] Yet, Kaplow's distribution-neutral income tax adjustment makes precisely that conclusion.

[14] A first-best case for the minimum wage can only be made in the presence of employer monopsony power, where the wage is used only to *correct* for market power, is set at the competitive level, and in that sense does not redistribute.

6.4 REDISTRIBUTION AND COLLECTIVE BARGAINING

This final section of the chapter considers how the argument I have just provided for the minimum wage can also be extended to collective bargaining.

The dominant picture of collective bargaining within law and economics has been the "cartel model" (Posner 1984). This model of wage bargaining is very similar to the traditional minimum wage analysis given previously. Instead of a government, a labor union representing the firm's workforce chooses the wage. In response, the employer chooses how many workers to employ, setting marginal cost – the wage – equal to the marginal productivity of labor, which is the employer's demand curve. The monopoly, or cartel, designation reflects the fact that the union has market power unilaterally to set the wage that maximizes its members' well being, subject to the employer's unilateral choice of the number of workers (Dunlop 1944). The employer's subsequent choice of labor acts as the main constraint on the union's objective, which the union anticipates when setting the wage. A variation on the monopoly-union model is the "right-to-manage" model. In this model, the union and the employer bargain over the wage, following which the employer unilaterally chooses the level of employment. Because the wage is negotiated, rather than set unilaterally by the union, the wage level is determined by the relative bargaining powers of the parties. Hence, the monopoly-union model emerges as a special case of the right-to-manage model, where the union has all of the bargaining power (Manning 1987). (Similarly, if the employer has all of the bargaining power, the market-determined wage emerges as the "bargained" wage.)

In fact, the monopoly-union model (and right-to-manage model) of wage setting is exactly analogous to the monopoly problem in the standard product-market setting. And, like monopoly models in general, the monopoly-union model predicts that collective bargaining is inefficient. As wages rise above their market-clearing level, output falls. In this respect, the monopoly-union model is identical to the simple minimum-wage analysis. There is, however, at least one small difference. Typically, collective bargaining is conceived as a single union bargaining with a single firm. Consequently, the monopoly wage in the union setting does not cover the entire industry or even the national economy. As workers are disemployed in the unionized firm, therefore, they increase labor supply in the rest of the industry's or economy's labor market and drive down wages. Thus, where a national minimum wage has a "pure" disemployment effect, increasing inequality between the employed and unemployed, the inequality effect of collective bargaining is more muted, disemploying only some workers and lowering wages for other workers elsewhere in the labor market. Nevertheless, as a proponent of the competitive labor-market model will point out, both scenarios increase inequality of some kind and amount.

But the monopoly-union model is not the only model of collective wage bargaining. In fact, if the union and the employer behave as the monopoly-union model predicts, they will fail to reach a Pareto optimal agreement with respect to themselves. The union, representing the interests of its members, could be made better off by lowering wages slightly in order to increase employment, and the firm could increase profits by doing so. Another model of collective bargaining, the "efficient bargaining" version, pursues the line of thought that, because the monopoly union contract is Pareto inferior, firms and unions are more likely to bargain to a more mutually beneficial agreement on wages and employment (McDonald and Solow 1981). Indeed, within this conception of collective bargaining, neither the union nor the employer act unilaterally with respect to wages or employment. Instead, the union and the employer bargain over both. As the bargaining model shows, there are in fact a whole range of points on the contract curve between the union and the firm that achieve a Pareto superior outcome to the right-to-manage model. Which combination of wages and employment is agreed upon depends on the relative bargaining powers of the parties.

The surprising and interesting insight of the efficient bargaining model of collective bargaining is that there may be no inefficiency at all. Indeed, if the firm and union want to fully exploit the gains from their joint enterprise they will have an interest in eliminating any waste. Hence, the contract curve typically starts at the efficient, market allocation of wages and employment and extends upwards in a vertical line, holding the level of employment fixed as wages are raised. As a result, the bargained agreement delivers higher wages to employees but without any loss of employment relative to the competitive market-determined wage. Collective bargaining can be just as efficient as the competitive labor market; only the distribution of rewards have changed.

The efficient bargaining model suggests that unions can increase wages without any loss of efficiency. But the model still retains some strong assumptions. Wage increases must come from somewhere, namely the firm's profits, and the efficient bargaining model does not model how the effect on profits affects other economic decisions. The remainder of this section will focus on two such decisions: (1) firms' entry-and-exit decisions and (2) firms' investments, including research and development.

With regard to the entry-exit decision, the bargaining model of collective bargaining takes the number of firms as fixed. There is no (long run) entry or exit of firms into the relevant product market in which firms and unions negotiate. However, this assumption is counterfactual: Because wages come at the expense of profits in the bargaining model, even though there is no loss of efficiency (in terms of employment), we should expect this to affect the entry and exit of firms. As profits decline in an industry where collective bargaining is prevalent, firms will tend to leave that industry and capital will be invested elsewhere. One can understood this effect to work like the taxes on labor-supply that we have encountered throughout this book. Just as an increase in the marginal tax rate causes individuals to reduce their labor supply, so too the supply of firms in the product market will decrease as wages go up and profits down.[15]

Note, however, that as long as collective bargaining is "efficient" (i.e., with respect to employment) there will be no second, or "double," distortion accompanying it. In this respect, collective bargaining will work just like taxes do, and have no immediate disadvantage relative to the tax system. Nevertheless, one potential drawback is that the redistribution undertaken by collective bargaining is not "targeted" in an ideal fashion. Because wage increases go to employed workers, rather than to the unemployed, redistribution through collective bargaining may not serve the welfare of those most in need. We will return to this issue, and show how collective bargaining may actually avoid this concern.

With respect to firms' investment decisions, this too is not included in the efficient bargaining model; it therefore assumes that wage negotiation has no effect on the firm's investment strategy. Yet, this is clearly incorrect. There is well-documented evidence that collective bargaining has a "holdup effect" on investment, capital, and research and development (Connolly, Hirsch, and Hirschey 1986; Denny and Nickell 1992; Hirsch 1992; Bronars, Deere, and Tracy 1994; Odgers and Betts 1997). As first analyzed formally by Grout (1984), because unions will raise their wage demands subsequent to a productivity-enhancing investment, this will discourage firms from undertaking the investments in the first place.[16] As long as negotiated wage levels are geared to the firm's productivity, wage bargaining acts as an additional, implicit cost of capital. This holdup effect functions as a "tax" on investment. Thus when workers appropriate part of the firm's investment through higher wages, firms will underinvest. I consider this holdup effect on investment as an independent "distortion"; but note that by further reducing profits – not just through higher wages, but through lower productivity – the holdup effect will also discourage firm entry into the relevant market.

Once we have incorporated the holdup effect into the analysis, collective bargaining may indeed induce a double-distortion in the Kaplow and Shavell (1994) sense. By changing the distribution of income, through higher wages and lower profits, collective bargaining, like the income tax, influences the supply of "labor" – the entry of firms, in this example. In addition, by distorting the level of investment – in

[15] Instead of analogizing the supply of firms to the labor supply of individuals, we could just as easily model the labor supply of wealthier individuals who (on average) receive capital income from their ownership of firm shares. Then, the higher profits and greater supply of firms would correspond to greater capital income and therefore greater individual labor supply. This is essentially the way that Kaplow (2021) brings firms into his distribution-neutral tax adjustment analysis.

[16] This is essentially a problem of credible commitments. The assumption that wage demands are made after investment reflects that fact that a union's promise not to make such demands is not credible. One function of "no-strike" or "peace" clauses in collective bargaining agreements is to ameliorate this commitment problem.

capital, technology, or research and development – collective bargaining also creates a second distortion. Note that this is true even under the efficient bargaining model of union-management negotiation, where the employment is chosen efficiently. Collective bargaining is efficient in this model only in a narrow sense, with respect to the level of employment. In any case, once we consider the hold-up problem, it would appear that collective bargaining is inferior to the income tax as a method of redistribution, because it generates a second distortion, rather than only one, like the tax system.

Before drawing that conclusion, however, we should reexamine an assumption mentioned before, one that is typically maintained in *every* model of collective bargaining, whether monopoly union, right to manage, or efficient bargaining. This is the assumption that bargaining takes place at a decentralized rather than a more centralized level. Decentralized collective bargaining occurs when a union negotiates with a single employer over an agreement that covers the employees of a single firm or, at an even more decentralized level, a single workplace, such as a plant, warehouse, or store of an employer that has many. Centralized bargaining takes place when a union negotiates for the employees of an entire industry, sector, or even for a national economy. When bargaining is centralized, the union negotiates with an employer's association that represents the employers of the industry or economy. In terms of both policy and practice, decentralized bargaining may be a reasonable assumption for the United States. But it is not a reasonable assumption outside of the United States, and particularly for collective bargaining in Western Europe. In those countries, it is more common for collective bargaining to be more centralized.

What happens when we change the assumption about where collective bargaining takes place, from the firm level to the sectoral level? Because collective bargaining continues to shift income from profits to wages, we can still anticipate it to have a "tax" effect on the supply of firms (or "labor supply," to emphasize the connection with double-distortion thinking). In fact, scholars have provided both theory and evidence for why centralized bargaining should more closely approximate the efficient-bargaining model than does decentralized bargaining (Calmfors and Driffill 1988). One can think of local bargaining as a negative externality on employment. Because local unions are too small to recognize the effect of their wage demands on macro-level employment levels, they do not take these effects into account, and favor wages over employment in negotiations. When unions bargain on a broader level – when they are sufficiently encompassing, for example, to be de facto representatives of the national workforce – they are forced to consider the effects of wage demands on aggregate employment levels. Taking employment into account, centralized bargaining is more likely to reach an efficient mix of wages and employment. There is therefore good reason for treating centralized bargaining as having a pure, distributive effect, at least between wages and profits.

What about the implications of centralized bargaining for technology and investment? As theory and research have also demonstrated, centralized bargaining has more favorable consequences for technology and investment than decentralized bargaining.[17] There are several possible mechanisms for this. When wages are set at an industry or national level, they are geared to the *average* productivity of firms in the sector, rather than the productivity of an individual firm. As a consequence, when individual firms undertake an investment in capital or R&D, those investments will have only a negligible effect on the wages they pay. We can also think about this positive investment effect in terms of firm heterogeneity. When firms have different productivities, centralized bargaining, by setting a uniform wage regardless of firm-level productivity, acts as a subsidy to productivity leaders and a tax on laggards, which further encourages investment (Moene and Wallerstein 1997). For either of these reasons, centralized bargaining is therefore more favorable to firms' investment behaviors than decentralized bargaining.

The next question that arises is whether collective bargaining can redistribute income more efficiently than the tax system. To answer this question, let us first compare decentralized with centralized collective bargaining. Moving from a decentralized to a centralized regime of wage setting, the first notable effect is a reduction in inequality. Although decentralized wage bargaining redistributes income, centralized bargaining has a significantly larger effect on income inequality reduction (Wallerstein 1999). Decentralized bargaining primarily redistributes within firms, but centralized bargaining redistributes both within and between firms. Thus, centralized bargaining will redistribute income more than decentralized bargaining, generating the first, "tax" distortion that influences labor supply (in this case, the supply of firms). Centralized bargaining also has a second effect, which is its positive effect on investment incentives. Because centralized bargaining reduces or eliminates the hold-up problem, compared to decentralized bargaining, and may even encourage investment, this effect offsets the first, tax distortion.

These combined effects make centralized bargaining more efficient than taxes in redistributing income compared with a regime of decentralized bargaining. The pure, redistributive effect of collective bargaining – shifting income from profits to wages – distorts the supply of labor (i.e., firms), just like the income tax. In this respect, centralized bargaining and taxes are identical. However, centralized bargaining encourages greater investment in capital, technology, or R&D, making firms more productive. This has a positive effect on firms' profits, and hence the supply of firms into the given sector, which counters the negative effect that follows the redistribution from profits to wages. This positive effect on firm supply is unavailable

[17] Menezes-Filho and Van Reenen (2003, 293, 328) report that North American (mostly U.S.) studies "find consistently negative impacts of unions on [research and development spending]," while unions in Europe by contrast do not appear to reduce spending on research and development. Hibbs and Locking (2000, 755) also showed that wage compression associated with centralized wage bargaining in Sweden was consistent with increases in productive efficiency as long as it focused on reducing wage inequalities between firms and did not compress within-firm wage differentials too much.

with the use of the single-distortion income tax change. As a result, centralized collective bargaining is more efficient than taxes in redistributing income.

To emphasize once more a crucial point, it is not necessary that the positive investment effect of centralized bargaining entirely offset its negative labor-supply effect. In fact, if it did, centralized bargaining would be efficient, independently of role of the income tax, and there would be no efficiency-equity trade-off. Centralized bargaining would be endorsed for its efficiency effects, regardless of its distributive impact, and would not falsify the double-distortion argument. If the investment effect of centralized bargaining only partially offsets the labor-supply effect, then it is inefficient. But because the investment effect partially offsets the labor-supply effect, which is equivalent to the effect of taxes, centralized bargaining redistributes more efficiently than the income tax.

Notice also the analogy between collective bargaining and the minimum wage analysis provided previously. Just as the minimum wage has a positive productivity effect on labor effort, in addition to a redistributive effect, centralized bargaining also has a positive productivity effect – not necessarily though increasing labor effort, but through the firm's investment in capital or technology. In either case, the productivity serves to offset the labor-supply distortions induced by redistributing income. A graphical analysis of centralized bargaining would therefore be roughly the same as for the minimum wage, as displayed in Figure 6.3.

Finally, one might ask whether centralized collective bargaining is better than no collective bargaining at all. Centralized bargaining may encourage greater investment, compared to decentralized bargaining, where the hold-up problem causes firms to underinvest. But what about investment incentives where there is no collective bargaining whatsoever? It may be tempting to draw the conclusion that investment decisions will be optimal in the absence of collective bargaining. If this is the case, taxes may beat centralized bargaining. If investment decisions are optimal when employees contract individually, but centralized bargaining still has some detrimental effect on investment – even if less detrimental than decentralized bargaining – then centralized bargaining will still present a double distortion. Relative to no bargaining, centralized bargaining will distort labor-supply incentives and investment incentives. In this scenario, the answer is not to substitute centralized bargaining for decentralized bargaining, but to abolish collective bargaining altogether.

But there is no reason to assume that investment incentives will be optimal without collective bargaining. As the literatures in labor economics and the theory of the firm have long recognized, the employment relationship is a good deal more complicated than the basic supply-and-demand model suggests, where nothing happens except an exchange of wages for labor. In an important contribution, Stole and Zwiebel (1996a, 375, emphasis in original) present a formal model of the "intra-firm bargaining process between the firm and its *individual* employees." Based on the "at will" nature of the employment relationship – classically cited as an advantage in law and economics scholarship (e.g., Epstein 1983) – employees can always renegotiate ex post, after investments have been made. It also matters that employees cannot be immediately and costlessly replaced; otherwise renegotiation would not be feasible. In order words, the individual employment relationship, like collective bargaining, is also susceptible to hold-up problems. Indeed, studying the implications of this model for labor and capital choice, Stole and Zwiebel (1996b, 197) "find striking implications of overemployment and capital underutilization."

Individual employment contracting therefore has no clear a priori advantage over centralized wage bargaining, as far as the firm's investment strategies go. And given the distortions in employment and capital utilization generated by individual contracting identified by Stole and Zwiebel (1996a, 1996b), centralized wage bargaining may well be superior. By taking wage-setting out of the hands of individual employees or local unions, the central union may be able to make credible and binding commitments that these others cannot. Under those circumstances, centralized bargaining will have an offsetting advantage over the distribution-neutral income tax alternative. Due to its favorable effect on investment, centralized wage bargaining will offset the labor-supply distortions generated by its redistributive effect. And, once again, the offset may not be total, in which case it will be inefficient from a wealth-maximizing point of view. But any offset will make centralized wage bargaining less inefficient than the tax system in redistributing income.

6.5 APPENDIX

The following presents a formal model of the minimum wage, and is reproduced in the online version. Section 6.5.1 specifies the nature of production, Section 6.5.2 discusses the nature of the firm's monitoring choice, and Section 6.5.3 formally establishes the redistributive value of the minimum wage. The final section's redistributive evaluation includes the cases where (1) the minimum wage is set at its efficient, competitive-market level (to prevent the incidence effects of wage subsidies); (2) the social welfare function is Rawlsian (where the minimum wage loses any redistributive rationale in the model of Lee and Saez (2012)); and (3) the minimum wage is eliminated and wage subsidies are allowed to have incidence effects.

6.5.1 *Production*

The model follows the redistributive minimum-wage literature with two types of skilled workers and endogenous wages. Stiglitz (1982) was the first to develop this model (in an optimal-tax setting) and others have used it to model the redistributive value of the minimum wage, including Allen (1987), Guesnerie and Roberts (1987), and Lee and Saez (2012).

The production process produces a unique consumption good $F(h_1, h_2)$ that depends on the amount of low-skilled labor, h_1, and high-skilled labor, h_2, employed.

Low-skilled workers receive a wage, w_1, and high-skilled workers receive, w_2. I assume throughout that $w_2 > w_1$. The production function exhibits constant returns to scale. For simplicity, I assume that the effort of low-skilled workers must be monitored but high-skilled workers is not (suppose, for example, that high-skilled work is more intrinsically rewarding). For now, I also assume that the cost of monitoring, $M(p)$, which is a function of a given amount of supervision, p, is fixed; later, these choices are endogenized.

For now, we can describe the firm's profit function as follows:

$$\pi = F(h_1, h_2) - (w_1 + M(p))h_1 - w_2 h_2. \tag{6.1}$$

Firms choose labor to maximize profits, where the marginal product will equal marginal cost. Demand for labor for high- and low-skilled workers respectively are given by:

$$w_2 = \frac{\partial F}{\partial h_2} \quad \text{and} \quad w_1 + M(p) = \frac{\partial F}{\partial h_1}. \tag{6.2}$$

Constant returns to scale implies that in equilibrium there are zero profits. This allows us to derive an important relationship between the wages of low- and high-skilled workers. Suppose, for example, that the production function takes a Cobb-Douglas form: $Y = Ah_2^{\alpha}h_1^{1-\alpha}$. Profit-maximizing labor-demand functions can then be written as:

$$h_2 = \frac{\alpha Y}{w_2} \quad \text{and} \quad h_1 = \frac{(1-\alpha)Y}{w_1 + M(p)}.$$

Imposing the zero-profit condition and substituting these labor-demand solutions into the profit constraint, $Ah_2^{\alpha}h_1^{1-\alpha} - (w_1 + M(p))h_1 - w_2 h_2 = 0$, we get:

$$A\left(\frac{\alpha}{w_2}\right)^{\alpha}\left(\frac{1-\alpha}{w_1 + M(p)}\right)^{1-\alpha} = 1.$$

This expression defines a decreasing relationship between w_2 and w_1 as can be seen after rearranging it:

$$w_2(w_1) = \left[\frac{A\alpha^{\alpha}(1-\alpha)^{1-\alpha}}{(w_1 + M(p))^{1-\alpha}}\right]^{\frac{1}{\alpha}}. \tag{6.3}$$

The most important implication of this decreasing relationship between high- and low-skilled wages is that increasing the minimum wage, which will directly affect low-skilled workers, will reduce the wages of high-skilled workers. In other words, the minimum wage is redistributive.

6.5.2 *The Firm's Monitoring Choice*

This section examines more closely how the firm chooses its level of monitoring intensity and (possibly) wages. Monitoring entails a per-worker cost $M(\cdot)$, which is a continuously increasing, twice differentiable, and convex function of the probability of detection, p, chosen by the firm: $M(0) = M'(0) = 0$ and $\lim_{p \to 1} M'(p) = \infty$. This relationship means that the cost of perfect monitoring (i.e., $p = 1$) is prohibitive. The effort of the worker is observable to the firm and the worker, but not to the government or the courts, and is therefore nonverifiable and noncontractible. The worker makes a binary effort choice: $e \in \{0, \bar{e}\}$ with $\bar{e} > 0$. Exerting zero effort, $e = 0$ costs nothing while exerting positive effort, $e = \bar{e}$, costs the worker the value of the leisure forgone, $X(\bar{e})$.

This model requires a distinction between the "voluntary" unemployment produced by individuals' labor-market choices and "involuntarily" unemployment induced by the minimum wage. Let workers' income be given by $y_1 = qw_1 + (1-q)b - T_1$, where q represents the probability of being employed and is a function of the ratio of jobs (demand) to job-seekers (supply): $q = h_1^D(w_1)/h_1^S(c_0, c_1, c_2)$. (Of course, in a perfectly competitive market, $q = 1$, but with a minimum wage, there will be excess supply, and therefore $q < 1$.) Intuitively, as the number of job-seekers entering the labor market increases, the probability of employment goes down. One can think of b as the income from unemployment, which can be unemployment benefits provided by the government, the value of home production, or some combination (say $b = v + c_0$). Indeed, it is useful to think of y_1 as *household* income and so q can be not only a probability but a share of household members employed or a proportion of time spent employed over a given period, say, a year.

If employed, and the worker exerts low effort, they are detected with probability p, terminated, and they receive $b - T_1$, which is household income while temporarily unemployed. With probability $1 - p$, they are not detected and receive the after-tax wage: $w_1 - T_1$ and the value of leisure. To ensure a level of high effort, $\bar{e}$, the following incentive-compatibility constraint must be satisfied:

$$w_1 - T_1 - X(\bar{e}) \geq p(b - T_1) + (1 - p)(w_1 - T_1). \tag{6.4}$$

In words, the value of employment less the cost of effort must be greater than that of "shirking" and the probability of termination. Taxes are included in this expression primarily to show how they do not affect the firm's wage-monitoring decision. Note that the incentive-compatibility constraint reduces to:

$$w_1 - X(\bar{e}) \geq pb + (1 - p)w_1$$

where taxes drop out of the equation. Also note that this constraint will always bind, otherwise the firm could lower the probability of detection and increase profits without affecting anything else. Thus, to ensure high effort at lowest possible cost, firms either adjust the wage (say, if the purely market-determined wage is too low) or the probability of detection so that the previous equation (6.4) reaches equality:

$$w_1 = \frac{X(\bar{e})}{p} + b \tag{6.5}$$

Equation (6.5) also establishes a convex relationship between the wage and the probability of detection. This implies that wages and monitoring are substitutes – that is, raising wages will induce a lower detection probability and hence lower monitoring costs. To see this, rearrange equation (6.5) to get:

$$p(w_1) = \frac{X(\bar{e})}{w_1 - b}. \tag{6.6}$$

It is easily checked that $p(w_1)$ is convex: $p'(w_1) < 0$ and $p''(w_1) > 0$. Because p is everywhere decreasing in w_1, monitoring costs, $M(p)$, which are an increasing function of p, are decreasing in w_1.

Workers also face a participation constraint. The wage the firm offers, less the costs of high effort, must exceed the worker's outside option, that is, what they can get from another firm in the market. Write this constraint as:

$$w_1 - X(\bar{e}) \geq \bar{u} \tag{6.7}$$

where $\bar{u} = q(w_1 - X(\bar{e})) + (1 - q)b$. Unlike the incentive-compatibility constraint, the participation constraint may or may not bind. This depends on whether the wage that the firm prefers to pay is above or below the market-determined wage.

We can now specify the firm's profit-maximizing choices of p and (possibly) w_1. There are two possibilities, depending on whether the participation constraint in equation (6.7) binds. If the participation constraint does not bind, the firm is free to choose both p and w_1. We can simultaneously solve for both by substituting the (binding) incentive-compatibility constraint solved for p given by equation (6.6) into the firm's profit function given by equation (6.1). Choosing w_1 to maximize this expression, we get:

$$-M'(p)p'(w_1^{**}) - 1 = 0 \tag{6.8}$$

where, recalling from the monitoring intensity equation (6.6), the sign of $p'(w)$ is negative. Letting $\hat{w}_1$ be the market-determined wage, if the supply of labor at w_1^{**}, $h_1^S(w_1^{**})$, exceeds the demand for labor, $h_1^D(w_1^{**})$, then the participation constraint does not bind and firms are free to pay their most preferred wage: $w_1 = w_1^{**} > \hat{w}_1$.

Otherwise, when the supply of labor at w_1^{**} is less than the demand for labor, the participation constraint binds. In this case, the wage is determined directly from the participation constraint, $w_1 = \bar{u} + X(\bar{e}) = \hat{w}_1 > w_1^{**}$. Moreover, from the w-p curve given by the incentive-compatibility constraint in equation (6.6), when firms pay a higher wage, they reduce their monitoring. Hence, for $\hat{w}_1 > w_1^{**}$, we have $\hat{p} < p^{**}$ and $M(\hat{p}) < M(p^{**})$.

Another very important conclusion follows from the above analysis. When the participation constraint does not bind, we can read the firm's cost-minimizing choice of wages and monitoring, given in equation (6.8), as equalizing the marginal costs of wages and monitoring at unity: $-M'(p)p'(w_1^{**}) = 1$. In other words, at the optimum, a unit increase in the wage implies that the marginal benefit of lowering monitoring costs will be a positive one. Furthermore, given the convexity of the wage-monitoring curve, this implies that the marginal-change to the costs of monitoring at a wage above the firm's most-preferred wage, w_1^{**}, (where the workers' participation constraint does not bind), will be less than unity; and that at a wage below this level, the marginal-change to the costs of monitoring are greater than one:

$$-M'(p)p'(w)dw = \begin{cases} 0 \leq 1, & \text{for } w_1 \geq w_1^{**} \\ > 1, & \text{for } w_1 < w_1^{**}. \end{cases}$$

This result has a few implications. On the one hand, it implies that the minimum wage is inefficient. Whether the participation constraint binds or not, the minimum wage increases the wage rate and reduces the cost of monitoring. However, from the incentive-compatibility constraint (the wage-monitoring curve), the reduction in monitoring costs will be less than the increase in wage costs, so that overall the marginal cost of employing a worker increases and employment for labor decreases. On the other hand, because these two effects offset each other, the redistributive effect can be more efficient than the use of taxes. We examine this second implication in more detail in Section 6.5.3.

6.5.3 *Minimum Wage versus Taxation*

With the basic elements of the model described in the previous sections, this section turns to the relative redistributive efficiency of the minmium wage compared with taxation.

First, returning to the redistributive nature of the minimum wage, I will show that a change in low-skilled workers' employment costs (i.e., wages and monitoring costs) are entirely compensated by changes in high-skilled workers wages. A change in low-skilled workers wages creates changes in all of our variables of interest, dw_1, dw_2, dh_1, dh_2, and dM. Using the profit function in equation (6.1), a small change in w_1 yields:

$$d\pi = \left(\frac{\partial F}{\partial h_1}\right) dh_1 - (w_1 + M(p))dh_1 - h_1(1 + M'(p)p'(w))dw_1 + \left(\frac{\partial F}{\partial h_2}\right) dh_2 - w_2 dh_2 - h_2 dw_2.$$

From the labor-demand equations given by equation (6.2), this expression simplifies to:

$$-h_1(1 + M'(p)p'(w))dw_1 - h_2 dw_2.$$

The zero-profit condition, $\pi = 0$, then implies that $d\pi = 0$ and thus:

$$h_1(1 + M'(p)p'(w))dw_1 + h_2 dw_2 = 0. \tag{6.9}$$

Thus, an increase in low-skilled workers through the minimum wage, $dw_1 = d\bar{w} > 0$ is entirely compensated by a reduction in wages of high-skilled workers.

Combination Wage Subsidy and Efficient Minimum Wage

A distribution-neutral income tax adjustment, used to replace the minimum wage policy (as described by Kaplow (2008) and the book appendix), can be carried out in a variety of ways. I first consider the case where a redistirbutive, but inefficient, minimum wage is replaced by a tax reform that increases the subsidy (or lowers taxes) for low-skilled workers, but lowers the minimum wage to its efficient level, without eliminating it entirely. Lowering the minimum wage, but not eliminating it, prevents an incidence effect that would otherwise transfer a portion of the wage subsidy to employers. This combination of wage subsidy and efficient minimum wage happens to be the preferred policy of Lee and Saez (2012) and, as shown in the next subsection, is relevant to the issue they raise about the value of a minimum wage when the social welfare function (specifically, Rawlsian) does not place any value on low-skilled workers because they are not the least well off.

The minimum wage is theoretically ambiguous, it is entirely plausible that it redistributes more efficiently than the tax system. The tax reform that replicates the redistributive effects of the minimum wage has two effects. First, it increases employer demand for low-skilled labor and therefore saves the government from paying more in subsidies (or losing less in taxes) than it otherwise would. (Incidentally, this is the same effect that Lee and Saez (2012) identify as the one that makes the combination of a minimum wage and positive taxes (second-best Pareto) inefficient.) Second, and however, taxes cannot replicate the productivity benefits of the minimum wage, which increases the cost of the tax reform. Thus, the minimum wage will be more redistributively efficient than taxes when the revenue losses of the second effect outweigh the revenue gains of the first.

To implement a distribution-neutral income tax adjustment, we hypothetically give low-skilled workers a wage subsidy (or tax reduction) and set the minimum wage at its efficient level (to prevent an incidence effect) so that they have the same well-being as they do with the higher, redistributive minimum wage. This subsidy, $\hat{T}_1$, is calculated as follows:

$$q(w_1^*)w_1^* + (1 - q(w_1^*))b - T_1 - \hat{T}_1 - \theta_1 = q(\bar{w}_1)\bar{w}_1 + (1 - q(\bar{w}_1))b - T_1 - \theta_1,$$

where $w_1^* = \max\{w_1^{**}, \hat{w}_1\}$. Because the minimum wage increases household income by raising hourly earnings, $\bar{w}_1 > \bar{w}_1$, the tax adjustment in this case will be negative, i.e., a tax reduction or a subsidy $\hat{T}_1 < 0$. Solving in terms of $-\hat{T}_1$ we have:

$$-\hat{T}_1 = q(\bar{w}_1)(\bar{w}_1 - b) - q(w_1^*)(w_1^* - b).$$

The reduction in the minimum wage increases employment exclusively on the demand side. The amount of labor supplied is constant because low-skilled jobholders or -seekers receive the same utility, c_1, under the minimum wage or the distribution-neutral tax adjustment. Adding $q(\bar{w}_1)(w_1^* - b) - q(\bar{w}_1)(w_1^* - b)$ to the previous expression and rearranging it:

$$-\hat{T}_1 = q(\bar{w}_1)(\bar{w}_1 - w_1^*) - (q(w_1^*) - q(\bar{w}_1))(w^* - b).$$

For high-skilled workers, the distribution-neutral adjustment takes the following form:

$$w_2 - T_2 - \hat{T}_2 - \theta_2 = \bar{w}_2 - T_2 - \theta_2,$$

where $\bar{w}_2 = w_2(\bar{w}_1)$ as defined in equation (6.3) and, from $\bar{w}_1 > w_1$, we necessarily have $\bar{w}_2 < w_2$. Note that in either case, the minimum wage or taxes, the number of high-skilled workers employed is supply-side constrained. So, $h_2 = h_2^S$ in either scenario. Because the minimum wage reduces the high-skilled worker's income, the tax adjustment in this case is positive, i.e., an increase in taxes $\hat{T}_2 > 0$. Solving in terms of $\hat{T}_2$ we obtain:

$$\hat{T}_2 = w_2^* - \bar{w}_2.$$

The condition for the minimum wage to be more efficient than the tax adjustment is for the budget constraint to be negative, that is, for expenditures (in tax reductions or subsidies) to exceed revenues (in tax increases). We can write this condition as $h_2\hat{T}_2 + h_1\hat{T}_1 < 0$. Plugging in the appropriate expressions, we can write the condition as:

$$h_2(w_2^* - \bar{w}_2) - h_1[q(\bar{w}_1)(\bar{w}_1 - w_1^*) - (q(w_1^*) - q(\bar{w}_1))(w^* - b)] < 0.$$

In this expression, $h_1 = h_1^S$, $q(\bar{w}_1) = h_1^D(\bar{w}_1)/h_1^S$, and $q(w_1^*) - q(\bar{w}_1) = (h_1^D(w_1^*) - h_1^D(\bar{w}_1))/h_1^S$. In addition, from equation (6.9) we know that $h_2(w_2^* - \bar{w}_2) = h_1^D(\bar{w}_1)(\bar{w}_1 + M(\bar{p}) - w_1^* - M(p^*))$. With these two facts the condition can be simplified to:

$$h_1^D(\bar{w}_1)\left[M(\bar{p}) - M(p^*)\right] + (h_1^D(w_1^*) - h_1^D(\bar{w}_1))(w^* - b) < 0.$$

This form expresses the condition in terms of the minimum wage's two main effects: the reduction of monitoring costs, specified in $M(\bar{p}) - M(p^*)$, and the costs of unemployment, captured by the term $(h_1^D(w_1^*) - h_1^D(\bar{w}_1))(w^* - b)$. As specified above, p is decreasing in w and by assumption M is increasing in p. Therefore, $\bar{w}_1 > w_1^* \Rightarrow \bar{p} < p^*$ and $M(\bar{p}) - M(p^*) < 0$. On the other hand, $(h_1^D(w_1^*) - h_1^D(\bar{w}_1))(w^* - b) > 0$. Hence, the condition will be satisfied, and the minimum wage will be more redistributively efficient than taxes, when $h_1^D(\bar{w}_1)[M(p^*) - M(\bar{p})] > (h_1^D(w_1^*) - h_1^D(\bar{w}_1))(w^* - b)$.

This is a possible outcome, for the following reasons. The minimum wage's effect on labor demand, $h_1^D(w_1^*) - h_1^D(\bar{w}_1)$, is given by equation (6.2). As seen in that equation, the marginal effect on labor demand, $\partial F/\partial h_1$, depends on the total costs of wages and monitoring: $w_1 + M(p)$. We also know from equation (6.8), the firm's monitoring choice, that wages and monitoring are substitutes. Indeed, as already shown, for a dollar increase in wages above the firm's most preferred level, monitoring costs are reduced by no more than one dollar. At the limit, a dollar increase in wages leads to a dollar reduction in monitoring costs. At that limit, from the firm's labor demand function, a dollar increase in wages causes no loss in employment. In other words, at that limit $M(p^*) - M(\bar{p}) = 1$ and $h_1^D(w_1^*) - h_1^D(\bar{w}_1) = 0$, which would satisfy the condition for the minimum wage to redistribute more efficiently than taxes. More generally, the larger the difference $M(p^*) - M(\bar{p})$ for a given wage increase, the smaller the loss in employment $h_1^D(w_1^*) - h_1^D(\bar{w}_1)$.

Value of a Minimum Wage with a Rawlsian Social Welfare Function

In Lee and Saez's (2008) model, the minimum wage only has policy value when an "intermediate" social welfare function places some weight on the working poor. Because the working poor are not the least well off, their welfare receives some weight only under such a social welfare function. By contrast, if the social welfare function is a Rawlsian one, the working poor receive no weight, and the combined wage-subsidy-wage-floor policy has no value.

Contrary to Lee and Saez, the previous subsection demonstrates that the minimum wage can have redistributive value even under a Rawlsian social welfare that places no weight on the welfare of low-wage workers. The condition that the minimum wage redistribute more efficienctly than taxes, namely $h_1^D(\bar{w}_1)[M(p^*) - M(\bar{p})] > (h_1^D(w_1^*) - h_1^D(\bar{w}_1))(w^* - b)$, holds whether or not low-wage workers are taxed or receive a subsidy. Therefore, if low-wage workers receive no positive social-welfare weight, and are taxed, it can still be social-welfare maximizing to implement the minimum wage. The basic intuition is that the minimum wage, by taking advantage of the cost-saving productivity benefits, can increase the efficiency of transfers to the least well off.

Wage Subsidy without a Minimum Wage

Very briefly, this section concludes by showing that the preceding rationale for the minimum wage is strengthened when the minimum wage is entirely eliminated. Without a minimum-wage floor set at efficiency, a distribution-neutral tax adjustment (whether tax reduction or subsidy increase) triggers an incidence effect that pushes low-skilled wages below their efficient level. As in Lee and Saez (2012), this allows employers to capture part of the wage subsidy intended for workers and increases the costs of tax redistribution. In addition, this incidence effect induces additional distortions in supervision costs.

Because of the incidence effect of the increased transfer (or tax reduction), the subsidy pushes low-skilled wages below their efficient level. Label this wage $\tilde{w}_1$ and note that $w_1^* > \tilde{w}_1$. Lower wages will of course increase demand for low-skilled labor: $h_1^D(\tilde{w}_1) > h_1^D(w_1^*)$. From the wage-monitoring curve in equation (6.6), the fall in the wage also implies $\tilde{p} > p^*$ and therefore $M(\tilde{p}) > M(p^*)$. Moreover, given the convexity of the wage-monitoring curve and monitoring costs, it is also the case that $M(\tilde{p}) - M(p^*) > M(\bar{p}) - M(p^*)$.

All other features are the same, and so the condition for the distribution-neutral tax reform to be less efficient than the minimum can be written as:

$$h_1^D(\bar{w}_1)\left[M(\bar{p}) - M(\tilde{p})\right] + (h_1^D(\tilde{w}_1) - h_1^D(\bar{w}_1))(\tilde{w}_1 - b) < 0.$$

There are three differences to pay attention to. First, more revenue is saved by increasing employment, $h_1^D(\tilde{w}_1) - h_1^D(\bar{w}_1)$, which makes the condition less likely to be satisfied. However, two other differences go in the opposite direction, making the condition more likely to be satisfied. The second difference is that the costs of monitoring, $M(\bar{p}) - M(\tilde{p})$, are also higher – significantly so, given the convexity already identified. And the third is that the difference $\tilde{w}_1 - b$ is smaller than the equivalent expression in the previous condition, $w^* - b$, which points to the greater government expenditures needed to offset the wage-subsidy's incidence effect and make low-skilled workers' expected utility equal to that with the minimum wage.

7

Antitrust

Writing at the dawn of the Internet age, Microsoft founder Bill Gates saw a bright future for competitive capitalism. Until then, markets had not achieved Adam Smith's vision of perfect competition because "would-be buyers and would-be sellers hardly ever have complete information" (Gates, Myhrvold, and Rinearson 1995, 180). However, the Internet would burst these constraints. According to Gates, "The Internet will extend the electronic marketplace and become the ultimate go-between, the universal middleman" (158). Unlike the stereotypical middleman, the Internet would be a benign one. Buyers and sellers will have an array of options and prices at their fingertips, provided by an Internet with low costs. Gates continued, "We'll find ourselves in a new world of low-friction, low-overhead capitalism, in which market information will be plentiful and transaction costs low. It will be a shopper's heaven" (158).

To say that things have not gone exactly as Gates predicted would be an understatement. Perhaps the most critical miscalculation is that idea that, by lowering the costs of information and transactions, the Internet would increase competition. Instead, lower transaction costs allow some retailers to sell in every market, at prices cheaper than local, "brick and mortar" sellers, and expand their scope enormously. Instead of more competition, the Internet has brought less competition and more monopolization.

Consider the digital behemoth Amazon. Many analysts were initially skeptical about Amazon's future success. Yet today, "nobody seriously doubts that Amazon is anything but the titan of twenty-first century commerce" (Khan 2016, 712). According to a trenchant exposé by Lina Khan (2016), who as of this writing is currently chair of the Federal Trade Commission, Amazon had captured nearly half (46 percent) of online retail by 2015 and had expanded its services far beyond its original debut in the mid-1990s as "Earth's Biggest Bookstore." Khan (2016, 713) wrote, "In addition to being a retailer, it is a marketing platform, a delivery and logistics network, a payment service, a credit lender, an auction house, a major book publisher, a producer of television and films, a fashion designer, a hardware manufacturer, and a leading provider of cloud server space and computing power."[1]

Khan titled her article "Amazon's Antitrust Paradox," both a reference to Robert Bork's famous book *The Antitrust Paradox* and to Amazon's own specific antitrust paradox. Bork helped generate a dramatic rethinking of antitrust policy by focusing solely on the consumer: Is the business practice being advanced harmful to the individual consumer, or not? Amazon's paradox is that despite its huge share of online retail, its strategy has been largely pro-consumer. Amazon slashes prices, gives away free shipping, and plows most of its revenues into expansion and new investments. These decisions all favor consumers' short-term interests in cheap goods. Thus the paradox: How can practices that are so good for consumers also be bad for the economy?

Khan resolves this paradox by demonstrating that there are indeed some troubling longer-term and structural concerns about Amazon's strategy. Its cutthroat pricing puts competitors – everyone from the mom and pop corner bookstore to the once-powerful Barnes and Noble – under threat of bankruptcy. Its size gives it negotiating power to strong-arm suppliers and vendors. Precisely as a result of the revolution in antitrust policy that Bork helped create, "antitrust law now assesses competition largely with an eye to the short-term interests of consumers, not producers or the health of the market as a whole; antitrust doctrine views low consumer prices, alone, to be evidence of sound competition" (Khan 2016, 716). As President Biden's chair of the FTC, Khan has tried to go beyond Bork's narrow focus on consumer welfare and restore a broader view of antitrust policy. It has not been easy going (Kang 2023).

Besides Amazon's own paradox there is the other paradox of digital capitalism, alluded to earlier. Indeed, the biggest paradox of twenty-first century capitalism is that the technology that was supposed to bring us a perfectly competitive "Friction-Free Capitalism" (Gates, Myhrvold, and Rinearson 1995, 157) has instead facilitated the further centralization and concentration of capital. And, of course, this new technology is not just confined to the FAANGs (Facebook, Apple, Amazon, Netflix, Google). According to John E. Kwoka (2017, 6) "Over the past 20 years, major sectors of the U.S. economy have undergone sweeping consolidation, from airlines to brewing, cable television to drug companies, eyeglasses to finance, and grocery stores to hospitals to industrial chemicals – nearly the entire alphabet of industries in the United States." Economists Grullon, Larkin, and Michaely (2019) find empirical evidence for this. Their research reports that since the late 1990s, over 75 percent of US industries have become more concentrated. They also find that firms in industries with the largest increases in product market concentration show higher profit margins and more profitable mergers and acquisitions deals. Despite those mergers,

[1] Since Khan's article, Amazon has continued to expand its portfolio, acquiring the grocery and health foods supermarket Whole Foods and the film studio MGM as well as many smaller companies, and diversifying its own businesses, from cloud computing to an online pharmacy.

which are often justified in terms of lowering operating costs, they find no evidence for a significant improvement in operational efficiency (2–3). Monopolization in turn has contributed to income inequality, specifically by causing wage stagnation. Wage stagnation refers to the problem of wages not keeping pace with the growth of economic productivity. Deb et al. (2022) examine the effects of both monopsony, where firms use their market power to pay lower wages to workers, and monopoly, which lowers wages through another channel: Charging higher prices to consumers lowers demand for the firm's product, which in turn lowers output and weakens the demand for labor, and thus lowers wages. Using firm-level data from the US Census Bureau between 1997 and 2016, they find evidence that both monopsony and monopoly contribute to wage stagnation, but with monopoly being the primary determinant. They find that monopoly accounts for 75 percent of wage stagnation and monopsony for 25 percent (2183).

* * *

Because of rising income inequality, and its link to the growth of monopoly, antitrust policy has moved from a place of arid, technocratic policy analysis back to the center of politics, where trust-busting politicians such as Theodore Roosevelt once staked and built their political legacies. Monopoly can be a tricky issue when viewed from a distributive perspective. After all, as we will discuss further, monopoly not only contributes to inequality but is also inefficient. For more traditionalists, such as Kaplow and Shavell, therefore, the redistributive case for antitrust is inapposite. If monopoly is inefficient, antitrust policy should oppose it on those grounds alone; any favorable distributive effects are incidental. But the double-distortion claim goes further: If a merger of two companies is accompanied by efficiency gains (for example, eliminating redundancies in the industry or increasing economies of scale), it should be allowed even where it results in a larger enterprise with greater market power.

It is the burden of this chapter to demonstrate the opposite. The chapter will show that some efficient mergers should be opposed on distributive grounds. More generally, antitrust policy should sometimes sacrifice efficiency for the sake of income equality. Section 7.1 begins with a diagnosis of the problem of monopoly and market power. For economists, the primary problem of monopoly is inefficiency. Thus, while monopolization and market power may also raise income inequality, this concern is secondary from an economists' perspective. From that view, recent public concern about monopoly is misplaced. That sets up a challenge to a distributive perspective on antitrust that I will resolve later in the chapter.

Following this, Section 7.2 then reviews current antitrust scholars' and policymakers' thinking about market power. This thinking is defined by Robert Bork's influential reorienting of antitrust policy in terms of a "consumer welfare" standard. The controversy over this standard, both in theory and judicial practice, is whether it implements an efficiency standard ("total welfare") or rather is meant to protect consumers, including in non-welfare ways. I argue that none of the prevailing standards or interpretations are very helpful if one prefers a direct, unqualified distributive orientation toward antitrust law, at least one expressed in terms of welfare economics.

The third section of the chapter, Section 7.3, examines the double-distortion approach to antitrust law. The double-distortion provides an even clearer and stronger case against using antitrust law for distributive goals. The reasoning should by now be familiar: Legal rules, including antitrust law, redistribute income less efficiently than the tax system; therefore, antitrust policy should favor legal rules that maximize wealth ("total welfare" in terms of antitrust policy debates) and leave distributive concerns to the tax system.

Finally, Section 7.4 shows why and when antitrust law can and should be used to redistribute income. In this argument, Kaplow's (2008) method of using distribution-neutral income tax adjustments as a way to evaluate policy, including antitrust law, acquires particular importance. I will argue that Kaplow's (2021) more recent conclusion, that antitrust policy should favor efficiency, is open to two objections. The first is a problem of interpretation. Using his method of distribution-neutral income from Kaplow (2008), Kaplow (2021, 332, 351) concludes that antitrust policy should be guided by efficiency, rather than distributive, concerns. But, in a spirit closer to Kaplow and Shavell (1994), one can interpret these distribution-neutral methods as showing, not that antitrust law should pursue efficiency, but that antitrust law can sometimes redistribute more efficiently than the income tax. The second problem is a special assumption Kaplow makes to ensure that the distribution of monopoly profits affects individuals' labor supply in the same way as earned income. Once that special assumption is dropped, there is no particular warrant for the argument that antitrust should pursue efficiency (under any interpretation of efficiency or standard of evaluation) rather than distributive concerns.

7.1 MONOPOLY: WHAT'S THE PROBLEM?

From the perspective of mainstream economics, and law and economics, the overriding problem of monopoly and oligopoly is inefficiency. Monopoly – and, more generally, oligopoly – represent a form of market power, one of the canonical departures from the ideal state of a perfectly competitive market. When actors – including firms, businesses, and corporations – have market power they are price-*makers* rather than price-*takers*. They can influence prices to benefit themselves, at the expense of other actors in the market, mainly and ultimately consumers, but also suppliers and vendors, among others. According to economists, this is not just a transfer of wealth from consumers to producers, but an overall loss of wealth to society. Monopoly is inefficient.

How does this work? In a perfectly competitive market, where neither buyer nor seller can influence the price of a good or service, any attempt by a business to raise its prices will simply send consumers elsewhere. This is a bad decision for the company. Because consumers can get equally good services or products from other companies offering the competitive price, the would-be price hiker is left with no buyers – and therefore no revenues and no profits. The rational decision for the producer is to offer its goods at the competitive price, one that is beyond the influence or control of any single actor (buyer or seller) in the market. The competitive price is determined by the price that "clears" the market, that is, the price that equalizes the amount supplied and the amount demanded so that there is neither unwanted supply or unmet demand.

Markets, however, might not always be perfectly competitive. In some markets, participants might have market power. We will focus on sellers having market power, though it is also possible for buyers to have market power, too – for example, firms with market power can influence wages in their guise as buyers of labor. One possible source of market power is when there is only one or few buyers or sellers in the market relative to the other side of the market. When there is one seller we have a *monopoly*; with few sellers, an *oligopoly* (a single buyer and few buyers are a *monopsony* and an *oligopsony*, respectively). In the case of a monopoly, for example, there is literally no one else consumers may buy from. This means the seller has the power to choose whatever price it wants. If the business cares only about how much money it makes, it will opt for the price that maximizes its profits. Now, because some buyers will not be willing to pay for the good as the price rises, the business will lose customers the moment it begins increasing the price. The firm therefore makes a trade-off: A higher price means more revenue (and more profit) per unit sold, but also fewer units sold. The firm will choose the price that balances this trade-off and maximizes its profit.

The critical result here is that fewer goods are sold. From an economic perspective, this is inefficient, because output is lower than it would be in a competitive market. There is indeed also a *transfer* of wealth – from those consumers who continue to purchase the good at the higher price. This transfer is equal to the difference between the competitive price and the monopoly price times the number of goods sold in the monopolistic market. But there are also consumers who do not pay for the good at all because they are only willing to purchase at a price lower than the monopoly price. Put another way, monopolists cannot capture surplus from every single customer who would have bought the good at its competitive price because some of these consumers drop out of the market. This is called *deadweight loss*. Hence, market power causes both a transfer of wealth as well as a loss of wealth.

Economists tend to focus on this deadweight loss – the inefficiency – as *the* problem of monopoly. But monopoly typically increases inequality as well, and this occurs through the wealth transfer. An increase in monopoly will raise inequality whenever the owners of the firms with market power are on average richer than consumers who purchase goods or services from them. Consumers are made poorer, because the price of the good is higher, which makes their real incomes lower.[2]

[2] As Deb et al. (2022) point out, monopoly power can also depress wages: Falling consumer demand for the higher-priced product lowers the firm's demand for labor, which depresses wages.

On the other side, firm owners' incomes rise with higher prices and profits. Because owners are more concentrated than consumers, the increased profits from market power offset the deadweight loss *for owners*. Of course, if the firms with market power are public companies and their shares distributed equally in society, then the existence of market power would just make everyone poorer, without exacerbating inequality. But this is certainly not the case. According to data from the Federal Reserve, in the third quarter of 2023, the top 1 percent owned 53.7 percent of corporate equities, directly or indirectly (Board of Governors of the Federal Reserve System (US) 2023b), while those in the 90th to 99th percentiles owned 39.2 percent (Board of Governors of the Federal Reserve System (US) 2023a). Combined, the top 10 percent directly or indirectly now own, as of this writing, 92.9 percent of corporate equities.[3] What goes for stock ownership generally almost certainly holds for the ownership of stock in monopolistic firms. Market power therefore not only reduces efficiency, but it increases inequality as well.

The inequality generated by monopolistic practices has therefore become at least as big a problem – certainly in the public's mind and in politics – as the problem of inefficiency. According to Wu (2019), "Excessive corporate size and power can be linked to many voter concerns, including stagnant wages, the invasion of privacy, the rise of fake news, the demise of the middle class and an unresponsive democracy."

7.2 ROBERT BORK, THE "CONSUMER WELFARE" STANDARD, AND CURRENT ANTITRUST POLICY

This section examines current antitrust law, policy, and scholarship, which is oriented around the concept of "consumer welfare," thanks to Robert Bork's fundamental reorientation of the field. There are at least two issues with the "consumer welfare" concept. The first is about what "consumer welfare" means, as well as the implications of that meaning. On the one hand, scholars remain divided on this issue. For some, consumer welfare is a synonym for consumer surplus, which we will define shortly. For others, consumer welfare means not just consumer surplus, but total surplus – the sum of consumer and producer surplus – which itself is just a synonym for efficiency. On the other hand, courts appear to employ a more settled meaning. Nevertheless, that meaning is restricted to the impact of alleged anticompetitive practices on consumers (arguably closer to the idea of consumer surplus), which, as hinted at in our earlier discussion, forecloses inquiry into larger questions about monopoly (e.g., Khan 2016). Second, and more fundamentally, the dispute about the meaning of consumer welfare cannot be settled without raising

[3] Corporate equity ownership was already highly concentrated in 1995, but has become more so in the roughly thirty years since. In 1995, the top 1 percent of those in the wealth distribution owned 51.4 percent of corporate stock (either directly or indirectly through mutual funds), and the top 10 percent owned 88.4 percent of corporate equity (Wolff 1998, 139, 140 tbl. 6).

larger questions about what the proper goals of antitrust should be. By addressing this second issue, I hope to show that none of the alternatives about the meaning of consumer welfare adequately incorporate a concern about income distribution, as conceived by a proper social-welfare analysis.

The scholarship on antitrust law has been racked by an interminable debate, starting with Robert Bork's controversial but highly successful reinterpretation of antitrust law through the lens of mainstream microeconomic analysis.[4] Viewing antitrust law at the time as hopelessly confused, Bork (1967, 242) argued that "existing statutes can be legitimately interpreted only according to the canons of consumer welfare" (quoted in Orbach (2010, 134)). He also contended that "[c]onsumer welfare is the only legitimate goal of antitrust, not because antitrust is economics, but because it is law" (Bork (1967, 244); quoted in Orbach (2010, 134–35)). The confusion begins here, because while Bork in context meant efficiency or "allocative efficiency," he instead used the term "consumer welfare." Consequently, the only consensus appears to be that there is no consensus on the meaning of "consumer welfare." For example, Salop (2010) acknowledges the "confusion that has resulted from Judge Robert Bork's usage of the term 'consumer welfare' in referring to aggregate welfare" (336). Orbach (2010) agrees, and "chronicles how academic confusion and thoughtless judicial borrowing led to the rise of a label ['consumer welfare'] that 30 years later has no clear meaning" (134). Finally, Stucke (2012) sums it up this way: "In 1987, one scholar remarked that the terms efficiency and consumer welfare 'have become the dominant terms of antitrust discourse without any clear consensus as to what they exactly mean' and that consumer welfare 'is the most abused term in modern antitrust analysis.' This remains true today" (571).

One reason Bork's invocation of the term "consumer welfare" to mean efficiency has produced intractable debate is because "consumer welfare" has a more limited meaning than efficiency within economic analysis. "Consumer welfare" can also be rendered "pure consumer welfare" or "consumer surplus." Efficiency on the other hand, might be rendered "total surplus" or "aggregate economic welfare." As the names suggest, consumer welfare rendered as consumer surplus would measure the effect of a potentially anti-competitive business practice on consumers only, and exclude that of producers. A total surplus approach, on the other hand, would measure the impact on both consumers and producers. It is indeed possible that Bork was confused about this distinction or that, even more probable, he believed that an enhancement in efficiency would always work in consumers' favor and vice versa. Indeed, Oliver Williamson (1968), one of the winners of the 2009 Nobel Prize in economics (along with Elinor Ostrom), famously wrote a response to Bork's

4 Orbach (2010, 135): "Bork is not a man of consensus. His analysis of the goals of antitrust laws is no exception: His views were fiercely debated by antitrust scholars and practitioners throughout the 1960s, 1970s, and early 1980s. The Supreme Court, however, quickly adopted Bork's 'consumer welfare prescription,' making it the stated law of the land."

argument precisely to refute that assumption. Williamson showed that, for example, the merger of two companies could raise efficiency but *reduce* consumer welfare.

The possibility that an efficient merger, as Williamson showed, could harm consumers also reveals that the difference between total and consumer surplus has rather significant policy implications. As Salop (2010) explains, "The aggregate economic welfare standard would condemn conduct only if it decreases the sum of the welfare of consumers (i.e., buyers) *plus producers* (i.e., sellers plus competitors); and *without regard to any wealth transfers*. … In contrast, the true consumer welfare standard would condemn conduct if it reduces the welfare of buyers, irrespective of its impact on sellers" (336; emphasis in original). For example, suppose a merger lowered the costs of production because a single factory had enough capacity to produce as much as two, separately owned factories; or, that the merger lowered advertising costs by eliminating a rival. As long as these costs were sufficient to raise the selling firm's profits by more than the aggregate harm to consumers, then the merger would be justified by the total surplus standard, regardless of the fact that consumers are worse off after the merger. In contrast, under the consumer surplus standard, this merger would fail because consumers would be worse off even though total or aggregate surplus is raised. This does not mean that the consumer surplus standard, which Salop calls the "true consumer welfare standard," is opposed to efficiency. Rather, "[e]fficiency counts under the true consumer welfare standard," says Salop, "but only if there is evidence that enough of the efficiency benefits pass through to consumers so that consumers (i.e., the buyers) would directly benefit on balance from the conduct" (336–37). As Orbach (2010) concludes, Bork ended the debate about the goals of antitrust, but started a debate about the meaning of "consumer welfare."

There appears to be only slightly more consensus on the standard that courts apply in practice. In 1979, soon after the publication of Bork's *The Antitrust Paradox* in 1978, the Supreme Court in *Reiter v. Sonotone Corp.*, quoting Bork's book, declared that "Congress designed the Sherman Act as a 'consumer welfare prescription.'"[5] Five years later, in *National Collegiate Athletic Association v. Board of Regents of University of Oklahoma*, the Supreme Court again approvingly quoted Bork's conclusion that the US antitrust laws were enacted as a "consumer welfare prescription."[6] In its decision in that case, the Court stated that "restraint that has the effect of reducing the importance of consumer preference in setting price and output is not consistent with this fundamental goal of antitrust law."[7] In Orbach's (2010, 150) interpretation of this statement, "the Court essentially held that antitrust law does not permit promoting efficiency while sacrificing consumer interests." Later,

5 Reiter v. Sonotone Corp., 442 U.S. 330, 343 (1979).
6 National Collegiate Athletic Ass'n v. Board of Regents of University of Oklahoma, 468 U.S. 85, 107 (1984).
7 *Id.*

in subsequent cases like *Brooke Group Ltd. v. Brown & Williamson Tobacco Corp.*[8] and *Weyerhaeuser Co. v. Ross-Simmons Hardwood Lumber Co.*,[9] the Supreme Court implicitly acknowledged the difference between consumer welfare and total welfare, or efficiency, and again concluded in favor of consumer welfare (150).[10] Orbach concludes that "the Court appears to believe that the 'consumer welfare' standard is about consumers, rather than about efficiency" (Orbach 2010, 150). In addition to the Supreme Court, "many courts and the federal enforcement agencies appear to have opted for the true consumer welfare standard" (Salop 2010, 339). Thus, there appears to be some consensus among courts and agencies that "consumer welfare" resembles something like consumer surplus, rather than efficiency or total surplus. However, some scholars dispute even that level of consensus. As Stucke (2012) says, "Some U.S. courts say that the 'reduction of competition does not invoke the Sherman Act until it harms consumer welfare.' This is nonsense. Courts have not arrived at a shared, specific definition of consumer welfare. Even if they did, courts cannot value, consistent with the rule of law, how much competition can be reduced before harming consumer welfare" (574).[11]

Whatever the degree of consensus among the courts, there is no doubt that Bork's consumer welfare interpretation fundamentally reoriented antitrust policy, which itself has had an outsized impact on the economy. Bork's emphasis dramatically narrowed the range of concerns that, according to some scholars, were part of Congress's original antitrust objectives (Khan 2016). For instance, Lande (1982) identified "[t]hese [alternative] goals [to] include promotion of small business and creation of entrepreneurial opportunity, encouragement of local control over business, prevention of industrial concentration, and the reduction of the political influence of large firms and promotion of individual liberty" (69). Lande has been a persistent critic of the efficiency or consumer welfare paradigm, and has insisted on a more capacious vision for antitrust. Most importantly for our discussion, Lande has argued that Congress passed the Sherman Act "to further economic objectives, but primarily objectives of a distributive rather than of an efficiency nature" (68). (As we will soon see, Lande has a special notion of distribution.) Averitt and Lande (2007) have also argued in favor of a "consumer choice" interpretation of the antitrust laws.

8 Brooke Group Ltd. v. Brown & Williamson Tobacco Corp., 509 U.S. 209 (1993).

9 Weyerhaeuser Co. v. Ross-Simmons Hardwood Lumber Co., 549 U.S. 312 (2007).

10 According to Orbach (2010, 150), both cases were about unsuccessful predatory pricing schemes, a business practice which may be socially undesirable, or inefficient, but may also be a benefit to consumers because of lower prices. As the Court in *Brooke Group* explained, "Recoupment is the ultimate object of an unlawful predatory pricing scheme; it is the means by which a predator profits from predation. Without it, predatory pricing produces lower aggregate prices in the market, and consumer welfare is enhanced. Although unsuccessful predatory pricing may encourage some inefficient substitution toward the product being sold at less than its cost, unsuccessful predation is in general a boon to consumers." 509 U.S. 209, 224.

11 Quoting Metro Indus., Inc. v. Sammi Corp., 82 F.3d 839, 848 (9th Cir. 1996) (quoting Rebel Oil Co. v. Atl. Richfield Co., 51 F.3d 1421, 1433 (9th Cir. 1995)) and citing several other cases.

Prior to the Borkean revolution in antitrust, courts also appeared to embrace a mix of economic and politico-economic goals for antitrust (Wright and Ginsburg 2012, 2405–07). For Bork (1978, 7), however, this mix of goals was part of the problem, for it produced "a policy at war with itself." "Coherence" is therefore often cited as one of the supposed benefits of elevating consumer welfare to pride of place within antitrust law (Wright and Ginsburg 2012, 2406).

Defenders of the consumer surplus, rather than total surplus (or efficiency), interpretation of the consumer welfare standard have sought to marshal it in favor of egalitarian objectives. For example, Lande (1982; 1989) always describes as distributive what is, for him, the central objective of antitrust law, which is to prohibit wealth transfers from consumers to producers. However, as Lande admits, that objective does not address the broader goal of intentionally shaping the overall distribution of income. Rather, it is more similar to the law's general prohibition on theft. For instance, Lande (1982) writes

> It should be stressed, however, that Congress did not pass the antitrust laws to secure the "fair" overall distribution of wealth in our economy or even to help the poor. Congress merely wanted to prevent one transfer of wealth that it considered inequitable, and to promote the distribution of wealth that competitive markets would bring (70)

Salop (2010) follows Lande in endorsing this limited redistributive interpretation of antitrust law. Salop explains that "the adoption of the consumer welfare standard does not mean that courts are using antitrust as a mechanism to redistribute wealth" (350). Rather, the consumer welfare standard has the more limited aim of preventing the redistribution of wealth *away* from consumers. Echoing the theft intuition as well as the apparently baseline "just" distribution of outcome generated by the market, Salop also writes, "Antitrust law instead involves giving consumers a property right in the competitive outcome" (350–51).

With growing concerns about income inequality and monopolization, we are entitled to question the narrow economic focus on consumer welfare. Indeed, in light of those concerns, the purportedly clarifying justification for consumer welfare looks pathologically single-minded. As we saw in the case of Amazon, an obsession with consumer welfare – price – has allowed other disturbing dimensions of Amazon's business practices to get overlooked (such as, for example, its relationship to vendors and suppliers, other competitors, and the "health of the market as a whole" (Khan 2016, 716)). And as already noted, Kwoka (2017) and other scholars have documented an increasing trend of industry consolidation in the years since the "Borkean revolution." Growing monopolization is in turn associated with wage stagnation and rising income inequality (Deb et al. 2022). Stucke (2012) scathingly assesses the current status of antitrust law and policy. "The quest in the United States for a single economic goal was a failure. ...The quest distanced antitrust from important policy issues (such as systemic risk) and rendered antitrust less relevant. Consequently, now is the time to reconsider antitrust's political, social, and moral concerns. In reconsidering the goals of competition as a means to secure political, economic, and individual freedoms, antitrust can be more responsive to citizens' concerns about promoting well-being" (624). Whether income inequality is one of those goals is an issue we turn to next.

7.3 ANTITRUST AND INCOME INEQUALITY

As Section 7.2 demonstrated, antitrust policy and scholarship is oriented around the "consumer welfare" standard. This section asks about the prospects for a more ambitious egalitarian role for antitrust law. We therefore move beyond antitrust law as it is presently applied by administrative agencies and the courts. Instead we will look at antitrust law exclusively from a welfare-economics perspective and ask whether it should be used to redistribute income – to, as Lande (1982, 70) expressed it earlier, "secure the 'fair' overall distribution of wealth in our economy." Thus, whether current antitrust law and statutes allow for a broader egalitarian role for antitrust is secondary to my concerns; if some competition-law scholars believe and argue that antitrust law should be concerned solely with maximizing wealth, or efficiency, it seems only fair to consider the alternative.

There are two existing objections against using antitrust law to redistribute income. The first is the "imprecision" argument; the second is the double-distortion argument. This section addresses each in turn.

7.3.1 *The Imprecision Objection to Redistributive Antitrust*

The imprecision argument against using antitrust law with distributive objectives is straightforward. Antitrust law redistributes from producers to consumers, but these categories only crudely map onto rich and poor, respectively. Some consumers are quite rich so that, to the extent that we are benefiting consumers, we are actually benefiting the rich as well as (or even rather than) the poor. Given this incongruity, it would be better to use the tax-and-transfer system to address the problem of income inequality. This is *especially* so in light of the choice of standards on offer. For instance, a "consumer welfare" standard that is equated with "consumer surplus" will disregard any producer surplus in the proposed change. In so doing, it could block mergers that increase efficiency (or, total surplus). Why not allow the efficient merger and then use the tax-and-transfer system to remedy any increase in income inequality? The objection, simply put, is that antitrust law is too blunt an instrument to use for ameliorating income inequality (see, for example Cooter and Ulen 2016, 8).

Before offering my own response to the imprecision objection, it will be instructive to see how other scholars have responded to it. Scholars such as Lande and Salop, who have sought to marshal a pro-consumer case from the existing consumer welfare standard, are well aware of the imprecision objection. Lande (1982) puts the objection as follows: "It should be noted that wealth redistribution caused by monopolies does not always transfer wealth from poor consumers to rich stockholders. Monopolized products almost always will be purchased by at least some consumers who are richer than at least some stockholders" (74 n.37) Nevertheless, the position taken by Lande and Salop is relatively immune to the imprecision objection. As Lande observes in response, "[T]he legislators passing these laws were concerned with preventing transfers from consumers to monopolists and did not premise these statutes on redistribution from rich to poor" (74 n.37).[12] Thus, whether antitrust law on balance shifts income from rich to poor, and not just from producers to consumers, is not really a problem for Lande's and Salop's antitrust position. In their view, antitrust law is meant to protect the distribution of income generated by a truly *competitive* market – to prevent transfers from consumers to producers rather than to facilitate transfers from rich to poor. The evaluation of the overall distribution of income is a different concern, and perhaps one best left to the tax system.

Lande's and Salop's answer to the imprecision objection may be successful on its own terms, but it obviously does not meet the complaint if one wants to use antitrust law to shape the overall distribution of income – to reduce income inequality between rich and poor, not just prevent theft-like transfers from consumers to producers. It is instructive to question Lande's and Salop's own antitrust premises. As we have already shown, Lande and Salop are more concerned about preventing a kind of theft. But, then, we have to ask: Why oppose theft? Why view the competitive market outcome as the consumer's property entitlement? Lande and Salop defend the consumer welfare standard on the grounds that antitrust law is intended to prevent wealth transfers from consumers to producers and to protect the distribution of wealth generated by the competitive market. Those may be satisfying answers to some, but for the more single-minded economist they simply beg the question. Why should we prevent theft? Why should the distribution of income generated by the competitive marketplace be protected? At least for an economist, the answer must be because preventing theft or protecting competition (and its distribution of income) is efficient. But, then, if efficiency is the goal, that would appear to weaken the case for a consumer welfare standard, which can produce inefficient outcomes. If efficiency is genuinely the aim, we should adopt the total welfare standard, which maximizes total wealth. The kind of argument developed by Kaplow and Shavell (1994) provides a challenging reason for this: Even if consumers are harmed under a total welfare standard, (1) there is no compelling efficiency argument for why consumers should be entitled to specific protection; and (2) to the extent consumers are poor or are made poorer, the tax system can correct for these deficiencies.

[12] Lande (1982) also notes that, "[o]n balance," the overlap between consumers and the poor is tight enough that the "redistributive effects of the antitrust laws would seem to favor the poor" (74 n.37). As discussed further below, even critics concede that antitrust laws benefit the poor as an empirical matter, and notwithstanding the imprecision objection.

Fortunately, there is another answer to the imprecision objection if one wants to use antitrust to redistribute income, rather than just to prevent producers from stealing from consumers. The gist of this answer is that the imprecision claim is one-sided. Whether a legal rule or policy, antitrust included, is imprecise, crude, or blunt is secondary. What matters is whether the value of redistribution, great or small, precise or imprecise, as measured by a given social welfare function, is worth its cost.

Consider this claim in the antitrust context. Surely, some consumers are rich, but it is almost certainly the case that in the aggregate monopoly increases income inequality. The effect may not be as strong as a "pure" redistributive transfer based solely on income, but this is not really the point. In fact, comparing the redistributive value, or "punch," of tax with that of antitrust is to compare apples and oranges. Specifically, evaluating the relative merits of tax and antitrust in terms of their precision is to compare the marginal benefits of *different* redistributive instruments without comparing their *corresponding* marginal costs. All that is said in this comparison is that the marginal benefit of a redistributive tax policy is larger than the marginal benefit of our antitrust policy. But, from an economics perspective, this is, at best, an incomplete, and, at worst, an ill-formed comparison.

Suppose for example that blocking a merger that would monopolize an industry has only a faint impact on income inequality; if permitted, the merger would raise income inequality only modestly. This could be because, for example, there is only a weak overlap between the rich and producers, on one hand, and the poor and consumers, on the other. Alternatively, we could drastically change the tax schedule and enact a much more substantial redistribution of income. Is the tax choice a better policy? Not obviously, because we have said nothing about the costs of either policy. If, say, the smaller cost of producing the good, post-merger, is effectively nil while the more dramatic tax change has substantial labor-supply or business-investment distortions, it is even less obvious that the tax plan is a clear winner. What really matters is whether the imprecise distributive benefits of blocking the merger outweigh the very small higher pre-merger product costs. Likewise, whether the dramatic change to the tax schedule raises welfare more than the economic distortions it causes is a separate and independent question. Only then does the comparison become meaningful.

Thus, evaluating different redistributive policies requires equating the marginal benefits and marginal costs of a given policy or decision, not comparing the marginal benefits of different policy choices. What we really need to know is whether the marginal benefit of a redistributive antitrust policy – however imprecise or "crude" (Cooter and Ulen 2016, 8) it is – is greater than its marginal cost. Even more precisely, it would make sense to compare the marginal benefits of taxation and antitrust *only if* the marginal cost of the antitrust and the tax policies were equal. Only then would comparing marginal benefits exclusively be meaningful. So the correct question is: Is the marginal benefit of our antitrust policy larger than or equal to its marginal cost?

To continue with the previous example, if the modestly lower, and "imprecise," level of income inequality before the merger was valued more (that is, by a social welfare function) than the lower production cost from merger efficiencies, then the merger should be blocked. Likewise if the tax-schedule change causes distortions in labor-supply or investment decisions that outweigh the comparatively larger (social-welfare measured) reduction in inequality, then the tax plan should be discarded. The redistributive value of each policy is evaluated independently of each other, by their costs, not their comparative value.

In fact, to its credit, this is what makes the double-distortion argument so effective. The double-distortion argument avoids the apples-and-oranges error made by the imprecision argument. Instead, the double-distortion argument essentially equates (hypothetically) the marginal benefit of both the tax and the legal redistribution (in this case, antitrust), and then argues that the marginal cost of the legal redistribution will always be greater. Because we are *equating* the marginal benefits of the two policy choices, the comparison, unlike the imprecision argument, focuses exclusively – and meaningfully – on the marginal cost. Note also that by equating the marginal benefit of each policy, the double-distortion side-steps the imprecision argument. It effectively assumes that whatever the redistributive "punch" of the legal policy or its imprecision, we can always come up with a tax schedule that is just as good in terms of distribution. Nevertheless, as we will see in Section 7.3.2, there is no reason to think that the marginal costs of antitrust policy will be greater than taxation, and this is where the double-distortion argument stumbles.

7.3.2 *The Double-Distortion Objection to Redistributive Antitrust*

If we want to use antitrust law for stronger redistributive goals, and are not convinced by the imprecision objection against doing so, we still have to address the double-distortion argument. This section focuses precisely on that objection.[13] Kaplow's (2012) specific argument against redistributive antitrust follows identically the logic of the claim laid out elsewhere. That claim is that "one can make all income groups better off by removing any redistribution through competition law (achieved by deviating from the maximization of total welfare) and substituting a similar degree of redistribution through the tax and transfer system" (Kaplow 2012, 10). Kaplow elaborates, "The fundamental reason is that indirect redistribution, to the extent

[13] It is surprising that there has not been a more extensive conversation between antitrust and double-distortion scholars. The most explicit discussions of the relevance of the double-distortion argument for the distributive effects of antitrust law are found in Kaplow (2012) and Kaplow (2021). In addition to outlining the double-distortion argument against redistributive antitrust, Kaplow (2012) also discusses the "imprecision," or what he terms the "targeting," argument. Interestingly, he concedes that, despite the "imprecision" associated with redistributing to consumers (rather than the poor), "it remains true that the distribution of producer surplus is significantly more favorable to the very wealthy and not very favorable at all to the lower half of the income distribution relative to the distribution of consumer surplus" (9).

that it is successful, distorts labor supply to the same degree as would accomplishing that amount of redistribution through the tax and transfer system" (12). Thus, using antitrust law to redistribute income would distort labor supply incentives just as much as tax policy, without any offsetting benefit that would make it more desirable than tax policy.

Defenders of the consumer surplus version of the consumer welfare standard have also responded to the the double-distortion claim. That response is again based on the notion that antitrust law should *prevent* transfers of wealth from consumers to producers, rather than attempt to shape the overall distribution of income. Thus, Salop asserts that antitrust law can prevent redistribution from consumers to producers more efficiently than the tax system can "neutralize" those same transfers over time. As Salop (2010, 351) explains, "The redistribution away from consumers is automatically dealt with by adoption of the true consumer welfare standard. That impact is not so difficult to gauge; and, the conduct of firms to prevent that redistribution also can be observed." Once again, as effective as this response is on its own terms, it obviously does not meet the double-distortion objection if we want to use antitrust law in a more thoroughgoing redistributive fashion.

We can easily enough analyze a redistributive antitrust policy in terms of taxes and transfers, as Kaplow (2012) does. A redistributive antitrust policy is one that would reduce producer surplus, setting aside the imprecision argument for the time being and assuming that producers and the rich are identical (an assumption Kaplow adopts as well). Simultaneously, this policy would raise consumer surplus where, likewise, we treat consumers and the poor as identical. The former effect – reducing producer surplus – would be equivalent to a tax on producers (or the rich); the latter would essentially be a transfer to consumers (or the poor). Kaplow asserts that "the result is tantamount to raising taxes on the rich to increase transfers to the poor. And, if that is the consequence, then we have the same distorting effect on labor supply" (12). Moreover, given that the redistributive antitrust policy distorts labor supply incentives in exactly the same way as a distribution-equivalent tax-and-transfer policy, Kaplow says the antitrust policy "is necessarily inferior" because "to accomplish additional redistribution, it was necessary to deviate from the maximization of total welfare" (13). In other words, if we are choosing antitrust policies that do not maximize total surplus but instead favor consumers (the poor) over producers (the rich), we are necessarily choosing policies where the increase in consumer surplus is less than the fall in producer surplus. Therefore, using antitrust policies to redistribute income causes a double distortion: "Society suffers from the inefficiency cost from redistribution per se *and also* the further inefficiency cost due to inefficient competition law outcomes" (13, emphasis in original).

Kaplow illustrates this argument with a simple example. To further clarify his claim, and my own subsequent view, and to avoid any misrepresentation of his claim, I reproduce the example in full:

> To illustrate, compare two competition law rules in the following setting. One rule (which aims to maximize total welfare) produces an outcome with consumer surplus of 10 and producer surplus of 10, for total welfare of 20. The other rule (which aims to maximize consumer welfare) produces an outcome with consumer surplus of 12 and producer surplus of 2, for total welfare of 14. Further suppose that producer surplus goes primarily to the very wealthy, so that the latter outcome seems superior on distributive grounds.
>
> Suppose we start with the second rule, aimed at consumer welfare. Let us consider substituting the first rule, aimed at total welfare, combined with an increase in explicit redistribution. To be concrete, suppose that we tax an additional five from the rich (perhaps through a higher profits [tax] or [a higher] corporate tax) and distribute an additional 5 to consumers (through a VAT reduction). The net effect on consumers is that they have only 10 rather than 12 in consumer surplus due to the change in the competition law rule, for a loss of 2, but they also gain by 5 from the tax reduction. In sum, consumers have a net gain of 3. Producers (really, their owners and ultimate beneficiaries) have producer surplus of 10 rather than 2, for a gain of 8, but pay more in taxes of 5. In sum, producers also have a net gain of 3. Therefore, both groups are better off as a consequence of moving to a competition law regime aimed at maximizing total welfare rather than consumer welfare, accompanied by a redistributive adjustment to the tax and transfer system (Kaplow 2012, 13–14).

It is important to point out in this example that Kaplow excludes labor-supply effects. This is evident because the only redistributive policy instruments contemplated are corporate and profit taxes, levied on producers, and sales taxes (the VAT) levied on consumers; there are no income taxes mentioned. Omitting labor supply and income taxation raises problems for the claim that legal rules should favor efficiency over distribution, as Section 7.4.1 demonstrates. Labor supply reappears in Kaplow's (2021) more recent work, which is critically analyzed in Section 7.4.2.

To help facilitate discussion, Kaplow's example is expressed in Table 7.1. Thus, under the first competition rule, which initially appears less redistributive than the second, consumers ultimately receive a welfare of 15 once taxes are factored in (higher than the 12 they receive under the second rule) while the rich obtain a welfare of five. Hence, the poor are better off under the first rule (plus taxes) compared to the second rule by three welfare points; meanwhile, the rich are better off by three welfare points. Overall then, Kaplow believes that a competition rule that maximizes total welfare or surplus (Rule 1) is superior to a rule aimed at maximizing consumer surplus (Rule 2). Although Rule 2 does increase consumer surplus compared to Rule 1, adopting Rule 1 and using the tax system to transfer five from producers (the rich) to consumers (the poor) yields an even more favorable outcome for the poor, precisely because it is more efficient.[14]

[14] There are a few oddities with Kaplow's example that are worth clarifying but do not make any difference to his main point. For example, presumably the rich also obtain income from other sources, which makes them wealthier than the poor, despite the fact that net producer welfare under the competition rule is 5, lower than the 15 going to consumers. Or, perhaps

TABLE 7.1 *Kaplow's antitrust example*

	Rule 1	Rule 2	Rule 1 + Taxes
Producers	10	2	5
Consumers	10	12	15
Total	20	14	20

There is nothing logically wrong with Kaplow's example. The idea that taxes can compensate for a competition policy that increases inequality, but also efficiency, is certainly a plausible scenario. But as will be illustrated in Section 7.4, Kaplow's example is primarily chosen to confirm the double-distortion argument. Nevertheless, it fails to generalize, and does not seal the case that competition law should be chosen to maximize wealth – or, total welfare in the antitrust sense – and eschew redistributive objectives.

More recently, Kaplow (2021) has taken an even closer look at antitrust policy. This article examines market power formally and in more detail, considering a number of subsidiary but important issues. Nevertheless, he arrives at the same basic conclusion: "The overall result is to leave largely intact some standard competition policy prescriptions that ignore distribution, labor supply distortion, and income taxation, and also to preserve familiar formulations for the optimal degree of redistributive income taxation that are predicated on models with no market power" (330). In other words, antitrust law should maximize total or general welfare and ignore distributive issues, which are better handled by the income tax system.

7.4 EFFICIENT REDISTRIBUTION THROUGH ANTITRUST

This section will now argue that antitrust law can be used for redistributive purposes. That is, not only should antitrust law be used to prevent illicit transfers from consumers to producers, but it should also be used to shape the overall distribution of income. The double-distortion argument does not defeat this claim. Contrary to that argument, antitrust law should sometimes sacrifice efficiency for the sake of distribution because (and when) these redistributive objectives can be accomplished more efficiently – or less inefficiently – than the tax system.

This section will approach this claim through two different perspectives. The first perspective stays within the framework of producer and consumer surplus, working

these numbers reflect total wealth by group, rather than per capita income. In addition, it also appears, counterfactually, that there is no loss in wealth from redistributive taxation. In the first rule with taxes, total welfare remains the same at 20; five is transferred from the rich to the poor without any loss in wealth. Perhaps Kaplow is applying his customary method of a distribution-neutral income tax adjustment, which holds labor supply constant and therefore negates the role of distortionary taxes. This method is more closely examined in Section 7.4.2.

with Kaplow's (2012) chapter on competition law and the example reproduced in Table 7.1. The second perspective "disaggregrates" consumer and producer surplus into individual-level utilities of rich and poor, using Kaplow's (2021) article on market power which relies on his distinctive method of distribution-neutral income tax adjustments (Kaplow 2008).

7.4.1 *Using Antitrust to Redistribute Income*

In general, the reason that antitrust law *can* be used to redistribute income more efficiently than taxes is that there is no a piori association between prima facie anticompetitive behaviors and efficiency, as Williamson (1968) recognized long ago. Thus, if a given competition policy tends to raise income inequality but have no or only marginally small positive effects on overall efficiency the redistributive costs of abandoning the policy may be smaller than the costs of taxation.

Consider merger policy, for instance. Antitrust administrators review mergers, rather than peremptorily blocking all of them, because of a belief that some mergers, despite their anticompetitive effects, may also produce efficiencies (such as greater economies of scale) (Hovenkamp 2016). This ambiguity is possible because potentially anticompetitive behaviors can have effects that move in opposite directions. Hence the need for merger review: We are not sure a priori whether mergers will increase or reduce efficiency.[15] Given that uncertainty, there is no reason why blocking a merger because of its inegalitarian consequences should always be more inefficient than taxes or not inefficient at all. There must be intermediate cases where blocking the merger is inefficient as a matter of total wealth but less inefficient than taxes as a matter of redistribution.

To illustrate this claim, consider the following two-step argument that uses Kaplow's (2012) model of producer and consumer surplus that was depicted in Table 7.1. To summarize the argument at the outset, suppose in step one that permitting a merger increases income inequality, by transferring surplus from consumers to producers, but results in the same total, consumer and producer, surplus (before any adjustments in corporate and sales taxes). This could be because the merger reduces competition and raises prices (leading to a transfer of surplus) but also generates production efficiencies because the merger creates greater economies of scale (keeping total surplus the same). Because the merger is efficiency neutral, it immediately follows that the merger should be blocked for distributive reasons. This is *necessarily* so because either blocking or permitting the merger yields the same

[15] Given the renewed concerns about monopolization and inequality, one is entitled to think that merger policy gives the presumption in favor of efficiency unjustifiable weight. Hovenkamp (2016, 705) observes that "[r]ecent empirical literature suggests that merger policy today is under deterrent." But even with those renewed concerns, we are unlikely to witness a new policy in favor of a total ban on mergers because the possibility of an efficient merger cannot be ruled out, even if they are less likely than previously imagined. Hence, the ambiguity remains.

amount of total (producer and consumer) surplus; any tax response to the merger's inequality increase must then lower total surplus. By that logic, in step two, there must be mergers that *marginally* raise efficiency, as well as inequality, before taxes are adjusted; but that are still overall less efficient and less equal even after taxes are adjusted, even optimally. That outcome simply depends on whether the merger's effect on efficiency is small enough and its effect on inequality is large enough. If so, blocking the merger is the social-welfare maximizing choice. Thus, sometimes legal rules may sacrifice efficiency for equality, and do so less inefficiently than taxes.

This two-step argument is illustrated in the following two tables. Table 7.2 reconstructs the case of an efficiency-neutral, but inequality-increasing, merger. Let us say that under the first rule (or, when a merger is permitted) consumer surplus is 10 and producer surplus is 10, for a total welfare of 20, just as in Kaplow's example. However, under the second rule (or, when a merger is blocked), let us suppose that consumer surplus is 15 and producer surplus is 5, also for a total welfare of 20. As we have argued, there is nothing implausible about this second scenario. It simply recognizes the efficiency trade-offs in antitrust law illustrated by Williamson (1968): Mergers may both enhance and reduce efficiency.

It necessarily follows that the second rule is better than the first on equitable, as well as social-welfare grounds. One might be tempted to argue that we can simply increase corporate taxes and reduce sales taxes (or increase subsidies) under the first rule and obtain an identical distribution of welfare as under the second rule. This proposal would tax five from the rich producers, leaving them with a net welfare of five, and transfer that same amount to the poor consumers, leaving them with a net welfare of 15. However, this option is *not* displayed in Table 7.2, because we can only make this argument if we assume that increased taxation has zero distortionary effects, which is clearly an impermissible claim, even by the double-distortion argument's own standards (Kaplow and Shavell 1994). Hence, a more plausible scenario is the case displayed in the rightmost column of Table 7.2. In that scenario, labeled Rule 1 + Taxes, suppose that the optimal-tax adjustment, in conjunction with the first rule, taxes four from the rich, for a net six. Also suppose that this tax transfers two to the poor, for a net 12. This delivers a total welfare of 18 with an implicit loss through tax distortions of two. Clearly, allowing the merger and compensating with taxes would be inferior to blocking the merger under any social welfare function because that choice provides both lower inequality and greater wealth.

TABLE 7.2 *Efficiency-neutral but inequality-increasing merger*

	Rule 1	Rule 2	Rule 1 + Taxes
Producers	10	5	6
Consumers	10	15	12
Total	20	20	18

Assuming that pre- and post-merger total welfare are identical is a useful benchmark. If total wealth is the same but inequality is higher under one rule compared to another, the rule that produces lower inequality is *necessarily* superior even when the optimal tax response is available to correct the other rule's higher inequality. Step two of the argument generalizes the claim. After all, mergers are unlikely to always be neutral with respect to efficiency. Furthermore, Kaplow is concerned not with competition policies that are indifferent to efficiency, but with *redistributive competition policies that fail to maximize efficiency*. So, let us now assume that blocking the merger still has pro-consumer welfare effects but that total surplus is now reduced, albeit by a loss that is arbitrarily small. Compared to permitting the merger, which gives higher total surplus, blocking the merger is now inefficient. Should the merger still be blocked, or should it now be permitted? The answer is that as long as the welfare loss associated with blocking the merger is less than the welfare loss associated with the optimal tax when permitting the merger, the merger should be blocked. When those conditions obtain, merger policy redistributes income less inefficiently than the tax system. Furthermore, these conditions are plausible because, as we have already established in step one, an efficiency-neutral outcome is also plausible. A fortiori, a blocked merger that only slightly reduces wealth is just as plausible as a blocked merger that makes no difference to total wealth, holding fixed any tax adjustments.

To illustrate the possibility that inefficient competition policy can still redistribute more efficiently than taxes, let us examine another example, displayed in Table 7.3. As in the previous example, suppose again that permitting the merger – Rule 1 – gives consumer welfare of 10 and producer welfare of 10, and total welfare of 20. However, now suppose that if the merger is blocked – Rule 2 – consumer welfare is 15, but producer welfare is four, for a total welfare of 19. In other words, the second rule is inefficient, and gives lower total wealth that the first rule. Should the merger be blocked or permitted? This depends on the wealth lost caused by the optimal tax response to the inequality-increasing merger. Assume again, as in the previous example (Table 7.2) that the optimal tax following the merger taxes four from the rich, for a net six, and transfers two to the poor, for a net 12. The tax distortions cause a loss of two and deliver a total welfare of 18. In this case, using an inefficient legal rule to block the merger still dominates permitting the merger with an optimal-tax

TABLE 7.3 *Efficiency- and inequality-increasing merger*

	Rule 1	Rule 2	Rule 1 + Taxes
Producers	10	4	6
Consumers	10	15	12
Total	20	19	18

adjustment. Clearly, Rule 2, which blocks the merger, is superior to Rule 1 coupled with the tax adjustment. Not only does Rule 2 give lower income inequality (15 for the poor and five for the rich, compared to 12 and six under the tax-adjusted second rule) but total wealth remains higher as well (19 compared to 18). Any pro-redistributive social welfare function would favor blocking, rather than permitting, the merger than permit it, *even though allowing the merger maximizes wealth*. The result contradicts Kaplow and Shavell's (1994) claim: legal rules, even inefficient legal rules, can redistribute more efficiently than taxes.

Of course, blocking a merger may reduce total wealth more than the optimal tax response to permitting the merger, as shown in Kaplow's original example in Table 7.1. In that case, the policy advice is straightforward, and the merger should be approved. Like merger policy, which makes no a priori judgment that mergers will always be good or bad, our approach to legal-rule distribution should be the same. If permitting the merger with an optimal-tax adjustment raises social welfare, it should be permitted. Conversely if the merger, even with the optimal-tax adjustment, lowers social welfare, it should be blocked. At the end of the day, the point is that even inefficient legal rules may redistribute income more efficiently – or, less inefficiently – than the tax system. We therefore reject Kaplow's (2012, 13; emphasis added) conclusion that "indirect redistribution through competition law [compared to] direct redistribution through the income tax and transfer system, ...is *necessarily* inferior."

7.4.2 *Evaluating Antitrust Policy with Distribution-Neutral Income Tax Adjustments*

Section 7.4.1's argument generalizes straightforwardly as long as the concepts of efficiency, or total wealth or total welfare, include labor-supply effects. That is, antitrust policies that fail to maximize total efficiency may sometimes be chosen because they redistribute income less inefficiently than taxes.

However, this conclusion *appears* to contrast with Kaplow's (2021) most recent statement regarding the distributive role of antitrust law. In that article, Kaplow endorses a policy prescription that "calls for the maximization of consumer plus producer surplus, regardless of the distributive effects of the reform" (Kaplow 2021, 332). This conclusion seems to hew to the traditional double-distortion reasoning that antitrust policy should ignore distributive consequences and focus only on efficiency – the maximization of consumer and producer surplus. Unlike his previous contribution (Kaplow 2012), which was silent on the issue of labor supply and focused on producer and consumer surplus, Kaplow's (2021) more recent contribution explicitly considers labor-supply effects and uses his method of "distribution-neutral income tax adjustments" to analyze them (see Kaplow 2004; 2008, as well as the book's appendix, for further discussion of this method).

This section contests Kaplow's most recent contribution from two angles. On the first angle, I show that Kaplow's conclusion rests on a contestable matter of interpreting his distribution-neutral income tax adjustments. What Kaplow presents as policy conclusions dictated exclusively by (truncated definitions of) efficiency are, when viewed more contextually, decisions about when legal rules versus taxes redistribute income more efficiently. On the second angle, I critically examine Kaplow's (2021, 334–35) assumption that capital income is solely a function of labor income. When that assumption is relaxed, taxes will not have distributionally equivalent labor-supply effects as antitrust rules. In that case, the efficiency judgments, such as they are, of distribution-neutral income tax adjustments do not apply, and we will want to choose antitrust policies that fail not just to maximize overall efficiency, as on the first angle, but that also *fail to maximize the sum of producer and consumer surplus*. That conclusion is not a matter of interpretation but directly contradicts Kaplow's (2021, 332) claim.

Interpreting Distribution-Neutral Income Tax Adjustments

In his most recent discussion of antitrust law, Kaplow (2021), as mentioned above, continues to endorse the double-distortion argument – or, at least, he appears to. He even writes, "This efficiency test, which sums allocative and productive efficiency – equivalently, consumer and producer surplus – applies regardless of the distributive consequences …" (351). Kaplow bases this conclusion on his method of distribution-neutral income tax adjustments. This is roughly the same method that Kaplow and Shavell (1994) use to argue that legal rules redistribute income less efficiently than the income tax. Kaplow elaborates this method further in Kaplow (2004) and Kaplow (2008), but a subtle shift takes place. In essence, although he does not say so, Kaplow no longer denies that legal rules should be used for redistribution. Instead, he argues that we should choose policies that are efficient *independent of their distributive and labor-supply effects*. This truncated definition of efficiency is close (but may not be identical) to what Liscow (2014, 2483) refers to as "i-efficient legal rules": a definition of efficiency that is "internal-to-legal-rule" and "ignores the tax system, imperfect private insurance, any desire to redistribute, and social welfare maximization." Similarly, Kaplow's "efficiency test" is one that ignores the distributive, additional wealth, and labor-supply effects that the underlying policy would otherwise generate.

The question is this: Is Kaplow's distribution-neutral method an efficiency test, or a *redistribtive* efficiency test? This is why I argue in this subsection that Kaplow's seeming pro-efficiency conclusion for antitrust rests on a matter of interpretation. The better interpretation is that distribution-neutral income tax adjustments determine when legal rules or the income tax redistributes more efficiently, not that one should always choose efficient legal rules or policies. Put this way, it should also be obvious that my interpretation preserves the spirit of Kaplow and Shavell's (1994) original use of distribution-neutral income tax adjustments.

The following discussion uses two examples to illustrate the preferred interpretation. In both examples, a proposed merger would raise efficiency in the broad sense, that is, when distributional and labor-supply effects are included. However, the first merger lowers total – consumer plus producer – surplus while the second merger raises total surplus. Accordingly, on Kaplow's judgment the first merger should be blocked but the second permitted, based exclusively on the idea – *using distribution-neutral income tax adjustments* – that the first lowers the sum of consumer and producer surplus while the second raises it. But blocking the first merger also fails to maximize total, overall efficiency, which suggests that something other than applying "first-best" efficiency principles is going on. Instead, I argue that the policy outcomes are determined by which policy is most *redistributively* efficient. In other words, legal rule and policy choice can be justified on distributive grounds.

Consider the following example, where antitrust officials are trying to determine whether to approve a proposed merger. Table 7.4 represents a hypothetical comparing consumer and producer surplus before and after a merger. The numbers are chosen solely to illustrate the qualitative claims about when antitrust law should be used to redistribute income. No weight should be given to the numbers' quantitative significance. In this scenario, there are five firms in the market. Two firms wish to merge and everyone anticipates that this consolidation, which will lower unit production costs, will drive another firm out of the market. The merger will therefore reduce the number of competing firms to three. Table 7.4 lists the consequences of a monopolistic competition model in terms of the total quantity of the good produced, the price, aggregate profits, consumer welfare, and total welfare (producer surplus and consumer surplus). One should also think about these numbers in per-capita terms, which will aid in the next stage of the analysis.

There are a few crucial observations contained in Table 7.4. As the table shows, the merger has production efficiencies: It lowers unit production costs, z, from 7 to 6.93. This could be, for example, because the merger allows the two companies to consolidate and expand production in fewer factories or facilities, which increases economies of scale. However, the merger also has anti-competitive effects (in other words, it has allocative inefficiencies). Thus, the total quantity, Q, of the good produced falls from 2.5 to 2.3025. The combined effect of these productive efficiencies and allocative inefficiencies is a redistribution of surplus from consumers to producers. Thus, consumer surplus, v, falls from 3.125 to 2.6508 while producer surplus, Π, climbs from 1.25 to 1.7672. Finally, Table 7.4 shows that the merger lowers

TABLE 7.4 *Merger lowers consumer and producer surplus*

	n	z	Q	p	Π	v	W
pre-merger	5	7	2.5	7.5	1.25	3.125	**4.375**
post-merger	3	6.946	2.2905	7.7095	1.7488	2.6232	**4.372**

Notes: n = number of firms, z = unit production cost, Q = total quantity, p = price, $\Pi = n \cdot \pi$ = producer surplus, v = consumer surplus, W = total surplus.

total (consumer plus producer) surplus (*W*). Pre-merger total welfare is 4.375; post-merger total welfare is 4.372.

On Kaplow's grounds, the merger depicted in Table 7.4 should be rejected for lowering the sum of consumer and producer surplus. However, this evaluation ignores the labor-supply responses of the merger's distributive effects. Do we make the same judgment when those responses are also considered? To answer this question, consider Table 7.5, which examines the same proposed merger, but from the perspective of individual welfare rather than producer and consumer surplus. Individuals' utility is affected by their consumption of the good (consumer surplus), but they may also own shares of the firms' stock. Table 7.5 reports the results of a model that includes income from labor, income from capital (share ownership), taxes, overall utility, and labor supply. These numbers are presented in per-capita terms. Three income groups are considered (rich, middle class, and poor) and to simplify the distributive dimension of the problem, suppose that only the rich own shares. The last two columns in Table 7.5 list respectively group-level (per capita) welfare ($h_i \cdot u_i$) and the revenues and expenditures of a distribution-neutral income tax adjustment ($h_i \cdot \hat{T}_i$).

Unlike the consumer-and-producer-surplus table (Table 7.4), the individual welfare table (Table 7.5) says the merger should be approved if we include labor-supply effects, and not just the sum of consumer and producer surplus, in our efficiency evaluation. Because of the unequal distribution of firm ownership, the net effect of the merger raises inequality. However, the increase in inequality also increases net labor-supply incentives. This makes sense: Just as an increase in marginal tax rates is predicted to lower labor supply, because by reducing inequality it discourages work, an increase in inequality increases labor supply. As a result, the merger *increases* total welfare, inclusive of labor supply responses as well as consumer and producer surplus. In the second-to-last column on the right in Table 7.5, pre-merger total welfare is 18.1454; post-merger welfare is 18.1496. This contradicts the evaluation in the prior table, Table 7.4, which evaluates the merger based only on consumer and producer surplus. Excluding labor-supply responses, the merger is considered inefficient and should be blocked. Including labor-supply responses, the merger is considered efficient and should be approved.

If we are judging, as Kaplow wants us to, on efficiency grounds, comparing Tables 7.4 and 7.5 reveals that including labor-supply effects changes that judgment. I will now argue that the merger should be blocked, not because it is inefficient – as we have just shown, that judgment depends on how we define efficiency – but because it redistributes income more efficiently than taxes. The rightmost column in Table 7.5 lists a distribution-neutral income tax adjustment. This adjustment is the taxes raised (on the rich, group 2) and the transfers spent (on the middle class and poor, groups 1 and 0) required to offset the distributive effects of the merger. This income-tax adjustment achieves the same level of utility – and, consequently, the same level of labor supply – as in the pre-merger scenario. (Hence, these tax adjustments,

TABLE 7.5 *DNITA evaluation of surplus-inefficient merger*

	i	w_i	σ_i	T_i	h_i	u_i	$h_i \cdot u_i$	$h_i \cdot \hat{T}_i$
	2	25	5.3261	5	0.2347	28.4511	6.6773	n.a.
pre-merger	1	15	0	2	0.6563	16.125	10.5820	n.a.
	0	0	0	−5	0.1091	8.125	0.8861	n.a.
total welfare							**18.1454**	
	2	25	7.4363	5	0.2352	30.0595	7.0691	0.3810
post-merger	1	15	0	2	0.6563	15.6232	10.2527	−0.3293
	0	0	0	−5	0.1086	7.6232	0.8277	−0.0547
total welfare							**18.1496**	
budget								**−0.0030**

Notes: DNITA = distribution-neutral income tax adjustment; i = group type, where 2 = rich, 1 = middle class, and 0 = poor; w_i = labor income; σ_i = capital income; T_i = taxes or transfers; h_i = labor supply (as population percentage); u_i = utility (comprising labor and capital income, taxes, and consumer surplus from Table 7.4); $h_i \cdot u_i$ = population weighted utility, $h_i \cdot \hat{T}_i$ = distribution-neutral tax adjustment.

measured by a change $\hat{T}_i$ are weighted by the *pre-merger* labor supply responses, h_i, in order to calculate the total budgetary effect.) Because labor-supply effects are negated, only the consumer and producer surplus effects of the merger remain. Not surprisingly then, the budget deficient (−0.0030) is exactly equal to the welfare difference recorded in the previous table, Table 7.4 (4.3720 − 4.3750 = −0.0030). This is what drives Kaplow's interpretation: The distribution-neutral income tax adjustment eliminates the labor-supply and distributional effects of the merger, allowing us to evaluate it solely in terms of consumer and producer surplus. However, there is another way of looking at the result. The budget deficient indicates that allowing the merger, and attempting to replicate the pre-merger distribution of income with the income tax, is too costly. Thus we can best preserve the pre-merger distribution of income by preventing the merger. Legal rules, and the policy of merger review, can be efficiently used for distributive purposes.

To underscore this distributional interpretation, consider the next example in Table 7.6. There is really only one crucial difference between the first consumer-and-producer-surplus table (Table 7.4) and this second. This is that the second merger has larger productive efficiencies than the second. In the second, the unit product cost, z, drops from 7 to 6.93 (rather than 6.946). Ultimately, the difference means that the merger raises consumer and producer surplus. Thus, while this merger still results in a restriction of output, an increase in prices, and an increase in inequality (that is, producer surplus increases and consumer surplus decreases), its aggregate effect is to raise the sum of consumer and producer surplus.

Following Kaplow's policy rule, this second merger should be permitted because it raises the sum of consumer and producer surplus, even though it does so unequally

TABLE 7.6 *Merger raises consumer and producer surplus*

	n	z	Q	p	Π	v	W
pre-merger	5	7	2.5	7.5	1.25	3.125	**4.375**
post-merger	3	6.93	2.3025	7.6975	1.7672	2.6508	**4.418**

Notes: n = number of firms, z = unit production cost, Q = total quantity, p = price, $\Pi = n \cdot \pi$ = producer surplus, v = consumer surplus, W = total surplus.

TABLE 7.7 *DNITA evaluation of a surplus-efficient merger*

	i	w_i	σ_i	T_i	h_i	u_i	$h_i \cdot u_i$	$h_i \cdot \hat{T}_i$
	2	25	5.3261	5	0.2347	28.4511	6.6773	n.a.
pre-merger	1	15	0	2	0.6563	16.125	10.5820	n.a.
	0	0	0	−5	0.1091	8.125	0.8861	n.a.
total welfare							**18.1454**	
	2	25	7.5138	5	0.2352	30.0595	7.0943	0.4059
post-merger	1	15	0	2	0.6563	15.6232	10.2527	−0.3112
	0	0	0	−5	0.1086	7.6232	0.8277	−0.0517
total welfare							**18.1957**	
budget								**0.0429**

Notes: DNITA = distribution-neutral income tax adjustment; i = group type, where 2 = rich, 1 = middle class, and 0 = poor; w_i = labor income; σ_i = capital income; T_i = taxes or transfers; h_i = labor supply (as population percentage); u_i = utility (comprising labor and capital income, taxes, and consumer surplus from Table 7.6); $h_i \cdot u_i$ = population weighted utility, $h_i \cdot \hat{T}_i$ = distribution-neutral tax adjustment.

(raising producer surplus while lowering consumer surplus). But before we are satisfied with following that prescription, let us use Table 7.7 to take a closer look at the labor-supply effects of the merger. Once again, the transfer of surplus from consumers to producers translates into higher utility for the rich (share earnings increase) while reducing the utility of the middle class and poor (prices increase and consumer surplus decreases). That leads to a net increase in labor-supply and an overall increase in welfare, for the same reasons as in the previous case. In the case of the second merger, welfare increases from 18.1454 to 18.1957. However, the crucial difference is that the balanced budget evaluation of the distribution-neutral income tax adjustment now yields a surplus, rather than a deficit. The budget surplus is 0.0429 which, again because the distribution-neutral tax adjustment eliminates the labor-supply effect of the merger, is exactly equal to the difference in pre- and post-merger total (consumer and producer) surplus.

Unlike Kaplow's interpretation, which says that antitrust policy should be chosen to maximize the sum of consumer and producer surplus, regardless of the distributive consequences, Table 7.7 suggests a different interpretation. The merger should be permitted because, although it increases inequality, the productive efficiencies (lower production costs) sufficiently outweigh the allocative inefficiencies (less competition and output, higher prices) such that the income tax system can maintain the pre-merger distribution of income more efficiently than blocking the merger. Thus, in both mergers, overall efficiency (which includes labor-supply effects) dictates permitting both mergers. Yet we block the first and permit the second. Why? Kaplow says that we should do so because each case maximizes the sum of consumer and producer surplus. But why choose that truncated measure of efficiency rather than the overall measure that includes labor supply? Obviously not for efficiency reasons because that interpretation comes down to the arbitrary choice of the efficiency measure. Rather, we block the first and permit the second precisely because of distributive implications. In the first case, taxes cannot preserve the pre-merger distribution of income more efficiently than blocking the merger – even though allowing the merger would maximize overall efficiency. That is, blocking the merger in the first case can only be justified because of its distributional effects. In the second case, taxes can preserve the pre-merger income distribution more efficiently than blocking the merger. Even though the second merger maximizes efficiency on either measure, the reason for permitting it is still distributional: In this case taxes redistribute more efficiently than legal rules.

This interpretation of distribution-neutral income tax adjustments is more in keeping with the original comparison of taxes and legal rules in Kaplow and Shavell (1994). That is, distribution-neutral income tax adjustments do not direct us to choose efficient legal rules and policies. Rather, they direct us to choose *redistributively* efficient legal rules and policies. Admittedly, this is difficult to see in the antitrust case, because that prescription happens to reduce to a familiar rule of efficiency: maximizing the sum of consumer and producer surplus. But if we were to accept Kaplow's bald efficiency interpretation of distribution-neutral income tax adjustments, that would require interpreting plainly inefficient policies, like the minimum wage, as efficient (see Chapter 6). In particular, Chapter 6, the labor and employment law chapter, examined the redistributive value of a minimum wage. Using Kaplow's method of distribution-neutral income tax adjustments, that chapter shows that the minimum wage will redistribute more efficiently than taxes when its productivity effect outweighs any loss of employment. Indeed, when using distribution-neutral income tax adjustments, a redistributively efficient minimum wage will also be "efficient," in the same way that an overall inefficient antitrust policy that nevertheless maximizes the sum of consumer and producer surplus is also efficient. But no one would really call the minimum wage efficient in the overall sense. Even a redistributively efficient minimum wage has all of the inefficient features of the typically conceived minimum: excess labor supply, involuntary unemployment, and reduced labor demand. The minimum wage is efficient only in the tautological sense that Kaplow's distribution-neutral income tax adjustment makes it so.

In summary, the results of the examples in Tables 7.4 through 7.7 support the conclusion that antitrust policy should be used to redistribute income, and can do so more efficiently than the income tax. In both cases, total efficiency, including labor supply effects, would be maximized if the merger is permitted. But we should block the first merger and permit the second, and that is only partially driven by the fact that doing so maximizes the sum of consumer and producer surplus in each case. In fact, a distribution-neutral income tax adjustment shows us that blocking the merger in the first case is a more redistributively efficient way to preserve the pre-merger distribution of income than permitting the merger and correcting the resulting inequality with taxes. A similar analysis shows us in the second case that allowing the merger and correcting inequality with taxes is, by contrast, a more redistributively efficient way to preserve the pre-merger distribution of income than blocking it.

Assumptions about Income from Capital and Labor

For those not convinced by the interpretative argument about distribution-neutral income tax adjustments – which is, after all, just the interpretation put forward in Kaplow and Shavell (1994) – Kaplow's antitrust efficiency argument is open to a more serious criticism. This criticism highlights Kaplow's strong assumption that capital income – say, dividends received through ownership of shares in a (monopolistic) firm – is a function of earned income – that is, income that is earned from wages or salaries.[16] This allows Kaplow to assume that changes in capital income have identical effects on labor supply as changes in labor income. More generally, that assumption permits Kaplow to maintain the pervasive hypothesis, inside the antitrust context as well as without, that the income tax is always and everywhere fully equivalent to generating an identical distribution of income, without any different labor-supply effects, as any redistributive legal rule. But that assumption also allows him to avoid the possibility of income (or wealth) effects that may reduce labor supply as a response to higher capital income. Relaxing Kaplow's assumption makes taxes more distortionary than antitrust rules and means that we may want to choose, for distributive reasons, policies that fail, not just to maximize overall efficiency, as in the previous discussion, but that also *fail to maximize the sum of producer and consumer surplus*.

Kaplow adopts the conventional assumptions that earned income, y, is a function of the wage rate, w, and the level of labor effort (for example, hours worked), l, so that $y = wl$. He also accepts the conventional formalization of taxes, where taxes paid are a non-linear function of earned income, $T(y)$, meaning that the tax rate may differ depending on your level of earned income, such as being in a different "tax bracket." So far, so good, but when it comes to income from capital, Kaplow

[16] Income from labor is still often referred to as *earned* income, as distinct from capital income which is thereby thought of, at least by implication, as unearned.

adopts a restrictive assumption that makes the share of profits received by individuals a function of income from labor. Thus, where Π is total, economy-wide profits, he writes $\theta(y)$ as the individual's share of profits, so that individuals receive $\theta(y)\Pi$ as capital income. Kaplow makes no specific assumption about the functional form of $\theta(y)$ (Kaplow 2021, 335). Thus, all individuals could receive the same, equal share of profits[17]; or the profit share could be increasing with income, $\theta'(y) > 0$, so that the distribution of profits would be unequal.[18]

This assumption crucially implies that changes in capital income will have identical labor-supply effects as changes in labor income and taxes. Kaplow says this assumption can be "motivated in a number of ways" (334). He settles on the idea that it reflects a "collapsed dynamic model" (334). For example, think of a model that divides a person's life into two periods, where a person works and consumes in the first period but only consumes in the second period (say, after retirement). Ownership of shares then reflects savings, and as long as savings (that is, second-period consumption) is a normal good – a good for which demand increases when income increases – then individuals who earn more will save more and receive higher shares of profits. (That interpretation does in fact entail that the share of profits increases with income, or $\theta'(y) > 0$.) Thus, capital income indeed "collapses" into labor income and this allows Kaplow to maintain the essential hypothesis, on which the double-distortion argument absolutely depends, namely that changes in the distribution of income through whatever source (legal rules, wages, share ownership, etc.) will have identical labor-supply effects. Thus, distribution-neutral income tax can correct for both changes in income distribution and labor supply, restoring the status quo ante without additional complications or distortions.[19]

[17] Kaplow expresses the possibility of equal shares as $\theta(y) = 1$ for all y, which is confusing because as a share function that would seem to indicate that *everyone* simultaneously receives *all* of the economy's profits.

[18] There is very likely, unsurprisingly, a positive correlation between wage rates and savings propensities (Diamond and Saez 2011, 180). But that is a weaker statement than collapsing capital income into savings from labor earnings (on this, see below). There are other possible sources for the correlation, including reverse causation. For example, children from wealthier families – in the capital-asset ownership sense – will generally have better educational opportunities and consequently higher labor earnings.

[19] I should clarify that Kaplow's assumption is not atypical for an older generation of tax economists. These scholars all share the proclivity to adopt unrealistic models of savings: infinitely lived lives; finite lives with overlapping generations, but no bequests or dynastic linkages; representative-agent models that minimize or eliminate the sources and implications of income inequality; and so forth. These assumptions are part of a larger conversation about whether the optimal tax scheme should tax capital income or not. Earlier wisdom suggested that capital income should not be taxed (Judd 1985; Chamley 1986). One reason that capital income should not be taxed is that it creates a double distortion: Because savings is construed merely as deferred consumption, taxing capital income distorts consumption choices in addition to labor-supply choices (Atkinson and Stiglitz 1976). Recent research increasingly calls the earlier wisdom into question (Diamond and Saez 2011; Gamage 2014, 2015). The realistic complexities this newer research identifies should increase our skepticism that the tax system can cleanly

Contrary to Kaplow, it is far more reasonable to assume that changes in non-labor income, including capital income, will not be functionally equivalent to dollar-equivalent changes in labor income. In fact, it is a basic result in labor economics that an increase in non-labor income will *reduce* labor supply (see, e.g., Borjas 2016).[20] The idea is that when sources of income other than from labor increase, you can raise your utility by increasing both consumption (through the higher income) and leisure (by reducing labor supply). Everyone would love to be able to work less and consume more; increased income from capital or other non-labor sources allows you to do that. But that implication goes against Kaplow's assumption which treats labor and capital income as equivalent.

For example, as we saw in the previous two examples, in Tables 7.5 and 7.7, the merger inequalities caused an increase in labor supply – as would be expected with a distributionally equivalent reduction in taxes. But that was because we assumed (implicitly) along with Kaplow that increases from monopoly-profit income would affect individuals just like an increase in labor income. With a more general labor-supply assumption, we expect the opposite, namely, that an increase in monopoly-profit income will reduce labor supply. Why might this happen? Perhaps ownership shares are inherited or unearned, or capital income is a large enough share of one's budget, or one is close to retirement. In each case, an increase in capital income will lead to reduced labor supply because, respectively, future consumption is not dependent on current labor, the value of additional leisure outweighs the value of increasing labor for future consumption, or earlier retirement is made more feasible. Ultimately, if gains in capital income cause labor supply to decrease, rather than increase, taxes will not be able to restore the status quo ante distribution of income without additional distortions. That in turn may make it redistributively efficient to block a merger that raises the sum of consumer and producer surplus, contrary to Kaplow's hypothesis.[21]

Consider the final table, Table 7.8, where we drop Kaplow's assumption and instead assume that changes in capital income have *no* effect on labor supply. This assumption is a simple way of capturing the heterogeneous effects of capital income on labor supply. Thus, I assume that changes in capital income have mixed effects

offset the problems of market power in ways that preserve Kaplow's (2021) truncated efficiency prescription.

[20] Empirical research usually finds that an increase in wealth, say, from winning a lottery (Cesarini et al. 2017) or a rise in home values (Disney and Gathergood 2018), reduces labor supply.

[21] Kaplow (2021) does suggest that the model can be elaborated to account for capital income effects. For example, he writes, "Taking a dynamic model with savings even further, one could allow for overlapping generations or other intergenerational linkages that feature bequests, in which event investment returns of heirs would arise in part from the labor earnings of prior generations and inheritance taxation would be another relevant policy instrument" (334 n.6). But because elsewhere Kaplow (2008) thinks of bequests like consumer preferences, estate taxation would seem to create additional distortions that would undermine Kaplow's policy prescription.

TABLE 7.8 *DNITA evaluation of a surplus-efficient merger with general labor supply*

	i	w_i	σ_i	T_i	h_i	u_i	$h_i \cdot u_i$	$h_i \cdot \hat{T}_i$
	2	25	5.3571	5	0.2333	28.4821	6.6458	n.a.
pre-merger	1	15	0	2	0.6563	16.125	10.5820	n.a.
	0	0	0	−5	0.1104	8.125	0.8971	n.a.
total welfare							**18.1250**	
	2	25	7.5736	5	0.2333	30.2243	7.0523	0.3500
post-merger	1	15	0	2	0.6563	15.6507	10.2708	−0.3112
	0	0	0	−5	0.1104	7.6507	0.8447	−0.0524
total welfare							**18.1679**	
budget								**−0.0136**

Notes: DNITA = distribution-neutral income tax adjustment; i = group type, where 2 = rich, 1 = middle class, and 0 = poor; w_i = labor income; σ_i = capital income; T_i = taxes or transfers; h_i = labor supply (as population percentage); u_i = utility (comprising labor and capital income, taxes, and consumer surplus from Table 7.4); $h_i \cdot u_i$ = population weighted utility, $h_i \cdot \hat{T}_i$ = distribution-neutral tax adjustment.

on labor-supply that effectively cancel each other out. The example in Table 7.8 is based on the second merger example, given in Table 7.6, where the merger raised the sum of consumer and producer surplus. As Table 7.8 shows, it also raises overall efficiency, labor supply included: Welfare increases from 18.1454 to 18.1957. Thus, on either standard of efficiency, we should approve the merger. However, with weaker assumptions on labor supply, the merger fails a hypothetical distribution-neutral income tax adjustment. Implementing changes to the tax schedule in order to maintain the pre-merger distribution of utilities yields a budget deficit: −0.0136. This deficit results precisely because, with weaker assumptions about labor supply, increased income from monopoly does *not* increase labor supply. The distribution-neutral income tax adjustment therefore only reduces labor supply, rather than preserving it at its pre-merger levels. In other words, changing tax rates to correct for the inequality just makes things worse.

When we relax Kaplow's assumptions about labor-supply, it may therefore be the case that we reject efficient mergers – on either definition of efficiency: overall efficiency, inclusive of labor supply, or the sum of consumer and producer surplus. When efficient mergers increase profits from monopoly and individuals do not respond similarly to changes in capital income as they do to labor income, income taxes cannot work as efficiently as law to redistribute income. Thus, contrary to Kaplow's (2021) policy prescription, for the sake of social welfare and distributive goals, in some cases we should *not* approve mergers that increase efficiency (again, on either measure).

7.5 APPENDIX

The appendix defends this chapter's claims with a formal analysis that is also reproduced in the online appendix. Section 7.5.1 builds a simple but tractable model of product-market oligopoly where firms compete in quantities (a model of so-called Cournot competition). The equilibrium is defined and then the basic trade-off in merger analysis is posed. Section 7.5.2 analyzes how a distribution-neutral income tax adjustment would evaluate the merger question and also why that method can be misleading.

7.5.1 *Model*

Assume that consumers have a simple quasi-linear quadratic utility function given by:

$$u(q) = q_0 + Aq - \frac{1}{2}q^2$$

where q_0 is the numéraire. With consumers having a budget constraint given by $p_0 q_0 + pq = y_i - T_i$ for $i \in \{0, 1, 2\}$, we can set p_0 equal to one, solve for q_0, and substitute into the utility function to get:

$$u(q) = c_i - pq + Aq - \frac{1}{2}q^2. \quad (7.1)$$

Choosing q to maximize $u(q)$ in equation (7.1), we get

$$-p + A - q.$$

Setting this expression equal to zero and solving for q, we get $q = A - p$. Plugging this back into the utility function in equation (7.1), we can write individual utility as:

$$u(q^*) = c_i + \frac{1}{2}(A - p)^2.$$

We can regard

$$v = \frac{1}{2}(A - p)^2 \quad (7.2)$$

as the subutility function for purposes of the consumer welfare or consumer surplus analysis. Aggregating across all consumers, the first-order condition $-p + A - q = 0$ also gives us the following price function:

$$p(Q) = A - Q, \quad (7.3)$$

where $Q = \int_0^n q_i dn$ is total quantity produced by n firms.

Each producer, i, faces a profit function given by:

$$\pi = (p(Q) - z)q_i$$

where z is the unit cost of production, assumed to be equal across firms. Maximizing this expression with respect to q_i leads to the following first-order condition for the profit-maximizing quantity choice:

$$-q_i + A - Q - z_i = 0.$$

In a symmetric equilibrium, $q_i = q_j$ for all $i, j \in n$, so $Q = nq$. Imposing this condition and solving for the individual firm's optimal quantity we get:

$$q^* = \frac{A - z}{n + 1}. \tag{7.4}$$

Summing individual firm quantities, it will be useful to write:

$$Q^* = nq^* = \frac{n}{n + 1}(A - z). \tag{7.5}$$

Substituting this profit-maximizing quantity back into the firm's profit function, we get the firm's equilibrium profits:

$$\pi^* = \left(\frac{A - z}{n + 1}\right)^2. \tag{7.6}$$

Aggregate profit, or producer surplus, is

$$n\pi = \Pi. \tag{7.7}$$

For given primitives of the problem, number of firms n and unit production cost z, one can derive all of the quantities given in Table 7.4 for quantity (equation 7.5), price (equation 7.3), producer surplus (equation 7.7), and consumer surplus (the subutility in equation 7.2). Interpreting producer and consumer surplus in per capita terms, total welfare is simply the sum of producer and consumer surplus.

We can now pose the trade-off faced in merger analysis. Let us suppose that the merger generates production efficiencies so that pre-unit costs of production fall: $z^* > \tilde{z}$, where z^* is the pre-merger production cost and $\tilde{z}$ is the post-merger production cost. However, because the merger also creates consolidation in the industry, it generates an entry cost, F, for all entering firms. This is a "barrier" to entry in McAfee et al.'s (2004) sense: "An economic barrier to entry is a cost that must be incurred by a new entrant and that incumbents do not or have not had to incur" (McAfee, Mialon, and Williams 2004, 463) Suppose further that this cost is sufficiently high that, including the merger of firms, the number of firms after the merger falls: $n^* < \tilde{n}$. Chapter 8, on intellectual property, builds a formal model that explicitly links these variables, showing how lowering production costs, increasing entry costs (via licensing), and fewer firms in competition can all be intrinsically related.

Hence, we have the merger dilemma: The merger increases (productive) efficiency by lowering production costs, but reduces (allocative) efficiency by lowering the number of competing firms. As can be seen in the quantity functions, equations (7.4) and (7.5), lower unit costs tend to increase output and lower prices. Lower unit costs also benefit consumers by lowering prices, as seen in equation (7.3), and benefit producers by increasing profits, as seen in equation (7.6). However, the smaller number of firms has the opposite effect. Also seen in the quantity equation, weaker competition lowers output. Lower output also has clearer distributive effects, because it increases firms' profits at consumers' expense.

Should the antitrust authorities take distributional considerations into account in their merger review policy, or should efficiency be the sole concern? (Note that we can provisionally think of $\tilde{z}$ as the pre-merger state and z^* as the post-merger state, but we need not give this a chronological interpretation, insofar as the antitrust regulators have authority to "break up" a large firm, for example.) We use a distribution-neutral income tax adjustment in Section 7.5.2 to answer these questions.

7.5.2 *Merger Evaluation with Distribution-Neutral Income Tax Adjustments*

Although Kaplow (2021) ultimately endorses the traditional consumer plus producer surplus approach to competition policy, he disaggregates the problem to the individual level in order to address the distributive problems of antitrust. Profits, or producer surplus, are then introduced at the individual level through their ownership of shares in firms. Furthermore, total disposable income is also included in the analysis, as in the utility equation (7.1), not just consumer surplus with respect to the products or industries of the merging firms, as in the subutility equation (7.2). Accordingly, let σ_i be the share of per capita profits going to members of group $i \in \{0, 1, 2\}$, and further assume, for simplicity, that middle class and poor individuals own no shares: $\sigma_1 = \sigma_0 = 0$. Rich individuals therefore get more than the per capita share of aggregate profits: $\sigma_2 = 1/h_2$.

As in Kaplow and Shavell (1994), the condition for blocking the merger to be more efficient than taxes is for the tax adjustment that replicates the distribution of pre-merger income be negative: $h_2\hat{T}_2 + h_1\hat{T}_1 + h_0\hat{T}_0 < 0$. The tax adjustment necessary to offset the net increase in income for the rich is:

$$c_2 + v(q^*) + \sigma\Pi^* - \hat{T}_2 - \theta_2 = c_2 + v(\tilde{q}) + \sigma\tilde{\Pi} - \theta_2.$$

Solving in terms of $\hat{T}_2$ we get:

$$\hat{T}_2 = \sigma\Pi^* + v(q^*) - (\sigma\tilde{\Pi} + v(\tilde{q})).$$

By assumption the merger increases the net well-being of group-2, $\sigma\Pi^* + v(q^*) - (\sigma\tilde{\Pi} + v(\tilde{q})) > 0$, so $\hat{T}_2 > 0$. That is, the tax adjustment increases taxes on the rich and generates revenue for the government's budget.

Next, the tax adjustments for groups 1 and 2 are respectively:

$$c_1 + v(q^*) - \hat{T}_1 - \theta_1 = c_1 + v(\tilde{q}) - \theta_1$$

and

$$c_0 + v(q^*) - \hat{T}_0 = c_0 + v(\tilde{q}).$$

Solving in terms of $\hat{T}_1$ and $\hat{T}_0$, we get:

$$\hat{T}_1 = -(v(\tilde{q}) - v(q^*))$$

and

$$\hat{T}_0 = -(v(\tilde{q}) - v(q^*)).$$

Because pre-merger consumer surplus is larger than post-merger surplus, we have $v(\tilde{q}) - v(q^*) > 0$, $\hat{T}_1 < 0$ and $\hat{T}_0 < 0$. In other words, the tax adjustments on groups 1 and 0 are tax reductions or subsidies and therefore debits in the government's budget.

Placing these expressions in the budget condition, $h_2\hat{T}_2 + h_1\hat{T}_1 + h_0\hat{T}_0 < 0$, we obtain:

$$h_2(\sigma\Pi^* + v(q^*) - (\sigma\tilde{\Pi} + v(\tilde{q}))) - h_1(v(\tilde{q}) - v(q^*)) - h_0(v(\tilde{q}) - v(q^*)) < 0.$$

Because $\sigma = 1/h_2$ and $h_0 + h_1 + h_2 = 1$, this conditions simplifies to:

$$\Pi^* - \tilde{\Pi} < v(\tilde{q}) - v(q^*).$$

Intuitively, and simply put, if the gains in profits from merger, $\Pi^* - \tilde{\Pi}$, are smaller than the gains in consumer surplus from halting the merger, $v(\tilde{q}) - v(q^*)$, blocking the merger is a more efficient way of redistributing income than the income tax.

As discussed in this chapter, Kaplow (2021) takes this result as an endorsement of economics' traditional efficiency analysis in competition law, namely to evaluate mergers based on whether they maximize the sum of consumer and producer surplus. But as also argued in this chapter, it is more plausible to interpret his result in terms of the *redistributive* efficiency of antitrust law. Indeed, as demonstrated in the text, Kaplow's interpretation makes sense only because the distribution-neutral income tax adjustment negates the effect of the merger on labor supply. When labor-supply responses are included in the evaluation, the merger may well increase net wealth in addition to raising inequality. Thus, the efficiency gain from blocking the merger merely indicates that antitrust law can be used to redistribute income more efficiently than taxes.

8

Intellectual Property

A "crisis in innovation" gripped the United States during the 1970s after a generation of post-war global dominance (Gallini 2002, 131–32). The Patent and Trademark Office (PTO) was so underfunded and understaffed that by 1979 the office temporarily discontinued granting patents (Jaffe 2000, 532). Political leaders believed reforms to the American patent system, both institutional and legal, were needed to confront the crisis and protect the country's position as a global leader in innovation in the world economy. Legislative, judicial, and executive reforms were enacted to strengthen intellectual property protections in the United States. The consequences, as we will see, were not wholly good; a recharged patent system has, among other things, exacerbated trends in income inequality, especially at the top of the distribution (Aghion et al. 2019).

The United States Constitution grants Congress the power "to promote the Progress of Science and Useful arts, by securing, for limited Times, to Authors and Inventors, the exclusive Right to their respective Writings and Discoveries."[1] Beginning in 1980, Supreme Court decisions and Congressional legislation expanded this power in three important ways: by "expanding patent protection to new subject matter; giving greater power to patent holders in infringement lawsuits; and lengthening the term of patents" (Gallini 2002, 133).

In two important decisions from the early 1980s, *Diamond v. Chakrabarty*[2] and *Diamond v. Diehr*,[3] the Supreme Court held that patent protection could be extended to genetically engineered bacteria as well as software. These extensions of patentable subject matter drastically increased patents in both biomedical

[1] U.S. Const. art. I, § 8, cl. 8.
[2] Diamond v. Chakrabarty, 447 U.S. 303 (1980).
[3] Diamond v. Diehr, 450 U.S. 175 (1981).

engineering, data processing,[4] and other fields.[5] Later, a federal circuit court upheld the patentability of business methods and financial service products,[6] which was then extended to include internet processes like Amazon's one-click internet ordering process and Priceline.com's reverse auction method for booking airline tickets (Gallini 2002, 133–34). The protection of "Writings and Discoveries" enumerated in the Constitution was transformed into: "all commercially important technological areas must be included within the realm of patentable technology" (Jaffe 2000, 536).

The expansion of patentable material coincided with a strengthening of patent laws and a privatization of publicly funded research. In 1982, Congress created the Court of Appeals for the Federal Circuit, which was empowered with exclusive appellate jurisdiction for all patent cases. The idea was to standardize patent law throughout the country and eliminate forum shopping (533). Results of patent infringement cases abruptly changed: Prior to 1980, patents were upheld on appeal in 62 percent of cases, but by 1990 this had risen to 90 percent. At the same time, appeals courts become more aggressive about overturning district courts' findings that patents were invalid (533). Thus, the probability that a litigated patent would be upheld rose by 54 percent over the period and patentees were much more likely to be granted a temporary injunction barring sale of their infringed product (533). The Court of Appeals for the Federal Circuit became a patent clearinghouse.

Meanwhile, two 1980 laws not only allowed but encouraged private companies to patent publicly funded research at universities and public labs. The Stevenson-Wydler Technology Innovation Act explicitly made technology transfer a mission for all public labs, in part by mandating that they adopt institutional procedures for this purpose (534). For instance, every lab with an annual R&D budget of over $20 million was required to create an Office of Research and Technology Applications to oversee technology transfer operations, staffed with at least one full-time employee (534). The Patent and Trademark Law Amendments (Bayh-Dole) Act allowed universities and public labs to retain the title to patents derived from federally funded R&D and "explicitly recognized technology transfer to the private sector as a desirable outcome of federally financed research" (535). The race for global preeminence

4 Jaffe (2000, 544) reports: "USPTO Class 435, Molecular Biology and Microbiology, accounted for about 0.5% of all patents in 1985, about the same as in 1977. This rose to about 1% in 1990, 1.3% in 1995 and then grew dramatically to 2.5% in 1998. Classes 600, 601, 602, 603, 604, 606, 607 and 623, all of which deal with 'Data Processing,' accounted for about 0.4% of all patents in 1977, 0.7% in 1985, 1.2% in 1990, 1.6% in 1995 and 2.6% in 1998."

5 Jaffe (2000, 537) again explains: "Thus, a long-term secular decline in the intensity of patenting activity in the U.S. reversed in the mid-1980s, and the trend since that time has been steadily upward. In the 1990s, U.S. inventors have been receiving patents in record numbers, with the 1-year total of over 80,000 in 1998 more than double the number received in any year from 1979 through 1986. The figures show that part, but not all, of this increase is associated with an increase in R&D expenditure."

6 *State Street Bank and Trust v. Signature Financial Group*, 149. F.3d 1368 (Fed Cir. 1998).

simultaneously transferred public knowledge into private hands and strengthened the right to enforce restrictions on its use.

After the collapse of the Soviet Union led to the closer integration global markets, patent protection became a key component of free-trade agreements. The Uruguay Round of the General Agreement on Tariffs and Trade (GATT) included the Trade-Related Aspects of Intellectual Property (TRIPs) agreement, which required the United States to extend patent protection for many technologies from 17 to 20 years (Gallini 2002, 134). The agreement also strengthened patents of American companies by standardizing laws abroad, as many developing countries at the time did not recognize drug patents or process patents (Jaffe 2000, 536). Patent protection now extended longer and further than before.

The newest major American patent law, the Leahy-Smith America Invents Act of 2011, continues to prioritize international coordination of patent protection over distributional concerns (Tramposch 2011). The Leahy-Smith Act aligns American patent law with the international community by transforming the system from "first to invent" to "first to file." In essence, "it shifts the system's emphasis from the date it was invented to the date an inventor dropped an application at the patent office" (Hurst 2013). Many commentators have suggested the system favors large companies that are familiar with the patent system, at the expense of the small inventor. The law does provide a few mechanisms to protect small inventors, but ultimately the law's purpose is to "provide the transparency that banks, venture capitalists, and other investors need to invest in new businesses while establishing the stability that companies need to bring new products to globalized markets" (Tramposch 2011). When it comes to patent protection, international competition, not domestic well-being, is the primary concern.

Does a recharged intellectual property law exacerbate inequality? According to Hughes and Merges (2016), at least one area of intellectual property law, copyright, "arguably provides the most robust mechanism for disadvantaged groups, particularly African Americans, to accumulate wealth in American society" (549). Unfortunately, the argument does not apply to the distribution of income as a whole. While intellectual property law may provide avenues of betterment for some individual members of society, the gains have been distributed highly unequally. Data and analysis generated by Aghion et al. (2019), displayed in Figure 8.1, provide support for this conclusion. The figure on the left-hand side, (a), vividly illustrates the relationship between income inequality and the strengthening of IP protection. Interestingly enough, both the number of patents granted and the share of income going to the top 1 percent exhibit no particular trend between the 1960s and the early 1980s. Since then, however, both variables exhibit a positive trend. The figure on the right-hand side, (b), provides a little more analysis. Between 1980 and 2005, there is a significant and positive correlation between the increase in the log of innovation in a state (measured by the number of citations within five years after patent application, by state per capita), and the increase in the share of income held by the top 1 percent.

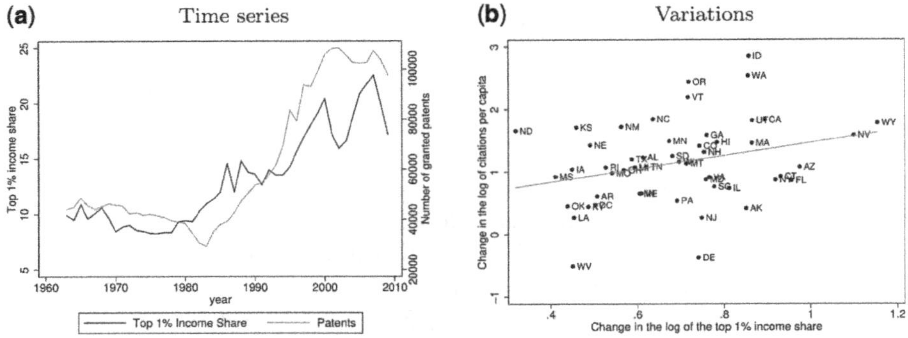

FIGURE 8.1 Innovation and inequality

Notes: (a) Plots the number of granted patents distributed by their year of application against the top 1 percent income share for the USA as a whole. Observations span the years 1963–2009. (b) Plots the difference of the log of the number of citations per capita against the difference of the log of the top 1 percent income share in 1980 and 2005. *Source*: Aghion et al. (2019)

The reason for innovation's bolstering of income inequality is not hard to fathom. Intellectual property has always been premised on a two-edged sword. Granting intellectual property creates a temporary monopoly. The rewards from winning the innovation race create incentives for discovery and invention; but the very mechanism by which these rewards are conferred has anti-competitive effects, which augurs in favor of inequality. The evidence that Aghion et al. (2019, 2) accumulate suggests that intellectual property protection has a causal relationship to the rise in the top 1 percent's share of income and therefore constitutes "certainly one such factor" in explaining this rise.

* * *

Is it possible that intellectual property law could be used to redistribute income more efficiently than the tax system? As we have seen throughout this book, Kaplow and Shavell (1994) famously said no; they argued that the tax system is always more efficient at redistributing income than the legal system. That claim applies to any set of legal rules, including intellectual property. This chapter makes the argument that intellectual property can be used to redistribute income.

Section 8.1 of the chapter briefly reviews the legal scholarship about the distributive implications of intellectual property law. As will be seen, this scholarship has not directly confronted the double-distortion argument. Section 8.2 shows how the double-distortion argument applies to the prospect of using IP to redistribute income and, at a general level, why that prospect is promising. The third and final section presents a simplified version of the chapter appendix's formal model of redistributive IP. Section 8.3 and 8.4 model the economics of patent scope and shows why Kaplow and Shavell's "double distortion" argument fails in this case.

The model's main insight shows that broadening the scope of patent protection generates greater incentives for innovation, which enhances efficiency, but also has stronger anti-competitive effects, which both increase income inequality and have offsetting, negative effects on efficiency. The model also allows the owner to license the patent, which has ambiguous anti-competitive effects but unambiguous and positive income inequality effects. Overall, adopting an *inefficient* legal rule that narrowed the patent's scope protection may have small (negative) effects on efficiency but large (positive) effects on income-inequality reduction. This means that IP law could be more efficient – or more precisely, less inefficient – at redistributing income than the tax system, against Kaplow and Shavell.

The model relies on an argument used elsewhere in the book (particularly in the chapters on labor and employment law and antitrust law) for why the "double distortion" claim fails as a general matter: In the patent-scope model, the distortions caused by adopting a more income equitable legal rule are not *cumulative*, but *offsetting*. In fact, the temporary monopolies granted by IP law confer the same kind of market power (which may nevertheless derive from other sources) that is regulated by antitrust law. There is therefore a great deal of overlap between this chapter and Chapter 7, on antitrust. What this chapter essentially adds is, if you will, another potential "distortion": innovation. In addition to labor supply and monopolistic competition, innovation is both a potential tool for market power and another countervailing source of efficiency that can be traded off against the others in order to redistribute income more efficiently than taxes.

8.1 INCOME INEQUALITY IN IP SCHOLARSHIP

The strengthening of patent and IP protection over the last several decades has certainly bolstered interest in IP scholarship, not least within the legal academy. Nevertheless, discussion of the distributional consequences of intellectual property has largely evaded sustained scholarly focus. This section will briefly describe the main exceptions to that state of affairs.

Legal scholars are certainly aware that intellectual property has distributive implications. For example, Kapczynski (2011) seeks to transcend what she calls "intellectual property internalism," by which she means the preoccupation of the production and distribution of scientific and cultural goods, or informational goods, through one particular institutional mechanism: price, or intellectual *property*. Scholarship takes intellectual property as a given, and then examines questions "internal" to IP, such as how broad or narrow IP rights, and their exceptions, should be. But there are other ways of governing the production and distributional goods, such as "commons-based production" and "government procurement" (such as financial prizes or awards for inventions). Kapczynski aims to broaden the discussion about the governance of informational-goods production as alternatives to IP.

In her view, one reason to look beyond intellectual property, in its narrow sense, is because of its distributional implications. Intellectual property regulates information and its production through prices, "it distributes resources in a way that is sensitive to the background allocation of resources" (996). If money is the ticket to accessing information, or informational goods, then those without money will be deprived of access. Kapczynski refers briefly to Kaplow and Shavell's argument that, in her interpretation, "efficiency should be maximized first, and … distributive issues should be attended to thereafter" (996). In the case of informational goods, however, the Kaplow-Shavell argument "has little purchase" "because sometimes we can give the poor access to information goods without substantially undermining innovation" (997). This is essentially the point that alternative forms of information production can be efficiency-neutral but have more favorable distributional implications: "If we can get the same or similar results in terms of efficiency, but intrinsically better distributive results (avoiding, for example, both the cost and the political uncertainty of post hoc redistribution), then there is no reason to accept the cost (in distributive terms) that price requires" (997). In this scenario, there is no trade-off between efficiency and distribution (997).

But, as pointed out already in this book, this response, while true and fair in its own right, does not exactly meet the Kaplow-Shavell objection. *If* in fact a different legal rule, or a different institution for governing the production of information, can achieve similar or better efficiency results than the current one, Kaplow and Shavell have no objection to it *because it is superior or equivalent on efficiency grounds*. Kaplow and Shavell would in fact endorse Kapczynski's proposal: If one IP rule happens to be more distributionally favorable than another, while also maximizing efficiency, then they have no objection, and the argument does not contradict their claim. The issue is not whether we can find rules that are superior on distributional grounds while also satisfying efficiency. Rather, the issue is whether, once such rules have been found and implemented, we should make sacrifices to efficiency for the sake of even greater income equality.

Hughes and Merges (2016) address specifically the distributional justifications for copyright law. Their perspective is somewhat unique, at least with respect to the law-and-economics literature. That perspective is a Rawlsian one, and they make the claim that copyright law satisfies Rawls's Difference Principle. That is, copyright law arranges social and economic inequalities "so that they are both: (a) to the greatest benefit of the least advantaged … and (b) attached to offices and positions open to all under conditions of fair equality of opportunity" (Hughes and Merges, 2016, 519, citing Rawls, 1971, 302). That is, Rawls's principles of justice endorse economic inequality if benefiting the wealthy improves the material standing of the "least advantaged" in income and wealth.

Hughes and Merges (2016, 528) say that insofar as copyright incentivizes the production of "music, literature, and audiovisual works that improve the lives of all or almost all" then even if copyright does generate economic inequality by concentrating wealth among creators and copyright owners, this is justified by making the least advantaged better off. However, they are more concerned about responding to what they call the "corporate trope," namely, that the "bulk of [copyright's] expansion has enriched copyright intermediaries, rather than creators and readers" (Hughes and Merges, 2016, 515, citing Litman, 2010, 27–28). This claim, as they note, is centered around copyright law's impact on the distribution of *income* (rather than, say, the distribution of well-being or other primary goods). They concede that copyright law "has little positive impact on the income of the economically least advantaged" (529). Nevertheless, they think that "copyright does have a positive impact on the income of individual citizens in middle income groups and, under the canonical Difference Principle, that may be enough to justify its distributive impact" (529).[7]

Hughes and Merges also address the second part of the Difference Principle, the "Fair Equality of Opportunity Principle," which requires that access to the "bountiful end of inequalities" be "attached to offices and positions open to all under conditions of fair equality of opportunity" (547). For this, they concentrate on the "hard-to-miss experience of African Americans" (547). They briefly review the evidence for racial wealth disparities in America, observing that the correlation between race and socio-economic disempowerment indicates that society is currently further from Rawls's "equality of opportunity" ideal than it ought to be. The question is whether current copyright law is neutral towards this correlation of socio-economic disempowerment, exacerbates the disempowerment, or ameliorates it. Hughes and Merges answer that question with "the strong claim that the copyright system as it presently functions, *warts and all*, arguably provides the most robust mechanism for disadvantaged groups, particularly African Americans, to accumulate wealth in American society"

7 Hughes and Merges (2016) support the claim that copyright has had positive impact on the income of middle-income groups by pointing to evidence from the Bureau of Labor Statistics where the link between a number of occupational categories and copyright protection is sufficiently close. All of the occupations they identify have incomes above the median level (with one exception: "photographers") (529–30). To get a closer look, they examine in greater detail "musicians, singers, composers, and the like" (530). The idiosyncrasies of musical copyright (described as a "labyrinth" (531)), as well as the disruptions to the music industry caused by streaming services and peer-to-peer downloading, create "an area of economic and creative activity where copyright should have failed creative individuals" (532). However, data from musical collecting societies show that from 2010 to 2014, at least $4.1 billion was distributed to American creative professionals through the copyright-based licensing system for musical compositions (532–33). Additionally, a 2013 survey of 5300 musicians concluded that working musicians as a whole generate between 12 to 22 percent of their income from copyright-based royalties (Hughes and Merges, 2016, 534, citing DiCola, 2013, 304–05). The survey indicates that while working musicians would not necessarily be penniless without copyright, copyright may make the difference between having a reasonable standard of living or not. According to Hughes and Merges, therefore, copyright serves not merely to enrich corporations or the wealthy; the income earned from copyright protection is widely enough shared to satisfy Rawls's Difference Principle.

(549, emphasis in original).[8] Despite Hughes and Merges' conclusion, that copyright works to the welfare advantage of the least well off and generates income for at least middle-income groups, they do not address the double-distortion problem. That is, insofar as copyright improves the lives of the least advantaged, they do not ask whether copyright does this more efficiently than the income tax system could. Hughes and Merges' argument could therefore be entirely compatible with the Kaplow-Shavell assertion. From a double-distortion perspective, we could say that inasmuch as the current copyright regime is efficient, any benefits to the least well-off or middle-income groups would be incidental. From Hughes and Merges, we are unable to tell whether an alternative copyright regime – one that was more equitable even if less efficient than the current one – would be desirable and why.

8.2 IP LAW AND THE "DOUBLE DISTORTION" ARGUMENT

At first glance, a double-distortion analysis would seem to disqualify intellectual property law as a redistributive legal tool. Indeed, this first glance would suggest that a redistributive change in IP law would produce a double-distortion in the exact manner that Kaplow and Shavell (1994) theorize.

Suppose, for example, that we start from an efficient, wealth-maximizing patent system, one that happens to also produce substantial income inequality. To be more exact, we can surmise that this patent regime protects against infringement both at its wealth-maximizing length – the amount of time the invention is protected against infringement – and its wealth-maximizing breadth – the "scope" of protection provided against infringement. In the next step, suppose the government introduces a new patent regime. This change is intended to ameliorate income inequality, but because it is a departure from the original, efficient regime, it evidently comes at a sacrifice to efficiency. Should this new regime be adopted?

Apparently not, from a double-distortion perspective, for the new regime would have two distortions that would be "additive" or "compounding" in exactly the way that Kaplow and Shavell dread. The first distortion is the familiar labor-supply distortion. An inequality-reducing patent rule will distort labor supply. This happens because reducing inequality discourages work incentives. The effect is exactly equivalent to a tax; it is as if the taxing authority decided to increase the tax rate on the income earned from patentable goods or services production. This could happen in a number of more concrete ways. For example, think of a cobbler who has invented a more comfortable sole and who, in turn, licenses the invention to a select number of shoe-making firms. Suppose the rich own a broad portfolio of stocks, including

[8] To support the claim that copyright provides the most robust mechanism for disadvantaged groups to accumulate wealth in American society, Hughes and Merges (2016) cite *Forbes* magazine's 2009 publication of the wealthiest African Americans in the United States. Of the top 25, 22 are in "traditionally identified 'copyright industries'" (553–54) Additionally, of those 22, nearly all of them were "self-made billionaires and millionaires" (554).

shares in those firms that license the patent. A shorter patent length or narrower patent scope will reduce the value of the firms that license the comfort-sole patent because competing firms will have an easier time replicating the invention, without infringing, or will enter into competition sooner, when the patent expires. The lower value of the licensing firms will cause the rich to reduce their supply of labor. In Kaplow's (2021, 334) parable, lower share values reduce labor supply because they reduce the incentive to use higher labor earnings earned today to save more for the future, where the value of savings is determined by share values.[9] Ultimately, the important distinction to make about this particular labor-supply effect is that it is economically distinct and independent from the incentives or resources spent on discovering the patented invention itself.

Of course, the new, inefficient patent regime also affects those same incentives to innovate. This is the second distortion. Thus, in Kaplow and Shavell's language, where the first distortion affects labor-supply incentives (the "tax" effect), the second distortion affects the behavior regulated by the legal rules themselves (the "legal rule" effect). So, while the value of the comfort-sole patent influences the labor-supply of those who own shares in firms that utilize the patent, it also affects the incentives of inventors – the cobbler in this case. Reducing the value of the patent will discourage, at least on the margin, the incentives of inventors to invent.

The patent-rule change presents us with a double distortion. The new patent regime reduces labor supply – just like a tax – but it also targets inventive activity, the behavior regulated by the legal rules of IP law. These effects moreover are compounding; they move "in the same direction," both constituting losses in total social wealth. This would suggest that, instead of implementing the new patent regime, we should instead change the tax schedule. The new tax schedule will generate the same distribution of income as the equity-informed patent regime. But by influencing only the labor-supply incentives, the alternative tax policy will eliminate the second distortion, the distortion that affects the incentives to invest time and resources into discovery of new, patentable knowledge. This putatively makes the tax policy superior to the egalitarian-inspired, second patent policy. The tax policy can achieve the exact same level of income distribution as the inefficient patent policy, while eliminating the distortion to inventive activity. The savings generated by the efficiency can be used to increase the well-being of the poor, making their welfare even greater than under the egalitarian patent regime. In other words, the

9 Think, for example, of a simple two-period model where people work today, but consume in both periods (we can call the two periods working age and retirement age). If common portfolio values increase, that will increase the inventive to work more today so that one can consume more in both periods. One is entitled to ask whether higher share prices would not rather *discourage* labor supply. The higher value of one's portfolio may encourage early retirement, for example. If that's the case, the labor-supply effects of changing patent rules will not be the same as a distribution-neutral change to the income tax schedule. Because those effects must be the same for the double-distortion argument to have any practical traction, so much the worse for the double-distortion argument.

tax system can do *all* the redistribution we want from the patent policy, without all of the negative side effects it creates for research and development.

Or so it would seem. This analysis would work perfectly, but only because we have entirely ignored the most conspicuous impact of intellectual property policy: its anticompetitive effects. Although the more equitable patent regime would discourage inventive activity, it would also encourage more competition. In the case of our cobbler, the stronger patent regime encourages the invention of more comfortable shoes, but it also makes infringement of the patent more likely, giving the inventor greater monopoly power in the market. For example, would-be competitors will find it safer to do business by licensing the comfortable-sole patent rather than run the risk of trying to duplicate those efforts. This also allows the inventor to charge a higher fee for the license, which in turn acts as a barrier to entry for further competition. In classic monopoly fashion, not only does income inequality increase, but output declines in the comfortable shoe industry. To put it another way, the inefficient patent regime creates not just a double distortion, but a *triple* distortion. Most importantly, the effect of this third distortion goes exactly in the opposite direction from the first two distortions, toward the creation of more wealth rather than its destruction. In sum, the more equitable patent regime reduces income inequality, thereby reducing labor supply, and also discourages R&D or other inventive activity. Both of these effects go in the direction of lower wealth. But by encouraging more competition, the third effect goes in the direction of greater wealth. The ultimate point is that, jointly, the effects of these three distortions are theoretically, a priori *indeterminate*.

This indeterminacy is important because it deprives the double-distortion hypothesis of its generality. When there are two distortions that go in the same direction, we can be certain that a distribution-equivalent tax policy will beat the proposed legal redistribution. Because the first, labor-supply distortion is always equivalent to the tax distortion, the existence of a second, behavioral distortion means that the tax alternative is *necessarily* more efficient than the legal redistribution. However, once we introduce a third distortion – *critically*, one that moves in the opposite direction than the others – that deductive necessity is destroyed. Now, the only relevant policy question is whether the aggregate distortion created by all three is greater or less than the distortion created by the distribution-equivalent tax alternative. More importantly, this statement implies the *possibility* that the new, egalitarian legal policy can be more efficient than the income tax at redistributing income.

For example, suppose that the first two, wealth-reducing distortions are exactly offset by the wealth-increasing distortion – the pro-competitive effect. On net, this gives us a "zero distortion" (Liscow 2014) reduction in income inequality, meaning that there is no compelling reason not to adopt the new regime. Not only is the redistributive effect more efficient than the income tax in this case, but it also comes "free of charge."

But if the more equitable regime is not neutral with respect to efficiency, but rather inefficient, that does not necessarily change the conclusion. Assume that the wealth-enhancing, pro-competitive effect of the new IP regime is net inefficient. Or, viewed conversely, that the old IP regime is more efficient than the new one, and is therefore, strictly on efficiency grounds, superior. In other words, despite the anti-competitive effects of the more restrictive IP regime – longer duration and broader scope in patent protection – the greater labor supply and the quicker or more effective discoveries in commercial knowledge more than offset these losses. Unfortunately, by itself, this fact does not allow us to conclude that the old IP regime should be adopted. Again, because the double-distortion argument does not apply in the case of "offsetting" distortions, we have no a priori confidence, either way, about which regime to endorse.

One way to settle the question about which IP regime to adopt is by using optimal-tax analysis.[10] Suppose that we begin with the older, less equitable and more patent-protective, IP regime, and also suppose we implement the optimal tax schedule. That is, the tax schedule that maximizes social welfare, which accounts for both total wealth and its distribution, subject to the wealth losses caused by redistributive taxation. We now know how costly the old IP regime is in terms of higher inequality because this is translated into and measured in dollars through the loss of wealth that comes through redistribution. The next step is to compare this with the optimal tax under the new IP regime. One conclusion we can immediately draw from this comparison is that the cost of taxation – equivalently, the labor-supply effect – will be smaller under the new IP regime. This is because the marginal social welfare value of redistribution is a function of inequality: The more inequality there is, the greater the value of redistribution, and therefore the larger costs of redistribution that are required to equalize that larger marginal benefit. (Recall, again, that in the double-distortion analysis we had the convenience of equalizing the costs of taxation choosing a distribution-neutral tax schedule that induces the same distortion in labor supply.) Gauged at the optimal-tax schedule for each regime, the regime that minimizes the costs of all three effects will tell us which regime should be adopted. For example, compared to the new IP regime, an old IP regime that has modest and positive inventive-incentive effects but large and negative anti-competitive effects coupled with high inequality (and therefore large and negative costs of taxation) will lose the policy horse race.

[10] See the book's appendix for a brief overview of optimal tax-analysis. For now, optimal-tax analysis is a different, and somewhat more demanding (computationally) approach than the straightforward double-distortion analysis and specifically Kaplow's (2008) distribution-neutral income tax adjustment analysis. In our context, however, the challenges are reasonably met. The optimal-tax problem sets a baseline for the cost of taxation. Knowing this cost, in addition to knowing which regime yields more or less income inequality, will be able to tell us which policy maximizes *welfare*, inclusive of both wealth and inequality, rather than merely which policy maximizes wealth (i.e., efficiency).

It is true that we still have no a priori way of determining whether taxation or legal rules are better at redistribution. The actual effects of policies, whether in theory or in practice, must be known before deciding.[11] More to the point, however, legal redistribution *can* be more efficient than distribution through legal rules. We know this possibility exists because of the "zero distortion" benchmark we have already mentioned. As the pro-competitive gains of the new IP regime approach, in measure, the costs of the labor-supply and inventive-incentive effects, the new IP regime *must* be superior on social welfare grounds. This is because when the effects of these three distortions "cancel out," the only costs that need to be compared are the costs of redistributive taxation, which are *necessarily* smaller under the new IP regime. Indeed, as long as the new IP regime is more equal than the old regime, then the costs of redistributive taxation of the old regime will be strictly larger – positive, non-zero – than those of the new regime. That gives us some room, the amount of which is determined exactly by the difference in costs of taxation, to adopt a more egalitarian, but less efficient IP regime, one where the pro-competitive effects may not exceed the costs of the labor-supply and inventive-incentive effects. In this case, the loss of efficiency is made up for by the gain in inequality, which comes with less costly taxation.

Before concluding, I remind the reader that it is entirely possible that a more egalitarian patent regime could also be a more efficient one, but that this does not defeat the double-distortion claim. It is plausible, for example, that with the new patent regime the reduction of the (inefficient) anticompetitive effects would entirely swamp the reduction of the (efficient) labor-supply and R&D-incentive effects. In that case, the old patent regime was not only inequitable, but also inefficient. (Of course, this possibility need not also imply that *no* intellectual property protection is efficient, although that argument could be saved for another day). The efficient policy could still protect patents with strictly positive length and breadth – that is, the efficient patent is greater than zero years and protects against some infringement, however slight.) But, again, the possibility of a new patent regime that is both more equitable and more efficient than the old does not defeat the double-distortion argument. Kaplow and Shavell would have no objection to an equitable change in IP if it was also more efficient. The double-distortion argument does not necessarily imply that every equitable change in the law is inefficient. Rather, such changes are the only cases that present a trade-off between equity and efficiency and therefore raise a question about which means of redistribution – taxes or legal rules – is a more efficient way to address income inequality.

[11] But such is economic policy-making. In most cases, the advice the policy maker can give is almost always "on one hand … on the other." It depends. In that respect redistributive policy advice is no different than any other kind of policy advice.

8.3 EFFICIENCY AND EQUITY IN AN INNOVATION MODEL WITH MONOPOLISTIC COMPETITION

This section offers a more formal analysis of the previous section's claim as a precursor to the fully formal treatment given in the appendix. The model examines specifically the issue of patent scope. Merges and Nelson (1990, 839) demonstrated the importance of scope issues in patents, saying, "The economic significance of a patent depends on its scope: the broader the scope, the larger the number of competing products and processes that will infringe the patent." It is this central observation that is important for the model, although Merges and Nelson are mainly concerned with subtler issues in both the law and economics of innovation. Other dimensions of patents, such as the length of patent protection, could have been chosen. I focus on patent scope primarily because of its tractability.

The model captures the three main effects we have been discussing. In one part of the model, firms invest in R&D in order to discover (with some probability) a lower-cost patentable production process. Discovery of this process not only lowers the firm's production costs, but can also be licensed to other firms in the market. This part captures the inventive incentives dimension of the problem. Another part of the model features monopolistic competition among firms that sell a homogeneous good to consumers. However, the firm's production costs will differ depending on whether they license the patent from the lead firm that has won the "patent race." This part of the model captures the anticompetitive effects of patent scope. A final part of the model allocates the producer and consumer surplus, that innovation and competition yield, to individuals who supply labor by making an occupational choice; this captures the third, labor-supply dimension of the problem. This last part of the model essentially recapitulates the model in Chapter 7 on antitrust, so readers are invited to read both in conjunction with one another.

8.3.1 *The Stages of the Innovation Model*

The sequence of events takes the following order. The first stage is the "labor supply" stage. In this stage, each individual, knowing their idiosyncratic occupational or skill cost and taking the income tax schedule as given, chooses one of three occupations differentiated by income. The sources of income are two: earned income from wages and capital income from share ownership. What is essential for the model's purposes is that share ownership is unequally distributed so that those with higher earned income also have higher capital income. (As mentioned in the Chapter 7, this assumption is abundantly confirmed empirically.) For simplicity, I will assume that only the richest of the three occupations by earned income owns stock. This stage is the "labor supply" stage.

The second stage is the innovation, or inventive-incentive, stage. In this stage, each firm in the product market makes an R&D investment in order to develop a new patentable production process that lowers the costs of production, denoted z, of some good or service. A larger investment by the firm increases its likelihood of successfully discovering a lower cost process.[12] The R&D race is assumed, for simplicity, to be symmetrical, so that the amount of each firm's investment is, in equilibrium, identical, and therefore "nature" selects at random the winner of the patent race from among the firms. The winner of the patent race, which I will call the innovation leader, decides whether to license the patent and what licensing fee, denoted F, to charge.

The third stage is the monopolistic competition stage, capturing the anticompetitive effects of IP. In this stage, all firms decide whether to engage in goods production.[13] Each non-winning firm must also decide whether to pay the innovation leader's licensing fee, which gives it access to the patented and lower-cost production technology; or instead to use existing, higher-cost but publicly available technology. Using the patented technology will allow the firm to produce one unit of the good at cost z_l while the public technology requires production with the higher cost $z_h > z_l$. The stringency of the legal rules governing patent scope explains the difference between these two costs: $\chi = z_h - z_l$. When patent scope is stronger (captured formally by a larger χ) it prohibits the use of any technology with a cost lower than $z_l + \chi$. (This is certainly not the only or even the most accurate way to model patent scope. But, in addition to being fairly standard within the economics literature, it captures some simple intuitions between patents, technology, and inequality.) Finally, firms in this product market engage in monopolistic competition, and profits, fees, wages, taxes, and transfers are distributed. Firms compete by choosing quantities of the produced good, in "Cournot" fashion.

8.3.2 *Main Results*

I will first describe some general characteristics of the resulting equilibrium, and then discuss the implications of patent scope for inequality, efficiency, and social welfare.

In general, an equilibrium exists and any competitive equilibrium has multiple firms, with all firms licensing the patented, low-cost production technology from the firm that wins the patent race (which we can call the "innovation leader"). In equilibrium, there are thus *multiple* firms, but *no* high-cost firms. The result obtains because this outcome maximizes the profits and licensing fee revenues of the innovation leader. A few steps are required to reach this conclusion. First, I assume the cost difference, $\chi = z_h - z_l$, is never so drastic that, if the innovation leader charges too high a licensing fee, high-cost competitors are deterred from entering

[12] Given expectations, it is always profit-maximizing to make an investment over no investment at all.

[13] Once the winner of the patent race is revealed some entrepreneurs will find goods production unprofitable. These entrepreneurs choose their next best occupation, worker or unemployed, and I assume they are able to discharge their R&D investment cost, for example, via bankruptcy.

the market. A lower production cost always allows a firm, even a monopolist, to raise profits by expanding output and lowering the price. A *drastic* cost difference could yield prices so low that a high-cost firm wouldn't be able to charge that price and make any profit. Thus, in equilibrium there are multiple firms in the market rather than a single, monopoly firm.

Second, there are no high-cost firms in the market. This is because it always pays the innovation leader to charge a fee that lets every competitor that enters the market become a low-cost firm. This may seem counterintuitive. After all, a low-cost competitor has higher output and therefore drives down the price of the good, which hurts the profits that the innovation leader gains through product sales (rather than licensing fees). But low-cost firms always earn higher profits than high-cost firms, for any given number of firms in the market, so the innovation leader can gain by charging a fee that exactly equals that profit difference: The licensing firm is then indifferent between being a low- or high-cost firm and the innovation leader gets to pocket the difference. The innovation leader always stands to gain from that kind of arbitrage, so the logic applies no matter how many high-cost firms are in the market. Therefore, because lowering the fee to induce a high-cost firm to become a low-cost firm always yields a gain to the innovation leader, the innovator continues to lower the fee until the last remaining high-cost firm is indifferent between staying in competition and going out of business. The licensing fee will therefore be set equal to the profit difference between a low-cost and a high-cost firm, with the marginal firm a low-cost firm just indifferent to being a high-cost firm and going out of business. To put this another way, aggregate producer surplus is maximized when all firms are low-cost producers. Because the innovation leader can appropriate that surplus through its licensing fees, its individual, profit-maximizing incentives are the same as a social planner who would choose to maximize aggregate producer surplus. Thus, not only are there multiple firms in the market, there are no high-cost producers: All firms in the market are low-cost producers.

In terms of the model's comparative statics, the stringency of patent scope is the most interesting variable. As already indicated, the greater scope for the protection of a patent, measured by a larger χ, the larger the difference between the production costs of the firms, $\chi = z_h - z_l$. Because profits are a direct function of production costs, greater patent scope gives rise to larger profit differentials between low- and high-cost producers. From our previous analysis, broader scope protection means that the innovation leader will be able to charge a higher licensing fee. Furthermore, the higher the cost of production is (for the high-cost firm), the fewer firms will compete in equilibrium: Given the higher cost, z_h the entry condition becomes binding for a larger number of excluded firms. With fewer firms in competition, the rents from oligopoly increase. Both of these facts – higher licensing fees and greater monopoly rents – mean that larger patent scope unambiguously increases the rewards to being an innovation leader (as one would probably expect). Higher innovation rewards, in turn, increase incentives for greater R&D investment, and greater investment will lead to the discovery of lower-cost production methods. Thus, more stringent scope protection leads to lower cost production methods. A trade-off is emerging: Greater patent scope protection increases efficiency by fueling the innovation process, but it also encourages monopolization and greater inequality.

We can now turn to the choice between using IP law and the income tax as redistributive instruments. Let us start with constructing the "baseline" case we described informally in the Section 8.3.1. To do this, compare two levels of patent scope protection: a broad level of patent scope, $\overline{\chi}$, which increases the range of infringing patents, and a narrow level of patent scope, $\underline{\chi}$, which does the opposite. We know from our benchmark results that under a broad level of patent scope, $\overline{\chi}$, (1) the amount of R&D investment will be higher; (2) the cost of the patentable production process, z_l, will be lower; (3) the publicly available production process, z_h, will be higher; (4) the licensing fee, F, will be higher; and (5) the equilibrium number of firms, n, will be lower.

What remains ambiguous, and dependent on parameters, is total output, $Q = nq$, the output of each firm, q, multiplied by the number of firms, n, and which is closely related to the sum of producer and consumer surplus (see Chapter 7 for more about this important concept). If broader patent scope protection lowers output, it will reduce consumer surplus and indirectly lower the income of the nonrich, due to higher prices, but will increase producer surplus and indirectly raise the income of the rich, due to fewer firms, n, and lower costs, z_l. To construct our benchmark suppose a move from IP regime $\underline{\chi}$ to $\overline{\chi}$ results in a fall in total output, and a loss of income to the nonrich (that is, the lower two occupation categories) that is exactly equal to the gain enjoyed by the rich. In other words, the broader scope patent regime, $\overline{\chi}$, is equally efficient to, but more unequal than, the narrower scope regime, $\underline{\chi}$.

When both patent regimes are equally efficient, the policy prescription is obvious: Choose the narrower scope patent protection. The narrower scope reduces inequality without any sacrifice to efficiency. But it is easy to see from this baseline case that even if narrowing the scope of patent protection reduces efficiency, it may still be a superior choice in terms of social welfare. For instance, if narrower patent scope is only slightly less efficient but substantially more egalitarian, the costs of redistributive taxation associated with broader scope protection, justified as a response to its greater income inequality, will fail to maximize social welfare. More broadly, given that the optimally redistributive tax associated with broader patent scope will produce strictly positive costs, any efficiency loss associated with narrower scope protection that is less than those higher costs of redistribution will make the use of IP law more efficient than taxes at redistributing income.

Beyond this example, the model helps us understand when IP law can redistribute income more efficiently than taxes. As we have seen, the model links patent-scope protection with income inequality. Greater scope protection increases both the likelihood that competitors will infringe and the discovery of lower-cost production methods; both of these give the innovation leader market power, which increases inequality. On the other hand, greater scope protection has ambiguous effects on efficiency. Greater scope protection encourages more investment in R&D and the discovery of lower-cost production methods, which improve efficiency; but, as just seen, it also increases market power and reduces competition, which diminishes efficiency.

These counteracting effects indicate that IP rules may be adjusted for reasons that favor redistribution over efficiency, while redistributing income more efficiently than taxes. A more equitable choice of patent scope protection will distort labor-supply incentives and lower R&D investment, but it will also increase competition. Even if the combination of effects is inefficient, the positive effects of more competition may outweigh the negative effects of labor-supply distortion and less innovation. If the offset is sufficiently large, without increasing overall efficiency, the legal rule will redistribute more efficiently than taxes. We can determine this more precisely with a hypothetical distribution-neutral income tax adjustment, discussed in the book's appendix and also in Chapter 7. Such an adjustment will yield a budget deficit if the legal rule redistributes more efficiently than taxes. A budget deficit indicates that taxes will be a less efficient substitute for legal rule redistribution; therefore, legal rules can redistribute more efficiently than taxes.

The argument that IP law should sometimes sacrifice efficiency in favor of equity is closely related to the argument made in Chapter 7. As discussed in that chapter, Kaplow's (2021, 332) recent analysis of market power concludes that one should choose competition rules to maximize the sum of "consumer plus producer surplus, regardless of the distributive effects." That is, Kaplow still prefers efficiency to equity. In Chapter 7, I discuss two reasons why I think Kaplow's conclusion is wrong; both reasons are relevant to the IP analysis.

First, Kaplow (2021) uses his method of distribution-neutral income tax adjustments (Kaplow 2008) to make the conclusion that competition rules should maximize the sum consumer and producer surplus. This method is discussed further in Chapter 7 and in the book's appendix. There is little reason to think that Kaplow would draw a different conclusion if evaluating IP law rather than antitrust law. However, the problem with distribution-neutral income tax adjustments is that they produce odd conclusions. As shown in Chapter 7, such hypothetical adjustments can lead to the conclusion that one should block a proposed merger between firms because it fails to maximize the sum of consumer and producer surplus, even though permitting the merger would maximize overall efficiency. (The discrepancy between these two efficiency measures arises because the hypothetical tax adjustments negate labor-supply responses to the policy's distributional effects.) It is not clear why, of the two different measures of efficiency, one should prefer total surplus over total wealth. Chapter 7 proposes that the only plausible solution to this conundrum is that blocking the merger is not efficient, but rather it is more *redistributively* efficient. One could easily make a similar claim about IP law. For instance, Kaplow might say that one should choose IP rules and policies that maximize the sum of consumer and producer surpluses. However, this prescription would lead to the same paradox as just described, as well as the same resolution of that paradox.

Second, Chapter 7 also shows how Kaplow's total-surplus prescription rests on very special assumptions. Because antitrust law, as well as intellectual property law, inevitably implicates questions of production and competition among firms, Kaplow needs a way to link the income of firms – profits and share ownership – to the individual labor-supply decisions that lie at the heart of the double-distortion argument. Kaplow's answer to this problem is to assume that individuals adjust their labor supply in response to changes in capital income in the same way they do to changes in labor income. The idea is that savings, invested in a stock portfolio, for example, are merely deferred consumption from an earlier period's labor earnings. Therefore, when share values increase because of inequitable IP rules, individuals who own shares work more now both to consumer more now and in the future (e.g., after retirement). However, this is not the only way to think about the relationship between labor supply and capital income. In fact, the starting assumption in labor economics is that a rise in non-labor income, which may include capital income, will decrease, not increase, labor supply. The logic is that when a person's non-labor income goes up, they can increase both consumption and leisure by working less. For example, think of the person who retires earlier (reducing their labor supply) because their stock portfolio's value rises. Thus, capital-income driven changes in income inequality, can, contrary to the required double-distortion assumption, reduce labor supply rather than increase it. That in turn makes the income tax more costly than legal rules for redistributing income. Kaplow and Shavell's (1994) idea is that increases in income inequality and labor supply can be cleanly offset with a change in the income tax schedule. But if a capital-income driven rise in income inequality already reduces labor supply, increasing taxes only compounds that problem. This possibility is entirely relevant to IP law, because firms, and individuals who own shares of firms, are the primary beneficiaries of IP protection. Thus, when capital income is involved, a more egalitarian IP regime may be more redistributively efficient than using the tax system. Those ideas are also discussed further in Chapter 7.

8.4 APPENDIX

This appendix produces a formal version of the innovation model presented in the text, and is reproduced in the online appendix. The model is similar to the Cournot, monopolistic competition model developed in Chapter 7, but the present version allows for heterogeneous firm costs and adds an explicit innovation stage wherein firms invest resources in a patent race to develop a lower cost production method. Inspiration for the model is credited to Suzuki (2019). The main purpose of the model is to show systematically how innovation and IP law can lower production costs but also reduce competition. Section 8.4.1 presents the basic model, Section 8.4.2 derives the equilibrium values of the key quantities, and Section 8.4.3 shows that stronger patent protection can increase both efficiency and income inequality.

8.4.1 *Model*

Assume that consumers have a simple quasi-linear quadratic utility function given by:

$$u(q) = q_0 + aq - \frac{1}{2}q^2$$

where q_0 is the numeraire. With consumers having a budget constraint given by $p_0 q_0 + pq = y_1 - T_1$, we can set p_0 equal to one, solve for q_0 and substitute into the utility function to get:

$$u(q) = c_1 - pq + aq - \frac{1}{2}q^2. \tag{8.1}$$

Aggregation across all consumers then gives rise to the following price function:

$$p(Q) = A - Q, \tag{8.2}$$

where $Q = \int_0^n q_i dN$ is total quantity produced. Each producer, i, faces a profit function given by:

$$\pi = (p(Q) - z_i)q_i$$

where z_i is the unit cost of production for firm i. Maximizing this expression with respect to q_i leads to the following first-order condition for the profit-maximizing quantity choice:

$$-q_i + A - Q - z_i = 0.$$

Given the choice of technology described previously, there will be two production techniques adopted in equilibrium. Let $z_h > z_l$, where z_h is the high-cost technology and z_l the low-cost technology, and let H be the number of high-cost producers and L the number of low-cost producers. Summing up the first-order condition across all producers, $n = H + L$, we obtain:

$$-Q + nA - nQ - Lz_l - Hz_h = 0.$$

Rearranging, we get total quantity produced as:

$$Q = \frac{nA - Lz_l - Hz_h}{n+1}. \tag{8.3}$$

Substituting the total quantity back into the first-order condition, we can derive the quantity produced by each type of firm:

$$q_l = \frac{A + Lz_l + Hz_h}{n+1} - z_l \tag{8.4}$$

and

$$q_h = \frac{A + Lz_l + Hz_h}{n+1} - z_h. \tag{8.5}$$

Clearly, because $z_h > z_l$, it follows that $q_l > q_h$.

Next, substituting Q and q_i into the profit function, $(A - Q - z_i)q_i$, we obtain a solution for each firm's profit:

$$\pi_l = \left(\frac{A + Lz_l + Hz_h}{n+1} - z_l\right)^2 \tag{8.6}$$

and

$$\pi_h = \left(\frac{A + Lz_l + Hz_h}{n+1} - z_h\right)^2. \tag{8.7}$$

As it turns out, profits are simply the square of the optimal quantity produced by each type of firm, $(q_i)^2$. For that reason it is clear that a low-cost firm earns higher profits than a high-cost firm: $\pi_l > \pi_h$.

8.4.2 *Equilibrium*

The owner of the patent can license the technology to other firms at a cost F chosen by the patent owner. By paying for the license, the licensee gets access to the lower-cost technology and, using it, can increase its profits. At the same time, the license does not come for free. Thus, each producer will pay for the license under the following condition:

$$\pi_l - F \geq \pi_h.$$

We will now determine the optimal fee, called F^*, chosen by the patent owner. I will show that the patent owner maximizes its own profits, and the revenues from licensees, by setting the fee such that it excludes all high-cost producers from the market and makes licensees (who become low-cost producers) just indifferent between being a licensee and being a high-cost producer. Any lower fee increases the number of fee-paying licensees, but this benefit is overwhelmed by the patent owner's lower direct profits from increased competition and the smaller size of the fee. Any higher fee increases competition from high-cost producers, which lowers licensees' profits and induces them to become high-cost producers, which reduces the number of fee-paying firms.

First, let us define the proposed optimal fee, F^*. Assume that producers can always redeploy their capital elsewhere and earn reservation profits equivalent to $\bar{\pi} \geq 0$. A firm cannot gain from becoming a high-cost producer when there are sufficient low-cost firms in the market, which drive down profits to the level of the reservation utility of occupation 1. Rearranging the expression for the high-cost firm's profits given by equation (8.7) where all other firms are low-cost firms, this condition can be written as:

$$\left(\frac{A - n^*(z_h - z_l) - z_h}{n^* + 1}\right)^2 = \bar{\pi}. \tag{8.8}$$

This equation determines the critical number of firms, n^*, supporting the patent owner's optimal licensing fee. Thus, also reexpressing the low-cost firm's profit function in equation (8.6), the fee must keep a high-cost firm from opting to become a high-cost firm and not pay the fee:

$$\left(\frac{A - z_l}{n^* + 1}\right)^2 - F^* = \left(\frac{A - n^*(z_h - z_l) - z_h}{n^* + 1}\right)^2.$$

From this expression, the licensing fee can be written as:

$$F^* = \left(\frac{A - z_l}{n^* + 1}\right)^2 - \left(\frac{A - n^*(z_h - z_l) - z_h}{n^* + 1}\right)^2. \tag{8.9}$$

Does the patent owner want to charge any higher fee, $F > F^*$? Suppose the owner chooses a fee higher than F^*. Starting from the previous equilibrium, with $n = n^*$ and $L = n^*$, the first consequence is that low-cost producers earn negative profit. However, holding the number of firms constant at n^*, a low-cost firm can choose to not pay the license, become a high-cost firm and earn profits above the reservation profit level, $\pi_h > \bar{\pi}$. This is because, again holding the number of firms constant, one low-cost firm switching to a high-cost production method raises profits for both low- and high-cost producers. This can be seen by a comparison of the profit functions of each, where the following conditions for low-cost and high-cost firms respectively hold:

$$\left(\frac{A + H(z_h - z_l) - z_l}{n^* + 1}\right)^2 \geq \left(\frac{A - z_l}{n^* + 1}\right)^2$$

and

$$\left(\frac{A - (n^* - H)(z_h - z_l) - z_h}{n^* + 1}\right)^2 \geq \left(\frac{A - n^*(z_h - z_l) - z_h}{n^* + 1}\right)^2$$

for any $H \geq 0$. In fact, the change in profits for a low-cost firm from a marginal change in the composition of firms is:

$$\frac{\partial \pi_l}{\partial H} = 2\left(\frac{z_h - z_l}{n + 1}\right) q_l.$$

However, now that high-cost firms earn greater than reservation profits, $((A - (n^* - H)(z_h - z_l) - z_h)/(n^* + 1))^2 \geq \bar{\pi}$ for $H \geq 0$, additional high-cost firms can enter the market. Firms continue to enter until high-cost firms once again earn reservation profits. But further entry of firms also lowers the profits of low-cost firms. The change in profit to a low-cost firm from a marginal increase in the number of firms is:

$$\frac{\partial \pi_l}{\partial n} = -2\left(\frac{1}{n + 1}\right) \pi_l.$$

In fact, this second, negative effect on profits (additional firms, $n > n^*$) outweighs the first, positive effect (switching from z_l to z_h). Using the previous two derivatives, this condition for the negative effect to dominate is:

$$2\left(\frac{z_h - z_l}{n+1}\right)q_l - 2\left(\frac{1}{n+1}\right)\pi_l < 0.$$

After some extensive algebraic manipulation, this condition becomes:

$$-2\left(\frac{1}{n+1}\right)\left(\frac{A - L(z_h - z_l) - z_h}{n+1}\right)q_l < 0.$$

Because $A - L(z_h - z_l) - z_h > 0$ is a necessary condition for high-cost firms to earn non-negative profits, the condition is satisfied. Consequently, low-cost firms earn lower profits once firms begin switching to high-cost production and additional high-cost firms enter the market. It therefore does not improve a firm's position to pay $F > F^*$ and remain a low-cost firm. And because the patent owner loses all revenue from licensing, and individual profits are reduced, the owner never charges $F > F^*$.

Does the patent owner ever want to charge a lower fee than F^*? Suppose the owner chooses some $F < F^*$. The patent owner earns the following: $\pi_l + (n-1)F$. Because high-cost firms are excluded from the market at F^*, $n = L$. And from equations (8.8) and (8.9) we can also express the fee as $F = \pi_l - \bar{\pi}$. The owner's earnings can therefore be expressed as:

$$\pi_i = \pi_l + (n-1)(\pi_l - \bar{\pi}).$$

A lower fee allows additional low-cost firms to become licensees and enter the market. We can therefore calculate the effect of lowering the fee by calculating the effect of an increase in the number of firms on the owner's total income:

$$\frac{\partial \pi_i}{\partial n} = -2\left(\frac{1}{n+1}\right)\pi_l + (\pi_l - \bar{\pi}) - 2\left(\frac{n-1}{n+1}\right)\pi_l.$$

Rearranging, we get the following expression,

$$\pi_l - 2\left(\frac{n}{n+1}\right)\pi_l - \bar{\pi} < 0,$$

which is unambiguously negative for any $n \geq 1$. Thus, the patent owner does not choose any $F < F^*$ and F^* is the optimal fee.

8.4.3 *Innovation*

Before firms know whether they are the technology leader, and a patent owner or a licensee, they compete in a patent race. Firms can spend κ resources that will produce a production process with unit cost

$$z(\kappa) = \frac{1}{\kappa}. \tag{8.10}$$

Note that $-z'(\kappa) > 0$ and $-z''(\kappa) < 0$. Because the patent is exclusive, only one firm wins the patent race. The contest-success function is given by:

$$\frac{\kappa_i}{\sum \kappa_i} \quad \text{for} \quad i \in n.$$

A larger R&D investment therefore lowers the cost of production, conditional on winning the patent race, and increases the likelihood of winning that race. That said, each firm is ex ante identical so the game is symmetric and in equilibrium, each firm will have an equal chance of prevailing in the patent race. Firms thus choose their R&D investments to maximize the following equation:

$$\frac{\kappa_i}{\sum \kappa_i}\left[\left(\frac{A - z_l(\kappa)}{n^* + 1}\right)^2 + (n-1)F^*\right] + \left(1 - \frac{\kappa_i}{\sum \kappa_i}\right)\left[\left(\frac{A - z_l}{n^* + 1}\right)^2 - F^*\right] - \kappa.$$

Choosing κ to maximize this expression, the first order condition can be written, using symmetry and after some simplification, as:

$$\left(\frac{n-1}{n}\right)F^* - \frac{1}{n}\left(\frac{\pi_l'(z_l(\kappa^*))}{\kappa^*}\right) = \kappa^*, \tag{8.11}$$

which determines each firm's (symmetric) optimal investment, κ^*.

We turn now to some comparative statics. Let χ be the scope of patent protection. Thus an imitator can use replicating technology without infringing as long as $z_h \geq \chi + z_l$. Clearly, a larger χ generates a larger disparity between the low- and high-cost technologies: $z_h - z_l = \chi$. Suppose there are two different levels of patent-scope protection, $\overline{\chi}$ and $\underline{\chi}$ with $\overline{\chi} > \underline{\chi}$.

What are the effects of choosing a higher level of patent-scope protection? The basic insight is that increasing patent-scope protection, χ, increases R&D investment, κ, which lowers the production cost of the innovating firms, z_l. To see this, suppose patent-scope protection is raised from $\underline{\chi}$ to $\overline{\chi}$. From the entry constraint in equation (8.8), this increases $z_h - z_l$ and therefore raises the costs of entry for high-cost firms. This reduces the number of firms in equilibrium, so $n^*(\underline{\chi}) > n^*(\overline{\chi})$. Next, because the identity in the entry condition in (8.8) still holds, and the number of firms decreases, the equation for the licensing fee in equation (8.9) indicates that the fee increases (even holding z_l constant, although, as we will prove, z_l also decreases), so that $F^*(\underline{\chi}) < F^*(\overline{\chi})$. In addition, a higher F^* dictates a larger R&D investment. By examining the optimal investment choice in equation (8.11), a higher F^* increases the left-hand side, which requires increasing κ^* to raise the right-hand side and lower the left-hand side to restore the equality. Thus, we also have $\kappa^*(\underline{\chi}) < \kappa^*(\overline{\chi})$. Finally, a greater investment, κ^*, lowers the production cost of the innovating firms, as indicated by equation (8.10). Hence, $z_l^*(\underline{\chi}) > z_l^*(\overline{\chi})$.

To conclude, Chapter 7 assumed the possibility of a merger that reduced competition but also lowered production costs. Now, the model of intellectual property just illustrated provides reasons for thinking that those opposing movements are more systematically related. Indeed, section 8.4.3 showed how an increase in patent-scope protection both reduces production costs and reduces the number of firms, which have opposing effects on output and prices.

From this point forward, the analysis essentially recapitulates the one provided in Chapter 7 on antitrust law. The core case, as illustrated in Chapter 7, is the Williamson (1968) example of merger that features production efficiencies (e.g., lower production costs) but allocative inefficiencies (e.g., less competition) – again, an efficient merger that raises income inequality, a possibility that this chapter's innovation model demonstrates is feasible as more than a mere assumption. As Chapter 7 also demonstrated, we may indeed want to block such a merger because doing so is a more efficient way to maintain the pre-merger distribution of income. Likewise, we can claim for identical reasons that an inefficient but more equitable patent regime – for example, one that reduces the strength of patent scope somewhat – may be an efficient way to reduce income inequality.

9

Housing Regulation

Perhaps no other event of the past forty to fifty years has magnified income inequality more than the Great Recession of the years 2007–2009. Similarly, no other event has underscored more the role of law in shaping the distribution of income.

Financial crises are typically preceded by a run up in debt financing. As economists Atif Mian and Amir Sufi (2010) crisply explain, there are essentially two different explanations for this relationship: a demand-side one and a supply-side one. The demand-side explanation follows from individuals' overoptimistic estimation about changes in technology or productivity. Businesses, for example, wanting to take advantage of a new technology, may borrow money to invest in that technology, only to find it not as productive or efficient as they anticipated. Default and financial crisis ensue. By contrast, the supply-side explanation follows from new ways of supplying credit, chiefly what we may call "financial innovation." According to the "maverick" economist Hyman Minsky, whose unheeded warnings about the finance industry were vindicated by the Great Recession (Cassidy 2008), financial innovation – the invention and reinvention of "new" forms of money, substitutions for money in portfolios, and other financing techniques – is not an aberration, but rather "is a characteristic of our economy in good times" (Minsky 1986, 199)

Evidence supports the supply-side view of the financial meltdown in the Great Recession of 2007–2009. A great deal of "financial innovation" took place leading up to the Recession. Financial institutions pooled mortgages to secure a new kind of financial instrument (mortgage-backed securities) and these and other kinds of asset-backed securities were further repackaged into collateralized debt obligations (CDO) with different tranches of risk to diversify investment options.[1] These innovations fueled the supply machine for subprime mortgages. According to Mian and

[1] As Fligstein and Goldstein (2012) illustrate in their history of mortgage securitization, the government also played a significant role in pioneering and promoting financial innovation through government-sponsored enterprises (GSE) like Freddie Mac and Fannie Mae.

Sufi (2010, 52), "The fraction of home purchase mortgages that were securitized by non-government-sponsored enterprise (GSE) institutions rose from 3 percent to almost 20 percent from 2002 to 2005, before collapsing completely by 2008."[2] Risky mortgage-lending created a boom in housing prices, which in turn spurred a rise in home equity-based borrowing (Mian and Sufi 2011). As we all know now, the universal growth of debt, underwritten by questionable financial engineering, did not end well.

Financial innovation on Wall Street was also a period of deregulation, non-regulation, and widening income inequality. The Glass-Steagall Act was repealed in 1999, which allowed banks to span both investment and commercial operations, and thereafter financial institutions of all types joined the housing party.[3] Infamously, the former Chairman of the Federal Reserve Bank, Alan Greenspan, misattributed the growth of debt financing to demand-side technological changes,[4] and opposed the regulation of the financial industry (Fligstein and Goldstein 2012, 351). Meanwhile, relative wages in the financial sector exploded, with economists later estimating that 30–50 percent of the increase from the mid-1990s until 2006 came from rent extraction, rather than technological developments or productivity increases (Philippon and Reshef 2012). Financiers generated wealth not by developing better products for more people, but by packaging and repackaging other people's assets and generating fees in the process. Abetted by legal changes, the American housing market became a primary target for engineering inequality.

The aftermath of the crisis was severe. Home values for the middle class dropped 30 percent from their peak in 2006, resulting in a 23 percent loss of wealth for the average American (Smeeding 2012, 2). For their part, while recession dealt the wealthy an initial setback, the wealthiest Americans have seen their stock-market wealth come roaring back since then (2).[5] This trend, too, has been aided and abetted by the financial sector's ascendancy. Research suggests that the growing role

2 See also Mian and Sufi (2009).

3 *See* Gramm-Leach-Bliley Act 113 STAT. 1338 PUBLIC LAW 106-102 (enacted Nov. 12, 1999).

4 In 2005, in remarks to the Federal Reserve System Community Affairs Research Conference, Alan Greenberg (2005) stated:

> With these advances in technology, lenders have taken advantage of credit-scoring models and other techniques for efficiently extending credit to a broader spectrum of consumers. The widespread adoption of these models has reduced the costs of evaluating the creditworthiness of borrowers, and in competitive markets cost reductions tend to be passed through to borrowers. Where once more-marginal applicants would simply have been denied credit, lenders are now able to quite efficiently judge the risk posed by individual applicants and to price that risk appropriately. These improvements have led to rapid growth in subprime mortgage lending; indeed, today subprime mortgages account for roughly 10 percent of the number of all mortgages outstanding, up from just 1 or 2 percent in the early 1990s.

5 Smeeding (2012) writes, "Wealth inequality has also increased. The wealthy did suffer large losses in wealth early on in the recession, as the financial crisis unraveled the stock market, but since then they have recovered. Meanwhile, middle class home owners lost much wealth with the housing crisis, especially the emerging Black and Latino middle class who bought first homes in the mid-2000s" (1).

of finance in the economy, facilitated by a favorable legal environment, is linked to income inequality. Lin and Tomaskovic-Devey (2013) explain that the economy's financialization not only transferred income to the finance sector – the finance sector share of profits tripled from a stable postwar average of 15 percent to a peak of 45 percent in 2002 – but that "firms' increasing reliance on financial, rather than production, income decoupled the generation of surplus from production and sales, strengthening owners' and elite workers' negotiating power against other workers" (1285).

* * *

Housing and finance reveal yet again how legal rules and government policy have enormous distributive implications. This chapter will examine policies even more directly related to the distributive stakes of housing law and policy. Section 9.1 of this chapter considers briefly and broadly some recent research on rent control. Like the minimum wage, research on rent control focuses on its efficiency effects. But efficiency is not the goal of rent control; equity and affordability are. Housing policies that are intended to help the poor are often blamed for causing the prevailing disparities in housing equity that harm them. Nevertheless, as we shall see, it is possible to ask whether the affordable housing crisis is not the result of well-meaning policy myopia, but rather the larger forces driving income inequality across the board.

After this brief discussion of rent control, Section 9.2 turns to housing standards and the warranty of habitability, which is a legal rule obligating landlords to maintain their properties according to minimal standards of livability. The warranty of habitability did not become the revolution in property law that advocates had envisioned (Super 2011, 458–59). However, it did spark some important debates in law-and-economic policy, including the "first debate" on the redistributive efficiency of legal rules, initiated by Ackerman's paper (1971), "Regulating Slum Housing Markets on Behalf of the Poor." This part of the chapter explores the key moments of this first debate.

Building on this work, including a paper by Duncan Kennedy (1987), Section 9.3 then asks whether there is life left in the warranty of habitability, especially in the midst of our current affordable housing crisis. The main contribution of this section is to explicitly address the issue of the redistributive efficiency of housing standards, as posed by the double-distortion argument. Arguments such as Ackerman's and Kennedy's have been typically pitched in terms of efficiency, showing how housing standards may have no efficiency costs or may even improve efficiency. This obviously addresses economists' core concern, but neither explicitly tackles the double-distortion argument conceptually, undoubtedly because both contributions appeared before Kaplow and Shavell (1994). I will therefore take up this challenge in Section 9.4 and show that housing standards can redistribute more efficiently than taxes, even if they are themselves *inefficient*.

The chapter in Section 9.5 concludes with some brief remarks about combining housing subsidies (a more pro-market solution to the lack of affordable housing) and rent control. This discussion is inspired by Lee and Saez's (2012) insights into the incidence effects of wage-subsidies in labor markets. Analogizing to that problem, housing subsidies can be expected to increase demand for housing. This effect causes housing prices and rents to increase, meaning that some portion of the subsidy is captured by property owners or landlords. In this context, rent control can prevent housing prices from exceeding their market-clearing level and ensure that every dollar of the subsidy remains with the tenants.

9.1 RENT CONTROL

Many economists adamantly oppose rent control, with an intensity that equals, and probably exceeds, their opposition to the minimum wage. Arnott (1995), citing Alston, Kearl, and Vaughan (1992), reports that, in a 1990s survey of 40 questions regarding economic theory and policy, the highest degree of consensus among economists – 93.5 percent – was agreement or qualified agreement with the statement: "A ceiling on rents reduces the quantity and quality of housing available." Consensus among economists may have eroded somewhat since the 1990s, but, in light of the empirical research reviewed below, probably not much.

The simple, "free market" case against rent control is straightforward and mirrors the argument against the minimum wage. Whereas the minimum wage sets a price floor on wages, with the aim of protecting sellers of labor services (workers), rent control sets a price ceiling on rents, with the aim of protecting buyers of housing services (tenants). As a price ceiling, rent control prevents rents from rising to their market clearing allocation. As a result, the quantity of housing services supplied is constrained by the short side of the market, in this case the landlords and developers supplying housing services. There will therefore be a shortage of housing services supplied to the market and an excess of demand. This is inefficient because the quantity of housing services supplied is suboptimal: Some of those excluded from the rent-controlled housing market would be willing to pay more than the price set by the rent-control measure.

Figure 9.1 gives a graphical depiction of the textbook model of rent control. Without rent control, the market is presumed to generate a competitive allocation of housing services, marked by the equilibrium point *a* where housing supply and demand intersect. This generates an efficient supply of housing services, q^*, and an efficient level of rent, r^*. The levying of rent control lowers the price of housing services to $\bar{r}$, below the efficient price. This lower price creates an excess demand for housing services. Demand for housing services increases to $\bar{q}_D$. However, because the supply curve binds, the actual level of housing services provided at the lower level of rent, $\bar{r}$, falls below its efficient level, to $\bar{q}_S$. In summary, the rent control policy

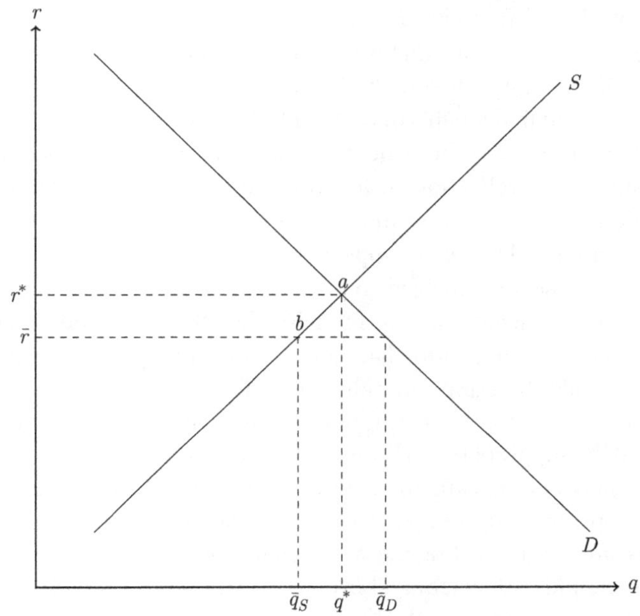

FIGURE 9.1 Rent control

Note: The horizontal axis measures the quantity of housing services, q, and the vertical axis measures the price of housing services, or rent, r. S labels the labor-supply curve, D labels the labor-demand curve.

generates a new equilibrium, represented by the point b, with lower rent, $\bar{r} < r^*$, less housing, $\bar{q}_S < q^*$, and excess demand, $\bar{q}_S < q^* < \bar{q}_D$.

Several recent studies empirically examine the effects of rent control. Sims (2007) surveys the results of a closely decided statewide initiative passed in Massachusetts in 1994 that ended rent control in the three cities that had it (Boston, Brookline, and Cambridge). Strong majorities in these three cities voted against the initiative. Sims finds that rent control had little effect on the construction of new housing but that it did prompt landlords to remove their properties from the rental market. After the end of rent control, units were more likely to become tenant-occupied, rather than owner-occupied (implying that during rent control, owners were more likely to remove their units from the rental market and convert them into condominiums): "units in decontrolled zones are about 7 percentage points more likely to become rental units after the end of rent control than units in zones that were never controlled" (143). Thus, rent control caused a reduction in the supply of rental housing, but not a reduction in the overall supply of housing. Sims also finds that the presence of rent control causes large decreases in rent but also "small but significant" decreases in the maintenance level of rental units.

Diamond et al. (2019) study the effects of an unexpected 1994 extension of a San Francisco rent control law that was initially adopted in 1979. This rent-control extension had cross-cutting effects. On the one hand, it did have substantial benefits for tenants. They find that tenants in rent-controlled units stayed in their apartments longer than tenants without the benefit of rent control. The authors infer that this decision to stay was a reflection of tenants' preferences, rather than a "lock in" effect, because beneficiaries were more likely to remain in San Francisco relative to the control group.[6] This effect appears to be substantial: "Indeed, we find the vast majority of those incentivized to remain in their rent-controlled apartment would have been displaced from San Francisco had they not been covered" (3366). On the other hand, rent control had some disadvantages for tenants. Diamond et al. (2019) find that the extension induced landlords to convert their properties to condominiums or to redevelop them, in order to escape the rent control strictures, which reduced the supply of rental housing. Diamond et al. suggest that this landlord response also increased housing inequality: "Ultimately, these endogenous shifts in the housing supply likely drove up citywide rents, damaging housing affordability for future renters, and counteracting the stated claims of the law" (3366).

Autor, Palmer, and Pathak (2014) also scrutinize the 1994 Massachusetts initiative. Unlike Sims (2007), who studies the impact of rent control on rental prices, Autor et al. analyze the effect of rent control on the market value of the entire residential housing stock. These authors are also interested in the "spillover" effects of rent control on housing that had never been subject to the law. They therefore also analyze the effects of rent control on decontrolled properties as well as never-controlled properties. Their evidence shows that the end of rent control increased the market value of both previously controlled and never-controlled properties. Before decontrol, the market value of rent-controlled properties were discounted by between 45 to 50 percent relative to never-controlled properties (with similar characteristics and in the same neighborhoods). After the end of rent control, the assessed values of decontrolled properties rose 18 to 25 percent relative to never-controlled properties. Using a measure of "rent control exposure,"[7] Autor et al. also find that the assessed values of properties in more densely rent-controlled areas (i.e., the 75th percentile) rose 13 percent more in value than units in less dense rent-controlled areas (i.e., the 25th percentile). Thus, value appreciation was greater in neighborhoods with a larger fraction of rent-controlled properties. Furthermore, rent control has "spillover"

6 "We further find that the beneficiaries are 4.5 percentage points more likely to remain in San Francisco relative to the control group, indicating that a large share of the renters who remained at their 1994 address due to rent control would have left San Francisco had they not been covered by rent control" (Diamond et al. 2019, 3367).

7 Calculated for each individual unit, this measure "is equal to the fraction of other residential units within a 0.20-mile radius that were subject to rent control as of 1994" (Autor, Palmer, and Pathak 2014, 667).

effects: The end of rent control affects not only the value of decontrolled units, but nearby, never-controlled units as well.

Finally, comparing decontrolled and never-controlled properties also allows Autor et al. to distinguish the direct from the indirect effects of rent control, namely, the value appreciation that results from the rise of rental prices following the end of rent control versus the appreciation that results from the greater capital investment in the properties. They show that the end of rent control contributed $2.0 billion to the total $7.7 billion increase in property appreciation in Cambridge between 1994 and 2004. However, the direct effect of increased rents accounts for only $300 million of this appreciation; the remaining $1.7 billion is due to greater investment. Furthermore, the majority of this indirect effect ($1.1 of $1.7 billion) comes from the differential appreciation of never-controlled units.

These studies largely appear to confirm the traditional economists' view of rent control. However, some context might be appropriate. For example, each study strongly demonstrates that rent control is successful at least in its primary objective to limit the rise of rent. Nevertheless, these studies are keen to show that rent control is self-defeating in its other objectives. For instance, recall that Sims (2007) demonstrates that rent control led to a decrease in the supply of rental housing. However his study also demonstrates that rent control did not cause a decrease in construction and therefore in the total supply of housing. This is important because most housing construction is, in any case, oriented toward those with the highest willingness to pay, and then eventually filters down to poorer housing consumers.

Diamond et al. (2019) make the bolder claim that rent control actually increases housing inequality. In the short run, rent control prevents the displacement of lower-income tenants. But in the longer run, it encourages landlords to substitute away from the rent-controlled provision of rental housing, and toward exempt forms of housing through conversion and redevelopment. In a formal, narrow way this seems true, at least according to their evidence. Diamond et al. show a decline of 24.6 percent in the number of renters living in rent-controlled housing relative to the average population in 1990 to 1994. This is significantly larger than the decline in renters overall during the same period (14.5 percent). This more dramatic decline in rent-controlled renters, Diamond et al. say, is driven by landlords' redevelopment decisions, which remove their properties from the rental market in order to avoid rent control. Consistent with this, the authors find that housing units that fell under the 1994 extension were 8 percentage points more likely to convert to a condominium or tenancy in common than the control group, and receive 4.6 percent more permits for additions or alterations.

In a broader sense, however, it is inaccurate to say that rent control *caused* housing inequality. Comparing conversion rates, from rental units to condominiums, is not the most accurate measure of inequality because it excludes the decision to raise rental rates in properties not covered by rent control. For example, it is also possible that the higher conversion rates in covered properties were *caused by* increasing income inequality, and a corresponding greater willingness to pay by wealthy housing consumers. Owners of uncontrolled properties had the opportunity to respond to this by raising rents; owners of controlled properties did not. Therefore, we would expect higher conversion rates in rent-controlled properties under this inequality explanation as well. One could also point out, as Mason (2019) does, that property conversion is not so much a cause of housing inequality as a loophole in existing rent-control legislation.

In that respect, the Autor, Palmer, and Pathak (2014) study offers more comparable evidence of the effects of rent control on housing inequality. Because ending rent control increased property values for both decontrolled and never-controlled properties, we should conclude that rent control *reduced* housing inequality. In a straightfoward, supply-and-demand model of rent control, we would expect rent control to increase the rental price or property value of never-controlled units while it decreases the rental price or value of controlled units. Autor et al. (2014) show that this is not the case. Rent control kept down housing values in both controlled and never-controlled units. This indicates a moderation of housing inequality; certainly the appreciation of property values in Cambridge following the end of rent control has led to greater housing inequality than during rent-control's reign.

We can also say something about the way Autor, Palmer, and Pathak (2014) present their evidence. As was indicated, they are careful to distinguish the pure, "mechanical" price effects of the rent control from other effects. They further specify that the price effects at decontrolled properties are composed of three elements: "a mechanical 'uncapping' effect, which reflects a transfer from renters to owners; a price increase reflecting improved maintenance, which generates increased landlord surplus net of the resource cost of maintenance; and a price increase reflecting greater neighborhood amenities due to improvements in maintenance and changes in resident types nearby" (674). While the first of these elements is a simple transfer, the latter two represent real "economic gains." In other words, Autor et al. are concluding that rent control is inefficient. Indeed, the efficiency loss of rent control is substantial. A full $1.1 billion (13 percent) of the appreciation in market value of never-controlled condominiums and houses over the period of 1994 to 2004 can be attributed to the indirect effects of rent control.

Nevertheless, one can question this conclusion by taking a closer look at the efficiency standard of evaluation. Thus far throughout the book, I have avoided doing so. However, this is as good a place as any to emphasize the biased nature of the efficiency standard.[8] As discussed a bit more extensively in the book's conclusion, efficiency (i.e., Kaldor-Hicks efficiency) depends on the "willingness to pay" concept. That is, utility is measured by one's willingness to pay for a good, service, or entitlement. At first glance, willingness to pay appears merely as a way to objectively, behaviorally reveal individually given preferences and well-being. But willingness to

[8] For a more extensive discussion of the pro-rich bias of the efficiency standard, see Liscow (2018).

pay is not a *direct* measure of well-being. Rather, it is an expression of preferences as mediated by money and income. A person's willingness to pay for a good, service, or entitlement *depends* on their income. Naturally, for normal goods, a person's willingness to pay increases with income. This is true for housing: As their income rises, a person will be willing to pay more for a home in a desirable location. Therefore, we need not interpret the economic losses attributed to rent control as a destruction of "real" economic gains. Rather, we should see these gains as driven by the factors underlying the overall enormous rise in property valuation: a bidding war for desirable housing locations aided and abetted by rising income inequality. These "real" economic gains need not reflect anything more than the wealthy outspending the poor for the most desirable housing locations and amenities, because a wealthy person's willingness to pay is greater than a poor person's exclusively by virtue of their wealth.

I conclude here without any ultimate evaluation of the redistributive value or efficiency of rent-control laws. I will return briefly to rent control, and its efficacy when combined with housing subsidies at the end of the chapter. The next section introduces the chapter's more central concern, the distributive utility of warranty-of-habitability standards, by showing that the debate over legal redistribution began with the topic of such standards.

9.2 THE FIRST DEBATE OVER EFFICIENCY AND EQUITY IN THE LEGAL LITERATURE

Legal scholarship has already given significant attention to the redistributive value of habitability standards. Indeed, the use of housing codes to benefit the poor marked the first "law-and-economics" debate over the use of law and policy for redistributive ends. Within legal scholarship, the debate begins in the 1970s. The origin can arguably be designated as Bruce Ackerman's (1971) "Regulating Slum Housing Markets on Behalf of the Poor." Although he did not identify himself as a law-and-economics scholar, Ackerman's analysis is straightforwardly economic.

Ackerman demonstrated that under certain conditions housing code enforcement could redistribute from rich to poor without any efficiency cost. He asks us to imagine a city named Athens that contains an area called Slumville, where all the town's slum tenancies are concentrated. Those who live within Slumville are "extremely mobile," and are able to move freely within the slum district. Those Athenians living outside Slumville, on the other hand, are "extremely reluctant" to move into the area, even if there was a significant improvement to the quality of the housing. In addition, Ackerman (1971) adopts the following assumptions:

> (1) both landlords and tenants act rationally in their self-interest; (2) no landlord or group of landlords has successfully established a monopoly or oligopoly position in the rental market; (3) tenants are aware of the range of prices and quality levels of

> accommodations offered for rent in Slumville and experience no significant cost in moving from one part of Slumville to another; (4) all of Slumville's accommodations are not only slums, but are equally slummy; (5) similarly, all of Slumville's tenants inflict equal damage upon the physical structures of the houses in which they reside; (6) a significant number of poor provincials are not entering Athens from the outlands nor are Slumvillites emigrating to the hinterlands; (7) each and every landlord in Slumville earns a rate of return on his investment which substantially exceeds the return available when the property is used for other purposes; indeed (8) even if the landlords are forced to bring their residential properties up to code, their rate of return would still exceed that available for any other use of the property; and (9) no landlord will find it more profitable to abandon his building entirely when faced with the necessity of investing substantial sums to bring his tenement up to code. (1102–03)

The first five assumptions are essentially the assumption of perfect competition: rational self-interest, no market power, perfect information, and housing of uniform quality. The sixth assumes perfect mobility *within* the area where all poor residents live ("Slumville") but no entry or exit outside this area. The last three assumptions do not imply that landlords are making extraordinary profits. They only mean that the next, best available use of the landlord's property is low enough to ensure that, even with the costs of housing code enforcement, the landlord will not convert or abandon (or destroy) the building. If, for example, a building was originally purchased for $100,000 and the owner is currently only making a one percent annual return, or $1000 per year, the assumption is that code enforcement does not alter the decision to continue operating the building for residential use. As long as the present discounted value of the future stream of rental income exceeds the costs, including those of housing code enforcement, the landlord will not convert or abandon the building.

To reach his critical result, Ackerman adopts one more condition. He assumes the existence of a small class of Slumville residents who are *not* willing to pay for improved housing. For instance, suppose two types of families live in Slumvilles's 100,000 residential units: 90,000 who would be willing to pay for improvements (called "homelovers") and 10,000 who would not (called "lukewarm" families). (It is not that these 10,000 families do not recognize that they would benefit from improved housing; it is just that their poverty makes them unwilling to allocate any more of their scarce funds to purchase it (1105).) In a competitive housing market, these 10,000 families essentially determine the price for housing. And because they are not willing to pay for housing improvements, landlords are unable to pass on the costs of code-enforced improvements to tenants. If landlords, for instance, attempted to pass on the costs of housing code enforcement by raising the price of rent by $25, the Slumville residents would "choose to pair up and share apartments instead, thus leaving 5000 units vacant" (1105). Because, on assumption, no new residents will move in from outside of Slumville, a landlord's only option is to attempt to induce one of the 90,000 "homelovers" to pay for the improvement. The landlord can do so by offering a rent slightly below $25. But this simply produces a new vacancy, and another cut in rents.

It is only when the lukewarm families are willing to (re)fill the existing vacancies that this competitive dynamic reaches an equilibrium. Because lukewarm families are unwilling to pay for improvements, this equilibrium will happen when landlords charge zero premium and rents return to pre-code levels. In the language of economics, lukewarm families are the marginal buyer and it is the marginal buyer, rather than the buyer willing to pay more for the unit, who determines the market price. In the end, therefore, the 90,000 poor Slumville tenants, who do value the improvements, are better off without any increase in rent. Landlords, who now face higher costs because of housing code enforcement, are worse off. The housing code is redistributive, with money flowing from richer property owners back to tenants.

Ackerman's article provoked a small firestorm about the efficiency and equity of housing regulation. Several criticisms appeared (Komesar 1973; Rabin 1983) as did several articles defending or extending Ackerman's analysis (Markovits 1976; Kennedy 1987). The focus of Komesar's (1973) objection was to Ackerman's assertion of a "leverage effect" of his proposal, namely the argument that the "in-kind" benefit of the housing code enforcement would provide dramatically larger benefits than, say, a negative income tax, for the same or lower government cost. Ackerman's "leverage effect" is that, while a "dollar spent on a negative income tax yields a dollar spent on the poor," housing code enforcement provides in-kind benefits that exceed the costs in government expenditures of cash (Ackerman 1971, 1122). Hence, the in-kind benefits provided by housing code enforcement could potentially exceed those of a simple cash-transfer program. Komesar questioned the conclusion of a leverage effect in housing code enforcement. For example, if the costs to landlords of maintaining code standards were instead explicitly taxed and transferred to tenants, the benefits of doing so could substantially exceed that of code enforcement, particularly if we believe – not unreasonably and consistently with Ackerman's assumptions – that the utility of cash is larger than that of improved housing quality.[9] For our purposes, Komesar's objection is significant for being an early example of the argument that income taxation can redistribute more efficiently than legal rules.

Komesar (1973) likewise provided additional reasons to question several of Ackerman's assumptions. First, Ackerman focused only on variable costs, rather than fixed costs. Over time, however, fixed costs become variable such that, in a more dynamic setting, adopting a housing code may sharply decrease the housing supply

9 Although the tone of Komesar's (1973) critique was a bit harsh, and characterized as "extremely critical" by Rabin (1983, 559), his later assessment, in Komesar (1983), was much more magnanimous. As Komesar (1983, 613) explained, "It was Professor Ackerman's analysis, not his conclusions, which concerned me." Komesar did not have a strong view of the ultimate desirability of housing code enforcement. Nor did he think housing code enforcement was an obviously inferior alternative form of redistribution. His "argument was only that it was not so obviously superior and costless as Professor Ackerman would have had his readers believe."

(1187–88). Second, Ackerman downplays the effect of the housing code on what economists sometimes call "filtering": the indirect effect on low-income housing supply created by the construction of high-income housing. While Ackerman thought those building high-income housing were very unlikely to incorporate the distant costs of code enforcement – as the building ages, "trickles down," and becomes low-income housing – Komesar argued that even small changes could make significant differences to the present discounted values of high-income housing (1188–91). Third, Komesar also questioned the assumption of a negligible effect of improved housing quality on in-migration to Slumville.

Other criticisms of Ackerman's analysis centered on his assumption that the housing supply was essentially fixed (Craswell 1991, 381 and 381 n.32). As we have just seen, this objection was raised by Komesar (1973), but it was also discussed by Posner (1998, 515–16), Hirsch, Hirsch, and Margolis (1975, 1116–19), and Markovits (1976, 1825–26). Most were convinced that the additional costs of code enforcement would reduce housing supply, even with a relatively durable commodity such as housing. Of course, a reduced housing supply would push up rents, harming and potentially erasing whatever benefits were conferred by improved housing quality. But this was not the only criticism. "Among the more questionable of these," wrote Rabin (1983), "is the assumption that non-slum-dwellers will refrain from moving into former slum buildings after they are brought up to code standards" (560). Clearly, as long as families from outside Slumville were willing to pay for the improvements, landlords would be able to fill the vacancies left by the doubling-up lukewarm families. In that case, landlords' strategy of passing on the costs of code enforcement could succeed, possibly washing out the redistributive effect of the policy. Rabin also pointed out that existing residents, who might choose to leave once their income increases, "would be more likely to stay if the area or building were brought up to code" (560). This phenomenon, too, would permit rents to rise, and hence possibly harm the intended beneficiaries of the code enforcement policy.

I will not attempt to provide a balance sheet of the ultimate outcome of this debate.[10] However, one should recognize Ackerman's contribution as a special case of Craswell's (1991, 380–83) analysis of inframarginalism in contracts. Indeed, Craswell notes explicitly that Ackerman's conclusion may still be true, even without his strong assumptions – which, as we have just seen, drew outsized attention. In Craswell's (1991) interpretation, Ackerman's two most important assumptions are: "(1) marginal consumers placed zero value on the warranty [i.e., of habitability, or the housing code] in the sense that they would be willing to pay no more for the product warranty than without it; and (2) the supply of the product was fixed, so sellers would not respond to any increase in costs by reducing the quantity they produced" (Craswell 1991, 380). As we have already seen, much of the criticism focused on

[10] See also Komesar's (1983) response to Rabin (1983), as well as Markovits's (1976) contribution to the debate.

the second assumption, that housing supply was essentially fixed. But what is more interesting to Craswell is the first assumption. He writes that "what is vital to Ackerman's analysis is not that marginal consumers place no value on the warranty, but rather that they value the warranty *less highly than all other consumers*" (382).

In other words, the "crucial assumption" is that those who are least willing to pay for housing are also the least willing to pay for improved housing standards, rather than the reverse correlation. That lukewarm families attach zero value to improvements is merely "a convenient way" of ensuring that they value the warranty least. "But Ackerman's key distributional result," continues Craswell, "would still hold even if the marginal consumers placed a high value on the warranty – as long as all the infra-marginal consumers valued the warranty even more highly" (382). That further implies that *even with* a "fairly substantial price increase" it is still valid to conclude that all Slumville residents would benefit or break even.

9.3 FILTERING AND THE DYNAMICS OF HABITABILITY STANDARDS

Having reviewed the history of debates about housing codes in the previous section, this section will discuss another important contribution to the redistributive merits of housing codes. This contribution will be a crucial step before we can bring the housing-code debate into direct conversation with Kaplow and Shavell's (1994) double-distortion argument, which only appeared subsequent to all of this discussion.

Appearing a bit later than the debate triggered by Ackerman's article, this other important contribution is Kennedy's (1987) article "The Effect of the Warranty of Habitability on Low Income Housing: 'Milking' and Class Violence." This article incorporates a dynamic element into the debate, a part missing from Ackerman's analysis which, as we have seen, left his defense of housing codes open to rebuttal.[11] This "dynamic element" bears directly on the issue of how code enforcement affects housing supply, which Ackerman assumed was essentially fixed.

In brief, Kennedy's argument is that landlords have strong incentives to under-maintain their units in neighborhoods where the value of building stock is in decline. To "under-maintain" means to extract the highest level of rent the market will bear while under-investing, or not investing at all, in building maintenance. It is not a controversial assumption to say that low-income people are more likely to live in areas where the value of the building stock is in decline. Kennedy's key idea is that enforcing a building code may prevent landlords from engaging in this under-maintenance strategy, with the effect of prolonging building life and increasing housing supply.

Let us pause to link to a point in this argument with the larger aims of the book. As demonstrated elsewhere, when we begin to concertize the analysis, unique features of specific markets emerge that reveal why legal interventions may be more

[11] See Craswell (1991, 381 n.32) and the sources cited therein.

redistributively efficient than income tax adjustments. This is certainly true in the market for housing, which differs significantly from other markets because of housing's durability and heterogeneity.[12] These differences have implications for housing regulation, and Kennedy builds the idiosyncrasies of the housing market directly into his model. In this case, the motivating feature of the housing market derives from its durability, and is referred to as "filtering."

Filtering, mentioned briefly before, is the idea that very little housing is built for the poor, and that new housing becomes available to the poor only after it "filters" down through the housing market, as previously built housing depreciates and higher-income tenants or owners abandon it for newer models. We can think of a cycle that begins with the construction of new buildings for upper- or middle-income tenants and ends when the building is abandoned or converted to other uses. As long as the rate of abandonment and conversion at the end of that cycle is greater than or equal to the rate of new construction at the beginning, then lower-income tenants will face a stock of available units that is either constant or decreasing. Kennedy (1987, 488) makes the insightful point that landlords owning units at the end of this cycle will "be able to charge rents that reflect the scarcity of units (quasi-rents) as well as location and maintenance costs." Part of the rent therefore includes an amount that reflects the scarcity of low-income housing. Kennedy continues, "As a matter of fact, low income rents generally reflect substantial scarcity payments, as is evident from the fact that dilapidated buildings in slums have positive market value" (488).

According to Kennedy, one of the facts that constrains the supply of low-income housing is the landlord behavior of "milking." Milking is the practice of reducing maintenance below the level required to keep the building in residential operation. The landlord essentially faces two choices: maintain the building and prolong its existence or save the costs of maintenance and shorten the lifespan of the building. The landlord gains from milking by saving the costs of maintenance. On the other hand, they lose current rents (because tenants will be less willing to pay for units with lower or zero maintenance) and future rents (because milking reduces the longevity of the income stream).[13]

Kennedy gives two reasons why the losses from milking should be smaller as the neighborhood declines. First, the difference in the rent the landlord can charge for a maintained versus an unmaintained building should be smaller as the building

[12] "There is an emerging consensus among housing economists that housing is, at least quantitatively, significantly different from other commodities, and that many of these differences derive from the heterogeneity and durability of housing" (Arnott and Igarashi 2000, 250, citing Stahl 1985).

[13] One point that Kennedy (1987, 490) makes is that it will sometimes be profit-maximizing for a landlord to embark on a milking strategy even before the time that rents will not be high enough to cover maintenance. But this should be obvious: Once rent is unable to cover maintenance, or variable costs, then abandonment or conversion are the only remaining rational choices. So for milking to be plausible in any scenario it would have to take place *before* rents failed to cover variable costs.

ages and poorer tenants filter into the market. These poorer tenants have a smaller willingness to pay – by virtue of their low income – for housing of a given quality. For example, a modest household with an annual income of, say, $35,000 might be willing to pay a monthly rent of $700 for an unmaintained unit, and be willing to pay a premium of $175 above this amount for a maintained unit. But a poor household, with an annual income of $20,000 might be willing to pay a monthly rent of $500 for an unmaintained unit and a $100 premium for a maintained unit. Thus, as the premium becomes smaller the loss of income from milking – not maintaining the unit – declines.

A second reason the losses from milking are smaller for older housing is that the difference in the future income streams between maintained and unmaintained units also declines. With a neighborhood entering decline, Kennedy supposes that a landlord chooses to maintain the building, but can expect at most fifteen years before rent payments fall below the threshold at which the landlord will abandon or convert the building – even while investing in maintenance. For instance, rent may cover maintenance for eleven years, but then falls below those costs. At this point, the landlord will start milking – stop maintaining the building, and charge whatever rent the market will bear – for another four years before the building is abandoned. In contrast, suppose that a landlord starts milking as soon as the neighborhood begins to decline, and that the building is abandoned or converted after four years. In this case, the landlord gives up eleven years of rental payments. However, for each year that the landlord delays the milking strategy, the amount of future income they give up is one year shorter. For instance, if the landlord starts milking in the sixth year (rather than the eleventh, or the first) and can expect four more years of milking payments, they only give up five years of income, rather than eleven. Thus, as the life of the building shortens, the expected premiums from maintaining the building become smaller and smaller. Eventually, the losses from milking decrease and milking becomes the dominant landlord strategy.

Policy-wise, Kennedy's main contention is that enforcement of the housing code can prolong the life of low-income housing and thereby *increase* its supply, offsetting or counteracting any reduction in supply caused by increasing enforcement costs. Because milking reduces the expected life of a building, it increases the rate at which housing leaves the low-income market and causes a reduction in supply, with correspondingly higher rents. On the other hand, if housing code enforcement increases building maintenance and extends the building's expected life, that policy will reduce the rate at which housing leaves the low-income market. As a result of code enforcement, therefore, low-income housing supply will increase, with an accompanying tendency for rent to fall.

Kennedy (1987) also believes that the policy of code enforcement would have to be selective. Ideally, the policy should only target those landlords who choose to milk their buildings *before* rents fall below the costs of maintenance. A policy of uniform enforcement might have the unintended effect of accelerating the rate at which buildings exit the low-income residential market, in particular for those buildings where maintenance costs (but not fixed costs) exceed rent. Selective enforcement would certainly increase the administrative cost of enforcement, requiring additional expenditures on investigators and inspections. Posner (1998, 518) even finds it "doubtful that a court or legislature" could discriminate between those buildings where enforcement would prolong or shorten their life. Though selective enforcement would raise the costs of the policy, with knowledge of rents and maintenance costs, it could still be a successful strategy.

More critically, however, selective enforcement seems to be important if one wants to ensure that housing codes have zero efficiency cost. But because, in terms of the double-distortion discussion, redistribution, through taxes or legal rules, is always costly, this issue is not decisive. In the following section, which brings the housing-code debate into direct conversation with the double-distortion argument, I ignore the issue of selective enforcement.

9.4 THE REDISTRIBUTIVE EFFICIENCY OF HABITABILITY STANDARDS

This chapter has reviewed the older debate about the economic justifications for housing codes and standards, the "first" debate over using legal rules to redistribute income, as well as Kennedy's (1987) important subsequent contribution to that discussion. We now bring the economics of housing standards into direct conversation with the double-distortion claim. The previous discussions sought to show that housing standards could redistribute and not cause any loss in efficiency. But if housing standards were efficient, they would not meet any objection from the double-distortion claim. Showing that housing standards can be (1) inefficient, (2) redistributive, but can also (3) redistribute more efficiently than the income tax, will address the double-distortion claim more directly.

To put the ultimate point plainly, housing standards can have offsetting effects that make them more redistributively efficient than taxes. This argument generalizes Kennedy's (1987) insight that housing standards can prolong the life of housing units, and thereby increase the supply of low-income housing, all else equal. As will be shown shortly, my argument relaxes Kennedy's strong assumptions and clarifies with more precision what I will call the nature of the landlord's maintenance-longevity trade-off. That trade-off goes directly to the offsetting effects of redistributive housing policy. On the one hand, housing standards increase the costs of maintenance, which reduces the supply of units. On the other hand, housing standards prolong the longevity of units, which increases their supply. If the landlord is making an optimal choice prior to the implementation of the regulation – balancing the cost of increased maintenance against the loss of future rental payments due to a unit's shorter lifespan – the housing standard will be inefficient; there will be some decrease in housing supply. In the limit, however, the decrease in supply, and with it the increase in rent, approaches zero. Hence, if the longevity effect is large enough, it can offset the costs of higher maintenance standards more efficiently than a tax-and-transfer scheme. Under these conditions, housing quality for the poor is improved more efficiently than with taxes.

Let me now provide a more detailed overview of the model. A formal model is given in the chapter appendix. The key assumption is the landlord's trade-off between maintenance and longevity. Maintenance is costly and reduces the profit from renting the unit. On the other hand, maintenance prolongs the life of the unit, offering the prospect of additional rental payments in the future.[14] I assume that landlords make an optimal, profit-maximizing choice of maintenance and longevity. The choice of maintenance is continuous, so this generalizes Kennedy's more dichotomous depiction of a landlord choosing to take a "milking" strategy (or not) at a definite period of time. Furthermore, Kennedy does not explain whether milking is an efficient choice for landlords. Is milking an efficient choice? Or is it a strategic choice with inefficient consequences? Kennedy is not entirely clear, but he does seem to believe that selective code enforcement is overall efficient. In this chapter's model by contrast, the landlord's pre-code choice is presumed to be uniquely efficient. Landlords are not trying to "game the system" or supply lower quality housing than promised. This implies that any habitability standard will be at least weakly inefficient. However, this assumption is the only way to effectively address the double-distortion argument. Furthermore, the landlord's maintenance choice is continuous, so there is no objective standard by which to judge whether the landlord is milking or not. Under-maintenance is in the eye of the beholder – or, rather, in the eye of the community that judges housing quality inadequate or not.

A second key assumption of the model is heterogeneity in preferences for housing quality among low-income tenants. This assumption simply follows Craswell's (1991) generalization of Ackerman's (1971) conjecture that the marginal tenant does not value an improvement in housing quality. As Craswell pointed out, justifying the redistributive value of habitability standards does not require Ackerman's stronger assumption. Accordingly, the model assumes a group of (inframarginal) tenants, perhaps a minority, that values the housing standard more than the other tenants, up to and including the marginal tenant. These marginal tenants may value the warranty more or less than its cost; but, again, the key expectation is that they value it less than inframarginal tenants.

A third assumption is that landlords, and the units they own, are free to enter and exit the housing market. This implies that landlords will earn a going rate of profit and the housing supply is variable. (In fact, this assumption views housing supply, strictly speaking, from a long-run perspective and therefore as perfectly elastic.) This is also

14 For simplicity I use a two-period model where the housing unit lasts for one period and may last for a second period. Landlords make a one-time maintenance decision that increases the probability that the unit will survive, and earn rent in the second period. A multi-period model where landlords make maintenance decisions in each period would yield a more realistic, but more complicated model without any additional insight.

a relaxation, and strong departure, from Ackerman's assumption that low-income housing supply is fixed. The implication, once again, will be that even when housing supply is variable, with the possibility of changing the price of housing, housing warranties may still be more efficient than a tax-and-transfer scheme. Finally, like Ackerman, I set aside the complicating possibility that higher-income tenants may enter the housing market following the application of the warranty; but, unlike Kennedy, I do not assume that the housing code is selectively enforced.

Given those assumptions, can habitability standards improve the welfare of the poor more efficiently than taxes? The model specifies four conditions under which the answer will be affirmative. The first condition depends on how effective the improved standards are at preserving the stock of housing. When modest upgrades in standards have a significant effect on prolonging the life of adequate housing, the smaller will be the standard's negative effect on housing supply and, hence, rents.

The second and third conditions depend on (1) the number of tenants whose welfare is improved by the habitability standard and (2) how large that welfare improvement is, for each tenant whose welfare is improved. The more that tenants prefer the warranty and the larger is their improvement in welfare, the more likely will the warranty redistribute more efficiently than taxes. This is because a larger aggregate welfare improvement will require larger tax expenditures for the tax alternative to the housing standard to be distribution neutral. Of course, in light of the previous discussion, there is substantial warrant to believe that the number of tenants who prefer the standard is no larger, and may indeed be smaller, than the number of tenants in the low-income housing market before the standard's imposition. This is because low-income tenants, precisely because of their poverty, probably have only a small willingness to pay for improvements in housing quality.[15] On the other hand, there strikes me with equal warrant that willingness to pay does not capture the *actual* welfare effects of housing improvements. The comforts of adequate shelter and one's willingness to pay for it, which depends on one's income, are two different things. Those differences are perhaps one justification for assuming heterogeneity in tenants' preferences for the warranty.

Finally, the costs of the warranty matter and these depend, intuitively, on the stringency of the warranty. When the warranty is stricter, for example, the costs of the warranty are higher. Inevitably, at least some of the costs of the warranty are passed on to the tenant in the form of higher rent. So, the more demanding the standard, the higher the rent increase. Of course, the countervailing factor is the first condition: the impact of the standard on the longevity, and supply, of housing. Hence, the first

[15] As Quigley (2008, 308) explains, "The high cost of rental housing, relative to the ability of low-income households to pay for housing, means that these households have few resources left over for expenditures on other goods – food, clothing, medicine – that are also necessities. Because housing represents a large share of household expenditures in market-based economies – for the middle class as well as the poor – small changes in the rent burdens faced by households can have large effects on their levels of well-being."

and the fourth conditions are the central trade-off in evaluating the redistributive efficiency of housing standards.

To summarize, a warranty of habitability will redistribute more efficiently than taxes when (1) it has a larger effect on prolonging the life of housing, which raises its supply; (2) a larger number of tenants are made better off by the warranty; (3) the amount of the welfare increase caused by the warranty is larger; and (4) the costs to landlords of the warranty are smaller. This result is still possible with modest declines in housing supply and increases in rent. The warranty is inefficient, but can still be less inefficient in redistributing welfare than the income tax.

9.5 RENTAL ASSISTANCE AND RENT CONTROL

There has been a significant shift in federal government support for affordable housing from the supply-side to the demand-side since its beginning during the New Deal. On the supply side, early housing policy provided direct or indirect support for the construction and operation of affordable housing. On the demand side, vouchers and subsidies for renters have more recently become important forms of housing support. Kazis (2022, 223) says that this divide is the "oldest, fiercest debate in low-income housing policy."[16] Hanlon (2017, 611) reports that while the public housing inventory administered by the U.S. Department of Housing and Urban Development (HUD) declined by 22.7 percent between 1991 and 2013, over the same period the number of units supported by tenant-based housing vouchers increased by 83 percent.

One rationale for government involvement in the provision of affordable housing is a concern about housing quality. The stated purpose of the supply-side-oriented Public Housing Act of 1937 was to "remedy the acute shortage" of decent housing and seek "elimination of substandard and other inadequate housing" (Quigley 2008, 300). However, it is possible that this policy objective is now antiquated. By 1975, Quigley (2008, 306) says, 11 percent of renter households lived in "severely inadequate housing;" by 2001 that fraction had fallen to 3.5 percent. In 1999, 5.3 percent of dwellings affordable to the poorest, defined as those earning less than 30 percent of area median income, were considered severely inadequate; of dwellings affordable to those earning 50–80 percent of area median income, 2.9 percent was severely inadequate (306–07). Substandard housing quality is thus arguably a problem of the past. This is not necessarily an argument against habitability standards themselves; the greater availability of minimally habitable housing may well be a result of such policies. But the trends do suggest that the federal government should step back from

[16] Kazis (2022, 223) also points out, however, that while this debate is lively at a federal level, at the state and local level "it is as if this debate had never taken place." Kazis explains that "federal government – having declared a truce in this decades-long fight – strikes a rough balance between project-based [supply-side] and tenant-based [demand-side] subsidies. But states and cities invest almost exclusively in project-based strategies" (223).

the construction and operation of affordable housing and should instead focus on the demand side.

Quigley (2008, 303) also reports evidence of a "gradual shift in low-income housing assistance from project-oriented to tenant-oriented subsidies" and cites the improvement in housing quality as a main justification for this shift (306–07). Another justification for the shift is cost: Supply-side policies are expensive. Accordingly to Quigley, "The cost of providing decent-quality housing through new construction is obviously much greater than the cost of providing it by using the existing depreciated stock of housing" (Quigley 2008, 310). He explains that "the first-year costs of subsidizing rental households through new construction programs are from 49 to 65 percent more than the costs of subsidizing the same households using vouchers, and the present-value life-cycle costs are from 19 to 38 percent more than the costs of voucher programs for comparable housing" (310).

But rental assistance has its own unique costs. If subsidies to renters increase the demand for housing at any given quality level, that should drive an increase in the rental price. That fact may support a rationale for continued supply-side government involvement, to help ensure that supply keeps pace with demand. But, perhaps more provocatively, that fact also provides a rational for the efficient use of rent control.

This argument in favor of rent control is analogous to Lee and Saez's (2012) argument in favor of the minimum wage. Recall from the chapter on labor and employment law that wage subsidies, like the Earned Income Tax Credit (EITC), are intended to increase the earnings of the working poor. But by increasing the supply of labor, they also lower its price. In fact, Rothstein (2010) finds that $1 of EITC spending raises after-tax incomes by only $0.73. In effect, employers capture $0.27 cents of a dollar of EITC spending through lower wages. This reduces the efficiency of the policy. For example, if policy makers want to ensure that the working poor achieve an extra dollar of income for income earned through work, they would have to increase transfers by more than a dollar in light of the EITC's incidence effect. Given that problem, Lee and Saez (2012) show that wage subsidies and the minimum wage are actually complementary policies. A minimum wage, set at its (competitive) pre-subsidy level, prevents the EITC from lowering wages and ensures that every dollar of the EITC goes to workers. The minimum wage therefore improves the efficiency of the tax-and-transfer system.

The complementary role of the minimum wage and wage subsidies can be applied to rent control and rental assistance. If rental subsidies increase housing demand, part of the subsidy intended for low-income renters will go to landlords in the form of increased housing prices. In the face of that problem, rent control could be used to keep housing prices at the (competitive) pre-subsidy level. That will ensure that every dollar the government spends on rental assistance will go to low-income tenants. This will be a more efficient rental subsidy policy because extra government spending will not be required to guarantee a certain level of disposable income for the poor. For example, as in the case of the minimum wage, if policy makers want a dollar

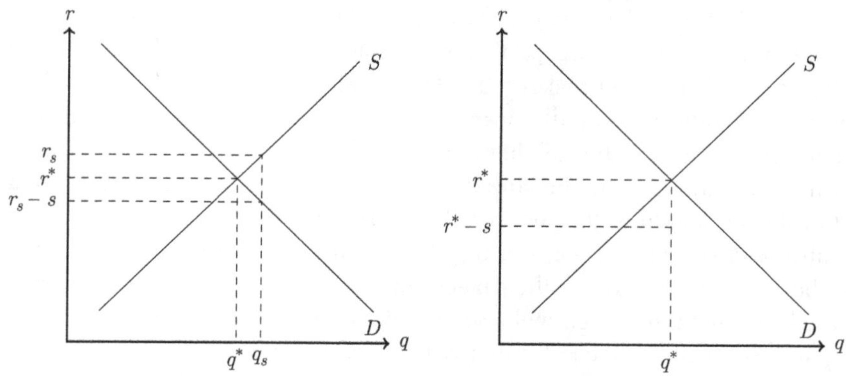

(a) No control (b) Control

FIGURE 9.2 Rental assistance and rent control

Note: This figure illustrates a rental assistance policy with (right) and without (left) rent control. Each horizontal axis gives the quantity of housing services, q, and each vertical axis gives the price of housing services, r.

of spending to go to low-income renters they will have to spend more than a dollar, because of the subsidy's effect on rent. A rent-control policy avoids this outcome by ensuring that low-income tenants receive every dollar of the subsidy.

Figure 9.2 illustrates a policy of rental assistance with and without rent control. Figure 9.2a depicts the subsidy without rent control. In that case, a rent subsidy lowers the cost of rent to the tenant, lowering the price of housing services from the market rate, r^*, to $r_s - s$. The subsidized rent also spurs an increase in demand, which increases from the market equilibrium, q^*, to q_s. However, the increase in demand also raises the market price of housing services, from r^* to r_s. Part of the subsidy, s, is then captured by landlords in the form of higher market rent. Figure 9.2b illustrates the use of rental assistance combined with rent control. Rent control holds the price of housing services at its competitive market price, r^*, and therefore landlords supply the same level of housing services as before the subsidy, q^*. However, tenants only pay for a portion of the rent, the market rate minus the subsidy, $r^* - s$. In this case, the entire subsidy stays with the tenant. Rent control makes the housing assistance more redistributively efficient.

Rent control has an even stronger salience in the context of rental subsidies than does the minimum wage in its own context. Unlike the minimum wage, which is intended to bind for all low-wage workers, rental assistance is not a "universal" program. Indeed, it is not even an entitlement program (Susin 2002, 113), like food stamps (the Supplemental Nutrition Assistance Program, or SNAP) or medical assistance under Medicaid (Quigley 2008, 309–10). Households that qualify for rental assistance are placed on a waiting list – eleventh months or even almost three years, depending on the situation (309) – and awarded according to a system of preferences.[17] As Quigley (2008, 310) explains, "The only form of welfare assistance that is awarded under the sweepstakes model, rather than the entitlement model, is rental housing." This fact makes the potential incidence effects of rental subsidies even more significant. Not all low-income households in the same rental market will receive assistance; but all households will have to pay the higher price of housing rents induced by the subsidy. Therefore, not only do landlords capture part of the subsidy from the subsidized, but they also capture pure transfers from the unsubsidized (Susin 2002, 110, 113). Furthermore, because potential recipients may be reluctant to give up their places on the waiting list, the program design also reduces mobility, which will also contribute to rising rents. With those sort of program-design effects, the redistributive benefits of rent control become even more important. Nevertheless, even if rental assistance was designed to be more like a welfare entitlement, so that all low-income households would receive it, rent control would still be a useful instrument to constrain the incidence effects of subsidies.

As it stands, empirical evidence about the effect of rental vouchers on housing prices is mixed. Early evidence from social experiments with housing allowances suggested that rental subsidies had little effect on prices (Susin 2002, 114).[18] By contrast, Susin (2002, 110) found that the voucher program "raised the rent paid by unsubsidized poor households in the average metropolitan area by 16 percent." Because not all poor households in the same housing market receive the subsidy, this implies a loss to the unsubsidized. Susin (2002, 111) estimates that the 16 percent increase in rent implied an $8.2 billion increase in the total rent paid by low-income non-recipients. As the subsidy only covers $5.8 billion of that cost to recipients, there is a net loss of $2.4 billion to low-income households. More recently, Eriksen and Ross (2015) have found more muted effects of vouchers. They do not find a meaningfully or statistically significant impact of vouchers on overall rents.[19] However, they did find significant effects on individual rents. Specifically, they find that the "18.2 percent nationwide increase in the supply of vouchers that occurred between 2000 and 2002 resulted in an average increase in monthly rents of $5.28 for medium-quality units near the [fair market rate] threshold and an average decrease in monthly rents of $13.47 for lower-quality units" (175). These results are consistent with a story where voucher recipients move from lower-quality to higher-quality housing after receiving the subsidy. Although they found no significant effect of vouchers

[17] According to Susin (2002, 113 n.9), "Priority is given to the homeless, those in substandard housing, and those with rent burdens (rent as a percentage of income) of 50 percent and higher."

[18] As Susin (2002, 114) notes, the original experiment changed household expenditures only minimally and most recipients stayed in place, unlike recipients of the current housing voucher program ("Section 8"), who move almost immediately and report more significant increases in total housing expenditures. Susin concludes, "Since HASE did little to increase demand, it is not surprising that rents were not bid up, and the experiment ultimately does not tell us much about the elasticity of supply" (114).

[19] Eriksen and Ross's (2015, 155) main concern with Susin's (2002) study is bias from unobserved determinants of rent that may have been correlated with the supply of vouchers.

on overall rent, Eriksen and Ross acknowledge that because they focus only on the short-term effects of a voucher expansion that took place between 2000 and 2002, their findings cannot speak to any longer-term effects (175).

Despite these mixed empirical findings, the main lesson has to do less with housing policy specifically. Rather, it is to call attention to the possible benefit of market interventions that are usually dismissed on efficiency grounds. Like the minimum wage's purported negative effects on employment, rent control is said to reduce housing supply, hurting the ones that need housing most. However, both of those responses evaluate policy in light of efficiency standards. These policies' positive role is more promising when evaluated from a redistributive perspective. From that angle, the minimum wage can stop the incidence effects of wage subsidies that reduce the efficiency of the tax-and-transfer system. Likewise, rent control can forestall the incidence effects of rental assistance, ensuring that government spending on poor tenants is not captured by landlords. Policymakers should be more open to the benefits of inefficient policies in redistributive contexts.

9.6 APPENDIX

The following appendix formalizes this chapter's argument for the redistributive efficiency of habitability standards. This appendix is also reproduced in the online version. Section 9.6.1 introduces the basic elements of the model; Section 9.6.2 establishes the competitively efficient allocation of housing supply and quality; and Section 9.6.3 shows how an inefficient habitability standard can redistribute well-being more efficiently than the tax system.

9.6.1 *Model and Implications*

We assume that housing consumers have a simple quasilinear utility function given by:

$$u(x, q) = x + v(q) \tag{9.1}$$

where x is consumption and v is the satisfaction derived from living in a rental unit of quality-level q. The next section discusses in more detail the relationship between v and q and the demand for housing. Individuals also have the following budget constraint: $px + r = c_i$. In this expression, p is the price of consumption, r is rent, and $c_i = y_i + \sigma_i - T_i$ is the disposable income of person with occupation $i \in \{0, 1, 2\}$, where y_i is labor income and σ_i is income from rent. For simplicity, I assume all rent income goes to the rich: $\sigma_2 > 0$, $\sigma_1 = \sigma_0 = 0$. Rewriting the budget constraint in terms of consumption, and normalizing the price of consumption at unity, we get

$$x = c_i - r.$$

Substituting this expression into the utility function, we obtain:

$$u(x,q) = c_i - r + v(q). \tag{9.2}$$

The durability of housing means that landlords make decisions with the future in mind. I assume a simple two-period model, where profits on rental income take the following form:

$$\pi(q) = r - q + \delta[\rho(q)r + (1-\rho(q))r_0]. \tag{9.3}$$

This expression says that the landlord's profit in the first period is a function of rent r and maintenance costs, which we take as direct function of the level of housing quality, q. The choice of quality (or maintenance costs) also determines the level of rent in the subsequent period. With probability $\rho(q)$ the landlord is able to maintain the unit at the previous period's level of rent; with probability $1-\rho(q)$ the rent falls to $r_0 \geq 0$, with $r - r_0 > 0$. I assume $\rho : [0,\infty) \rightarrow [0,1]$ with $\rho'(m) > 0$ and $\rho''(m) < 0$.

Finally, δ in the profit equation (9.3) captures landlords' discount rate. Landlords are homogeneous, wish only to maximize profits, and discount the future based on a common interest rate. In the long run, landlords earn the going rate of profit (defined as $\pi_0 > 0$) and, for simplicity, I assume that supply is (again, in the long run) perfectly elastic. This assumption is not essential to the results, but illustrates the basic intuition of the model. (Also note that this is exactly the opposite assumption that Ackerman (1971) makes.) The equilibrium rental price of housing, r^*, is then determined implicitly by the profit function in equation (9.3) set to the going rate:

$$r^* - q + \delta[\rho(q)r^* + (1-\rho(q))r_0] = \pi_0. \tag{9.4}$$

9.6.2 *Efficient Allocations and Housing Warranties*

Before considering the redistributive efficiency of housing warranties, we will examine the efficient allocation of quality and the effects of the warranty of habitability.

A warranty of habitability imposes a higher standard of quality than what the market will generate. Thus we can define the legal imposition of such a warranty as $\bar{q} > q^*$, where q^* defines the competitively determined, efficient level of housing quality, derived below. The warranty has several effects. First, it changes the valuations of tenants. As already mentioned, an individual tenant's valuation for a housing unit is a function of the unit's quality: $v(q)$. I will assume that tenants are heterogeneous in their valuations. Thus, let the cumulative distribution of valuations for a unit at the market rate and under the warranty of habitability be defined, respectively, as $D(v)$ and $F(v)$ on the intervals $[0, v^*]$ and $[0, \bar{v}]$. I make no prior assumptions about the change in valuations for each particular tenant. Some tenants may value the unit with the warranty more than without, others less. This heterogeneity of tenants' preferences will allow us to pin down the equilibrium quantity of housing along with the rental price, as determined by equation (9.4).

Profit-maximizing landlords will choose the level of maintenance (or quality) to maximize the stream of rental income, taking the rental price of housing as given. From equation (9.3), the first-order condition for this choice gives:

$$\delta\rho'(q^*)(r - r_0) = 1. \tag{9.5}$$

The maintenance variable has two effects on profits. First, it has a direct negative effect on profits, $-dq$. However, it also has a positive effect on future rental earnings. Increasing a unit of maintenance will increase the discounted probability, $\delta\rho'(q^*) > 0$, that the unit will earn a premium given by $r - r_0 > 0$. Hence the positive effect is $\delta\rho'(q^*)(r - r_0)$. The profit-maximizing maintenance level equalizes these two effects and thus equation (9.5) implicitly defines the efficient level of maintenance at q^*.

The warranty also impacts the cost and price of housing. Intuitively, raising the quality or maintenance requirements of housing raises its costs and price. However, this cost is partially offset by preserving the stock of low-income housing, which has the opposite effect on supply and therefore price. Recall that the marginal housing unit earns a fixed level of lifetime expected profit, as given in equation (9.4). Using the implicit function theorem, the relationship between quality and rent, q and r, is defined by:

$$\frac{dr}{dq} = -\frac{\delta\rho'(q)(r - r_0) - 1}{1 + \delta\rho(q)} \geq 0 \quad \text{for} \quad q \geq q^*.$$

When maintenance is at its efficient level, $q = q^*$, the effect of maintenance on rent is zero. This follows from the landlord's profit-maximizing quality choice, given by equation (9.5), which implies $\delta\rho'(q^*)(r - r_0) - 1 = 0$. Hence, when $q = q^*$, the numerator in the previous expression is zero and $dr/dq = 0$. Equation (9.5) also shows that, given the concavity of $\rho(q)$, an increase in quality has a positive effect on rent, $dr/dq > 0$ for $q > q^*$. However, notice that, when above the efficient level, a unit increase in quality raises rent by less than a unit. For $q > q^*$, the numerator is less than one, $\delta\rho'(q^*)(r - r_0) < 1$, and the denominator is greater than one, $1 + \delta\rho(q) > 1$ for any $\delta > 0$ and $q > 0$. Thus, an increase in housing quality, as through a warranty of habitability, has two, offsetting effects. Increasing quality has a direct, negative effect on landlord costs, which raises the rent. However, quality standards make it more likely that the unit will survive into the future at an adequate quality. This effect preserves the low-income housing stock, which raises housing supply and reduces the rent. Nevertheless, the main conclusion is that raising quality has some positive effect on rent: $\bar{q} > q^* \Rightarrow \bar{r} > r^*$.

With the effect of quality on rent determined, we can now examine the effect of quality on the equilibrium quantity. Tenants make welfare-maximizing housing decisions by equalizing marginal costs and marginal benefits. Hence, the marginal tenant receives $r = v(q)$. Let $\bar{v}$ and v^* respectively define the marginal valuations under the warranty and no-warranty legal rules. In each regime, every prospective tenant with $v \geq v^*$ ($v \geq \bar{v}$) is willing to pay for a unit of the respective quality,

q^* ($\bar{q}$). Hence, if h_1 is the number of prospective tenants, $D(v^*)h_1$ ($F(\bar{v})h_1$) is the number active tenants, and along with the distribution functions and marginal tenants, determines the equilibrium quantity of housing units in the market.

To connect all of the points in this section, although the warranty raises the rental price, the effect of the warranty on equilibrium quantity is ambiguous. For example, it is possible that the marginal tenant under the no-warranty rule values the housing warranty despite the increase in rent: $v(\bar{q}) - \bar{r} > v^* - r^* = 0$. This implies a marginal tenant further out in the tail of the distribution and an increased demand for housing: $F(\bar{v})h_1 > D(v^*)h_1$. Or, the no-warranty's regime marginal tenant could value the warranty less, $v(\bar{q}) - \bar{r} < v^* - r^* = 0$, in which case the demand for housing decreases: $F(\bar{v})h_1 < D(v^*)h_1$. The impact on housing demand is one factor that will influence the efficiency of redistribution through the warranty of habitability. But, as will be shown, also of importance is the difference in valuations by inframarginal tenants between each legal rule.

9.6.3 *The Redistributive Efficiency of Housing Standards*

This section now examines the redistributive efficiency of housing standards. This evaluation will use distribution-neutral income tax adjustments. For tenants, the adjustment, $\hat{T}_1$, gives well-being in the no-warranty regime equal to that of the warranty regimes. This gives:

$$y_1 - T_1 - \hat{T}_1 - r^* + v(q^*) - \theta_1 = y_1 - T_1 - \bar{r} + v(\bar{q}) - \theta_1.$$

Because tenants are heterogeneous with respect to v, I will assume counterfactually that the government can observe these valuations and make tax adjustments accordingly. This assumption serves mainly to simplify the analysis, but it also favors the conclusion that taxes are better redistributive instruments than legal rules, rather than the opposite. For each v, the adjustment therefore resolves to:

$$-\hat{T}_1 = v(\bar{q}) - \bar{r} - (v(q^*) - r^*).$$

Summing over all tenants, the total tax adjustment is:

$$-h_1\hat{T}_1 = \int_{\bar{v}}^{\bar{\nu}} (v(\bar{q}) - \bar{r})dF(v) - \int_{v^*}^{\nu^*} (v(q^*) - r^*)dD(v).$$

This can also be written as:

$$-h_1\hat{T}_1 = \int_{\bar{v}}^{\bar{\nu}} v(\bar{q})dF(v) - \int_{v^*}^{\nu^*} v(q^*)dD(v) - h_1(F(\bar{v})\bar{r} - D(v^*)r^*).$$

For the rich, the tax adjustment takes the following form:

$$y_2 + \sigma^* - T_2 - \hat{T}_2 - \theta_2 = y_2 + \bar{\sigma} - T_2 - \theta_2.$$

Rearranging, the adjustment is equivalent to the difference in rental income:

$$-\hat{T}_2 = \bar{\sigma} - \sigma^*.$$

Income from rent is total rental profit, $h_1F(\bar{v})\pi_O$ and $h_1D(v^*)\pi_O$, divided by the rich population share, h_2. The previous expression can therefore be rewritten as:

$$-\hat{T}_2 = \frac{h_1F(\bar{v})\pi_O}{h_2} - \frac{h_1D(v^*)\pi_O}{h_2}.$$

In order for the warranty to be redistributive, $-\hat{T}_2 > 0$ must be positive (i.e., revenue raising) and $-h_1\hat{T}_1 < 0$ must be negative (i.e., revenue spending). Furthermore, the warranty will be more redistributively efficient than taxes when there is a budget deficit. That is, when expenditures exceed revenues: $h_2\hat{T}_2 + h_1\hat{T}_1 < 0$. Using the above expressions for the tax adjustments, this condition can be written as:

$$h_2\left(\frac{h_1D(v^*)\pi_O}{h_2} - \frac{h_1F(\bar{v})\pi_O}{h_2}\right)$$
$$-\left(\int_{\underline{v}}^{\bar{v}} v(\bar{q})dF(v) - \int_{v^*}^{v^*} v(q^*)dD(v) - h_1(F(\bar{v})\bar{r} - D(v^*)r^*)\right) < 0.$$

Using the expression for π_O in equation (9.4), the condition can be simplified to:

$$\left(h_1D(v^*)(\pi_O - r^*) - h_1F(\bar{v})(\pi_O - \bar{r})\right) - \left(\int_{\underline{v}}^{\bar{v}} v(\bar{q})dF(v) - \int_{v^*}^{v^*} v(q^*)dD(v)\right) < 0,$$

where $\pi_O - r^* = \delta[\rho(q^*)r^* + (1-\rho(q^*))r_O] - q^*$ and $\pi_O - \bar{r} = \delta[\rho(\bar{q})\bar{r} + (1-\rho(\bar{q}))r_O] - \bar{q}$. $\pi_O - r$ therefore captures specifically the effect of quality or maintenance on profits; note that the difference $\pi_O - r^* - (\pi_O - \bar{r})$ is expressed in derivative form in equation (9.5). From the previous analysis, we have $\bar{r} \geq r^*$ for $\bar{q} \geq q^*$ and thus $\pi_O - r^* - (\pi_O - \bar{r}) > 0$.

Note that the expression in the first set of parentheses can be positive or negative, depending on $F(\bar{v})$. The sign of the expression in the second set of parentheses is unambiguously positive (by assumption that the warranty is redistributive). Hence the condition will be satisfied (i.e., negative, a deficit) the smaller is the first expression and the larger the second expression. This will be the case under the following more specific conditions:

(1) First, the more effective housing standards are at preserving the stock of housing – that is a smaller increase in q has a larger positive effect on ρ – the smaller the rise in rent and the smaller the difference in $\pi_O - r^* - (\pi_O - \bar{r})$. This makes the set of terms in the first set of parentheses smaller.
(2) The second condition is when as many tenants as possible prefer the quality improvement; formally this is ensured when the marginal tenant, $\bar{v}$, is lower in the distribution, so that $F(\bar{v})$ is as large as possible. This reduces the size of the

expression in the first set of parentheses and increases the size of the expression in the second set.

(3) The third condition is that $v(\bar{q}) > v(q^*)$ is larger for each tenant that prefers the quality improvement, that is, for each tenant in $[\bar{v}, \bar{\nu}]$. In other words, if the increase in well-being is larger for those tenants that prefer the quality improvement. This increases the size of the expression in the second set of parentheses.

(4) The fourth condition is when the warranty is more modest. When housing standards are not too drastic, the difference $\bar{q} - q^*$ is smaller and hence the difference $\pi_0 - r^* - (\pi_0 - \bar{r})$ is also smaller.

Simply assuming that housing codes have a large effect on tenants' well-being would be sufficient to make the entire expression negative and satisfy the condition that housing codes are more redistributively efficient than taxes. Such an assumption would make $F(\bar{v}) > D(v^*)$ large enough so that the terms in the first set of parentheses become negative – and thus the entire expression negative. But such an assumption would also imply that the no-warranty regime is not efficient. If tenants universally prefer higher housing standards, landlords would provide for them voluntarily. It is therefore more plausible to assume that the effect of the warranty is heterogeneous for tenants – which follows the reasoning of Ackerman (1971) and Craswell (1991). Indeed, a good way of capturing the notion that tenants would prefer higher quality housing but are limited, monetarily, in their ability (and therefore willingness) to pay for it, is to assume that only inframarginal tenants, $v > v^*$, prefer the warrantied housing. Given an increase in rent, $\bar{r} \geq r^*$, this necessarily implies $F(\bar{v}) \leq D(v^*)$, which makes a budget deficit less likely. However, provided that the other conditions (1), (3), and (4) are met, the budget condition can still be net negative even when the expression in the first set of parentheses is positive.

10

Conclusion

This book has never questioned the role of efficiency and social welfare in the analysis of social policy. Even when legal rules are justified by something other than efficiency – by welfare, which may require the sacrifice of wealth, as in the classic optimal tax problem (for example Mirrlees 1971) – Kaplow and Shavell (1994) and Kaplow (2008) have shown us that more *efficient* methods of redistribution can make Pareto improvements to welfare and well-being. Thus, this book has offered an "internal" critique of the law and economics of redistribution, never questioning the role of efficiency in the means of social-welfare maximization, even if we may agree that efficiency should not be the ultimate goal of legal and social policy. For that matter, this book has also not questioned the idea that welfare or well-being should be the endmost aim of policy. Thus, the book has assumed throughout that redistribution is "good" because it raises social welfare and has concentrated entirely on the question of whether and when legal rules can pursue that objective more efficiently than the income tax.

This assumption has been a deliberate choice on my part. I have not wanted to introduce contestable premises into the debate, but have preferred to stay firmly within the law-and-economics framework and show that specific conclusions do not follow from the same, shared set of premises. Nevertheless, in the course of writing this book and presenting material from it, that choice has always been met by questions and skepticism about those premises, especially from those outside of the law and economics tradition. In other words, audiences have often asked for an "external" critique. Even where the internal critique is able to contest received conclusions, such as the double-distortion argument, there remains a nagging suspicion about the unintended or downstream consequences of using the "master's tools," as one commentator put it.

I conclude this book with some highly tentative and preliminary thoughts on the "external" critique of efficiency and social welfare. Before delving into that subject, Section 10.1 summarizes the book's main argument and implications. Section

10.2 evaluates the concepts of efficiency, social welfare, and their maximization. My concern is that kind of welfarism defended by Kaplow and Shavell (2002) assumes an independent existence between the aggregation of well-being and the judgment of the analyst that simply does not exist. Welfarism is therefore no less of an "extrinsic" imposition on *others'* choices than are the supposedly qualitatively distinct "fairness" judgments that Kaplow and Shavell criticize.

10.1 SUMMARY OF THE BOOK'S ARGUMENT

The argument of this book is that it is quite possible, even reasonable, to expect that legal rules can redistribute income more efficiently than the income tax. There is a global, general reason for this expectation. The income tax is costly – it entails a single (at least) distortion in labor-supply decisions. Therefore, if we do not like the existing distribution of income, changing it by adjusting the income tax will always entail some loss of efficiency. If the book supplies a general lesson, it might be "mind the gap." What do I mean? Think of it this way. The efficiency effect of legal rules might fall on either side of this gap. On one side, some legal rules or policy prescriptions may reduce income inequality but also *increase efficiency*. Think, for example, of antitrust law which seeks to eliminate market power. Such legal rules may redistribute, by benefiting (poorer on average) consumers at the expense of (richer on average) producers, but also raise efficiency, by encouraging greater labor supply and increasing total (consumer and producer) surplus. On the other side of the gap, legal rules may redistribute income but generate *more inefficiency* than the tax system itself. One example is the income-dependent damages rule in tort used by Kaplow and Shavell (1994) in their pioneering analysis. Redistributively efficient legal rules fall into the "gap" between those extremes. If a legal rule redistributes income but increases efficiency, it does not contravene the double-distortion argument because it poses no efficiency-equity trade-off. A legal rule that redistributes income but reduces efficiency more than that tax system should be discarded in favor of the latter. But legal rules that redistribute income less inefficiently than taxes fall into the "gap" that makes them both redistributive in a nontrivial sense and better distributive instruments than taxes. A minimum wage with offsetting productivity effects (labor, Chapter 6) would be an example, as would the decision to block a proposed merger with more ambiguous efficiency effects than the preceding antitrust example (antitrust, Chapter 7).

This book is not the first to identify this general-level argument (see, e.g., Liscow 2014). However, the main point of this book has been to descend from this rarefied plane and examine specific legal domains, particularly those where the distributive stakes are greatest. Such an examination confirms in each area the general intuition that legal rules may fall in the less redistributively inefficient-than-taxes gap. But the reason for this result in each case can differ and these differences only emerge when examining legal rules more concretely or contextually than research has done in the past. Thus, as this book has shown, property rules may elicit information and behavior more subtly than taxes, making labor-supply responses different for otherwise distribution-equivalent changes to the tax schedule (property, Chapter 3). Or, tort rules can address the inequality-increasing ex post realization of risk that ex ante taxation ignores and that increases the cost of ex post taxation (torts, Chapter 4). Or, the minimum wage has offsetting productivity effects that make it more redistributively efficient than taxation (labor, Chapter 6). Or, capital income may have different effects on labor supply than labor income, eliminating the identity in labor-supply effects between income taxation and antitrust policy (antitrust, Chapter 7). Or, loosening IP protection may have pro-competitive effects that offset its negative effects on innovation incentives (IP, Chapter 8). Finally, habitability standards can improve the quality of low-income housing and prolong its life, offsetting the increased rents from the regulation (housing, Chapter 9). And so forth.

It is possible to generalize a little from these results. Legal rules may redistribute income more efficiently than taxes for one of two reasons, each highlighting a different assumption of the general double-distortion argument. First, the labor-supply effects of legal rules may not be identical or symmetric with those of taxation. We saw this for example in the case of property rules, tort law, and antitrust law. One assumption of the double-distortion argument is that a redistributive legal rule will distort labor-supply by the *same amount* as the income tax, where they redistribute the same amount of income. Nevertheless, as we have seen in this book, that identity need not hold. In those cases, legal rules may have a redistributive advantage. Second, legal rules may redistribute less inefficiently than taxes because the additional distortions created by the legal rule may *offset* rather than compound the first, labor-supply distortion. We saw this in the case of contracts, labor, and housing regulation. Another assumption of the double-distortion argument is that the legal rule will generate *more* economic waste than the income tax. However, as this book has illustrated, legal rules may create less *net* waste than taxation, because its distortions offset rather than compound one another, and for that second reason, legal rules may redistribute less inefficiently than taxes.

This book has not demonstrated *empirically* that legal rules do, in fact, redistribute more efficiently than taxes. But that is not the point. There is also zero empirical support for the double-distortion claim. Thus, the point of this book's theoretical exercise is to meet that argument on its own terms and dislodge the purely – and equally – *theoretical* presumption that income taxation redistributes more efficiently than legal rules. In fact, by critiquing that presumption on theoretical grounds, the book's goal is to ensure that the debate over the relative redistributive efficiency of taxes and legal rules becomes an a posteriori, empirical question rather than an a priori, predetermined conclusion. I hope the book has made that case by examining more concretely a range of distributionally pertinent legal domains. The fact that it is relatively easy to question the double-distortion argument in many cases where the distributive stakes of legal rules are high, should bolster the empirical validity of the book's theoretical argument. Given the notoriously poor track record of broad, general theories in economics, I would be surprised if income taxes performed better than legal rules in more than half the cases, should they be studied empirically.

10.2 THE EXTERNAL CRITIQUE OF WELFARE ECONOMICS

Kaplow and Shavell (2002) boldly assert that we should evaluate social policies based "exclusively" on how they effect the well-being of individuals and that notions of fairness "should receive no independent weight" in that assessment (3–4). Why should we give exclusive weight to well-being? They primarily emphasize that employing independent notions of fairness will reduce individual well-being; in fact, such notions can make "*everyone* worse off" (8, emphasis in original). But that claim is at least partly motivated by the concern that fairness notions involve substituting one person's judgment of well-being for another's. That is, applying ideals of fairness involve a kind of authoritarianism.

For instance, Kaplow and Shavell target normative standards that are independent of well-being, such as John Rawls's primary goods or Amartya Sen's "capabilities." Kaplow and Shavell (2002) object that "when the analyst decides which goods are primary or which capabilities are to count, and what importance each is to have, and then weights them differently from how the actual individuals in society weight them … individuals will be made worse off" (Kaplow and Shavell 2002, 29 n.27).

My argument is simply that any notion of social welfare, Kaplow and Shavell's included, entails precisely the same kind of substitution of one person's evaluation of well-being for another's, and hence the imposition of one person's judgment over another's or others'. The very act of weighting – and, furthermore, aggregating and maximizing – requires an independent act of judgment that is over and above whatever it might mean to give exclusive effect to persons' "actual" well-being.

One reason for this conclusion is that social welfare evaluations require aggregating individual well-being. Comparing and aggregating individual well-being requires commensurating the incommensurable. Social welfare functions in particular presume both the ability to measure well-being and a common, homogeneous metric or ranking according to which all such measures can be aggregated. There is no such metric or ranking – none, that is, that exists independently or objectively from any one person's own judgment of that metric or ranking. Hence, the positing of any such measure will entail the substitution of one person's judgment of social welfare for another's.

Both efficiency and the more general concepts of social welfare illustrate the necessity of making value judgments, and that any such judgment entails substituting one set of tastes for another. The following two subsections examine each in turn.

10.2.1 *Efficiency*

One way of comparing and aggregating different individuals' well-being is by using their "willingness to pay" for some good or legal entitlement. Willingness to pay implies the goal that law and policy should maximize efficiency. There is no obvious, unmediated way of directly measuring or even comparing different individuals' "levels" of well-being. Nevertheless, economists have argued that we can infer individual well-being from their behavior, namely, by observing what they would be willing to pay for a given good or legal entitlement. Knowing what an individual would be willing to pay allows us to measure, in dollars and cents even, how much a good our outcome is worth to that person. And with a common monetary metric, we can also compare how the good or entitlement would affect aggregate well-being. Also recall that willingness to pay is an essential part of the Kaldor-Hicks test. If the winners would be willing to compensate the losers monetarily, so that the losers are no worse off after the policy change than they were before, we have a way of measuring aggregate well-being. That is, willingness to pay is what makes well-being comparable in Kaldor-Hicks efficiency, by reducing welfare to a single, quantitative unit of measure.

Unfortunately, willingness to pay has some serious problems as a metric of individual well-being – assuming in principle the possibility or desirability of a standardized measure of well-being. Several scholars have argued that the efficiency standard has a pro-rich bias (see, e.g., Baker 1975; Dworkin 1980; Liscow 2018). In other words, one might say that willingness to pay imposes the preferences of the wealthy on society and the poor. This bias arises because a person's willingness to pay depends on their wealth. With a declining marginal utility of money or consumption, the rich become more willing to give up their money for a given good or entitlement, as their income increases. The rich therefore have, in general, a greater willingness to pay than the poor.[1] Policy making that is dependent on Kaldor-Hicks efficiency and the willingness-to-pay concept is therefore biased in favor of the rich.

Liscow (2018) uses a simple numerical example to underscore the rich-biased nature of the willingness-to-pay metric. Suppose that a government and its policy-makers are deciding where to shut down some polluting factories. There are two communities of equal population size, Richtown and Poortown. The residents of Richtown have an income of $y_R = \$9$ and those of Poortown have $y_P = \$1$. The residents of each town also have an identical utility function given by $u = \log(1+x) + \log(c)$. Utility is thus the addition of the logarithmic functions of consumption, c,

[1] Of course, there are some things that the poor may be more willing to pay for than the wealthy are. The poor may be more willing to pay for municipal bus services than the rich. But this is also because the poor are less likely to have better means of transportation while the rich, because of their wealth, are. (The rich own an automobile and, more often, automobiles.) Thus, while policy may not be universally biased toward the rich, rich persons' greater willingness to pay for most things places a very heavy thumb on the side of the rich in the scale of policy making.

and the cleanliness of the environment, x. Importantly, the logarithmic functions capture the declining marginal utility of consumption. Suppose that all income is spent on consumption.[2] Finally, suppose that the status quo policy is that Richtown and Poortown each have one unit of "cleanliness," $\bar{x}_R = \bar{x}_P = 1$. However, the government can reduce pollution by ten units in either location (but not both); thus, however the credits are allocated between the two locations, they sum to ten units: $x_R + x_P = 10$. How should the government allocate these credits? What is a cleanliness credit's value or price, labeled g?

Before seeing how different measures of wealth and welfare affect the government's allocation of the credits, we can get a brief glimpse of how willingness to pay depends on income. Both rich and poor have a budget that they can divide between consumption and cleanliness. If we assume that they spend their entire budget (no more, no less) and normalize the price of consumption to one, we can write this balanced budget constraint as $y + g\bar{x} = c + gx$, with the initial endowments of the left-hand side, and expenditures on the right. We can solve that equation in terms of c, which then gives $c = y + g(\bar{x} - x)$. Now, we can substitute this equation for c into the utility function, which becomes:

$$u = \log(1 + x) + \log(y + g(\bar{x} - x)).$$

Applying some basic calculus, we can differentiate this new utility expression with respect to cleanliness, x, set the result equal to zero, and solve for g in order to find the individual's willingness to pay for a unit of cleanliness.

$$\frac{y}{2x + 1 + \bar{x}} = g^*. \tag{10.1}$$

Willingness to pay is often defined as the maximum price for which a person is willing to pay for a unit of the good (or for the entitlement). Because residents of each town have one unit of cleanliness credit, $\bar{x}$, to spend, we can assume that that amount is actually spent so that x is also equal to one. Hence, equation (10.1) tells us the price an individual with income y would pay for that additional credit of cleanliness.

Equation (10.1) is thus the general willingness-to-pay expression for individuals in both towns. On the left-hand side of that equation, the denominator is the same for residents of Richtown and Poortown. Thus, with $\bar{x} = x = 1$, income, y, is the only variable that distinguishes them. The equation then clearly tells us that as income rises, the price that person would be willing to pay will also increase. Therefore, because $y_R > y_P$, or, more specifically, \$9 > \$1, the residents of Richtown would be willing to pay a higher price, g^*, for a unit of cleanliness than the residents of Poortown. For that reason, Richtown residents have a higher willingness to pay than Poortown residents. Indeed, carrying through the calculations, Richtown residents

[2] Why is income spent only on consumption rather than environmental amelioration? One reason is collective-action problems. For instance, because everyone benefits from reduced pollution the individual costs may exceed the individual benefits.

are willing to pay $g_R^* = \$2.25$ for a cleanliness credit, while Poortown residents would only be willing to pay $g_P^* = \$0.25$. One should already see the problem with interpreting these values as the unfiltered "preferences" that residents of each town have for a clean environment.

Following Liscow (2018), we can now compare two different measures of aggregate well-being that are used to determine how the government's cleanliness credits should be distributed. These two measures are, first, efficiency (determined by a person's willingness to pay) and, second, utility (on the assumption that individuals have the same utility function and hence a common metric for utility). When choosing utility, Liscow also compares the outcomes when individuals are allowed to exchange the cleanliness credits that they receive from the government.

Table 10.1 reports the results of Liscow's comparative exercise. The first column tells us which measure is being maximized: either efficiency or utility (both with and without trading credits). The next two columns show how the government allocates credits according to which measure is maximized. The final column uses total utility to evaluate each case.

As can be seen in Table 10.1, if the government wants to maximize efficiency (i.e., Kaldor-Hicks efficiency), it should allocate all credits to the rich. The rich have more money than the poor which makes their willingness to pay greater. They would gladly give up more income than the poor in order to improve the environment. All of the cleanliness credits are therefore awarded to Richtown, even though they do not actually have to pay anything. Consequently, this result produces greater inequality in the well-being of rich and poor than was the case in the status quo.

What if the government wants to maximize well-being as measured by utility rather than wealth? In the first case, the government does not allow trading. Because the status-quo policy assigns both Richtown and Poortown each one unit of "cleanliness," the marginal benefit of an additional unit of cleanliness is equal for residents in both towns. Utility, or well-being, is therefore maximized by distributing the cleanliness credits equally, five to each town.

Finally, how should the government allocate cleanliness credits to maximize utility if these credits can be traded? Now the marginal utility of consumption matters in addition to the marginal utility of a clean environment. And as already indicated,

TABLE 10.1 *Allocating cleanliness credits*

	Credits		
	Poor	Rich	Total Utility
Efficiency	0	10	2.00
Utility, no trading	5	5	2.51
Utility, with trading	9.8	0.2	2.95

the marginal benefit of an additional unit of consumption for the poor is much higher than for the rich (indeed, nine times as much). Accordingly, the government maximizes utility by giving 9.8 credits to the residents of Poortown and 0.2 credits to the residents of Richtown. Poortown then sells some of their credits to Richtown in order to increase consumption.[3]

Each of these policy choices yields stark differences between rich and poor. Referring again to Table 10.1, the efficient decision, which gives all ten credits to Richtown and zero to Poortown, produces a total utility of 2.00. The utility-maximizing decision, without the ability to trade credits, gives five credits to Richtown and five to Poortown, and delivers a total utility of 2.51. When credits can be traded, the results are almost the complete opposite of the efficient allocation. With tradeable credits, Poortown gets 9.8 credits and Richtown 0.2. The resulting total utility is 2.95. The point Liscow (2018) makes with this example, and the point that others have insisted on in other criticisms of the efficiency norm (e.g., Baker 1975; Dworkin 1980), is that the efficiency norm is biased toward the wealthy. This example illustrates that bias powerfully. The efficiency standard produces a massive inequality of wealth, well-being, and environmental cleanliness, poles apart than if the government's objective was to maximize total well-being or utility.

More interesting than efficiency's pro-rich bias is the process by which this bias inserts itself into the analysis, which cannot be explained so easily in terms of bad faith. After diagnosing the bias in the efficiency standard, Baker (1975) invites readers "to consider how, by favoring both the rich and the productive claimants," Kaldor-Hicks efficiency "would correlate with the ideological needs of a rising bourgeois" (21). With that invitation, it is tempting to interpret the efficiency standard in cynical terms, as a consciously calculated, bad-faith effort by economists, the paid mouthpieces of said bourgeoisie, to advance a pro-rich policy agenda with the thinly veiled patina of scientific facticity and quantitative rigor. But the "correlation" between efficiency and the interests of the capitalist class need not be so instrumental and crass as this. The Pareto principle begins innocently enough, stepping around the problem of aggregating the well-being of many different people by simply requiring that at least one person be made better off and no one worse off. As clever as this response is, Pareto efficiency raises a series of other complications, not least among them the inevitability of the aggregation problem that comes with the biased *consequences* of virtually any implemented policy – the fact that policies normally produce winners as well as losers. Kaldor-Hicks efficiency attempts to come to the rescue by offering a seemingly value-free, neutral answer. Classically, economists construe "tastes" or preferences as simply given, themselves simply value-free economic data – de gustibus non est disputandum. Stigler and Becker (1977) famously wrote:

[3] In fact, Poortown sells 4.8 cleanliness credits to Richtown at $0.83 per credit, yielding a revenue of $4. Because this exchange results in a transfer of money from rich to poor, it results in a complete equality of both consumption ($5 each) and environmental cleanliness (5 units each). Liscow (2018) derives this result in Appendix F of his article.

> Tastes are the unchallengeable axioms of a man's behavior: he may properly (usefully) be criticized for inefficiency in satisfying his desires, but the desires themselves are *data*. … [T]astes neither change capriciously nor differ importantly between people. On this interpretation one does not argue over tastes for the same reason that one does not argue over the Rocky Mountains – both are there, will be there next year, too, and are the same to all men. (Stigler and Becker 1977, 76, emphasis in original)

We can supposedly infer these preferences in a similarly factual, value-free way by observing individuals' behaviors, specifically by what they are *willing to pay* for a given good, service, or entitlement. "Willingness to pay" therefore seemingly gives us access to individuals' preferences, which in the logic of welfare economics acquire a foundational status. The elicitation of these preferences provides the factual givens on which policy decisions can be formed. It appears to achieve ulitarianism's long-wished for dream: a method of evaluation rooted in something physical rather than metaphysical, such as the notion of natural rights that Bentham described as "nonsense upon stilts"[4]

Of course, as we have just seen with Liscow's (2018) example, preferences, as measured by willingness-to-pay, are not neutral or free of interpretation. Willingness to pay depends on how much income someone has, which immediately raises issues of comparison: Some individuals have more income than others. But the dependence of preferences on income is even less innocuous than first appears. In nominal terms, a person's income is relatively meaningless. And in real terms, a person's income depends on the whole array of prices in a given economy, which themselves are a complex *social* function of society's tastes, choices, and technology. In that sense, there is nothing foundational about willingness to pay as an expression of preferences. Rather, willingness to pay is only one possible – and possibly a highly biased and distorted – expression of preferences.[5]

10.2.2 *Social Welfare*

The stark differences between the standards of efficiency and utility illustrated in the previous problem make it tempting to turn to the latter as an answer to the former's pro-rich bias. But this option is illusory because it does not address the fundamental problem. Liscow's example assumed a common metric and functional form for utility, but such a metric does not in fact exist. The purported appeal of efficiency, as we saw, was that willingness-to-pay behavior could be measured in the common metric of money. The problem with utility, or any other notion of

4 "*Natural rights* is simple nonsense: natural and imprescriptible rights, rhetorical nonsense, – nonsense upon stilts" (Bentham 1843, 501, emphasis in original).

5 For roughly similar thoughts on the limiting nature of prices in efficiency judgments, see Coleman (1980, 523–26).

well-being, is that it also requires some homogeneous measure in order to make the same kinds of comparisons. Traditionally, the stumbling block to this is that the utility or well-being of any two individuals are heterogeneous. If so, how are we justified in choosing a single, homogeneous metric by which different persons' well-being can be compared?

This concern is closely bound up with the challenge of making interpersonal comparisons of well-being. That challenge is whether some amount of pleasure or pain experienced by one person can be compared to another person's. Whatever we call it – utility, happiness, pleasure, well-being, preference satisfaction – is an inherently subjective experience. How can that experience be measured and compared across different people? As the father of utilitarianism, Jeremy Bentham, put it:

> 'Tis vain to talk of adding quantities which after the addition will continue to be as distinct as they were before; one man's happiness will never be another man's happiness: a gain to one man is no gain to another: you might as well pretend to add 20 apples to 20 pears. (Binmore 2009, 540)

To put this in terms expressed in this book, how do we know a poor person values an additional dollar more than a rich person? Perhaps because the rich and poor have different utility functions the rich, despite their greater wealth, value an additional dollar *more* than the poor? Maybe the rich are rich because they value riches more?

Curiously, efficiency came to predominate in economic evaluations because of the perceived inability to make interpersonal comparisons of well-being. In the 1930s and 1940s, when economics was concerned with its status as a "science," it was common to dismiss interpersonal comparisons because they entailed value judgments rather being based on cool, factual "observation" (Adler 2012, 185–86). Ethical judgments were thought to "have no objective validity whatsoever ... They are pure expressions of feeling and as such do not come under the category of truth and falsehood" (Ayer, (1936) 1971, 144, quoted in Hammond, 1991, 204). Infecting one's facts with value judgments was a cardinal sin within the reigning logical positivism of the times (Binmore 2009, 549) much as it remains so now among many economists and other social scientists (Barry 1986, 35). An oft-cited source for the opposition to value judgments is Lionel Robbins's (1935) book *An Essay on the Nature and Significance of Economic Science*, which many took to assert that interpersonal comparisons of well-being were inadmissible to economics as a positive science (Adler 2012, 185). Kaldor-Hicks efficiency was thus perceived as a way to make evaluations without entertaining interpersonal comparisons of utility.[6] Yet, Kaldor-Hicks efficiency is far from "neutral" or "objective," as demonstrated in the previous section.

[6] According to Adler (2012), "Kaldor and Hicks endorsed Robbins' argument – seeing it as a central justification for developing a new form of welfare economics that would abstain from interpersonal comparisons and instead be oriented around the Pareto(-superiority) principle and, by extension, the potential-Pareto (Kaldor-Hicks) tests" (186). One can also trace the discussion in Robbins (1938), Hicks (1939), and Kaldor (1939).

Today, economists appear to be much more comfortable making interpersonal comparisons of well-being. Among other factors, the drawbacks of the Kaldor-Hicks criterion were a motivation for taking more seriously interpersonal comparisons of well being and even for the development of a *new* new welfare economics, including the specification and elaboration of social welfare functions (185). There seems to be essentially two reactions to the erstwhile rejection of interpersonal comparisons by economists. The first is that *making* interpersonal comparisons of well-being is not subjective, or value-laden, but can be determined objectively, based on the observation of people's behavior. The second is that *evaluating* interpersonal comparisons is a value judgment, one that should not be rejected but rather embraced for that reason; indeed, interpersonal comparisons are, in some sense, thought to be "inevitable."

With regard to the first claim, that interpersonal comparisons can be made objectively, it turns out that observing people's well-being, or at least their preferences, is not as difficult or unscientific as once thought. Rather, individuals' actions, their choices, *reveal* their preferences. We need not even speculate about actual causes of individuals' behavior or whether something like "utility" really exists. As Binmore (2009) explains, "We accept that people are infinitely various, but we succeed in accommodating their infinite variety within a single theory by denying ourselves the luxury of speculating about what is going on inside their heads. Instead, we pay attention only to what we see them doing" (542). Modern utility theory abandons any attempt to explain why people do what they do. Rather it is thoroughly descriptive and "rooted in observed behavior" "because the data we use in determining what people want is not what they say they want – or what paternalists say they ought to want – but our observations of what they actually choose when given the opportunity" (542–43). Once individuals' preferences can be observed, then it presumably becomes a straightfoward exercise to compare their levels or differences of well-being – or, perhaps, more precisely, their levels or differences of preference satisfaction. One can argue that we make such "objective" interpersonal comparisons all of the time in daily life (Davidson 1986). For instance, judges compare the effects of their rulings on the well-being of the litigants; parents compare the well-being of their children to their own experience, when a child contemplates a "bad" decision. Thus, according to Adler (2012, 185), "the possibility of interpersonal comparisons seems relatively uncontroversial among philosophers."

As for the second reaction, economists no longer eschew making value judgments based on interpersonal comparisons of well-being. For example, Kaplow and Shavell (2002, 27 n.20) reject the prevailing interpretation that Robbins (1935) thought that interpersonal comparisons were impossible. Instead, they argue that Robbins thought that interpersonal comparisons, while not "scientifically verifiable" hypotheses, were nevertheless not a "deficiency" but an "inevitability" in economic policymaking. Thus, Kaplow and Shavell emphatically state that "the approach of welfare economics involves value judgments" (Kaplow and Shavell 2002, 25). This appears to be the accepted position among economists today. After all, the branch of economics known as welfare economics is *normative*, not positive. As a question of welfare economics, rather than positive economics, interpersonal comparisons do not entail an inappropriate confusion of facts and values. The disciplinary division allows us to retain the fact-value distinction, but recognizes, as a normative enterprise, that the welfare economics wing *requires* making value judgments, just as any other philosophy of ethics or morality.

Numerous difficulties remain. Among them, *which* interpersonal comparison of well-being should policymakers use to evaluate law and policy? Which is the normatively *correct* way to evaluate aggregate well-being? Economists essentially have no compelling answer for this. In their book-length defense of well-being as an evaluatively superior enterprise, Kaplow and Shavell confess, "[W]e do not defend any specific way of aggregating individuals' well-being; that is, we do not endorse any particular view about the proper distribution of well-being or income" (27). Thus, even when economists do straightforward welfare – that is, normative – economics, they often do not defend a normatively preferred social welfare function but instead simply talk about, in the third-person, the "tastes" of the government or some (disembodied) social planner.[7]

Harsanyi is often cited for the endorsement of utilitarianism as the preferred social welfare function. (Utilitarianism is the social welfare function that is simply the sum of individuals' well-being, without any weights assigned based on income or any other characteristic.) However, he generates this conclusion by appeal to a "veil of ignorance" counterfactual: We should choose the normatively compelling social welfare function by ignoring our own individual preferences and proclivities. It is of course telling, however, that Rawls (1971) uses – indeed, is famous for using – a very similar procedure to arrive at a very different framework for evaluating policy. Rawls's criterion does not maximize a weighted or unweighted aggregate of society's utilities but rather requires that any social or economic inequalities be permitted only to the extent that they benefit the least advantaged in society. We cannot rely on a veil of ignorance, because that procedure presumes what is required: an "objective" standpoint from which well-being can be ideally and normatively evaluated. The argument implies a "view from nowhere" (Nagel 1986), one which is sadly unavailable to us finite human creatures, especially in normative matters.

In his review of Kenneth Arrow's (2012) famous book, *Social Choice and Individual Values*, Ian Little (1952) explained why there is no behavioral or objective way to choose an aggregate measure of social welfare.[8] Suppose we ask everyone in a country

7 For example, see Saez (2002a, 1045), who describes the social marginal welfare weights derived from a social welfare function as "a sufficient statistic for the redistributive tastes of the government in the optimal transfer formulas that we derive," without making any claim to the exact values these weights should take.

8 For other reflections on the difficulty of determining an ethically objective interpersonal comparison of well-being, see Hammond (1991) and Hausman (1995).

to choose whether they prefer policy x or policy y. We then feed these answers into a machine which generates an answer "x is better than y" (or vice versa). Does the machine-generated "master" ranking have any significance? The answer is, not really. For one thing, the machine's answer cannot be a value judgment. As Little writes, "Every value judgment must be *someone's* judgment of values. If there are n people filling in cards to be fed into the machine, then we have n value judgments, not $n+1$" (427, emphasis in original). One could assert that if the machine produced x instead of y then x would yield greater welfare than y. You could then call the result a value judgment, but it would only be the value judgment of the person calling the machine a social welfare function. Otherwise, a person whose own value ranking that did not coincide with the machine's would be contradicting themselves. Formally, instead of writing a social welfare function as $W = W(u_1, u_2, \ldots, u_n)$ it would be more accurate to write $W_i = W_i(u_1, u_2, \ldots, u_n)$, where i refers to any particular individual in a group or society of n individuals (424). There is no need to introduce a further social welfare function of the form $W = W(W_1, W_2, \ldots, W_n)$. "We can deduce the whole effective corpus of welfare economics," Little writes, from, say, $W_{10} = W_{10}(u_1, u_2, \ldots, u_n)$, "remembering only to put 'in the opinion of individual No. 10' after 'welfare' whenever we use the term" (424).

The social-welfare alternative therefore does not appear to offer any more "neutral," "objective," or "impartial" metric of aggregation than efficiency itself. If we reject efficiency because it imposes the preferences of the rich on the rest of society, there seems little guarantee that any other metric of social well-being will avoid a similar problem. What welfare economics offers us is the machine – it can tell us *how* we should aggregate different persons' well-being – but it cannot tell us *which* method of aggregation we should use and *why* we should use it. Without that, we cannot guarantee that social welfare judgments will not be biased, that is, that they will not benefit some members of society at the expense of others.

Based on these reflections, I find it difficult to sustain the distinction between welfare and fairness that Kaplow and Shavell (2002) make. To admit that evaluations of well-being are value judgments is already to give "independent" weight to a specific notion of fairness. To claim that one should give exclusive weight to "how the actual individuals in society" weigh a policy is a non sequitur, for two reasons. First, nothing normative follows from the mere satisfaction of people's actual preferences (Hausman 1995). Second, any normative case for well-being judgments will inevitably overrule "actual" individuals' judgments. This will be the case when they act irrationally, or in uninformed ways, or when only their ex ante rather than ex post well-being is considered, or when they have "bad" preferences (for example, the preferences of white citizens for Jim Crow legislation during the era of segregation in the southern United States). Kaplow and Shavell (2002, 48–51, 410–13, 418–31) must constantly edit and correct people's actual preferences in precisely such cases without pausing to recognize that doing so obliterates the distinction that is the premise of their argument: There is no fundamental difference between fairness and welfare. For those reasons, I see no difference between Rawls's primary goods, Sen's capabilties, or Kaplow and Shavell's welfare in terms of their failure to give exclusive weight to actual individuals' well-being.

10.2.3 *Freedom and Welfare*

These problems would seem to place us in a difficult position. On the one hand, there is no purely "factual," descriptive way of comparing and aggregating different individuals' well-beings. At best, individual well-being is merely a part of a broader normative judgment about a policy or course of action. Thus, the problem that a policy making will override individuals' "actual" preferences – the problem of "dictatorship," the imposition of some people's preferences on others – is ever present if not guaranteed. On the other hand, the likelihood the legal rules, policies, and other official action will create winners and losers is just as inevitable, as are the interpersonal comparisons of well-being we make, in individual life and in matters of social policy (as voters, judges, officials, politicians). Perhaps the answer to this problem is not in trying to identify whose social-welfare tastes are the objectively, normatively correct ones, but to design a set of institutions in which no one person's or group's preferences dominate over the others.

This assertion opens a large number of issues that cannot be addressed here. Foremost among them is the question that motivates Arrow's (2012) aforementioned, *Social Choice and Individual Values*: Is the market or democracy the best way to further social welfare? The libertarian appeal is that one can entirely avoid questions of social welfare because individuals are the best judges of their own well-being and a perfectly competitive market yields a Pareto-optimal allocation of resources. In the libertarian vision, no social planners – no dictators, benevolent or otherwise – are required to make social-welfare trade-offs on behalf of others. However, the unregulated free market often looks anything but efficient (e.g., environmental costs, monopoly, and so forth) and even Pareto-optimal allocations may be judged by many people to be horrifically oppressive. Hence, as government and regulation have expanded during the twentieth century, public officials and agency bureaucrats have been called upon to make welfare judgments on behalf of society. At the same time, the administrative state contradicts our most basic notions of self government and democracy, placing the decisions that have profound effects on people's lives at a remove from their elected representatives and in the hands of appointed bureaucrats in remote corners of Washington, DC, office spaces.

Thus, it is understandable why neither laissez faire capitalism nor the administrative state has terribly great widespread appeal, which is why, when I say that we should be concerned with the design of institutions, neither should be exempt from fundamental rethinking. What such a profound reordering would look like cannot be addressed in this book, but it may require a massive redistribution of productive *assets*, so that well-being accrues to individuals in a way that preempts asking whether legal rules redistribute more efficiently than the income tax system. Until that question can be avoided, however, this books concludes that the legal system cannot be categorically excluded as always less redistributively efficient than the tax system.

APPENDIX

A Primer on Welfare Economics

This appendix is intended as a brief introduction and resource to basic ideas in welfare economics, including some of the formal and mathematical tools used in economics and in this book. Readers are encouraged to use it on an "as needed" basis.

This book uses a variety of familiar, and not-so-familiar, terms: efficiency, inequality, redistribution, social welfare, and so forth. Within economic discourse these terms have specific, often very technical, meanings. This is no less true for a concept as widely employed as "efficiency," whose meaning, as we will see, can change depending on its technical exposition. In other cases, it is not always clear how particular terms are being used. A case in point, as will be shown, is the concept of "redistribution," whose meaning is often taken as obvious in the law-and-economics literature, but is not so obvious upon reflection. To avoid confusion about how these terms will be used in this book, this chapter sets out to define these concepts as clearly as possible and to specify which meanings will be favored in the book, and when.

Sometimes, getting a good grasp of the central concepts requires a capacious enough context. How to think about "inequality" using Lorenz curves, for example, is often best understood when compared with other, sometimes competing concepts (such as, say, the Gini coefficient). This chapter presents the impossible task of presenting a broad but concise overview of concepts in welfare economics. It thus goes beyond what is strictly needed, perhaps, to comprehend the concepts used in the book, while at the same time only covering the most central topics.

Beyond simply defining terms, this exercise will also provide the reader with context to some of the more fundamental substantive debates in law-and-economics scholarship. For instance, we will see again, but at a different level, how the so-called fundamental theorems of welfare economics motivate Kaplow and Shavell's (1994) double-distortion argument. Even at the level of definitions, economics concepts are not free of distributive implications.

A.1 EFFICIENCY

The definitions of efficiency – specifically, Pareto efficiency and Kaldor-Hicks efficiency – are perhaps the best known and most widely cited within the law-and-economics literature.

A.1.1 *Pareto Efficiency*

Beginning with the concept of Pareto efficiency, we can subdivide this into two subconcepts: Pareto optimality (or Pareto efficiency) and Pareto superiority. Pareto *superiority* says that one allocation of society's resources is Pareto superior to another if it makes no one worse off and at least one person better off. In other words, it requires that there be at least some improvement in total social welfare. Hence a change in allocation that is Pareto superior to another is also called a Pareto improvement. Similarly, but conversely, we can say that one allocation is Pareto inferior if it makes no one better off and at least one person worse off. Note also that the metric used in this concept – worse off, better off – is well-being, rather than wealth, or money. That said, the comparison can be ordinal (that is, just "better than" in terms of ranking) and need not be cardinal (that is, "better than" by a quantitative amount, say, in "utils.")

Next is the idea of Pareto *optimality*, or Pareto efficiency. An allocation of society's resources is Pareto optimal if no one can be made better off without also making someone else worse off. Thus, when an allocation is Pareto optimal, we have exhausted all the Pareto superior, or Pareto-improving possibilities – it is no longer possible to make all persons or at least one person better off without making anyone worse off. To put this another way, a Pareto optimal allocation has no allocations Pareto-superior to it. However, just because no one can be made better off does not imply that a Pareto optimal allocation is necessarily *unique* – there may be many Pareto optimal allocations, perhaps an infinite number. Because of these many possibilities it is said that the collection of all Pareto optimal allocations constitutes the Pareto *frontier*. This frontier is also called the utility possibilities frontier, because it also defines the highest feasible allocations of utility among individuals (e.g., Hindriks and Myles 2013, 425).

One crucial fact about the Pareto criterion is that it can make no judgment about the distribution of the allocation. Call this the *equity* problem. It is possible that an allocation that makes everyone equally well off could be Pareto optimal. Likewise, an allocation that is extremely unequal could also be Pareto optimal. But Pareto efficiency has no way of judging the fairness or equity of different Pareto optimal allocations.

Related to this shortcoming, but even graver, is the problem that Pareto optimality does not have *any* criteria for choosing among the set of Pareto optimal allocations, that is, those allocations that are *on* the Pareto frontier. Call this the *indifference* problem. Instead of giving us a unique, determinate social choice, we are given a set of options, with no basis for choosing among them. As long as there are no unexploited gains – or no "waste" to put it a bit more casually – Pareto efficiency is indifferent between any two allocations.

A third drawback of the Pareto criterion is that it cannot exhaustively rank *all* allocations. That is, in addition to not being able to say which of the allocations *on* the Pareto frontier are more equitable, it also cannot tell us which of those allocations *within* the Pareto frontier are more preferable to others. Call this the *comparability* problem. Pareto superiority can only rank allocations where no one is made worse off. If a change in the allocation made one person much better off and a second person only slightly worse off, we might be willing to accept such a change, particularly if the "winner" in this change was willing and able to compensate the "loser," a possibility we will also consider shortly. But in fact, neither Pareto optimality nor Pareto superiority can say anything about this change because, after all, someone is made worse off, an outcome that is unintelligible from the perspective of the Pareto criterion. For this reason, some allocations are incomparable under Pareto efficiency. Also note that incomparability is not the same as indifference. When we say that we are indifferent between two Pareto optimal allocations we mean that they are equally good. When we say that two allocations are incomparable, we mean that nothing can be said about them at all.

The concepts of Pareto optimality and Pareto superiority are also illustrated in Figure A.1. The figure compares the utility of two people. The *x*-axis measures the

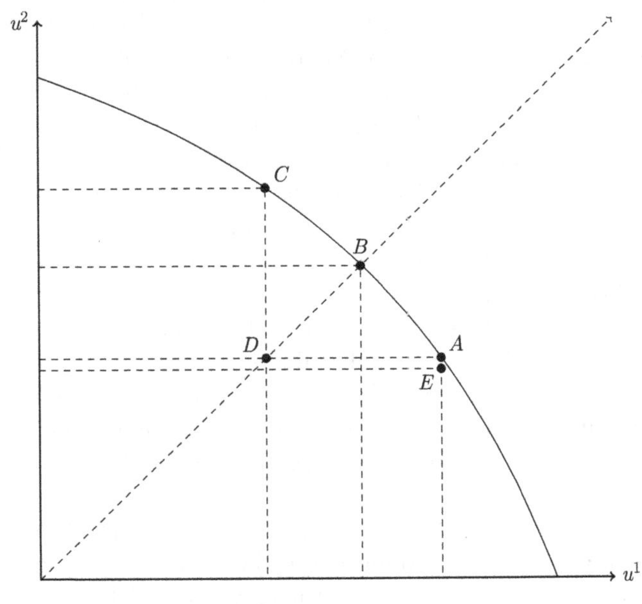

FIGURE A.1 Pareto efficiency and Pareto superiority

utility of person 1, u_1, and the y-axis measures the utility of person 2, u_2. The solid, curved line represents the utility possibilities frontier, or the Pareto frontier, the set of all Pareto optimal allocations of society's resources. The dashed line on the 45-degree angle is the set of all allocations that give each person equal utility. Points A, B, C, D, and E all represent different possible allocations. The principle of Pareto superiority can be illustrated by comparing allocation D with allocations A, B, and C. A change from D to allocation A, B, or C would all represent Pareto improvements. Compared to D, allocations A, B, and C would each make one person better off without making anyone worse off. Therefore A, B, and C are each Pareto superior to D; conversely, allocation D is Pareto inferior to each of those other three allocations. The equity problem can be illustrated by comparing allocation B with allocations A or C. Although utility is distributed more equally under allocation B than under allocation A or C, they are all Pareto optimal; Pareto efficiency has no basis for judging allocation B better than the others. For similar reasons, because allocations A, B, and C are all Pareto optimal, Pareto efficiency is indifferent between them. Each is as equally good as the others. Finally, we can illustrate the incomparability problem by highlighting allocations D and E. Allocation E dramatically improves the welfare of person 2, relative to allocation D, with only a small cost in utility to person 1. Moving from D to E also gets us much closer to the Pareto frontier. Yet because that move also makes person 1 slightly worse off, Pareto efficiency cannot compare the two allocations. Allocation E is not a Pareto improvement compared to E; nor is D Pareto inferior to E. Allocations D and E are incomparable.

Formal Defintion

To illustrate the concept of Pareto efficiency formally, we can depict a simple economy with an arbitrary number of consumers and goods. Suppose that there are a total of H different kinds of goods, indexed by $h \in \{1, 2, \ldots, H\}$, and I different consumers, indexed by $i \in \{1, 2, \ldots, I\}$. The total endowment of good h is $\omega_h \geq 0$ for $h \in \{1, 2, \ldots, H\}$. Suppose next that consumer i's consumption of each good is given by a vector $x^i = (x_1^i, x_2^i, \ldots, x_H^i)$. The preferences of consumers are described by each's utility function, denoted by $u^i(x^i) = u^i(x_1^i, x_2^i, \ldots, x_H^i)$ and define an allocation as a vector of each consumer's own consumption vector, $x = (x^1, x^2, \ldots, x^I)$. Finally, the set of feasible allocations for each good, is given by

$$\sum_{i=1}^{I} x_h^i \leq \omega_h \quad \text{for} \quad h \in \{1, 2, \ldots, H\}.$$

We can now give a formal definition of Pareto efficiency.

Definition 1. Pareto optimality. *A feasible allocation x_A is Pareto optimal (or Pareto efficient) if there does not exist an alternative feasible allocation x_B such that $u^i(x_B^i) \geq u^i(x_A^i)$ for all $i \in \{1, 2, \ldots, I\}$ and $u^i(x_B^i) > u^i(x_A^i)$ for some i.*

A.1.2 *The Fundamental Theorems of Welfare Economics*

Understanding Pareto efficiency makes it possible to discuss the first and second fundamental theorems of welfare economics. As suggested in the introductory chapter, these concepts are important because they inform a kind of presupposition about how law and economics approaches the issue of redistribution. To be sure, this link is often only in the background. But the family resemblance is unmistakable and, on occasion, made explicit.

The first fundamental theorem of welfare economics states that a perfectly competitive economy achieves a Pareto optimal allocation of resources. In other words, in a perfectly competitive economy we have reached the Pareto frontier, all Pareto improvements have been exhausted, and it is not possible to make anyone better off without also making someone worse off.

Following on this, the second fundamental theorem states that *any* Pareto optimal allocation of resources within a perfectly competitive economy can be achieved with lump-sum taxes. (Although, remember, we still have not been given a criterion for choosing which Pareto optimal allocation we want.) Since it is possible for some Pareto optimal allocations to be highly, even perfectly, equal, the idea is that one can obtain any desired distribution of income solely through the tax system without sacrificing economic efficiency.

The second theorem's purported appeal is that there is no need to reorganize the economy to achieve distributive objectives. The economy achieves both an optimal level of output in a decentralized fashion, while the tax system is the sole instrument necessary for influencing the distribution of economic rewards. It is precisely this distinction that informs the policy presuppositions of many law and economics thinkers on matters of taxation and distribution. This division was expressed in Musgrave's famous treatise, where an "Efficiency branch" of government and a "Distributive branch" of government have clearly defined, discrete tasks, and exist as institutional analogs of the first and second theorems of welfare economics (Musgrave 1959). Authors such as Louis Kaplow (2004, 168), who has argued against using legal rules for redistributive purposes, have taken explicit inspiration from Musgrave and the separation of policy tasks he endorsed.

If redistributive lump-sum taxes were feasible, this strict division of labor between the Efficiency and Distributive branches of the government could be directly translated into practical policy. However, in general, redistributive lump-sum taxes are infeasible. Intuitively, a lump-sum tax is one that has no distortionary impact on economic behavior. This is certainly a necessary feature of the tax system if one wants to achieve a desired distribution of resources without causing any loss to economic output. A more formal, but slightly less intuitive definition says that lump-sum taxes are those where the consumer cannot vary the amount of tax paid by changing her behavior. Under this definition, just about every tax instrument fails to be lump sum. A person can change the amount of income tax they pay by working less.

One can also change the amount of commodity taxes paid by changing saving and consumption patterns. Estate taxes can be avoided by making inter-vivos transfers. In the late 1980s, the United Kingdom implemented a poll tax, which came close to a lump-sum tax because it levied the same amount on every individual. No matter one's economic response, the amount of tax levied would be the same. Therefore, in principle, the tax would not induce any (distortionary) change in behavior. Yet even in this case, individuals could vary the amount of tax they paid by moving, not making any official declaration about the new address, and therefore failing to appear on local tax registers (Hindriks and Myles 2013, 428).

Even if poll taxes did not influence behavior, they would not be *optimal* lump-sum taxes. Because the appeal of the second fundamental theorem is that any desired distribution of income can be achieved, optimal lump-sum taxes will in general redistribute and therefore necessarily vary across persons of different tastes and abilities. In principle, one could achieve optimal lump-sum taxation if one had exact knowledge about each individuals' consumption preferences and economic endowments (e.g., their ability or productivity). But since this is private information for each individual, and cannot be known with certainty by a policy maker, redistributive lump-sum taxation is thought to be impossible in practice. Stiglitz (1987) sums it up the best: "It is sometimes assumed that lump-sum taxes are not feasible. Uniform lump-sum taxes are clearly feasible (provided they are not too large). What is *not* feasible are lump-sum taxes at different rates for individuals of different abilities; this is not feasible because the government does not have the requisite information to implement such a tax" (1006, emphasis in original)

Despite the infeasibility of lump-sum taxes, the policy division evoked by the second fundamental theorem – embodied in the Efficiency and Distribution Departments – lives on. Indeed, Kaplow and Shavell's double-distortion argument offers another rationale for maintaining this separation between distribution and efficiency. According to that claim, the legal system should not be used for distributive purposes. Rather, the legal system should merely serve to support the efficient production of goods and services. Distributional objectives should be left entirely to the tax system.

Formal Definition

To give the fundamental theorems of welfare economics a bit more rigor, let us begin by defining a competitive equilibrium. First, suppose that consumer i initially owns ω_h^i of good h, where $\sum_i \omega_h^i = \omega_h$, and denote consumer i's vector of endowments by $\omega^i = (\omega_1^i, \omega_2^i, \ldots, \omega_H^i)$. Then, an allocation $x^* = (x^{1*}, x^{2*}, \ldots, x^{I*})$ and price vector $p^* \in \mathbb{R}^H$ constitute a competitive, or *Walrasian*, equilibrium if the following two conditions are satisfied: (1) utility maximization, where for each consumer i, x^{i*} maximizes $u^i(x^i)$ subject to the constraint $p^* \cdot x^i \leq p^* \cdot \omega^i$; and (2) market clearing, where for each good $h \in \{1, 2, \ldots, H\}$, $\sum_{i=1}^I x_h^{i*} = \omega_h$. In addition, these conditions entail, or are entailed by, a full set of markets and perfect information.

With a competitive equilibrium defined, we can state the first fundamental theorem:

Proposition 1. First Fundamental Theorem of Welfare Economics. *If the price p^* and allocation x^* constitute a competitive equilibrium, then this allocation is Pareto optimal.*

The second fundamental theorem follows:

Proposition 2. Second Fundamental Theorem of Welfare Economics. *For any Pareto optimal levels of utility $(u^{1*}, u^{2*}, \ldots, u^{I*})$, there are transfers of the numeraire commodity $(T^1, T^2, \ldots, T^I)$ satisfying $\sum_i T^i = 0$, such that a competitive equilibrium reached from endowments $(\omega^1 + T^1, \omega^2 + T^2, \ldots, \omega^I + T^I)$ yields precisely the utilities $(u^{1*}, u^{2*}, \ldots, u^{I*})$.*

Formal proofs of these two propositions can be found in Mas-Colell, Whinston, and Green (1995, 326–328, 549–554).

A.1.3 *Kaldor-Hicks Efficiency*

As we saw, the Pareto criterion faces a comparability problem. That is, Pareto optimailty cannot say anything about allocations within the Pareto frontier where at least one person is made better off and at least one other is made worse off. Yet policy changes, and legal changes above all, often produce losers as well as winners. Strictly speaking, these cases are Pareto-incomparable because someone is made worse off yet, in many cases, we might think those trade-offs are worth making, depending on who the losers are and the magnitude of the losses. In cases where Pareto optimality confronts this comparability problem, the concept of Kaldor-Hicks efficiency comes in handy.

Prompted by Robbin's (1938) famous paper on interpersonal comparisons of utility, Kaldor (1939) responded that there was in fact "no such arbitrary element" involved in assuming equal capacity for satisfaction of utility among individuals. All the economist need show is that, when the states of affairs before and after the policy implementation are compared, the winners would be able to compensate the losers and still prefer the new policy. In that case, "it is *possible* to make everybody better off than before, or at any rate to make some people better off without making anybody worse off" (550, emphasis in original). Hicks (1939) essentially endorsed Kaldor's assessment.[1]

Intervening in the discussion, De Scitovszky (1941) pointed out a paradox. Suppose that when moving from allocation x_A to allocation x_B, the winners from B are able to compensate the losers. According to Kaldor's criterion, this would be an efficient

[1] "Mr. Kaldor's contribution is to have shown that these cases are not the mere trifling exception they appear to be at first sight, but that they do actually offer a sufficient foundation for at least the more important part of welfare economics" (Hicks 1939, 700).

move. However, the paradox is that under some conditions, once we arrived at x_B, the original allocation, x_A, would then be preferable, because the winners from moving back to A would be able to compensate the losers. This problem arises particularly in cases of wealth effects or technological changes that shift the endpoints of the utility possibilities frontier in opposite directions.[2] However, Scitovsky also solved this problem by adopting a "double-criterion." First, we ask whether the winners from the new allocation are able to compensate the losers, so that everyone is better off, or at least as well off, as under the original allocation. Second, we ask whether the losers from the new allocation are able to compensate the winners in order to forgo the move and remain at the initial allocation. If the first is possible and second impossible, the new allocation is an improvement; if the first is impossible and the second possible, the new allocation is not an improvement. If both are either possible or impossible, no welfare judgment can be made.[3]

Thus, as long as Scitovsky's "double criterion" is employed, the Kaldor-Hicks test can consistently compare allocations: allocation A is a Kaldor-Hicks improvement over *B* if those that are made better off in moving from *A* to *B* could in principle compensate those that are made worse off; and those made worse off would not be willing to compensate the winners to not move from A to *B*. Note that the possibility of compensation is merely hypothetical. If compensation did actually occur, the change in allocation would be Pareto superior as well. For this reason, Kaldor-Hicks improvements are sometimes described as *potential* Pareto improvements. To underscore the key point, the major advantage that Kaldor-Hicks efficiency is said to have over Pareto efficiency is that it allows us to evaluate changes where some are made better off and others worse off, because most economic policies – for example, free trade – involve both winners and losers.

At the same time, although Kaldor-Hicks efficiency can solve the comparability problem, it cannot address the distributional or indifference problems. Like Pareto efficiency, Kaldor-Hicks efficiency is indifferent between an allocation change that either increases or reduces inequality, so long as the winners can hypothetically compensate the losers in either case. Likewise, once we reach an allocation in which the gains of the winners equal the losses of the losers – and there may be many

[2] For details of these claims, see De Scitovszky (1941). Scitovsky presented his intervention as extending the efficiency insights from problems of allocation to those of production. In the former, the amount of goods or "stuff" is essentially fixed; in the latter, these quantities are variable. Economic policy will affect both allocation and production, but Scitovsky's paradox will arise (among other reasons) only outside of allocation problems. For a simple illustration of the Scitovsky paradox, see Coleman (1980, 519 n.14). For an extensive discussion of the Scitovsky paradox in the context of cost-benefit analysis, see Adler and Posner (1999).

[3] Arrow (2012, 38–45) shows that even with Scitovsky's "double criterion," Kaldor-Hicks efficiency cannot consistently rank allocations transitively. In particular, Arrow shows that with allocations *x*, *y*, and *z*, Kaldor-Hicks efficiency can be indifferent between *x* and *y* and between *y* and *z*, but that it could prefer *z* to *x*. If the Kaldor-Hicks text was transitive, then we should be indifferent between *z* to *x* if we are indifferent between *x* and *y* and between *y* and *z*.

– we have a set of equally good allocations, about which the Kaldor-Hicks test is indifferent.

Richard Posner argued that Kaldor-Hicks efficiency coincides with a principle of wealth maximization so that, for Posner, the concepts are interchangeable (Posner 1980, 491). Wealth, writes Posner (1979, 119), is the value in dollars, or dollar equivalents, of "everything in society." Wealth in turn is measured by people's willingness to pay for something (if they do not already own it) and what they would demand in money to give it up (if they do). The connection between wealth maximization and Kaldor-Hicks is then revealed by the fact that the Kaldor-Hicks test is satisfied when the winners would be willing to pay the losers to make the change and the losers would not be willing to pay the winners not to make the change. Because the "conditions for Pareto superiority are almost never satisfied," Posner (1998, 14–15) asserts that when economists talk about efficiency, "nine times out of ten" they mean Kaldor-Hicks efficiency. As others have argued, however, it is a more controversial claim to go from Kaldor-Hicks efficiency to wealth maximization.[4] Nevertheless, within the domains that economists apply the concept, including this book, Posner's claim has some force. At the very least, it will sometimes be helpful in this book to distinguish what is efficient, as in wealth maximization, from what is optimal, as in welfare maximization.

The advantages and disadvantages of Kaldor-Hicks efficiency can be illustrated by turning to Figure A.2. Figure A.2 is identical to Figure A.1, except that it contains an additional allocation, *F*, whose importance will be explained shortly. As was shown in Figure A.1, Pareto efficiency cannot compare allocations *D* and *E*, because it makes person 2 better off and person 1 worse off, even though the move puts us closer to the Pareto frontier. By contrast, under the Kaldor-Hicks test, the choice is an easy one. Because person 2 can easily compensate person 1, and still be made better off, we would judge the move as Kaldor-Hicks efficient. Indeed, as seen in Figure A.2, if the compensation was made – although compensation is not *necessary* under the Kaldor-Hicks test – we would be at allocation *F*, and the change would be a Pareto improvement: one person better off and nobody worse off.

However, while Kaldor-Hicks efficiency solves Pareto efficiency's comparability problem, Kaldor-Hicks efficiency cannot make any distributive judgments. For example, in Figure A.2 a move from allocation *D* to *E* increases inequality. Under allocation *D*, persons 1 and 2 have equal utility; under allocation *E*, person 2's utility increases dramatically, while person 1's utility decreases slightly. Inequality (of welfare) has increased. Yet, because the Kaldor-Hicks criterion is satisfied, an increase in inequality is not a concern under that standard. We could also imagine, of course, changes in allocations that were Kaldor-Hicks efficient and also reduced inequality. Nevertheless, whether inequality increases or decreases is irrelevant to Kaldor-Hicks efficiency.

4 See, for example, Coleman (1980) and Markovits (1980).

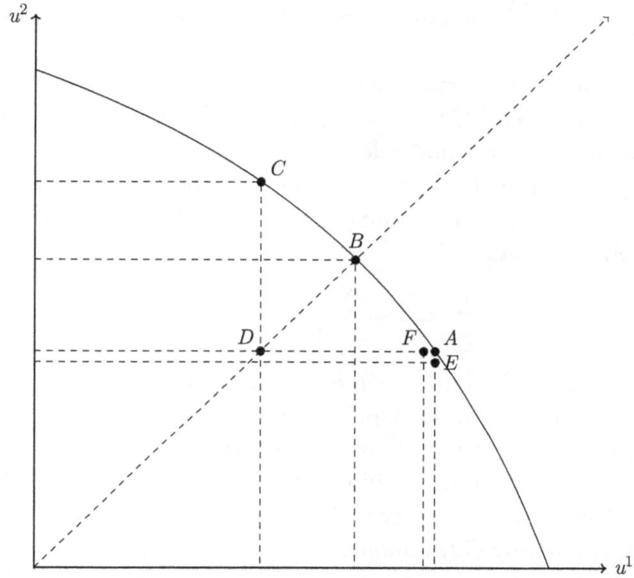

FIGURE A.2 Kaldor-Hicks efficiency

A.2 INEQUALITY

The law-and-economics literature has not paid very significant attention to the analysis and measurement of inequality. And only recently has the economics discipline given these issues more front-page attention. However, there has been a persistent body of scholarship that has developed concepts for the study of inequality, and this section will introduce them.

A.2.1 *Lorenz Curves*

Perhaps the most general, and easily grasped, notion of inequality is the Lorenz curve. The Lorenz curve is not, strictly speaking, a *measure* of income inequality but it does play an important role in its measurement. The Lorenz curve is a graph that relates the proportion of total income, given on the *y*-axis, that goes to a given share of the population, given on the *x*-axis. (See A.3, discussed further below.) To construct a Lorenz curve, one must first order individuals in terms of increasing levels of income (or wealth). If each person (or household) in the population held the same amount of income, the Lorenz curve would then be a straight, 45-degree line connecting points (0, 0) and (1, 1) in the graph. However, inequality will be present (and in the real world it always is) whenever a certain percentage of the population (less than 100 percent) holds less than that same percentage of the income. In that case, the Lorenz curve will lie below the diagonal line because, when there is inequality, the poorer share of the distribution must receive strictly less than that same share of total income.

For some it may help to express the Lorenz curve mathematically. The Lorenz curve is typically denoted $L(p)$, where $0 \leq p \leq 1$ refers to the population share.[5] If we take a population of size n, and order each individual by their income, y, such that: $y_1 \leq y_2 \leq \ldots y_n$, then p defines the share of the population $p = 1/n, 2/n, \ldots n/n$ ordered by increasing income. Letting $Y = \sum_{i=1}^{n} y_i$ denote total income, we can write the Lorenz curve as:

$$L(p) = \frac{\sum_{i=1}^{j} y_i}{\sum_{i=1}^{n} y_i} = \frac{\sum_{i=1}^{j} y_i}{Y} \quad \text{for} \quad 1 \leq j \leq n.$$

Thus, for any individual within the income-rank-ordered population, the Lorenz curve will give us the share of total income at each population share p. $L(p)$ in this discrete version is not continuous, but it is mathematically convenient to consider continuous income and population distributions. Let $f(y)$ be the probability density function, which gives the percentage of the population f at each income-level y. The corresponding cumulative distribution function, $F(y)$, then tells us the percentage of the population at or below each income level y, so we can write $p = F(y)$. We can then write the Lorenz curve as:

$$L(p) = L(F(y)) = \frac{\int_0^y xf(x)dx}{\int_0^{y_n} xf(x)dx} = \frac{\int_0^y xf(x)dx}{\mu}$$

where μ is mean income.

With two different distributions of income, we can construct two different Lorenz curves, and compare income inequality. Comparison of income distributions with Lorenz curves gives us a way to compare income inequality. This is the concept of *Lorenz dominance*. In words, distribution A will Lorenz dominate distribution B if the Lorenz curve of A lies everywhere above that of B. We then say that there is less inequality in distribution A (which is closer to the 45 degree line of equality) than in distribution B. In this case, a given percentage of the population under A always holds a larger percentage of the income than under B. Thus Lorenz dominance between distributions will occur when the poorer fraction of the population holds more of the income in one than in the other. Formally, say that we have two income distributions, which we call $A(y)$ and $B(y)$ and their associated Lorenz curves, $L_A(p)$ and $L_B(p)$.

Definition 2. Lorenz dominance. *Assuming $L_A(p) \neq L_B(p)$, distribution A Lorenz dominates distribution B, denoted $A \succ_L B$, if*

$$L_A(p) \geq L_B(p) \quad \textit{for all} \quad p \in [0, 1].$$

5 For further analysis of Lorenz curves, on which this formal section is based, and associated topics, see Lambert (2001, 23–35).

The idea of Lorenz dominance has strengths and weaknesses. The main strength is that when Lorenz dominance occurs, it allows a unanimous ranking of income distributions. There are many different measures of inequality. And depending on the kind of change in the income distribution, one index might conclude that inequality has fallen, while another might reach the opposite conclusion. But if one distribution Lorenz dominates another, all indexes will agree on whether inequality has increased or decreased.

On the other hand, Lorenz dominance does not supply an answer to the evaluation of changes in distribution in all cases. An income distribution can change without us being able to say whether the old distribution Lorenz dominants the new. This can happen, for example, when the poor receive a lower share of the income but the lower middle class gains a larger share, both relative to the rich. In this case, the Lorenz curve of the second distribution may not lie everywhere above the curve of the first. In this case, the Lorenz curves cross, and it is not possible to say whether one distribution dominates the other. Thus, similar to Pareto optimality, Lorenz dominance does not give us a complete ordering. In the real world this problem arises frequently, as when trying to compare inequality across different countries (Lambert 2001, 49–52).

Figure A.3 represents the use of Lorenz curves to rank income distributions. The horizontal axis represents the proportion of the population, arranged in order of increasing income, while the vertical axis represents the proportion of income (or wealth). If a society enjoyed perfect equality, each person would own an equal fraction of income, and the proportion of the population would always equal the

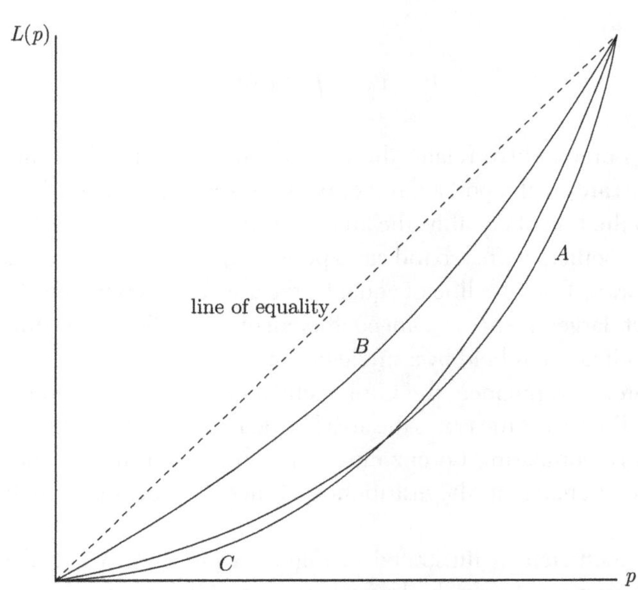

FIGURE A.3 Inequality and Lorenz dominance

proportion of income. This condition is represented in Figure A.3 by the dashed, "line of equality." But unless the income distribution is perfectly equal, the Lorenz curve will be convex, with a given proportion of the population possessing less than an equal proportion of the income. The three different curves, A, *B*, and *C*, represent different distributions of income. In the figure, distribution *B* Lorenz dominates distributions A and C because *B* lies everywhere above both A and C. Intuitively, income is distributed more equally, because any (poorer) proportion of the population below the richest person holds a greater share of the income in *B* than in *A* or *C*. In contrast, we cannot rank distributions A and C where the curves representing distributions A and C cross. Up to some proportion of the population, curve A lies above curve C, indicating that for that part of the population, income inequality is lower (i.e., closer to the line of equality) in distribution A than in distribution C. However, beyond that proportion of the population, curve C lies above curve A, indicating that for that part of the population inequality is lower in distribution C than in A. Lorenz dominance cannot therefore rank all income distributions.

A.2.2 *The Gini Coefficient*

The shortcomings of Lorenz dominance are a major reason why alternative measures of income distribution have been proposed. One of these alternatives is the Gini coefficient, one of the most popular measures of inequality. The Gini coefficient measures the *area* between the Lorenz curve and the "line of equality." Formally, we can write this as:

$$\Gamma = 1 - 2\int_0^1 L(p)dp.$$

Because the Lorenz curve relates the population share with the share of income, measuring this area will report a number between zero and one. As the Lorenz curve gets closer to the line of equality, the area measured by the Gini coefficient shrinks. Thus, a Gini coefficient of zero indicates perfect equality. Conversely, as the Lorenz curve moves away from the line of equality, the area between the curve and the line of equality gets larger. Hence, a Gini coefficient of one indicates maximal inequality: all of society's income is held by a single person.

Unlike Lorenz dominance, the Gini coefficient supplies a complete ordering of distributions. Because it measures the area between the curve and the line of equality, rather than just comparing Lorenz curves, it can give an unambiguous judgment about whether a change in the distribution of income increases or reduces income inequality.

The Gini coefficient is illustrated in Figure A.4. Figure A.4 is identical to A.3 except that the areas between the Lorenz curves and the line of equality are shaded, which indicates how the Gini coefficient measures the area between the Lorenz

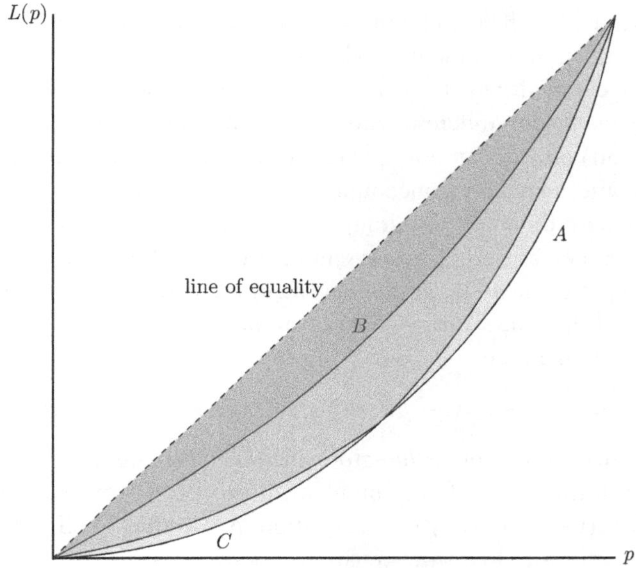

FIGURE A.4 Inequality and the Gini coefficient

curve and the line of equality. Clearly, the area between Lorenz curve *B* and the line of equality is the smallest (recall that when Lorenz dominance exists, all other measures of inequality will agree). As we saw in Figure A.3, Lorenz dominance cannot rank distributions A and C. However, by measuring the area between each curve, the Gini coefficient allows us to make such comparisons. As shown in Figure A.4, the intersection of curves A and *C* creates two areas between the two curves (indicated by the lightest shade of gray). These two areas tell us the difference between each distribution's Gini coefficient. Using an eye-ball test, the area to the right of the intersection appears larger, which would indicate that the area between curve A and the line of equality is larger than the area between curve C and the line of equality. In other words, income inequality is higher under distribution A than under distribution *C*. This gives us a complete, transitive ranking of income distributions, with distribution *B* having lower inequality than *C* and distribution *C* having lower income inequality than A.

A.2.3 *Income Shares*

Despite its advantages, the Gini coefficient is not without its own problems. Most conspicuously, the Gini coefficient is more sensitive to transfers in the middle of the distribution than at its "tails" (Alvaredo 2011). The top 0.1 percent, or even the top 1 percent, of income-earners is infinitesimal on the scale mapping the Lorenz curve. Yet if a large amount of income is concentrated within these small groups, changes in income inequality will be underestimated. In fact, this problem is directly relevant to recent discussions of income inequality. In recent years, most income gains have been very concentrated at the top of the income distribution. This raises the concern that the Gini coefficient underestimates the recent rise in inequality in the USA.

Alvaredo (2011) provides an example to illustrate how the Gini coefficient underestimates income inequality concentrated at the far ends of the distribution. For simplicity, suppose there are two groups, $j = \{1, 2\}$, with group 1 representing the "top" income earners and group 2 representing everyone else. Let p be the population share of the top-income group and S their income share; the rest of the population is $1 - p$ and their income share $1 - S$. We can then decompose the Gini coefficient Γ in the following manner:

$$\Gamma = \Gamma_{11} pS + \Gamma_{22}(1 - p)(1 - S) + \Gamma_{12}(p(1 - S) + (1 - p)S). \tag{A.1}$$

In this equation, Γ_{jj} represents *within*-group income inequality and Γ_{jk} *between*-group inequality. To further simplify the problem, it can be shown that between-group inequality, $\Gamma_{12}(p(1 - S) + (1 - p)S)$ in equation (A.1), reduces to $S - p$. Simplifying subscripts, this allows us to rewrite equation (A.1) as:

$$\Gamma = \Gamma_1 pS + \Gamma_2(1 - p)(1 - S) + S - p.$$

Now, if we let the population share of the top-income group get infinitesimally small ($p \to 0$) but still possess a finite share of total income, the equation $\lim_{p \to 0}[\Gamma_1 pS + \Gamma_2(1 - p)(1 - S) + S - p]$ can be written as:

$$\Gamma = \Gamma_2(1 - S) + S.$$

What this last equation shows is that *without* the decomposition of the Gini coefficient, given in equation (A.1), any change in S would be reflected only in group 2's income share, $1 - S$, and not group 1's share, S. This would underestimate the change in income inequality in any non-decomposed Gini coefficient, which is typically how that measure is reported. (A handy feature of the Gini coefficient, after all, is that income inequality can be reported in a single number.) The decomposition of the Gini coefficient avoids this underestimation, by allowing for changes in group 1's income share to be measured, even when that group's population size is effectively zero. For this reason, recent research has focused on measuring income shares of different groups in the population, as in the well-known studies of Piketty and Saez (see, e.g., Piketty and Saez 2003).

Despite the drawbacks of various measures of inequality, none of them will present any serious obstacles to the arguments made in this book. There may well be a debate about whether a change in legal rules will increase or decrease inequality according to one or another inequality index. But this problem exists independently of the question of whether the legal system should be used to redistribute income. In order to focus on the debate that matters for this paper, I assume that all distributional changes can be ranked according to the Lorenz dominance criterion. Since Lorenz dominance implies unanimous agreement, what this means essentially is that we only consider distributional changes on which all income-inequality indices would agree.

A.2.4 *Redistribution*

The law-and-economics literature does not have a very clear concept of redistribution. The term redistribution is typically used in a way that implies that it is *necessarily* inefficient.[6] We can accept the assumption that redistribution is always inefficient in two different senses. First, there is sometimes a distinction made, if only implicitly, between redistribution and distribution (or, predistribution). For example, Hacker (2011) writes, "When we think of government's effects on inequality, we think of redistribution – government taxes and transfers that take from some and give to others. Yet many of the most important changes [leading to the growth of income inequality] have been in what might be called 'pre-distribution' – the way in which the market distributes its rewards in the first place" (35). This understanding easily maps onto the distinction this book has made between legal rules and the income tax. After all, the income tax is itself a set of legal rules. But Hacker's distinction captures the idea that some legal rules are components – even conditions – of the legal architecture that supports and defines the market system, including the rewards it generates. Government shapes the distribution of income even where it is simply protecting property, enforcing contracts, and otherwise preserving the rules of the market. On the other hand, other legal rules (the tax system) intervene after the market has generated these rewards. Once the distinction between redistribution and predistribution is drawn, it is easy to equate redistribution with inefficiency because tax redistribution entails a loss of efficiency by changing people's labor-supply decisions.

The presumed inefficiency of redistribution can also be made acceptable because, for example, when a legal-rule change both reduces inequality and increases efficiency there is no trade-off between the two objectives. Such a change is a "win–win," and is uncontroversial. For Kaplow and Shavell seemingly, a legal-rule change that is efficient and also happens to reduce income inequality poses no problem to the double-distortion hypothesis. For that reason, it is only worth talking about distributive legal rules that are inefficient.

In a more general sense the assumption that redistribution is necessarily inefficient is unjustified and even ideologically freighted. To assume that redistribution is necessarily inefficient supports the false idea that law and government are not present in the basic functioning of the market and economy and that legal or regulatory

6 Kaplow and Shavell (1994) simply assume redistribution is inefficient without discussing this assumption. Craswell (1991, 377–80) also assumes that the redistribution is inefficient but is more explicit about it than Kaplow and Shavell.

intervention is meddlesome, unproductive, and unjustified. Instead, all "redistribution" should really mean is a change in the distribution of income, sans phrase. Whether the change is also inefficient or efficient, or whether it is accomplished through taxation or legal rules is a wholly contingent matter. As just indicated previously, this does not mean that it is impossible to draw a distinction between (pre)distribution and redistribution, nor that the distinction is always analytically or philosophically irrelevant. But it comes with less ideological baggage to talk simply about distribution without further distinction, and to emphasize the contingent rather than assumed relationship between distribution and efficiency.

We can define redistribution by recourse to our earlier introduction to Lorenz curves. Let $L_X(p)$ be the Lorenz curve associated with a pre-policy income distribution, X. "Pre-policy" here just means "prior to" a change in the tax *or* legal policy. (It does not mean prior to a "government intervention" insofar as property protection and contract enforcement are also "government interventions.") Designate the post-policy Lorenz curve as $L_{X-T}(p)$. Then we can define a redistributive policy intervention in the following way.

Definition 3. Redistribution. A *policy, T, is redistributive whenever the post-policy distribution Lorenz dominates the pre-policy distribution, or:*

$$L_{X-T}(p) \geq L_X(p) \quad \textit{for all} \quad p \in [0,1].$$

Implied in this definition of redistribution is that policy has an *equalizing effect* on the distribution of income. We could define redistribution to refer to any change in the distribution of income, one that increases or decreases income inequality, but because redistribution usually refers to a policy that has an equalizing effect on income distribution, I will maintain that sense in this book. It is interesting to note that one can prove that the income distribution is less unequal after the policy intervention than before if and only if the policy burden (e.g., tax remittances to the government in the case of a tax policy) is distributed more unequally than the incomes to which they apply (Lambert 2001, 37–39). Formally, we can express this as:

$$L_{X-T} \geq L_X \Leftrightarrow L_T \leq L_X.$$

Another virtue of the Lorenz-dominance definition of redistribution is that it corresponds closely to the ways economists measure the redistributive effects of taxation. The redistributive effect of taxation is essentially equivalent to the level of progressivity in the system. And one of the most frequently used measures of tax progressivity employs the ideas of the Lorenz curve and Lorenz dominance (Musgrave and Thin 1948; Kakwani 1977a, 1977b). There is therefore a compelling reason to make inequality the basis on which to define redistribution either through legal rules or tax-and-transfer systems. We can, moreover, do this sensibly without making any assumptions about the effect of redistribution on efficiency.

A.3 SOCIAL WELFARE

The idea of social welfare – and, in particular, maximizing social welfare – can solve the distribution and indifference problems of our concepts of efficiency. However, embracing the social-welfare paradigm comes at a significant philosophical cost, an issue I addressed very briefly in Chapter 10, the book's conclusion. For the book's purposes, these drawbacks do not have a direct bearing on the specific debate within the law and economics literature on how to address economic inequality.

A.3.1 *Social Welfare Functions*

Maximizing social welfare – as opposed to maximizing wealth, as in Posner's interpretation of the Kaldor-Hicks test – requires thinking about a social welfare function. A social welfare function aggregates individuals' welfare or utility. The crucial feature of the social welfare function is that it embodies the equity considerations of the policy maker, or "social planner." The basis for this idea of equity is the bedrock economics' view that people experience diminishing marginal utility. According to that notion, ten dollars are more valuable to me if I am poor and less valuable to me if I am rich. Likewise, equity is captured in a social welfare function insofar as a transfer of ten dollars from a wealthy to a poor person, for similar reasons, will *increase* total, or aggregate, social welfare. The key assumption is that a low-income person, whose marginal utility for money is high, will value ten dollars more than a high-income person, whose marginal utility for money is low.

Using a social welfare function to choose among income distributions solves all of the shortcomings of the efficiency concepts listed previously. Although there may be more than one allocation that achieves the same, and the highest, level of social welfare, under mild assumptions the social welfare criterion does not face the problem of an infinite indifference between allocations. It also fills the void of the absence of distributional judgments left by Pareto and Kaldor-Hicks efficiency. As just suggested, if we take a dollar away from a wealthy person and give it to a poor person, we will increase social welfare. Hence, unlike Pareto or Kaldor-Hicks efficiency, social-welfare maximization is not indifferent to the level of economic inequality. Finally, social welfare maximization can also address the incomparability problem. Suppose the difference between two different allocations is that the welfare of a poor person is much higher in the first than in the second, while the welfare of the rich is only slightly lower in the second than in the first. As we previously saw, Pareto efficiency cannot compare these two allocations. Kaldor-Hicks would endorse the first as long as the poor could compensate the rich. In addition, the social-welfare criterion would also endorse the first as long as total social welfare is higher in the first than in the second – which is arguably likely given diminishing marginal utility of money.

Although both social welfare maximization and Kaldor-Hicks efficiency can address the Pareto problem of comparability, they may well disagree about which allocation is more desirable. For example, Kaldor-Hicks efficiency clearly endorses an allocation change that increases inequality, but in which the rich can compensate the poor. Yet such a change may or may not be social welfare maximizing. For example, if the income gain of the rich exactly offsets the income loss of the poor, the allocation would reduce social welfare. For the same reason, for an increase in inequality to also increase social welfare, the gain of the rich must be substantially *larger* than the loss to the poor. In general then, the social welfare criterion and Kaldor-Hicks efficiency will give different answers about whether an economic allocation should or should not be endorsed relative to another. Yet the fact that they might agree also indicates that social welfare incorporates both equity *and* efficiency (wealth) into its evaluation of an economic allocation.

We can illustrate these ideas with the help of Figure A.5. In addition to the utility possibility (Pareto) frontier, which we first encountered in Figure A.1, social welfare introduces the social indifference curve. A social indifference curve represents all of the allocations that give the same level of social welfare – in this case, the same total welfare for persons 1 and 2. In Figure A.5, there are three social indifference curves, with the more northeastly curves representing higher levels of social welfare. Intuitively, as curves move outward from the origin, they give greater welfare to both individuals. Social indifference curves help us make judgments that efficiency concepts are not able to do. For example, while allocations A and *B* are both Pareto efficient, our social welfare index would easily prefer allocation *B* to A, since it moves

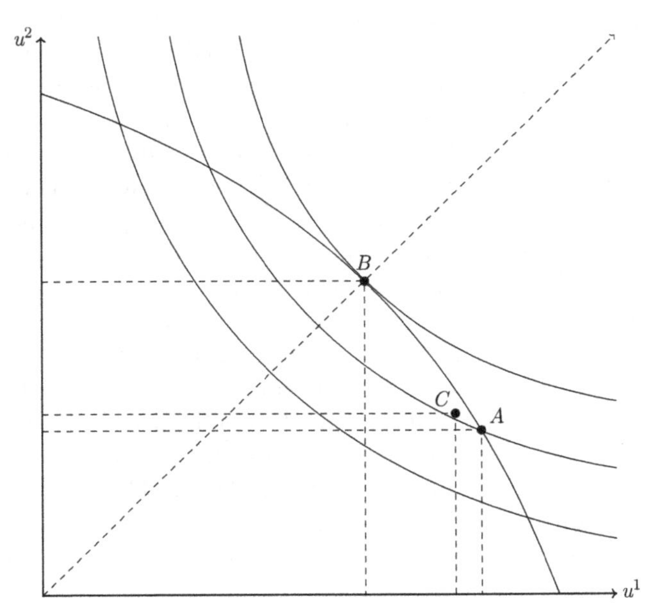

FIGURE A.5 Social welfare maximization

society to a higher indifference curve and unambiguously increases social welfare. Indeed because allocation *B* is on the Pareto frontier and gives equal utility or welfare to each person, the social welfare index judges *B* as the unique and "best" possible allocation of resources. The Pareto frontier indicates the outer possibility of feasible allocations of resources and, with the "lens" created by the Pareto frontier and the social indifference curve reduced to a mere point of tangency, it is not possible to increase social welfare any further beyond allocation *B*.

It is no mistake that the absolute social optimum indicated by allocation *B* – the allocation of society's resources that identifies the *unique* location on the Pareto frontier that maximizes social welfare – also happens to require *equal* well-being from both persons 1 and 2. This conclusion reflects Edgeworth's (1897) explorations into the early "pure theory of taxation." The principle of diminishing marginal utility dictates that social welfare can be increased by transferring income or resources from the rich to the poor. Based on that principle, the poor value an additional dollar more than the rich; therefore, social welfare can be improved through a transfer of income from rich to poor. Taken to its logical conclusion, this principle also dictates an allocation of resources that produces complete equality of well-being. According to Edgeworth (1897, 553), "The solution of this problem in the abstract is that the richer should be taxed for the benefit of the poorer up to the point at which complete equality of fortunes is attained." This simplified conclusion rests on two assumptions. First, that individuals have identical utility functions, by which equal incomes ("fortunes") produce equal levels of well-being. Second, that it is possible to transfer income without also discouraging work or other income-generating activities.[7] The issue of interpersonal comparisons of well-being is explored briefly in the conclusion (Chapter 10); the effect of taxation on work incentives is discussed in Section A.4.1, on optimal tax theory, which recognizes the trade-off between increasing social welfare through redistribution and the loss of social wealth through the discouragement of work incentives.

Returning to our illustration of social welfare functions in Figure A.5, also notice that a social welfare function and Kaldor-Hicks efficiency sometimes deliver a unanimous judgment. For instance, Figure A.5 shows that the social indifference curves indicate a preference for allocation *B* to allocation C. Allocation *B* is also evidently Kaldor-Hicks efficient relative to C. Nevertheless, Kaldor-Hicks is indifferent to the distribution of income, so the evaluations of social welfare functions and Kaldor-Hicks efficiency will sometimes diverge. Thus, a move from C to A would be Kaldor-Hicks efficient insofar as person 1 could compensate person 2 for the change. However, lying just above the indifference curve on which A lies, our social welfare index would prefer allocation C. In this case, the gain in wealth would not justify the

7 Edgeworth (1897) clearly recognized the constraints imposed on "complete equality of fortunes" by the disincentive effects of taxation. But without the modern apparatus of optimal tax theory, he was not able to reconcile the two objectives formally.

increase in inequality. Thus, social welfare and Kaldor-Hicks efficiency agree on the move from C to B, but disagree on the move from C to A.

Let us now consider social welfare functions formally. If we have a pair of utility or welfare levels, $\{u_1, u_2\}$, a general social welfare function can be written as $W(u_1, u_2)$, and this function determines the aggregate level of welfare. A similarly general expression, but with an indeterminate number of individuals n, can be written as $W(u_1, u_2, \ldots, u_n)$. In this general form, the social welfare function is called a *Bergson-Samuelson* social welfare function.

How strong the equity considerations of the social welfare function are depend on the specific form of the function that is chosen. At one extreme we have a *utilitarian* social welfare function, which is simply the summation of all individuals' utilities: $W = u_1 + u_2$. At the other extreme we have a *Rawlsian* or *maximin* (for maximize the minimum) social welfare function, which is defined as: $W = \min\{u_1, u_2\}$; only the utility of the person with the lowest level of welfare is considered. Between these extremes are a continuous range of *intermediate* social welfare functions. An example of a specific functional form for an intermediate social welfare function is given by the following, where y refers to income (of persons 1 and 2, respectively) and u is the common utility function:

$$W = \frac{1}{1-\rho}\left[(u(y_1))^{1-\rho} + (u(y_2))^{1-\rho}\right] \quad \text{for} \quad \rho \in [0,1) \cup (1,\infty). \qquad \text{(A.2)}$$

In this social welfare function, the term ρ captures the degree of "inequality aversion," or how sensitive the social welfare function is to inequality. To see how inequality aversion works, suppose that we raise a dollar of tax revenue from each person's disposable income. This can be done by totally differentiating the previous equation with respect to each person's income:

$$W' = (u(y_1))^{-\rho}u'(y_1) + (u(y_2))^{-\rho}u'(y_2).$$

Each $u'(y_i)$ describes the direct marginal welfare impact of a policy change on that individual, while each $(u(y_i))^{-\rho}$ term is described as the *social marginal welfare weight*. Note that as $\rho \to 0$, each $(u(y_i))^{-\rho} \to 1$. In that case, the social welfare function just becomes the utilitarian social welfare function. On the other hand, as $\rho \to \infty$, the social welfare function becomes the Rawlsian case in the limit. For example, suppose that $u(y_1) < u(y_2)$, with $u(y_1)$ arbitrarily close to zero. In that case, as $\rho \to \infty$, the social marginal welfare weight $(u(y_2))^{-\rho}$ approaches zero much faster than $(u(y_1))^{-\rho}$, implying that only the welfare of the least well-off matters in the aggregate. This is the Rawlsian case. Hence, we label the utilitarian and Rawlsian social welfare functions as extremes because the utilitarian social welfare function is the least equity-preferring and the Rawlsian the most.

Figure A.6 visually displays the way different social welfare functions weight equity into their evaluations. Each figure, A.6a through A.6c, depicts three different social indifference curves: each point on an indifference curve gives the same level of total

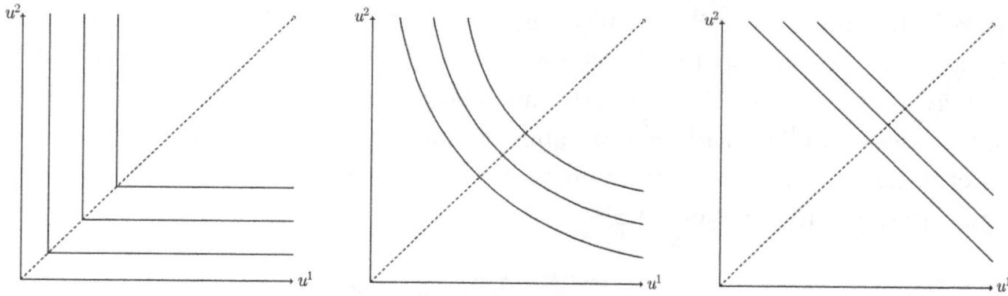

(a) Rawlsian (b) Intermediate (c) Utilitarian

FIGURE A.6 Inequality aversion and social welfare functions

social welfare. The utilitarian indifference curve, in Figure A.6c, is the least sensitive to inequality. The utility of each person is weighted the same as the other, regardless of the level of inequality. Hence, the social indifference curves are straight, sloped lines: a unit decrease in person 1's utility is equal to a unit increase in person 2's utility, independent of the level of inequality.[8] An "intermediate" social welfare function is more sensitive to the level of inequality. When inequality is high, the utility of a wealthy person gets smaller weight than the utility of a poorer person. For example, suppose person 1 is richer than person 2, which puts us somewhere below the line of equality in Figure A.6b. As indicated by the shape of the curves in that figure, we can maintain the same total level of social welfare and increase the utility of person 1 even if the decrease in the utility of person 2 is (metrically) larger. Hence below the line of equality the social indifference curves are "flatter." For similar reasons, the indifference curves are "steeper" when person 2 is richer than person 1. When person 2 is wealthier, increasing the welfare of the poorer person (person 1) justifies greater decreases in the welfare of the richer person (person 2). Notice that it is only when there is an exact equality of welfare, represented by the dashed line of equality, where each person's utility is weighted equally. The Rawlsian social welfare function is the most sensitive to inequality. When person 1 is richer than person 2, increasing person 2's welfare justifies any amount of decrease in person 1's welfare. Hence, Rawlsian indifference curves are maximally "flat" when person 1 is richer than person 2 and maximally "steep" when inequality is reversed.

A.3.2 *The Atkinson Index*

One way of seeing more clearly how social welfare functions measure both efficiency and distribution is with the Atkinson Index. The Atkinson Index was introduced by

[8] Note that with the assumption of decreasing marginal utility, a utilitarian social welfare function would depict curved lines, as in an intermediate social welfare function, if *income* rather than utility was measured on the axes of the graph. Therefore, even a utilitarian social welfare function is sensitive to the distribution of income, if not to the distribution of utility or well-being.

the British economist Anthony Atkinson in his 1970 article "On the Measurement of Inequality" (Atkinson 1970). Atkinson uses a standard welfare function, of the kind given by equation (A.2), to derive an "abbreviated social welfare function" that captures social welfare with two variables, income and its distribution.

Let W be a social welfare function with n individuals, a generalization of the two-person function in equation (A.2):

$$W = \frac{1}{1-\rho}\sum_{i=1}^{n}[u(y_i)]^{1-\rho}. \tag{A.3}$$

Define y_e as *equally distributed equivalent income*, that is, an amount of income received by everyone that would yield the same level of welfare as the actual, unequal distribution of income:

$$\frac{1}{1-\rho}\sum_{i=1}^{n}[u(y_i)]^{1-\rho} = \frac{1}{1-\rho}n[u(y_e)]^{1-\rho}. \tag{A.4}$$

Because social welfare measures distribution, equally distributed equivalent income, y_e, will be smaller when inequality is high (and larger when inequality is lower). Intuitively, it requires a smaller level of equal income to yield the same amount of social welfare when inequality is high. For that reason, it can be shown (by Jensen's inequality and the concavity of the social welfare function) that equally distributed equivalent income, y_e, will be less than average income, $\bar{y}$: $y_e \leq \bar{y}$. This allows us to construct an inequality index, which we can call Q:

$$Q = 1 - \frac{y_e}{\bar{y}}. \tag{A.5}$$

This expression is essentially the Atkinson Index, another measure of inequality captured by a number between zero and one. As inequality increases, equally distributed equivalent income, y_e, decreases, and Q becomes larger. As the income distribution becomes more equal, y_e approaches per capita income, $\bar{y}$, and Q becomes smaller.

With the inequality index Q it is then possible to write the social welfare function[9] as follows:

$$W = \frac{1}{1-\rho}[u(\bar{y}(1-Q))]^{1-\rho}. \tag{A.6}$$

This expression depends on two variables: average income, $\bar{y}$, we can take as our measure of wealth, and Q, which is our measure of inequality. Thus, when efficiency declines, per capita income, $\bar{y}$, becomes smaller and social welfare decreases.

9 To show that this version of the social welfare function is equivalent to the social welfare function in equation (A.3), use the expression for equally distributed equivalent income in equation (A.4) to solve explicitly for y_e. Substitute the explicit solution for y_e into the inequality index in equation (A.5). This gives the explicit version of the Atkinson Index, Q, which when substituted into the abbreviated social welfare function in (A.6) becomes the original social welfare function in (A.3).

Similarly, if holding wealth constant, inequality increases and Q becomes larger, social welfare also decreases. Hence, social welfare depends on both wealth and its distribution.

A.4 RESPONDING TO INEQUALITY

In addition to refining the definitions and concepts associated with efficiency, inequality, and social welfare, economists in particular have developed a formal apparatus for *responding* to inequality. Foremost among these is what goes under the name of "optimal tax theory."[10] As indicated in the introduction, the income tax has a special role to play in the debate over using legal rules to redistribute taxes. Not only does the double-distortion claim take the tax system to be the most efficient means of redistributing income, but even when the double-distortion argument is contested, the optimal income tax often serves as a useful, evaluative benchmark. In addition to optimal income taxation, the use of "distribution-neutral income tax adjustments" have been used and advocated, especially by Kaplow (2008), as a way of evaluating alternative policy and legal prescriptions. This section introduces the reader to both optimal tax theory and distribution-neutral income tax adjustments.

A.4.1 *Optimal Tax Theory*

The concept of social welfare and its maximization are critical in what is called the "optimal tax" literature. The optimal tax literature takes as given the problem that taxation will distort behavior and create disincentives that lower efficiency. The objective is to find that tax function that maximizes social welfare subject to the efficiency costs. On the one hand, taxation can increase social welfare by reducing inequality. On the other hand, taxation can reduce social welfare by distorting economic incentives and lowering wealth. The objective is to then find that tax schedule that optimally balances this trade-off – to achieve the highest level of social welfare consistent with the smallest cost to wealth or efficiency.

Optimal tax theory makes it possible to revisit the issue of taxation as an instrument for redistributing income. We previously encountered two different principles that led to dead ends. First, the second fundamental theorem of welfare economics tells us that any Pareto efficient allocation of resources is achievable with the use of lump-sum taxes. However, Pareto efficiency cannot tell us *which* allocation from among the set of Pareto efficient allocations we should choose; because each Pareto efficient allocation is "equally good" from its own standpoint, we have no way of ranking them (Section A.1.1). Second, in our discussion of social welfare functions, we learned from the principle of diminishing marginal utility that the allocation that maximizes social welfare gives each person exactly equal income

[10] For a recent overview of optimal tax theory, see Tuomala (2016).

(Section A.3.1). This is the Edgeworth (1897) insight. Putting these two principles together yields a unique, determinate solution: a scheme of differential lump-sum taxes that gives everyone equal income. However, we also previously encountered the insurmountable problem that differential lump-sum taxation is not possible.

The impossibility of differential lump-sum taxation gives rise to theory of optimal taxation. The form of the optimal tax problem is identical to that of every other optimization problem in economics: the maximization of some desired objective subject to constraints. Elsewhere in economics, for instance, consumers maximize utility subject to a budget constraint and firms maximize profits subject to a production constraint. In the optimal tax problem, the thing to be maximized – the maximand – may vary. Sometimes the objective is simply to maximize revenue. Given our concern with income inequality, we will focus on maximizing social welfare. Thus, the optimal tax problem seeks to find the tax schedule that maximizes the maximand (equity or revenue) subject to the government's budget constraint. However, unlike the Edgeworth (1897) problem introduced in Section A.3.1's discussion of social welfare functions, the optimal tax problem explicitly acknowledges the government's limited information about individual abilities. Because of that limited information, taxes are not lump sum and individual behavior will change in response to taxes. The optimal tax problem incorporates these behavioral responses as part of the constraints on the social welfare objective. Redistributive taxes can therefore increase social welfare by equalizing incomes, but redistributive taxes also negatively affect incentives to work and earn income, reducing the amount of wealth available for redistribution. Thus, the optimal tax problem gives rise to the classic trade-off between equity and efficiency.

Note that optimal tax theory is a case where it makes sense to distinguish optimality, welfare maximization, from efficiency, wealth maximization. Clearly, what is being maximized is not wealth. The social welfare function necessarily assumes that either individuals of different incomes or the "social planner" will value wealth, measured in dollars or some other currency, differently. Yet the resource constraint, to which the maximization problem is subject, is measured in currency or dollars, this being the necessary medium through which taxes are raised and transfers are made. To be sure, optimal tax theory typically takes the wealth-dependent concept of "willingness to pay" as its measure of well-being or welfare. Nevertheless, not everyone will value a dollar equally, which will justify some sacrifice in wealth in order to increase social welfare. If not, redistributive taxation, which lowers total social wealth, would never be justified.

The next two subsections will address, first, some of the scholarly history of optimal tax theory for context and background to explain why the taxation of labor income is so central for economists; and, second, they will provide a simple but general formal mode of the optimal tax problem. But before delving into those more particular details, I want to review two broad conclusions drawn from optimal tax theory that will be very useful for subsequent chapters of the book. The first is that

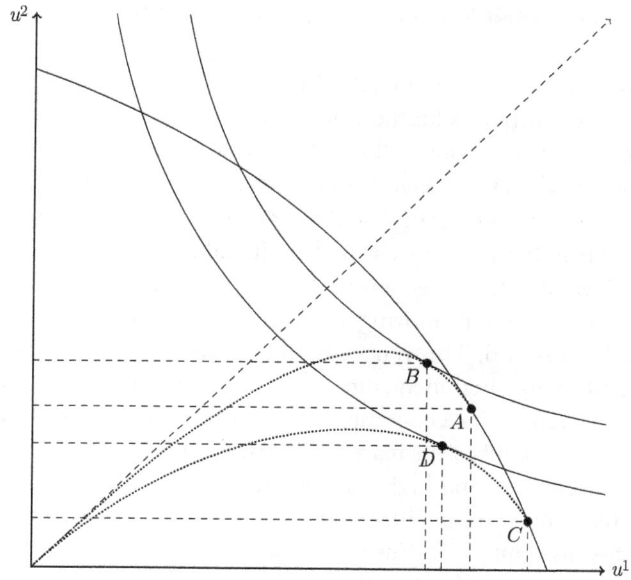

FIGURE A.7 Inequality and optimal redistributive taxation

higher inequality *by itself* can justify greater taxation – and hence larger economic distortions. When inequality is high, more redistribution becomes more desirable according to a social welfare function. More redistribution requires more taxes, and hence a larger distortion, but this is justified by the greater welfare benefit of redistribution in the context of high inequality. Conversely, if incomes were perfectly equal, there will be no welfare benefit to redistribution and only an economic cost. In that case, no taxation is justified.

This insight is illustrated in Figure A.7. Figure A.7 displays two initial, "pre-tax" income distributions, A and C, and their associated, "post-tax" income distributions, *B* and *D*. As in previous figures, this figure displays a utility possibilities (Pareto) frontier, a line of equality, and two social welfare indifference curves. In addition, there are two dotted "tax loss" curves, each starting from the initial distribution, A and C, and ending at the origin of the graph. One can think of these "tax loss" curves as new Pareto possibility frontiers generated by the costs of redistributive taxation. Beginning from the initial allocations on the original Pareto frontier, redistributive taxation moves the incomes and utility of persons 1 and 2 closer to the line of equality. However, on the assumption that perfect equality of welfare completely destroys work incentives, the tax loss curves eventually bend toward the origin. At the origin, nothing is produced, nothing redistributed, and therefore welfare is also at nil. This assumption may be stronger than necessary, but it nevertheless captures the fundamental trade-off in the optimal tax problem. The optimal tax problem is then to obtain the highest level of social welfare subject to this "tax loss" resource constraint.

A few insights emerge from Figure A.7 by comparing the two initial distributions, A and C. First, redistributive taxation increases social welfare. The social welfare indifference curves that are drawn through the post-tax distributions, *B* and *D*, are clearly higher than the curves that would go through the initial allocations, A and C, if they were to be drawn. Second, and this is the main point, more redistribution takes place when initial inequality is higher. Initial allocation C is more unequal than initial allocation A; consequently the post-tax changes are more dramatic. The reduction of inequality moving from C to *D* is larger than the reduction when moving from A to *B*. This is because the social welfare function places more value on redistribution when inequality is higher; higher inequality justifies greater redistributive intervention. In economists' terms, if optimizing social welfare requires equating marginal benefits with marginal costs, the higher (marginal) benefits of redistribution (because of the higher inequality) requires higher (marginal) taxes. Finally, note that final, post-tax inequality is still higher in after-tax distribution *D* than in after-tax distribution *B*. Further reducing inequality – achieving the same level of social marginal welfare weights as in distribution *B* would require greater costs. In that case, marginal costs would exceed marginal benefits, and this would violate the principle of optimality. Perhaps more simply, as seen by comparing the tax-loss curves, tax-induced income-earning disincentives make it impossible to start from a high level of inequality, like C, and move to a dramatically lower level of inequality, such as *B*.

The second conclusion from optimal tax theory worth emphasizing is that the optimal tax schedule depends not just on the level of inequality, but also on how much we (or the social planner) care about any particular level of inequality. It depends, that is, on which social welfare function is used to evaluate the optimal tax problem. For example, a utilitarian cares only about aggregate welfare. This means that there will be some gain to income redistribution, insofar as well-being implies a diminishing marginal utility of consumption, but zero weight is added to each person's marginal welfare. The utilitarian problem will then result in the least amount of redistribution, for a given level of income inequality. On the other hand, a Rawlsian cares only about the welfare of the least well-off person. This objective places a great deal of weight on inequality and chooses the tax level that maximizes the welfare of the poorest citizen, giving no weight to the welfare of any richer member of society. Any other social welfare function – reflecting the amount of consideration we give to equity – lies between these two extremes.

Figure A.8 illustrates this second important insight of optimal tax theory. The previous figure, Figure A.7 compared two different, initial levels of pre-tax inequality using the same social welfare function. Now, Figure A.8 compares the same initial level of pre-tax inequality with three different social welfare functions, one utilitarian, another intermediate, and a third Rawlsian. Each social welfare function imputes

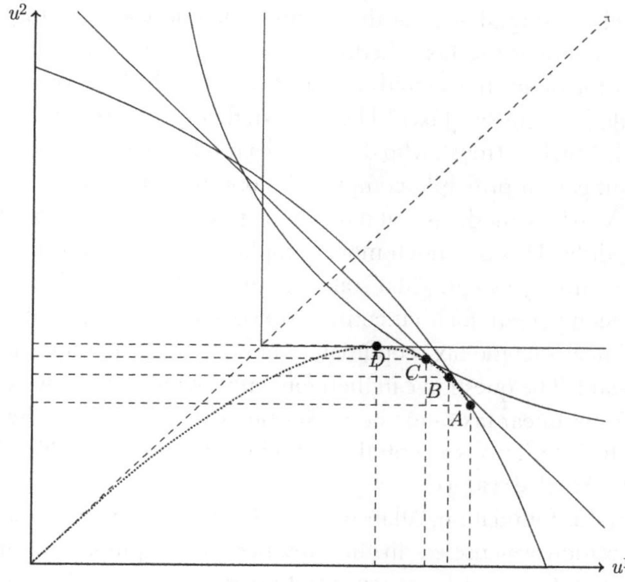

FIGURE A.8 Social welfare and optimal redistributive taxation

different social marginal welfare weights to the same, initial level of inequality. The utilitarian social welfare function is the least sensitive to inequality; the Rawlsian, the most sensitive. Therefore, as expected, the more inequality-sensitive the social welfare function, the more redistribution is justified. For example, the optimal amount of redistribution under the utilitarian social welfare function moves the welfare distributions of persons 1 and 2 from allocation *A* to *B*. An intermediate social welfare function moves us from *A* to *C*. And a Rawlsian social welfare function moves us from *A* to *D*. As those changes illustrate, the intermediate social welfare function entails more redistribution than the utilitarian, and the Rawlsian more than the intermediate (as well as the utilitarian). Thus, depending on which social welfare function society, or the social planner, adopts, more or less redistribution may be justified.

Some Background to Optimal Tax Theory

Optimal taxation of *labor income* has a privileged place within welfare economics. In the real world, policy makers choose and use a variety of taxes. There are sales taxes or value-added taxes, which are kinds of consumption or commodity taxes; there are taxes on income earned from labor and taxes on income earned on returns to capital investment; and there are also estate and gift taxes which are kinds of wealth taxes. Taxes on income earned from labor stand out as special, however.

The trajectory of optimal tax theory's development explains this special treatment. Shifting with the ideological winds through history, there has been a perennial debate in tax policy about the "shape" of the optimal income tax. Is a single rate, "flat" tax the best? Or should the tax schedule possess some "progressivity" with higher marginal rates for richer households and individuals? Or, less commonly, is there even a rationale for regressive taxes? The modern theory of the optimal labor income tax begins with Mirrlees (1971), who developed a model that, given the data brought to the problem, can in principle compute the optimal labor income tax schedule. The power of Mirrlees' model is that it makes no prior assumption about the "shape" of the tax schedule. This is a much more complicated mathematical problem than, for example, assuming a single, "flat" rate and then computing what this single rate should be. Fifteen percent for all income earners? Thirty-five percent? Thus, even if in practice a linear income tax is optimal, or close to it, the point is that this should be a *derived* result. The question can therefore only be properly answered in a model that allows for nonlinear tax rates and makes no assumption about the shape of the optimal tax schedule. This is a central question in the optimal tax literature that was inaugurated by Mirrlees (1971).

Building on this foundation, Atkinson and Stiglitz (1976) then demonstrated that commodity taxation was useless in the presence of an optimal nonlinear income tax. When excise taxes exist on consumption goods (except leisure, which is a consumption "good" but is considered non-taxable) and an income tax exists for earnings, individuals can respond to changes in taxation in two ways. They can either reduce their labor (and increase their leisure) or they can shift consumption to goods taxed at a lower rates. Note that the labor-leisure response is available for a change in *either* form of tax, excise or income. When an excise tax is raised on a consumption good, for example, this is equivalent to a tax on income, because any given level of (nominal) income can now only purchase less total consumption goods. Hence, whenever *differential* taxation of commodities exist, two distortions are caused as consumers both shift behavior from labor to leisure and consume more of the lower taxed goods and less of the higher-taxed goods. By contrast, a *uniform* excise tax is equivalent to an income tax and produces only a single distortion: when all goods are taxed at the same rate, say 10 percent, this is identical to a ten-percent tax on income. Hence, the exact same amount of revenue can be raised, and efficiency increased, by eliminating any differential rates on commodities and the double-distortion they cause.

However, this useless-commodity-tax conclusion rests on some nontrivial assumptions. One is that preferences are "weakly separable" between consumption and leisure, meaning that the marginal rate of substitution between goods i and j is independent of the amount of labor performed. In other words, the proportion of disposable income spent on each good will not change with the amount of labor required to earn that level of income. Another assumption is homogenous preferences across consumers, meaning that all individuals would buy the exact same bundle of goods when provided with the same amount of disposable income. Both of these assumptions are standard, but unrealistic. For example, it stands to reason that some goods are complementary to leisure (e.g., outdoors equipment). In this case, the weak separability assumption will be violated because the proportion of income allocation to the consumption of goods that are complementary to leisure will change as more, or less, time is allocated to work rather than leisure. Not surprisingly, the Atkinson-Stiglitz result breaks down when these assumptions are relaxed (see, e.g., Saez 2002b).

Nevertheless, the combined influence of Mirrlees (1971) and Atkinson and Stiglitz (1976) has had palpable effects on economists' policy advice. Prior to Atkinson and Stiglitz's paper, the prevailing orientation was that commodity taxes could be used for redistributive purposes, with different rates set for goods depending on whether they were consumed more frequently by the rich or the poor. The Atkinson-Stiglitz result provided a practical "rationale for eliminating preferential taxation of necessities on redistributive grounds, and using instead a uniform value-added-tax combined with income-based transfers and progressive income taxation" (Piketty and Saez 2013, 402). The Atkinson-Stiglitz result was also influential in the argument against the taxation of capital income and in favor of solely taxing either earnings or consumption (Saez 2013, 62 n.3).[11] Because in a (simplistic) dynamic framework saving is just deferred consumption, taxation of capital income results in unnecessary distortions just as in the static Atkinson-Stiglitz model. Finally, the Atkinson-Stiglitz result has served as inspiration, direct or indirect, for Kaplow and Shavell's double distortion argument.

Given these arguments against the unnecessary, additional distortions generated by taxes on commodities and capital, the taxation of labor income has come to assume a central place within public economics. The prescriptive message generated by these results has been that an ideal tax system should tax labor income exclusively. Taxing only labor income will reduce waste and inefficiency and allow more revenue to be targeted to society's needs, whether that be for redistribution, publicly provided goods, or whatever.

A General Model of Optimal Income Taxation

This brief history of optimal tax theory explains why the taxation of labor income is so central to welfare economics. Because of that importance, labor income taxation will serve a central role throughout this book. Even if the reader does not believe the income tax deserves such a prominent place, it will serve as an invaluable benchmark for evaluating the superiority or inferiority of other redistributive policies.

This subsection will present a simple, but general model, of the optimal (labor) income tax. This model follows the general optimal income tax model described in both Saez (2002a) and the three-occupation version in Lee and Saez (2012). As

[11] Judd (1985) and Chamley (1986) also show that, in the long-run, the optimal linear capital income tax should be zero. For the argument that capital income tax rates should be non-zero, see Saez (2013) and Straub and Werning (2020).

in those papers, the model here will concentrate on an important benchmark case with no income effects. Complete proofs of the optimal tax equations are given in this chapter's final section, A.6.1. For a model with income effects, which does not change the basic results or fundamental intuition, please see the working paper by Lee and Saez (2008).

Individuals have the choice of working in two different occupations: $i \in \{1, 2\}$. There are costs $\theta = (\theta_1, \theta_2)$ of working occupations 1 and 2. In addition, individuals can also choose not to work in either occupation; the costs of not working, designated as labor supply option 0, are normalized to zero: $\theta_0 = 0$. The vector of earnings for the occupations is: $y = (0, y_1, y_2)$, with $y_2 > y_1 > 0$. Hence, an individual can work in occupation 2 and earn y_2 at cost θ_2, work in occupation 1 and earn y_1 at cost θ_1, or remain unemployed. The individual cost of work vector θ is smoothly distributed across individuals in the population with cumulative distribution $H(\theta)$ and support Θ. Heterogeneity in θ represents differences in taste or ability for work, or entrepreneurial talent. The cost of work also has a long-term human capital interpretation as the cost of acquiring skills through education.

The tax authorities establish a tax schedule prior to individuals' labor supply decisions. As is normally assumed, the government can observe incomes, but not the individual costs of work or consumption decisions. Since there are three earnings outcomes, let T_i denote the tax (or if $T_i < 0$, the transfer) associated with each earnings outcome i. Each person's disposable income is then given by $c_i = y_i - T_i$. Each individual then chooses an occupation to maximize her utility, specified by $c_i - \theta_i$. (For contrast, a model with income effects will consider the utility function written as $u(c_i) - \theta_i$.) Define $\Theta_i = \{\theta \in \Theta | v_i = \max_j v_j\}$ as the subset of individuals choosing occupation i. Also define $h_i(\theta) = |\Theta_i|$ as the fraction of the population working in occupation i as a function of the disposable income vector $c = (c_0, c_1, c_2)$.

Despite its simplicity, this model describes a fully general nonlinear labor income tax model because it allows for labor supply responses on both the intensive and extensive margins. Individuals respond on the intensive margin by varying the number of hours they work or the intensity of their work effort. They respond on the extensive margin by deciding whether to work or not. In this model, the extensive margin is captured by the decision to work (either in either occupation 1 or 2) or not (remain unemployed 0). The intensive margin is captured in the decision to work in either occupation 1 or 2.

To get a view of the optimal tax problem, we will consider a basic version of the problem that we will refer back to elsewhere in the book. For now, let us simply focus attention on the intensive margin. In most cases, this will help us adequately address the behavioral response issue that is at the heart of the optimal tax problem in a world of imperfect information. In this case, we will consider the choice between occupations 0 and 1 and between 1 and 2 as reflecting responses to the intensive margin.

To complete the problem, we need to add a few more elements. First, we define the government's budget constraint. Assuming no exogenous spending requirement, this constraint is:

$$\sum_i h_i T_i = 0, \quad \text{for} \quad i \in \{0, 1, 2\}. \tag{A.7}$$

Second, in the discrete model with no income effects, the government's social welfare objective looks like this:

$$W = h_0 G(c_0) + \int_{\Theta_1} G(c_1 - \theta_1) dH(\theta) + \int_{\Theta_2} G(c_2 - \theta_2) dH(\theta) \tag{A.8}$$

where $G(\cdot)$ is a social welfare function that embodies society's, or the government's, redistributive preferences. As such, $G(\cdot)$ is concave, $G'(\cdot) > 0$, $G''(\cdot) < 0$, and so features diminishing marginal value of disposable income.

Third, we define what we call our *normalized* social marginal welfare weights. In our problem, these are given by:

$$g_0 = \frac{G'(c_0)}{\lambda} \quad \text{and} \quad g_i = \frac{\int_{\Theta_i} G'(c_i - \theta_i) dH(\theta)}{\lambda h_i} \quad \text{for} \quad i \in \{1, 2\}. \tag{A.9}$$

As a result of the social welfare function, these weights essentially describe the value of redistribution across groups. Therefore, g_i is decreasing in income or wealth, c_i. The added fact is the term in the denominator, λ, which is the marginal value of public funds. (For some discussion of the meaning of the marginal value of public funds and an equation that defines it, see Section A.6.1 and equation (A.19).) Thus the value of redistribution across groups is standardized by the cost of public funds. Standardizing in this fashion will allow us to show that the (population-weighted) normalized social marginal welfare weights sum to one:

$$h_0 g_0 + h_1 g_1 + h_2 g_2 = 1. \tag{A.10}$$

This result will have some useful analytic properties, as will be seen below. See Section A.6.1 for its full derivation.

Finally, we need to define the behavioral elasticity of labor supply with respect to taxes. This is:

$$\zeta_i = \frac{c_i - c_{i-1}}{h_i} \frac{\partial h_i}{\partial (c_i - c_{i-1})} \quad \textit{for} \quad i \in \{1, 2\}. \tag{A.11}$$

Most simply, this elasticity measures the change in the supply of labor to a given occupation when taxes on that occupation are changed. More technically, it measures the percentage increase in the supply of occupation i when the difference in the disposable incomes of adjacent occupations (say, i and $i - 1$), is increased by 1 percent.

The optimal tax equations are derived by combining the social welfare objective, in equation (A.8), with the government's budget constrain, in equation (A.7). Forming the LaGrangian, we have:

$$W + \lambda \sum_i h_i T_i.$$

Maximizing this expression with respect to each T_i and using the expression for labor-supply elasticity on the intensive margin given by equation (A.11), allows us to derive the optimal marginal tax rates, which are:

$$\frac{T_2 - T_1}{c_2 - c_1} = \frac{1 - g_2}{\zeta_2} \tag{A.12}$$

and:

$$\frac{T_1 - T_0}{c_1 - c_0} = \frac{1}{\zeta_1}\left[\frac{(1 - g_1)h_1 + (1 - g_2)h_2}{h_1}\right]. \tag{A.13}$$

To make these expressions for the optimal marginal tax rates a bit more intuitive, we can define an implicit marginal tax rate as $\tau_i = (T_i - T_{i-1})/(y_i - y_{i-1})$, or equivalently $1 - \tau_i = (c_i - c_{i-1})/(y_i - y_{i-1})$. Equations (A.12) and (A.13) can then be expressed as as:

$$\frac{\tau_2}{1 - \tau_2} = \frac{1 - g_2}{\zeta_2} \tag{A.14}$$

and

$$\frac{\tau_1}{1 - \tau_1} = \frac{1}{\zeta_1}\left[\frac{(1 - g_1)h_1 + (1 - g_2)h_2}{h_1}\right]. \tag{A.15}$$

Two immediate observations can be made about these two expressions. First, consider the effect of labor supply elasticity, ζ_i. In either equation (A.14) or (A.15), a larger elasticity means that people are more responsive to changes in taxes. The more responsive they are, the less room the government has to raise rates for fear that everyone will reduce their labor supply and shrink the tax base. Thus, higher elasticity means a lower marginal tax rate. Second, consider the effects of the social marginal welfare weights, g_i. As seen in either equation (A.14) or (A.15), a smaller g_i, together or individually, implies a larger marginal tax rate. In the first instance, the size of g_i is a function of individual wealth (disposable income c_i). Furthermore, given the shape of the social welfare function $G(\cdot)$, which is concave, g_i features a diminishing marginal value of wealth. Therefore, the higher a person i's wealth, c_i, the smaller is the social marginal welfare weight, g_i. This gives the result, from equations (A.14) or (A.15), that higher relative wealth gives a higher marginal tax rate.

It should also be fairly evident that the signs of both marginal tax rates are positive. Seeing this depends on the critical insight that the social marginal welfare weights sum to one, as given in equation (A.10). Inequality of incomes, $c_2 > c_1 > c_0$, implies social marginal welfare weights that are declining in income, $g_2 < g_1 < g_0$. And because the social marginal welfare weights sum to one, the weight on the richest members of society, g_2 will be less than one, $g_2 < 1$. Hence, equation (A.14) indicates a positive marginal tax rate at the top of the income distribution. The marginal tax rate at the bottom, τ_1, is also positive and, in fact, dictates a Negative Income

Tax policy. This is a little less immediate because of the ambiguity of the size of g_1 (greater or less than one?) and because of the different population weights, h_1 and h_2, as reflected in equation (A.15). However, the result that the social marginal welfare weights sum to one is again critical. Rearranging that expression, given in equation (A.10), we get $(1 - g_1)h_1 + (1 - g_2)h_2 = -(1 - g_0)h_0 = (g_0 - 1)h_0$. This allows us to rewrite the expression for τ_1 in equation (A.15) as

$$\frac{\tau_1}{1 - \tau_1} = \frac{1}{\zeta_1}\left[\frac{(g_0 - 1)h_0}{h_1}\right]. \tag{A.16}$$

Because the social marginal welfare weights sum to one, we have $g_0 > 1$. Hence, this implies in equation (A.16) that the marginal tax rate between groups 1 and 0 ought to be positive. To put this in slightly different terms, the optimal policy for the poor is to make the transfer to group 0, $-T_0$, as large as possible, and then impose large phasing-out tax rates as household income increases at the bottom of the income distribution. The classic instantiation of this policy is the Negative Income Tax.

A brief aside about this Negative Income Tax result. This result is a standard one within an intensive model of labor supply, and informs much thinking about the optimal tax structure, especially at the bottom of the income distribution. However, it contrasts significantly with the result when the extensive margin of labor supply is added to the analysis. When that is done, the marginal tax rate at the bottom of the income distribution may well be *negative*, in contrast to the positive rate we just adduced in equation (A.16). Translated into plainer language, this means that when the extensive margin is included, the optimal tax schedule may have a "bubble" at the bottom, with higher wage subsidies for low-income workers than for the unemployed, and thus possibly negative marginal tax rates at the bottom. The classic instantiation of such a policy is the Earned Income Tax Credit (EITC).[12] This choice between the NIT and the EITC is further discussed in Chapter 6.

Building on these immediate observations, we can see how these expressions for the optimal marginal tax rates imply the two key insights from optimal tax theory that were explained intuitively and graphically at the beginning of Section A.4.1. The first is that higher inequality yields more redistribution (illustrated in Figure A.7). In equations (A.14) or (A.15), greater redistribution is indicated by larger marginal tax rates, τ_2 and τ_1; intuitively, when marginal tax rates are higher, the progressivity of the tax schedule increases, and more income is redistributed from the top of the income distribution to the bottom. Thus, when inequality is higher for a fixed amount of total wealth, the differences between $c_2 > c_1 > c_0$ become greater. Those greater differences will in turn imply greater differences in the social marginal welfare weights $g_2 < g_1 < g_0$. Hence, equation (A.14) indicates that a larger share of income going to the richest group, group 2, implies a larger c_2, a smaller g_2, and thus a larger

[12] For further discussion of the intensive versus extensive margins of labor supply, and their implications for the shape of the tax schedule at the bottom of the income distribution, see Saez (2002a).

marginal tax rate between groups 2 and 1, that is, a larger τ_2. The marginal tax rate between groups 1 and 0, τ_1, will also increase. This is made most evident by inspecting the expression for τ_1 given by equation (A.16). Because greater inequality implies a larger g_0, that in turn justifies a larger marginal tax rate between groups 1 and 0. For example, this marginal-rate change can be accomplished by increasing transfers to the poor, which will increase the marginal rate between the poor and middle-income groups.

Our second key result of optimal tax theory is that the optimal tax schedule also depends on the chosen social welfare function (illustrated in equation A.8), which is said to embody society's, or the government's, or the social planner's preferences, or "tastes," for redistribution. Consider a change in preferences in a Rawlsian direction, toward favoring more redistribution. For a given level of total wealth and its distribution, preferences for more redistribution generate greater differences in the social marginal welfare weights. For reasons just given, these changes in social marginal welfare weights – in particular, a smaller g_2 and a larger g_0 – imply larger marginal tax rates, τ_2 and τ_1, indicated by equations (A.14) and (A.16), and hence more redistribution.

A.4.2 *Distribution-Neutral Income Tax Adjustments*

The second method we have for evaluating policies' distributive effects comes from the line of work first used in Hylland and Zeckhauser (1979) and Kaplow and Shavell (1994) and then elaborated in Kaplow (2008). Kaplow calls this the method of "distribution-neutral income tax adjustments." Part of the challenge of the Mirrlees framework is that it is mathematically cumbersome, requiring not only constrained optimization, but also the more exotic tools of optimal control theory. The method of distribution-neutral income tax adjustments requires nothing more than simple arithmetic. Furthermore, distribution-neutral income tax adjustments can evaluate any sort of policy with distributive effects, not just tax policy. This makes it uniquely useful for addressing the challenge of analyzing the distributive effects of legal rules. Although Kaplow has since subsequently elaborated on the method significantly (see, e.g., Kaplow 2004, 2008), a subtly different approach to distribution-neutral tax adjustments lie at the heart of Kaplow and Shavell's (1994) famous critique of using legal rules to redistribute income.

Suppose that we want to evaluate some change in policy – for example, a change in the amount of a public good provided by the government, a new environmental regulation, or the adoption of a new legal rule in tort. Such a policy will have a mix of effects that we need to consider before passing final judgment on its adoption. First, the policy will in general have some sort of positive welfare effect on individuals, which we assume can be translated into a dollar amount. These benefits need not be uniform across the population; they might even be negative for some members of the population. (Although if uniformly negative for all, we would not even consider the policy.) Second, this policy is probably not costless to implement and enforce, and therefore must be financed in some fashion from which we have a range of options to choose from (income, sales, payroll taxes, etc.). The method of finance will likewise have different distributive effects. While we know the policy will have distributive and efficiency effects, evaluating the complex mix of those effects, however, is a difficult question.

These difficulties can be alleviated by using the idea of distribution-neutral income tax adjustments. In addition to the welfare and distribution effects of the policy, suppose we levied an income tax on each individual – specifically, a tax or a transfer – so that the policy is *distribution neutral*. This hypothetical adjustment is a compensating variation, set at every level of income so that the total policy – welfare change, fiscal change, and the adjustment – provides individuals who initially earned that income the same level of utility as before the policy change. Because it keeps every person's utility the same, we can treat (again, at this point, hypothetically) the policy change as distribution neutral in a strong sense. That is, we do not need a definition of "distribution neutral" that would require making comparisons across different distributions with changed levels of income or utility.

Because this proposed policy "package" is distribution neutral, it completely isolates the efficiency effects of the policy and, indeed, the policy can be assessed entirely on grounds of a traditional cost-benefit test. Furthermore, this also means that we can assess the policy independently of whatever social welfare function is chosen (Kaplow 2008, 48–50). There is no change in distribution, no redistribution, and therefore no "equity" effect that must be included in the analysis and whose magnitude would depend on the choice of a social welfare function. Further simplifying the problem, we only need to determine whether the complete policy package yields a budget surplus or deficit – a simple cost-benefit test. By using taxes and transfers to maintain the same levels of utility as existed prior to the policy, all distributional effects are transformed into budget effects. Thus, if there is a budget surplus, it can be rebated – pro rata, for instance – and yield a strict Pareto improvement: everyone is made better off and no one worse off. Conversely, if there is a budget deficit, the policy idea can be abandoned, confirming that the status quo ante is preferred, or, if already enacted, reversed, which will likewise yield a Pareto improvement. This illustrates yet another implication of the method, which is that because it depends only on individuals' utilities, and is independent of the social welfare function, it does not matter what the initial income tax and transfer schedule is or even whether it is optimally set, following Mirrlees (1971), according to that social welfare function.

For an example of this method, we can turn to one offered in Kaplow (2008, 182–85). Suppose that the government wants to build a public park and that the benefits, measured (and, by assumption, measurable) in dollars, is distributively unequal. For example, suppose that the benefits of the public park rise with income, but at a less-than-proportional rate, as illustrated in Figure A.9. A standard

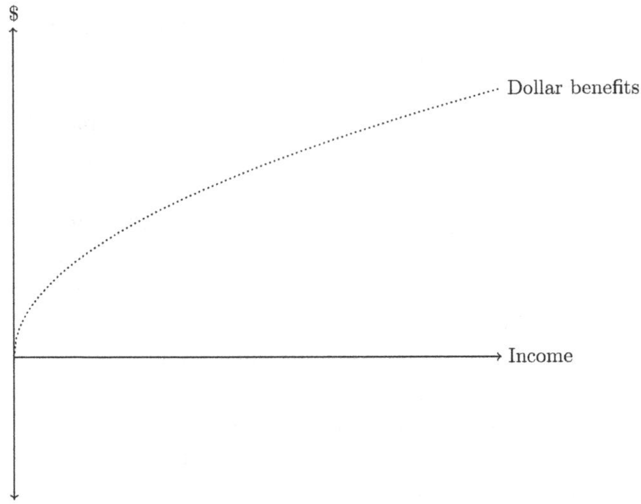

FIGURE A.9 Distributive incidence of a public good

cost-benefit analysis would evaluate this project by totaling dollar benefits, regardless of their distributive incidence, and ask whether they outweigh the expenditures required to build the park. But the unequal distribution of benefits makes this form of evaluation questionable. Should we treat the dollar benefits of the rich equal to those of the poor? A social welfare function, even a utilitarian one, would not treat these values equally because the rich would value a dollar less than the poor. However, introducing the distributive incidence of the public park also substantially complicates the evaluation.

A distribution-neutral income tax adjustment (Kaplow 2004, 2008) can address this complication. Suppose that we wanted to use adjustments to the tax schedule in order not only to finance the public park but also to offset some (or all) of the inequality it creates. Figure A.10 illustrates the possible ways of accomplishing this objective. In order to highlight a distribution-neutral tax adjustment, this option is contrasted with two alternatives: first, a uniform tax adjustment and, second, a proportional tax adjustment. Figure A.10a shows the effects of a uniform tax adjustment. In this case, in order to finance the building of the park, each individual, regardless of income, pays the same amount, which is equal to the average benefits of the public park. Clearly, this method does not change the distributive incidence of the project, and the net effect is to make the poor worse off and to redistribute to the rich.

Figure A.10b illustrates a proportional tax scheme used to finance the park's construction and offset its distributive incidence. Now, each individual is taxed in proportion to their income, and the same percentage is added to everyone's marginal income tax rate. The total revenue raised is again assumed to equal the total dollar

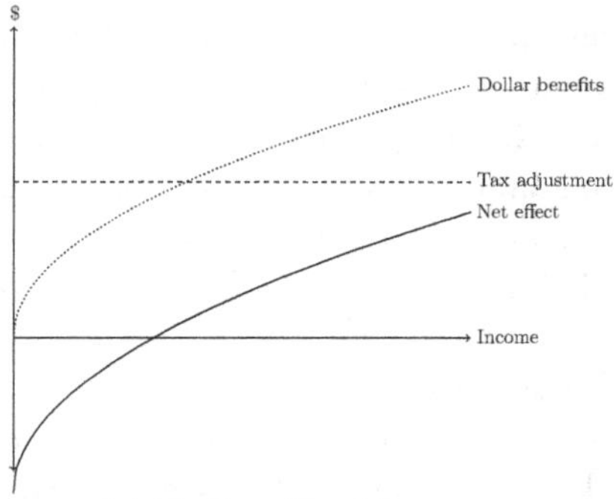

(a) Uniform Tax Adjustment

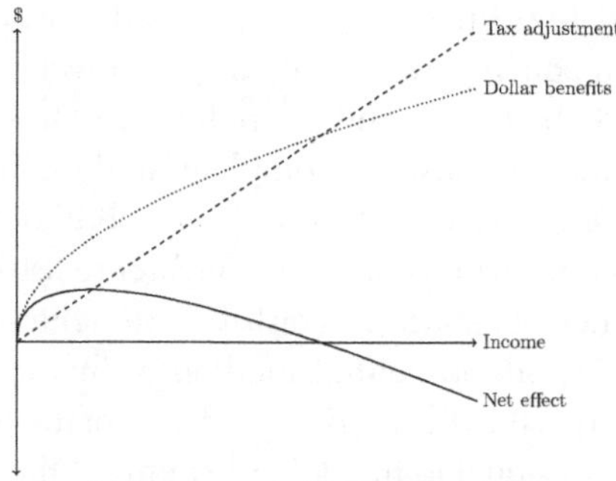

(b) Proportional Tax Adjustment

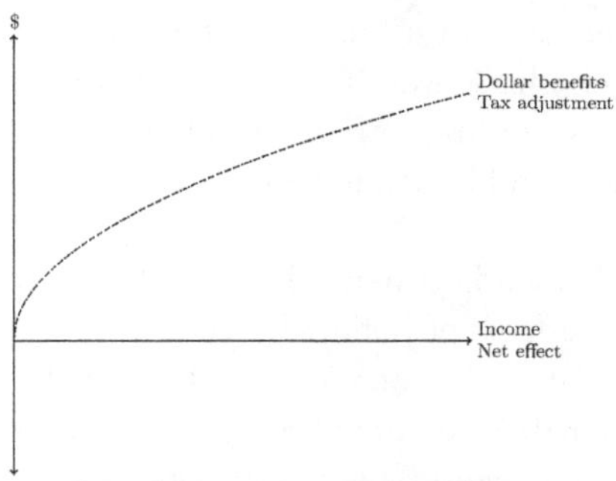

(c) Distribution-Neutral Tax Adjustment

FIGURE A.10 Financing a public good with tax adjustments

amount of benefits. Now, as Figure A.10b shows, the net effect of this financing method is to redistribute in favor of the poor.

The proportional tax adjustment represents another point worth highlighting. As Kaplow (2008) likes to insist, one should not evaluate a policy by focusing one-sidely either on its cost (that is, the way it is financed) or its benefits. It is very common to do this when evaluating tax policy. For example, we commonly ask whether a proposed tax change will be progressive or regressive without talking about how the revenue it raises will be spent. Instead of asking such a narrow question, one should evaluate the entire policy, its financing and its expenditure, as a package.[13] For instance, by ignoring the way it is financed, the public park project appears to favor the rich because its benefits rise with income. On the other side of the ledger, tax analysts routinely describe a proportional tax scheme as a "flat tax." And because proportionality is the standard benchmark for evaluating how redistributive a tax schedule is, the conventional answer is that a flat tax is not redistributive at all, being neither progressive nor regressive (17). Thus, neither the benefits of the park, nor

[13] In a similar vein, Murphy and Nagel (2002) emphasize that one cannot evaluate the justice or fairness of a tax policy without considering how those taxes are used.

its flat-tax financing, when viewed in isolation, appears to favor the poor. But when both policies are combined, the project is unambiguously "progressive": the poor are made better off, and the rich worse off. Kaplow thus emphasizes that proper policy evaluation must be "complete" and include all dimensions of the policy or project.

One may want to stop here and choose the proportional tax-financing scheme, given its (when combined) greater redistributive effect. Before making that decision, we need to consider a distribution-neutral tax adjustment, displayed in Figure A.10c. A distribution-neutral method of finance chooses taxes and transfers that are just equal to the distributive incidence of the public park. The tax adjustment is therefore exactly equal to the dollar benefits of the park, and the net effect is to give everyone the same level of well-being (or, measured in dollars, income) they had before the park was built. Now, there is no distributive (or, for that matter, redistributive) effect of the combined project whatsoever. The advantage of this method of finance – and policy evaluation – according to Kaplow is that "the distributive incidence of government expenditures would seem to be irrelevant for the simple reason that the net incidence is zero" (185).

A distribution-neutral tax adjustment allows us to sidestep the thorny issue of the unequal distributive effects of policy. Indeed, the problem then reduces to a simple cost-benefit calculation. Suppose that the benefit of the park to those earning \$100,000 is \$50, while for those earning \$20,000 the benefit is \$30. A distribution-neutral method of finance would then increase taxes (or reduce transfers) by exactly the same amount. If the total revenues exceeded or are equal to the cost of building the park, the public project would pass a cost-benefit test. For example, suppose the wealthy make up 25 percent of the population, the poor 75 percent. Then, the per-capita benefit of the park – equal to the per-capita revenue raised through the distribution-neutral income tax adjustment – is $0.25(\$50) + 0.75(\$30) = \$35$. Therefore, if the per-capita cost of constructing the park is \$20, the park would be a clear cost-benefit winner: $\$35 - \$20 = \$15$. Furthermore, in view of the sizable net gain, tax revenues could be rebated or tax rates adjusted downwards according to an appropriate social welfare function. That step aside, however, the central point is that a distribution-neutral income tax adjustment dramatically simplifies the evaluation of the public park project by eliminating its complicated distributive incidence and turning the problem into a simple cost-benefit calculation.

One might still favor the proportional tax adjustment: it *appears* to be the more pro-poor policy. But Kaplow's answer is that the proportional scheme may actually leave the poor worse off, for reasons elaborated by the double-distortion argument: it is too inefficient. Among other reasons, perhaps the income-tax schedule is already at its redistributive optimum. In that case, further redistribution is not only inefficient but unwarranted by whatever social-welfare metric we are using. Even if the the tax schedule is not at its redistributive optimum, we face Kaplow and Shavell's main claim: the income tax schedule *should* be set optimally, which will save resources, and allows us to evaluate other public policies in simple, cost-benefit terms. Using a distribution-neutral income tax adjustment may yield a policy that makes the poor better off than the proportional income tax adjustment.

The method of distribution-neutral income tax adjustments is a remarkably powerful insight and one that will be used repeatedly throughout this book. However, it does have some conspicuous limitations. The first, and most obvious, is that the welfare effects of the policy under consideration must be *identical* to utility-equivalent income (or monetarily valued consumption) effects, so that the income tax can be harnessed to distributionally "neutralize" them. For example, the individual benefit of the public park must have a dollar value that is in every respect equivalent to that amount in earned income. This is an extraordinarily strong assumption. It is plausible enough in certain cases, especially where the primary effects of the policy influence the distribution of income or material goods. The effect of a minimum wage policy, for instance, is to directly change the amount of income workers receive. But in a variety of other settings, the assumption easily collapses. Among other leaps, it requires the assumption that consumption and leisure are "weakly separable," one that was mentioned earlier in connection with Atkinson and Stiglitz's (1976) famous paper in Section A.4.1. That assumption is hard to accept, for example, in the public park case. Kaplow assumes that the benefits of the park can be measured like increases in wages or reductions in taxes, leading to an increase in labor supply. But because public parks are associated with recreation, they make leisure more attractive than labor and will have an indirect, negative effect on labor supply, one that is independent of the taxes used to finance the park.[14] That implication runs directly against Kaplow's hypothesis. The weak separability assumption serves to resolve such problems theoretically, by keeping consumption (enjoyment of the park) "separate" from leisure and therefore labor decisions. But as should be clear by now, that is an extraordinarily strong assumption and as several authors have recognized, once the weak separability assumption is dropped, the income tax may no longer be the uniquely desirable form of redistribution (see, e.g., Sanchirico 2010). More importantly, it calls into question that labor-supply responses between policies and distribution-neutral tax adjustments will be identical.

A less-widely recognized problem with distribution-neutral income tax adjustments is the changing ways that Kaplow and Shavell have interpreted them over the years. In Kaplow and Shavell (1994), they are used to argue that taxes are more efficient than legal rules for redistributing income. Later, in Kaplow (2004, 2008, 2021), they are used to argue that regulation and public policy should follow standard first-best, cost-benefit analysis while ignoring their distributive consequences. The problem is that the second interpretation can sometimes contradict the first.

[14] Kaplow (2004, 166) points out that public goods may also have an independent, positive effect on labor supply: "Conversely, public goods and environmental regulations that enhance the ambience of central cities may increase labor supply because they increase the utility associated with work." However, that possibility just underscores the point that the relationship between labor supply and environmental (and other public) goods is wildly indeterminate.

TABLE A.1 *Interpreting distribution-neutral income tax adjustments*

	Income Effect (Rich)	Income Effect (Poor)	Labor-Supply Effect	DNITA Budget	Total Effect
Public Park	\$50	\$30	\$15	\$15	\$30
Damages Rule	−\$1,200	\$366.66	−\$50	−\$25	−\$75
Minimum Wage	\$140	\$100	−\$35	\$20	−\$15
Merger	\$1,000	−\$350	\$20	−\$12.50	\$7.50

Consider the following examples to illustrate this claim, displayed in Table A.1, which compares four different legal rules, or policies. The first is Kaplow's (2008) park example just discussed; the second is the tort example used in Kaplow and Shavell (1994); the third is a minimum wage, which is further explored in Chapter 6, on labor and employment law; and the fourth is the evaluation of a proposed merger of firms under antitrust law, which is further explored in Chapter 7, on antitrust. The first column reports the effect of the policy, in direct income terms, to the rich; the second column reports the policy effect for the poor. In all cases, I assume that "the rich" compose 25 percent of the population and "the poor" 75 percent. The third column displays the net, per-capita labor-supply effect of the given policy. The fourth column tells us how the budget balances (or does not) when a distribution-neutral income tax adjustment (hence, "DNITA") is used to evaluate the policy. The final column reports the net wealth, or efficiency, effect of the policy if it were to go through without any distribution-neutral tax adjustment; as an "overall" measure of efficiency, it includes the labor-supply effects of the given policy. As will be illustrated in just a moment, it is possible to see the final column as another way of evaluating policies, as an alternative to distribution-neutral income tax adjustments. One point that I hope will become clear is that these two forms of evaluation do not always agree: for the policies in the first two rows they do, but for those in the bottom two rows, they do not. It is this disagreement that makes distribution-neutral income tax adjustments interpretively ambiguous.

The first example in Table A.1, the public park example, establishes a baseline for the others. In that case, recall that the direct, per-capita effect of the proposed project is valued at \$50 by the wealthy (column 1) and \$30 by the poor (column 2), for an average value of \$35. Because the park benefits everyone, and especially the rich, which effectively lowers the marginal tax rate, we can assume that the project would cause individuals to substitute work for leisure and increase labor supply (on Kaplow's strong assumption that preferences are weakly separable in consumption and leisure). Say that the added labor supply raises wealth by \$15 per capita (column 3). As already assumed, the cost to build the park is \$20 per capita. Thus, if income taxes were adjusted to exactly equal the benefit of the park to each individual, it would raise \$35 and, given the cost, yield a budget surplus of \$15 (column 4), which could be rebated pro rata, distributed to the poor, or used to lower everyone's taxes. Also note in the final column that the total value of the project, if undertaken without a distribution-neutral income tax adjustment and therefore having labor-supply effects, is: \$35 (direct benefit) + \$15 (labor supply effect) – \$20 (cost of building the park) = \$30.

By turning distribution effects into budget effects via the tax system, the public park proves itself to be a cost-benefit winner. Despite the complicated distributive effects, it can nevertheless be evaluated on the basis of a simple, first-best efficiency test. However, before distribution-neutral income tax adjustments were used to make cost-benefit evaluations, they were used in a subtly different way to test the *redistributive* efficiency of alternative tax and legal policies. To mark this interpretive shift, consider the wealth-dependent damages rule used by Kaplow and Shavell (1994) and displayed in the second row of Table A.1. In their hypothetical, the damages rule is intended to be redistributive. Suppose that the higher damages the wealthy must pay to poor victims transfers an additional \$1,000. In terms of the rule's direct effect, therefore, the per-capita amount, being purely distributive, is zero: $0.25(-\$1,000) + 0.75(\$333.33) = \$0$. However, the legal rules also generate additional costs. The rich spend more on precaution and are not fully compensated if they are injured by a poor person; the poor, on the other hand, spend less on precaution and pay less in damages if they injure a rich person. By hypothesis the rule is inefficient, so the costs to the rich are not offset by the benefits to the poor. Let us say the additional costs to the rich are –\$200 and the gains to the poor are \$33.33, so that the net per-capita cost of the rule is –\$25. Finally, because these total income changes to the rich and poor are equivalent to an increase in marginal tax rates, individuals substitute more leisure for labor, and labor supply falls, causing a per-capita loss of say –\$50. The total cost of the rule – the double distortion, which is the cost of the legal rule itself, –\$25, plus the labor-supply distortion, –\$50 – is therefore –\$75.

Now, there are two ways to evaluate the damages rule using distribution-neutral income tax adjustments. The first is as a test of redistributive efficiency, as in Kaplow and Shavell's (1994) original contribution. The second is as a cost-benefit test, as in the public-park case borrowed from Kaplow (2008). In the first case, a tax adjustment is used to *replicate* the post-reform, redistributive effects of the rule, in order to determine whether taxes or legal rules redistribute more efficiently. In this sense, the tax adjustment is distributively neutral with respect to the effects of the redistributive legal rule. Thus, because the redistributive legal rule's total cost to the rich is $-\$1,200$ and the total gain to the poor is \$366.66, when we adopt the efficient legal rule we adjust taxes by precisely that amount. The government's budget, when those amounts are raised and spent is $0.25(\$1,200) + 0.75(-\$366.66) = \$25$, which is, as should be expected, the savings the government accrues by adopting the efficient legal rule rather than inefficient, redistributive one. As usual, those savings can be rebated pro rata or used to lower everyone's taxes or spent entirely on the poor. Thus, in this perspective, the government can achieve *more* redistribution by using taxes and the efficient legal rule in place of the redistributive legal rule.

In the second form of evaluation, Kaplow (2008) uses income tax adjustments to *preserve* the status quo ante income distribution rather than *replicate* the income distribution created by redistributive rule. For instance, instead of taxing the rich and subsidizing the poor in order to achieve the redistributive legal rule's distribution of income, we subsidize the rich and tax the poor in order to *preserve* the less equal distribution of wealth. One difference that makes is that, by locking in the pre-reform income distribution, there is never any additional labor-supply distortion. In this way, a distribution-neutral income tax adjustment produces a budget deficit of $0.25(-\$1,200) + 0.75(\$366.66) = -\$25$.

The difference between the two forms of evaluation is subtle. Indeed, the result of the second tells us essentially the same thing as the first: if we want to evaluate the rule on a purely cost-benefit basis, controlling for (or negating) its distributive effects, it fails such a test by yielding a deficit. In the first case, replicating the distributive effects of the redistributive legal rule with taxes produces a budget surplus, which tells us that taxes are more redistributively efficient than the legal rule. In the second case, evaluating the redistributive legal rule on a cost-benefit basis by using distribution-neutral income tax adjustments tells us that it fails a cost-benefit test. To put this another way, the first method tells us that the income tax, compared to the legal rule, saves money; the second tells us that the legal rule, compared to taxes, loses money. In both cases, the tax adjustment – either to preserve the pre-reform distribution of income or to replicate the post-reform distribution of income – allows us to evaluate exclusively the efficiency effects of the policy itself while holding constant its distributive and labor-supply effects. Thus, the answer is the same under either form of evaluation.

However, while the interpretation of the two forms of policy evaluation agree in the damages case, it becomes more ambiguous in other cases. Consider the next example, the minimum-wage, displayed in the third row of Table A.1. A simple and accepted way to model the minimum wage is to think of the production of a unique consumption good that uses two labor inputs: low-skilled, low-waged workers and high-skilled, high-waged workers (see, e.g., Stiglitz 1982; Lee and Saez 2012). The two forms of labor are imperfect substitutes and on reasonable assumptions the minimum wage is redistributive: raising the wages of low-skilled workers lowers the wages of high-skilled workers. Following a large literature on information problems in labor markets, I also assume that there is a negative association between wages and the costs of monitoring workers' effort on the job; higher wages reduce monitoring costs. (For further details, the reader may consult Chapter 6.)

The minimum wage then has the following effects. First, suppose that the minimum wage increases low-skilled (annual) wages by \$100 (raising them from an initial \$300). Second, also suppose that the minimum wage lowers monitoring costs, per worker, by −\$50. Notice that the joint consequence of these effects will be to increase involuntary employment. The net cost of the minimum wage is still positive: $\$100 - \$50 = \$50 > 0$, raising the cost of employment above its marginal productivity. Thus, employers will lower their demand for low-skilled labor, even though there are more workers willing to work at the minimum wage than positions are available. Let us suppose that only 93.33 percent of low-skilled workers are employed, so that the percentage of low-skilled workers employed is now seventy percent of the total population ($0.70/0.75 = 93.33$). If the joint effect of these two changes is "paid for" entirely by high-skilled employees, then their wages fall by $-\$140$ ($0.25(\$140) = 0.70(\$100-\$50)$). Finally, because the minimum wage reduces income inequality it affects labor-supply the same as an increase in the marginal tax rate. Say that the minimum wage's labor-supply distortions amount to \$35 per capita.

The ambiguity of distribution-neutral income tax adjustments can now be seen more clearly. Suppose we use the first approach, the one that evaluates the redistributive efficiency of different policies. That approach entails, in this case, replicating the distribution of income achieved by the minimum wage by replacing it with an income tax adjustment that yields the same income distribution as the minimum wage. To do this, the minimum wage is lowered to its market-clearing, pre-minimum-wage level; because there would consequently be no involuntary unemployment, the government can spend less on subsidizing low-skilled workers to give them the same expected utility they have with the minimum wage.[15] As a share of wage earners, the government spends per employed low-skilled worker 0.93(\$400) but saves \$300 per low-skilled worker (whether employed or not). This captures the amount the government must spend in order to give low-wage workers the same utility as they have with the minimum wage. Likewise, the government taxes high-skilled workers by \$140, the amount each loses under the minimum wage. In this case, the government's budget comes out to $(0.25)\$140 - (0.75)((0.93)\$400 - \$300) = -\$20$, a deficit. Further analysis will show (in Chapter 6) that this deficit is generated by precisely the two efficiency effects it has, namely the lost savings from the minimum wage's productivity effect (weighted by the percentage of workers employed at the minimum wage) plus the savings gained by reducing unemployment. This equation is $-(0.70)\$50 + (0.75 - 0.70)\$300 = -\$20$. In any case, the deficit tells us that the income tax cannot redistribute income as efficiently as the minimum wage.

[15] I assume that the minimum wage is lowered, rather than abolished, to avoid the possibility of incidence effects that worsen the efficiency of income taxation; thus, the assumption works against my favored hypothesis. Also, workers with the minimum wage are treated as having an expected utility because, as in the standard treatment, the minimum wage creates excess labor supply – more workers are willing to work for a higher minimum wage than there are positions available. Therefore, utility for a wage-earner is an expected average of income in the employed and unemployed states. That treats the unemployment effect of the minimum wage as random, which is contestable, but has some justification, particularly if those whom the minimum wage benefits have a stronger likelihood of remaining employed. See Lee and Saez (2012) for more discussion.

The first interpretation of distribution-neutral income tax adjustments therefore concludes that the minimum wage redistributes income more efficiently than the income tax. But the ambiguity of such adjustments becomes apparent when we use the second, cost-benefit version. This second version uses the income tax system to negate the minimum wage's distributive effects, to restore the pre-reform, pre-minimum-wage distribution of income. This is just the reverse of the previous analysis: subsidize high-skilled workers income by \$140 and tax low-skilled employment workers by \$100 with an adjustment to account for unemployment: $-(0.25)\$140 + (0.75)((0.93)\$100 - (1 - 0.93)\$300) = \$20$. The budget is positive, which tells us that the minimum wage passes a cost-benefit test. So, which interpretation should we adopt? Should we endorse the minimum wage because it passes a cost-benefit test and is therefore efficient? Or should we endorse it, not because it is efficient, but because it redistributes more efficiently than the tax system? Indeed, when the labor-supply cost of the minimum wage is included, the minimum wage is inefficient, from an overall perspective: $\$20 - \$35 = -\$15$. It is admittedly difficult to accept the view that the minimum wage passes a cost-benefit test. The minimum wage is not a "first-best" efficient policy intervention. All of the effects for which the minimum wage is criticized are attendant: involuntary unemployment, reduced labor demand, and lower output. Yet, judging the minimum wage as "internally" efficient is precisely the conclusion one must draw according to Kaplow's framing of distribution-neutral income tax adjustments.

For a final, comparative example that underscores the ambiguity of distribution-neutral income tax adjustments, consider the antitrust, merger-evaluation case, displayed in the fourth row of Table A.1. In this case, suppose that two companies are proposing a merger that will have acknowledged anti-competitive effects, leading to a loss of allocative efficiency. However, the merger also generates benefits that lead to gains in productive efficiency (e.g., greater economies of scale). Suppose that merger, if undertaken, would increase the income of the rich by \$1,000 (by increasing profits and thus dividend payments) and decrease that of the poor by −\$350 (by raising prices). Because the merger increases income inequality, it functions like a reduction in the marginal tax rate, and therefore increases labor supply, say by \$20. Note that the net, per-capita effect of the rule is $0.25(\$1,000) - 0.75(\$350) = -\$12.50$. Should the merger be undertaken? If we use a distribution-neutral income tax adjustment to offset the distributive effects of the merger, we would tax the rich by \$1,000 and reduce taxes on (or increase subsidies to) the poor by −\$350. The budget result is, not surprisingly, a deficit of −\$12.50. The merger fails a cost-benefit test. The net effect of the merger's productive efficiencies and allocative inefficiencies is to lower the sum of consumer plus producer surplus. However, if the merger is permitted, the total effect, including enhanced labor-supply incentives, raises wealth by a per-capita \$7.50. The ambiguities should be evident. Why do we care about the sum of consumer and producer surplus rather than overall efficiency? If we block the merger, do we do so because the merger is inefficient or because it is more efficient than the income tax at maintaining the pre-merger distribution of income? Indeed, another way of looking at the distribution-neutral income tax adjustments in this case is as a way of replicating the pre-merger distribution of income. (Indeed, what if, say, we are contemplating the break-up of a monopoly rather than evaluating a proposed merger?) In that interpretation, the budget deficit reveals that the income tax is a less efficient way of redistributing income than using antitrust law.

To summarize, in the first two cases, the park and the wealth-dependent damages rule, there is no interpretive ambiguity. The judgments of distribution-neutral income tax adjustments align with overall efficiency evaluations, whether we are evaluating the redistributive efficiency of legal rules or putting the policies to a cost-benefit test. However, the ambiguities are stark in the minimum wage and merger cases. Do we adopt the minimum wage because it satisfies a cost-benefit test? Without distribution-neutral tax adjustments, the opinion has always been that the minimum wage is not efficient. The minimum wage saves on monitoring costs but these are swamped by labor-supply distortions. The proper interpretation therefore seems to be that the minimum wage, though not first best, redistributes income more efficiently than the income tax. But then, why should we adopt any different interpretation for the merger evaluation? The merger lowers the sum of consumer and producer surplus. On first-best efficiency judgments we should therefore reject the merger; it fails a cost-benefit test. But that is only true because the distribution-neutral income tax adjustment obviates labor-supply effects. When those effects are included, the merger is overall efficient. Arguably, the better interpretation is that the merger should be blocked because doing so is more efficient than taxes at maintaining the pre-merger distribution of income. But the ambiguities of distribution-neutral income tax adjustments remain.

A.5 THE GENERAL THEORY OF THE SECOND BEST

One last conceptual issue ought to be addressed. This idea is called the general theory of the second best (Lipsey and Lancaster 1956). The term "second best" is in contrast to the term "first best," a situation where all of the conditions for a competitive economic equilibrium are satisfied, and thus a Pareto optimal allocation of resources exists. Thanks to economists, we are familiar with this first-best world. The theory of the second-best explains what is possible when one or more of those Pareto conditions is not satisfied.

Definition 4. Theory of the Second Best. *The theory of the second best says that if one of these conditions for Pareto optimality fails to be satisfied, then even if the other Pareto optimal conditions are attainable, they are in general no longer desirable.*

To put it more sharply, if one of the conditions for Pareto optimality fails, then a second-best welfare maximizing allocation can be achieved *only by departing* from the other Pareto optimality conditions.

The theory of the second best grew out of the literature on trade and tariffs. For one example, among others, it was shown that "the adoption of a free trade policy by one country, in a multi-country tariff ridden world, may actually lower the real income of that country and of the world" (Lipsey and Lancaster 1956, 14) Thus, the existence of tariffs violates one of the Pareto optimality conditions. But the lowering of trade barriers by one country, instead of leading to an incremental improvement in welfare, actually lowers it. Another example comes from the analysis of a production problem. Typically, profit maximization requires, from the familiar textbook condition, that marginal productivity equal marginal cost. Suppose one of the inputs of a multi-input production process used by a firm is fixed at some minimum amount, above that which the firm would prefer to employ to maximize profits. Then the second-best maximization of profits requires not only that marginal productivity not equal marginal cost for this particular input, but that marginal productivity not equal marginal cost for all of the other inputs as well.

In the trade example, one might argue that it would be better if all countries eliminated trade barriers, thus removing all of the barriers to Pareto optimality. Yet, some violations of the Pareto-optimality conditions may not be possible to surmount even in principle. Think of all of the reasons a Pareto-efficient allocation of resources may fail – any of the canonical cases of "market failure," for example. Positive or negative externalities led individuals away from Pareto efficiency because they either do not receive all of the benefits or do not pay for all of the costs associated with the activity. Pollution is the most famous example. Ideally, policy, such as "internalizing" or Pigovian taxes, can correct for externalities. A carbon tax, for example, may help correct for the Pareto inefficient levels of fossil fuel emissions. But it seems legitimate to ask whether *all* externalities can in principle be solved through policy, tax or otherwise.[16] The same can be said for other market failures. Antitrust policy regulates and attempts to reduce market power. But can all anti-competitive behavior ever be entirely eliminated? In current economic analysis, product-differentiation is a chief source of monopolistic power in the product market. It is hard to see how such behavior can ever be completely extinguished. Think also of information problems. Adverse selection and moral hazard also violate the conditions of Pareto efficiency. But achieving perfect and complete information seems a fantasy, and is probably undesirable. For all of these reasons, getting to a first-best world, even with thoughtful policy interventions, is unreasonable or impossible. We thus live in a second-best world and should tailor policy accordingly.

One interpretation of the theory of the second best offered by economists and others is that if there are departures from perfect competition, economic theory has nothing to say. Joseph Stiglitz says this conclusion is incorrect. "Economic theory can tell us under what circumstances two small distortions are preferable to one large

[16] For some of the challenges facing the regulation of externalities through Pigovian taxes, see Fleischer (2015).

one; when it is better to have inefficiencies in both consumption and production; and when it is better not to have inefficiencies in production" (Stiglitz 2000, 551). The real lesson of the second best is not that economic theory is useless. Rather, it tells us that we cannot blindly apply first-best policy advice if we are in a second-best world. Finding the second-best solution may be difficult, because when one Pareto condition fails, nothing in general can be said about the direction or magnitude of the departure from the secondary optimum conditions that will implement the second best. This means that figuring out the best policy to take requires, as discussed in the introduction, an a posteriori, rather than an a priori, approach.

A.6 MATHEMATICAL APPENDIX

A.6.1 *Optimal Taxes in the Intensive Model*

This section presents the intermediate steps necessary to derive the optimal tax rates from the government's constrained maximization problem. Combining the social welfare function in equation (A.8) with the government's budget constraint in equation (A.7), we can form and maximize a Lagrangian equation with respect to each tax component, T_i. The Lagrangian looks like this:

$$W + \lambda \sum_i h_i T_i.$$

To maximize this expression, differentiate it with respect to each T_i. For each T_i, the first-order condition is:

$$-\int_{\Theta_i} G'(c_i - \theta_i) dH(\theta) + \lambda \left[h_i - \sum_j T_j \frac{\partial h_j}{\partial c_i} \right] = 0. \tag{A.17}$$

Where the first term on the left-hand side is $G'(c_0)$ for $i = 0$. Then, using the definition of social marginal welfare weights in equation (A.9), the first-order conditions in equation (A.17) can be rewritten as:

$$(1 - g_i) h_i = \sum_j T_j \frac{\partial h_j}{\partial c_i}. \tag{A.18}$$

In the model without income effects, increasing the after-tax income levels c_i by a constant amount does not change individuals' occupational-choice decisions and therefore does not change the distribution of occupations, h_i. Summing up equation (A.18) across all i, therefore gives:

$$(1 - g_0) h_0 + (1 - g_1) h_1 + (1 - g_2) h_2 = 0.$$

Because the population shares sum to one, $h_0 + h_1 + h_2 = 1$, this expression simplifies to equation (A.10) given in the text. Also notice that if we multiply equation (A.10) by the Lagrangian multiplier, λ, which in our model is an expression for the marginal value of public funds, we obtain:

$$\lambda = h_0 G'(c_0) + \int_{\Theta_1} G'(c_1 - \theta_1)dH(\theta) + \int_{\Theta_2} G'(c_2 - \theta_2)dH(\theta). \qquad \text{(A.19)}$$

This expression gives some intuition to the meaning behind the marginal value of public funds and also aids in understanding why the social marginal welfare weights sum to one, because each g_i, as defined in equation (A.9), is simply i's marginal welfare as a fraction of total marginal welfare.

According to Saez (2002a), the intensive model can be obtained by assuming that an individual i can only choose to work in adjacent occupations $i-1$ and $i+1$ (where available).[17] Therefore, the share or quantity of individuals h_i is a function of c_{i-1}, c_i, and c_{i+1}. In that context, equation (A.18) becomes:

$$(1 - g_i)h_i = T_{i+1}\frac{\partial h_{i+1}}{\partial(c_{i+1} - c_i)} - T_i\frac{\partial h_i}{\partial(c_{i+1} - c_i)} + T_i\frac{\partial h_i}{\partial(c_i - c_{i-1})} - T_{i-1}\frac{\partial h_{i-1}}{\partial(c_i - c_{i-1})}.$$

Using the fact that $\partial h_{i+1}/\partial(c_{i+1} - c_i) = -\partial h_i/\partial(c_{i+1} - c_i)$, we can rearrange the previous equation to get:

$$(1 - g_i)h_i = -(T_{i+1} - T_i)\frac{\partial h_{i+1}}{\partial(c_{i+1} - c_i)} + (T_i - T_{i-1})\frac{\partial h_i}{\partial(c_i - c_{i-1})}. \qquad \text{(A.20)}$$

For $i = 2$ in our three person model, $i \in \{0, 1, 2\}$, this expression becomes:

$$(1 - g_2)h_2 = (T_2 - T_1)\frac{\partial h_2}{\partial(c_2 - c_1)}. \qquad \text{(A.21)}$$

Using the expression for labor-supply elasticity on the intensive margin given by equation (A.11), we can rewrite equation (A.21) to derive the optimal top marginal tax rate given by equation (A.14) in the text. For $i = 1$, we sum equation (A.20) over $i = 1, 2$ and use the elasticity equation (A.11) to derive the optimal marginal tax rate given by equation (A.13) in the text.

17 For further discussion, see Saez (2002a). In a working paper, Saez (2000) shows how this discrete model of intensive labor supply converges to the more familiar continuous Mirrlees (1971) optimal tax model.

References

Acemoglu, Daron. 2001. "Good Jobs versus Bad Jobs." *Journal of Labor Economics* 19 (1): 1–21.

Acemoglu, Daron, and Robert Shimer. 1999. "Efficient Unemployment Insurance." *Journal of Political Economy* 107 (5): 893–928.

Ackerman, Bruce. 1971. "Regulating Slum Housing Markets on Behalf of the Poor: Of Housing Codes, Housing Subsidies and Income Redistribution Policy." *Yale Law Journal* 80 (6): 1093–97.

Adler, Matthew D. 2012. *Well-Being and Fair Distribution: Beyond Cost-Benefit Analysis*. Oxford: Oxford University Press.

Adler, Matthew D. and Eric A. Posner. 1999. "Rethinking Cost-Benefit Analysis." *Yale Law Journal* 109 (2): 165–247.

Adler, Matthew D., and Chris William Sanchirico. 2006. "Inequality and Uncertainty: Theory and Legal Applications." *University of Pennsylvania Law Review* 155 (2): 279–377.

Aghion, Philippe, Ufuk Akcigit, Antonin Bergeaud, Richard Blundell, and David Hémous. 2019. "Innovation and Top Income Inequality." *Review of Economic Studies* 86 (1): 1–45.

Allen, Stephen P. 1987. "Taxes, Redistribution, and the Minimum Wage: A Theoretical Analysis." *Quarterly Journal of Economics* 102 (3): 477–89.

Alston, Richard M., James R. Kearl, and Michael B. Vaughan. 1992. "Is There a Consensus among Economists in the 1990's?" *American Economic Review* 82 (2): 203–09.

Alstott, Anne L. 1999. "Work vs. Freedom: A Liberal Challenge to Employment Subsidies." *Yale Law Journal* 108 (5): 967–1058.

Alvaredo, Facundo. 2011. "A Note on the Relationship between Top Income Shares and the Gini Coefficient." *Economics Letters* 110 (3): 274–77.

Appelbaum, Benyamin. 2017. "This Is Not Arthur Laffer's Famous Napkin." *The New York Times* (October 13, 2017). Accessed March 22, 2024. www.nytimes.com/2017/10/13/us/politics/arthur-laffer-napkin-tax-curve.html.

Arlen, Jennifer H. 1992. "Should Defendants' Wealth Matter?" *Journal of Legal Studies* 21 (2): 413–29.

Arnott, Richard. 1995. "Time for Revisionism on Rent Control?" *Journal of Economic Perspectives* 9 (1): 99–120.

Arnott, Richard, and Masahiro Igarashi. 2000. "Rent Control, Mismatch Costs and Search Efficiency." *Regional Science and Urban Economics* 30 (3): 249–88.

Arrow, Kenneth J. 2012 [1951]. *Social Choice and Individual Values*. New Haven: Yale University Press.

Atkinson, Anthony B. 1970. "On the Measurement of Inequality." *Journal of Economic Theory* 2 (3): 244–63.

Atkinson, Anthony B., and Joseph E. Stiglitz. 1976. "The Design of Tax Structure: Direct versus Indirect Taxation." *Journal of Public Economics* 6 (1–2): 55–75.

2015. *Lectures on Public Economics*. Updated edition. Princeton: Princeton University Press.

Autor, David H., David Dorn, and Gordon H. Hanson. 2013. "The China Syndrome: Local Labor Market Effects of Import Competition in the United States." *American Economic Review* 103 (6): 2121–68.

Autor, David H., Alan Manning, and Christopher L. Smith. 2016. "The Contribution of the MinimumWage to US Wage Inequality over Three Decades: A Reassessment." *American Economic Journal: Applied Economics* 8 (1): 58–99.

Autor, David H., Christopher J. Palmer, and Parag A. Pathak. 2014. "Housing Market Spillovers: Evidence from the End of Rent Control in Cambridge, Massachusetts." *Journal of Political Economy* 122 (3): 661–717.

Averitt, Neil W., and Robert H. Lande. 2007. "Using the Consumer Choice Approach to Antitrust Law." *Antitrust Law Journal* 74 (1): 175–264.

Avraham, Ronen, David Fortus, and Kyle Logue. 2003. "Revisiting the Roles of Legal Rules and Tax Rules in Income Redistribution: A Response to Kaplow & Shavell." *Iowa Law Review* 89 (4):1125.

Ayer, A. J. 1971 [1936] *Language, Truth and Logic*. Harmondsworth: Penguin Books.

Ayres, Ian. 2007. "Market Power and Inequality: A Competitive Conduct Standard for Assessing When Disparate Impacts Are Unjustified." *California Law Review* 95 (3): 669–720.

Ayres, Ian, and Robert Gertner. 1989. "Filling Gaps in Incomplete Contracts: An Economic Theory of Default Rules." *Yale Law Journal* 99 (1): 87–130.

Ayres, Ian, and Eric Talley. 1995. "Solomonic Bargaining: Dividing a Legal Entitlement to Facilitate Coasean Trade." *Yale Law Journal* 104 (5): 1027–117.

Baker, C. Edwin. 1975. "The Ideology of the Economic Analysis of Law." *Philosophy & Public Affairs* 5 (1): 3–48.

Baker, Dean. 2020a. "A World With a $24 Minimum Wage." *Jacobin*. January 27. https://jacobinmag.com/2020/01/higher-minimum-wage-inflation-productivity.

2020b. *This Is What Minimum Wage Would Be If It Kept Pace with Productivity*, January. https://cepr.net/publications/correction-this-is-what-minimum-wage-would-be-if-it-kept-pace-with-productivity/.

Bankman, Joseph, and Thomas Griffith. 1987. "Social Welfare and the Rate Structure: A New Look at Progressive Taxation." *California Law Review* 75: 1905.

Barry, Brian. 1986. "Lady Chatterly's Lover and Doctor Fischer's Bomb Party: Liberalism, Pareto Optimality, and the Problem of Objectionable Preferences." In *Foundations of Social Choice Theory*, edited by Jon Elster and Aanund Hylland, 11–43. Cambridge, UK: Cambridge University Press.

Bebchuk, Lucian Ayre, and Steven Shavell. 1991. "Information and the Scope of Liability for Breach of Contract: The Rule of *Hadley v. Baxendale*." *Journal of Law, Economics, & Organization* 7 (2): 284–312.

Belli, Melvin M. 1951. "The Adequate Award." *California Law Review* 39 (1): 1–41.

Bentham, Jeremy. 1843. "Anarchical Fallacies; Being an Examination of the Declarations of Rights Issued during the French Revolution." In *Works of Jeremy Bentham*, edited by John Bowring, II:489–534. Edinburgh: William Tait.

Berliner, Dana. 2006. *Opening the Floodgates: Eminent Domain Abuse in the Post* Kelo *World*. Arlington, VA: Institute for Justice.

Bhaskar, Venkataraman, Alan Manning, and Ted To. 2002. "Oligopsony and Monopsonistic Competition in Labor Markets." *Journal of Economic Perspectives* 16 (2): 155–74.

Bhaskar, Venkataraman, and Ted To. 1999. "Minimum Wages for Ronald McDonald Monopsonies: A Theory of Monopsonistic Competition." *Economic Journal* 109 (455): 190–203.

Binmore, Ken. 2009. "Interpersonal Comparison of Utility." In *Oxford Handbook of Philosophy of Economics*. Oxford: Oxford University Press.

Blumkin, Tomer, and Yoram Margalioth. 2005. "On the Limits of Redistributive Taxation: Establishing a Case for Equity-Informed Legal Rules." *Virginia Tax Review* 25 (1): 1–29.

Blumkin, Tomer, and Efraim Sadka. 2005. "Income Taxation and Wage Policy: An Application to Minimum Wage." *International Tax and Public Finance* 12 (6): 713–22.

Blundell, Richard, and Thomas MaCurdy. 1999. "Labor Supply: A Review of Alternative Approaches." In *Handbook of Labour Economics*, edited by Orley Ashenfelter and David Card, vol. 3A, 1559–695. Amsterdam: North-Holland.

Boadway, Robin. 1997. "Public Economics and the Theory of Public Policy." *Canadian Journal of Economics/Revue canadienne d'economique* 30 (4a): 753–72.

Boadway, Robin, and Katherine Cuff. 2001. "A Minimum Wage Can Be Welfare-Improving and Employment-Enhancing." *European Economic Review* 45 (3): 553–76.

Boal, William M., and Michael R. Ransom. 1997. "Monopsony in the Labor Market." *Journal of Economic Literature* 35 (1): 86–112.

Board of Governors of the Federal Reserve System (US). 2023a. "Share of Corporate Equities and Mutual Fund Shares Held by the 90th to 99thWealth Percentiles [WFRBSN09149]." Retrieved from FRED, Federal Reserve Bank of St. Louis; https://fred.stlouisfed.org/series/WFRBSN09149. Accessed December 27, 2023.

2023b. "Share of Corporate Equities and Mutual Fund Shares Held by the Top 1% (99th to 100th Wealth Percentiles) [WFRBST01122]." Retrieved from FRED, Federal Reserve Bank of St. Louis; https://fred.stlouisfed.org/series/WFRBST01122. Accessed December 27, 2023.

Borjas, George J. 2016. *Labor Economics*. 7th ed. New York: McGraw-Hill Education.

Bork, Robert H. 1967. "The Goals of Antitrust Policy." *American Economic Review* 57 (2): 242–53.

1978. *The Antitrust Paradox: A Policy at War with Itself*. New York: Basic Books.

Boudette, Neal E. 2024. "VW Workers in Tennessee Vote for Union, a Labor Milestone." *The New York Times* (April 19, 2024). Accessed May 8, 2024. www.nytimes.com/2024/04/19/business/economy/volkswagen-united-automobile-workers-union.html.

Bronars, Stephen G., Donald R. Deere, and Joseph S. Tracy. 1994. "The Effects of Unions on Firm Behavior: An Empirical Analysis Using Firm-Level Data." *Industrial Relations: A Journal of Economy and Society* 33 (4): 426–51.

Bruenig, Matt. 2023. *The Starbucks Union Has Now Won 300 Elections*. People's Policy Project. www.peoplespolicyproject.org/2023/05/11/the-starbucks-union-hasnow-won-300-elections/.

Burdett, Kenneth, and Dale T. Mortensen. 1998. "Wage Differentials, Employer Size, and Unemployment." *International Economic Review*, 39 (2): 257–73.

Burke, Marcilynn. 2006. "Much Ado about Nothing: Kelo v. City of New London, Babbitt v. Sweet Home, and Other Tales from the Supreme Court." *University of Cincinnati Law Review* 75 (2): 663–723.

Cahuc, Pierre, and Guy Laroque. 2014. "Optimal Taxation and Monopsonistic Labor Market: Does Monopsony Justify the Minimum Wage?" *Journal of Public Economic Theory* 16 (2): 259–73.

Cahuc, Pierre, Anne Saint-Martin, and André Zylberberg. 2001. "The Consequences of the Minimum Wage When Other Wages Are Bargained Over." *European Economic Review* 45 (2): 337–52.

Calabresi, Guido. 1991. "The Pointlessness of Pareto: Carrying Coase Further." *Yale Law Journal* 100 (5): 1211–237.

2016. *The Future of Law and Economics: Essays in Reform and Recollection*. New Haven: Yale University Press.

Calabresi, Guido, and A. Douglas Melamed. 1972. "Property Rules, Liability Rules, and Inalienability: One View of the Cathedral." *Harvard Law Review*, 85 (6): 1089–128.

Calmfors, Lars, and John Driffill. 1988. "Bargaining Structure, Corporatism and Macroeconomic Performance." *Economic Policy* 3 (6): 13–61.

Card, David. 2001. "The Effect of Unions on Wage Inequality in the US Labor Market." *ILR Review* 54 (2): 296–315.

Card, David, and Alan B. Krueger. 1994. "Minimum Wages and Employment: A Case Study of the Fast-Food Industry in New Jersey and Pennsylvania." *American Economic Review* 84 (4): 772–93.

2000. "Minimum Wages and Employment: A Case Study of the Fast-Food Industry in New Jersey and Pennsylvania: Reply." *American Economic Review* 90 (5): 1397–420.

2015. *Myth and Measurement: The New Economics of the Minimum Wage. Twentieth-Anniversary Edition*. Princeton: Princeton University Press.

Carpenter, Dick M., II, and John K. Ross. 2007. *Victimizing the Vulnerable: The Demographics of Eminent Domain Abuse*. Arlington, VA: Institute for Justice.

Cassidy, John. 2008. "Comment: The Minsky Moment." *The New Yorker* 83 (46): 19.

Cesarini, David, Erik Lindqvist, Matthew J Notowidigdo, and Robert Östling. 2017. "The Effect of Wealth on Individual and Household Labor Supply: Evidence from Swedish Lotteries." *American Economic Review* 107 (12): 3917–46.

Chamley, Christophe. 1986. "Optimal Taxation of Capital Income in General Equilibrium with Infinite Lives." *Econometrica*, 54 (3): 607–22.

Chimerine, Lawrence, and Ross Eisenbrey. 2005. *The Frivolous Case for Tort Law Change*. Economic Policy Institute. https://files.epi.org/page/-/old/briefingpapers/157/bp157.pdf.

Coase, R. H. 1960. "The Problem of Social Cost." *Journal of Law & Economics* 3:1–44.

Coleman, Jules L. 1980. "Efficiency, Utility, and Wealth Maximization." *Hofstra Law Review* 8:509–51.

Colvin, Alexander J. S. 2014. "Mandatory Arbitration and Inequality of Justice in Employment." *Berkeley Journal of Employment and Labor Law* 35 (1–2): 71–90.

2017. *The Growing Use of Mandatory Arbitration*.Washington, DC: Economic Policy Institue, September 27, 2017. http://epi.org/135056.

Colvin, Alexander J. S., and Mark D. Gough. 2015. "Individual Employment Rights Arbitration in the United States: Actors and Outcomes." *ILR Review* 68 (5): 1019–042.

Congressional Budget Office. 2004. *The Effects of Tort Reform: Evidence from the States*. Washington, DC. www.cbo.gov/sites/default/files/108th-congress-2003-2004/reports/report_2.pdf.

Connolly, Robert A., Barry T. Hirsch, and Mark Hirschey. 1986. "Union Rent Seeking, Intangible Capital, and Market Value of the Firm." *Review of Economics and Statistics* 68 (4): 567–77.

Cooter, Robert, and Thomas Ulen. 2016. *Law and Economics*. 6th ed. Boston: Addison-Wesley.

Craswell, Richard. 1991. "Passing on the Costs of Legal Rules: Efficiency and Distribution in Buyer-Seller Relationships." *Stanford Law Review* 43 (2): 361–98.

2003. "Kaplow and Shavell on the Substance of Fairness." *Journal of Legal Studies* 32 (1): 245–75.

Davidson, Donald. 1986. "Judging Interpersonal Interests." In *Foundations of Social Choice Theory*, edited by Jon Elster and Aanund Hylland, 195–211. Cambridge, UK: Cambridge University Press.

De Scitovszky, Tibor. 1941. "A Note on Welfare Propositions in Economics." *Review of Economic Studies* 9 (1): 77–88.

Deb, Shubhdeep, Jan Eeckhout, Aseem Patel, and Lawrence Warren. 2022. "What Drives Wage Stagnation: Monopsony or Monopoly?" *Journal of the European Economic Association* 20 (6): 2181–225.

Denny, Kevin, and Stephen J. Nickell. 1992. "Unions and Investment in British Industry." *Economic Journal* 102 (413): 874–87.

Diamond, Peter A. 1980. "Income Taxation with Fixed Hours of Work." *Journal of Public Economics* 13 (1): 101–10.

1982. "Wage Determination and Efficiency in Search Equilibrium." *Review of Economic Studies* 49 (2): 217–27.

Diamond, Peter A., and Emmanuel Saez. 2011. "The Case for a Progressive Tax: From Basic Research to Policy Recommendation." *Journal of Economic Perspectives* 25 (4): 165–90.

Diamond, Rebecca, Tim McQuade, and Franklin Qian. 2019. "The Effects of Rent Control Expansion on Tenants, Landlords, and Inequality: Evidence from San Francisco." *American Economic Review* 109 (9): 3365–94.

DiCola, Peter C. 2013. "Money from Music: Survey Evidence on Musicians' Revenue and Lessons about Copyright Incentives." *Arizona Law Review* 55 (2): 301–70.

Dimick, Matthew. 2019. "The Law and Economics of Redistribution." *Annual Review of Law & Social Science* 15:559–82.

DiNardo, John, Nicole M. Fortin, and Thomas Lemieux. 1996. "Labor Market Institutions and the Distribution of Wages, 1973–1992: A Semiparametric Approach." *Econometrica* 64 (5): 1001–044.

Disney, Richard, and John Gathergood. 2018. "House Prices, Wealth Effects and Labour Supply." *Economica* 85 (339): 449–78.

Dixit, Avinash K., and Joseph E. Stiglitz. 1977. "Monopolistic Competition and Optimum Product Diversity." *American Economic Review* 67 (3): 297–308.

Dorff, Michael B. 2001. "Why Welfare Depends on Fairness: A Reply to Kaplow and Shavell." *Southern California Law Review* 75 (4): 847.

Drazen, Allan. 1986. "Optimal MinimumWage Legislation." *Economic Journal* 96 (383): 774–84.

Dube, Arindrajit. 2019. "Minimum Wages and the Distribution of Family Incomes." *American Economic Journal: Applied Economics* 11 (4): 268–304.

Dube, Arindrajit, T. William Lester, and Michael Reich. 2016. "Minimum Wage Shocks, Employment Flows, and Labor Market Frictions." *Journal of Labor Economics* 34 (3): 663–704.

Dunlop, John T. 1944. *Wage Determination under Trade Unions*. New York: Macmillan.

Dworkin, Ronald M. 1980. "Is Wealth a Value?" *Journal of Legal Studies* 9 (2): 191–226.

Eaton, Jonathan, and Harvey S. Rosen. 1980. "Optimal Redistributive Taxation and Uncertainty." *Quarterly Journal of Economics* 95 (2): 357–64.

Edgeworth, F. Y. 1897. "The Pure Theory of Taxation." *Economic Journal* 7 (28): 550–71.

Eisenberg, Theodore. 2015. "Four Decades of Federal Civil Rights Litigation." *Journal of Empirical Legal Studies* 12 (1): 4–28.

Ellickson, Robert C. 1991. *Order without Law: How Neighbors Settle Disputes*. Cambridge, MA: Harvard University Press.

Engbom, Niklas, and Christian Moser. 2022. "Earnings Inequality and the Minimum Wage: Evidence from Brazil." *American Economic Review* 112 (12): 3803–47.

Enghagen, Linda K., and Anthony Gilardi. 2002. "Putting Things in Perspective: McDonald's and the 2.9-Million Dollar Cup of Coffee." *Cornell Hotel & Restaurant Administration Quarterly* 43 (3): 53–60.

Epstein, Richard A. 1975. "Unconscionability: A Critical Reappraisal." *Journal of Law and Economics* 18 (2): 293–315.

1983. "A Common Law for Labor Relations: A Critique of the New Deal Labor Legislation." *Yale Law Journal* 92 (8): 1357–408.

2015. "*Kelo v. City of New London* Ten Years Later." *National Review* (June 23, 2015). Accessed June 23, 2015. www.nationalreview.com/2015/06/kelo-eminent-domain-richard-epstein/.

Eriksen, Michael D., and Amanda Ross. 2015. "Housing Vouchers and the Price of Rental Housing." *American Economic Journal: Economic Policy* 7 (3): 54–176.

Estlund, Cynthia. 2018. "The Black Hole of Mandatory Arbitration." *North Carolina Law Review* 96 (3): 679–710.

Fennell, Lee Anne, and Richard H. McAdams. 2016. "The Distributive Deficit in Law and Economics." *Minnesota Law Review* 100 (3): 1051–129.

Fleischer, Victor. 2015. "Curb Your Enthusiasm for Pigovian Taxes." *Vanderbilt Law Review* 68 (6): 1673–713.

Fligstein, Neil, and Adam Goldstein. 2012. "A Long Strange Trip: The State and Mortgage Securitization, 1968–2010." In *Oxford Handbook of the Sociology of Finance*, edited by Karin Knorr Cetina and Alex Preda, 339–56. Oxford: Oxford University Press.

Flinn, Christopher J. 2006. "Minimum Wage Effects on Labor Market Outcomes under Search, Matching, and Endogenous Contact Rates." *Econometrica* 74 (4): 1013–62.

Freeman, Richard B. 1980. "Unionism and the Dispersion of Wages." *ILR Review* 34 (1): 3–23.

Freeman, Richard B. and James Medoff. 1981. "The Impact of the Percentage Organized on Union and Nonunion Wages." *Review of Economics and Statistics* 63 (4): 561–72.

Gabuthy, Yannick, and Eve-Angéline Lambert. 2018. "Legal Advertising and Frivolous Lawsuits." *Journal of Institutional and Theoretical Economics* 174 (3): 570–93.

Gallini, Nancy T. 2002. "The Economics of Patents: Lessons from Recent US Patent Reform." *Journal of Economic Perspectives* 16 (2): 131–54.

Gamage, David. 2014. "How Should Governments Promote Distributive Justice?: A Framework for Analyzing the Optimal Choice of Tax Instruments." *Tax Law Review* 68 (1): 1–87.

2015. "The Case for Taxing (All of) Labor Income, Consumption, Capital Income, and Wealth." *Tax Law Review* 68:355–441.

Gates, Bill, Nathan Myhrvold, and Peter Rinearson. 1995. *The Road Ahead*. New York: Viking Press.

Greenberg, David. 1980. "Easy Terms, Hard Times: Complaint Handling in the Ghetto." In *No Access to Law: Alternatives to the American Judicial System*, edited by Laura Nader, 379–415. New York: Academic Press.

Greenspan, Alan. 2005. *Remarks by Chairman Alan Greenspan*. At the Federal Reserve System's Fourth Annual Community Affairs Research Conference, Washington, D.C. April

8, 2005. Accessed November 25, 2023. www.federalreserve.gov/BoardDocs/speeches/2005/20050408/default.htm.

Grout, Paul A. 1984. “Investment and Wages in the Absence of Binding Contracts: A Nash Bargaining Approach.” *Econometrica* 52 (2): 449–60.

Grullon, Gustavo, Yelena Larkin, and Roni Michaely. 2019. “Are US Industries Becoming More Concentrated?” *Review of Finance* 23 (4): 697–743.

Guesnerie, Roger, and Kevin Roberts. 1987. “Minimum Wage Legislation as a Second Best Policy.” *European Economic Review* 31 (1-2): 490–98.

Hacker, Jacob. 2011. “The Institutional Foundations of Middle-Class Democracy.” *Policy Network* 6 (5): 33–37.

Hale, Robert L. 1923. “Coercion and Distribution in a Supposedly Non-Coercive State.” *Political Science Quarterly* 38 (3): 470–494.

1943. “Bargaining, Duress, and Economic Liberty.” *Columbia Law Review* 43 (5): 603–28.

Hamada, Koichi. 1976. “Liability Rules and Income Distribution in Product Liability.” *American Economic Review* 66 (1): 228–34.

Hammond, Peter J. 1991. “Interpersonal Comparisons of Utility: Why and How They Are and Should Be Made.” In *Interpersonal Comparisons of Well-Being*, edited by Jon Elster and John E. Roemer, 200–54. Cambridge, UK: Cambridge University Press.

Hanlon, James. 2017. “The Origins of the Rental Assistance Demonstration Program and the End of Public Housing.” *Housing Policy Debate* 27 (4): 611–39.

Hasen, David. 2006. “Liberalism and Ability Taxation.” *Texas Law Review* 85 (5): 1057.

Hausman, Daniel M. 1995. “The Impossibility of Interpersonal Utility Comparisons.” *Mind* 104 (415): 473–90.

Hibbs, Douglas A., Jr., and Håkan Locking. 2000. “Wage Dispersion and Productive Efficiency: Evidence for Sweden.” *Journal of Labor Economics* 18 (4): 755–82.

Hicks, John R. 1939. “The Foundations of Welfare Economics.” *Economic Journal* 49 (196): 696–712.

Hindriks, Jean, and Gareth D Myles. 2013. *Intermediate Public Economics*. 2nd ed. MIT Press.

Hirsch, Barry T. 1992. “Firm Investment Behavior and Collective Bargaining Strategy.” *Industrial Relations: A Journal of Economy and Society* 31 (1): 95–121.

Hirsch, Werner Z., Joel G. Hirsch, and Stephen Margolis. 1975. “Regression Analysis of the Effects of Habitability Laws upon Rent: An Empirical Observation on the Ackerman-Komesar Debate.” *California Law Review* 63 (5): 1098.

Hosios, Arthur J. 1990. “On the Efficiency of Matching and Related Models of Search and Unemployment.” *Review of Economic Studies* 57 (2): 279–98.

Hovenkamp, Herbert. 2016. “Appraising Merger Efficiencies.” *George Mason Law Review* 24 (3): 703–41.

Hua, Xinyu, and Kathryn E. Spier. 2020. “Product Safety, Contracts, and Liability.” *RAND Journal of Economics* 51 (1): 233–59.

Hubbard, F. Patrick. 2006. “The Nature and Impact of the ‘Tort Reform’ Movement.” *Hofstra Law Review* 35 (2): 437–538.

Hughes, Justin, and Robert P. Merges. 2016. “Copyright and Distributive Justice.” *Notre Dame Law Review* 92 (2): 513.

Hungerbühler, Mathias, and Etienne Lehmann. 2009. “On the Optimality of a Minimum Wage: New Insights from Optimal Tax Theory.” *Journal of Public Economics* 93 (3): 464–81.

Hurst, Nathan. 2013. “How the America Invents Act Will Change Patenting Forever.” *Wired Magazine* (March 13, 2013). Accessed March 13, 2013. www.wired.com/2013/03/america-invents-act/.

Hylland, Aanund, and Richard Zeckhauser. 1979. "Distributional Objectives Should Affect Taxes but Not Program Choice or Design." *Scandinavian Journal of Economics* 81 (2): 264–84.

Hylton, Keith N. 2013. "The Law and Economics of Products Liability." *Notre Dame Law Review* 88 (5): 2457–514.

Irwin, Neil. 2016. "A New Movement in Liberal Economics That Could Shape Hillary Clinton's Agenda." *The New York Times* (November 4, 2016). Accessed March 22, 2024. www.nytimes.com/2016/11/06/upshot/monopsony-liberal-economics-policyhillary-clintons-agenda.html.

Jaffe, Adam B. 2000. "The US Patent System in Transition: Policy Innovation and the Innovation Process." *Research Policy* 29 (4-5): 31–557.

Johnston, Jason Scott. 1990. "Strategic Bargaining and the Economic Theory of Contract Default Rules." *Yale Law Journal* 100 (3): 615–64.

Jolls, Christine. 1998. "Behavioral Economics Analysis of Redistributive Legal Rules." *Vanderbilt Law Review* 51 (6): 1653.

Jones, Stephen R. G. 1987. "Minimum Wage Legislation in a Dual Labor Market." *European Economic Review* 31 (6): 1229–246.

Judd, Kenneth L. 1985. "Redistributive Taxation in a Simple Perfect Foresight Model." *Journal of Public Economics* 28 (1): 59–83.

Kakwani, Nanak C. 1977a. "Applications of Lorenz Curves in Economic Analysis." *Econometrica* 45 (3): 719–27.

1977b. "Measurement of Tax Progressivity: An International Comparison." *Economic Journal* 87 (345): 71–80.

Kaldor, Nicholas. 1939. "Welfare Propositions of Economics and Interpersonal Comparisons of Utility." *Economic Journal*, 49 (195): 549–52.

Kang, Cecilia. 2023. "F.T.C.'s Court Loss Raises Fresh Questions about Its Chair's Strategy." *The New York Times* (July 11, 2023). Accessed December 26, 2023. www.nytimes.com/2023/07/11/technology/lina-khan-ftc-strategy.html?searchResultPosition=7.

Kantor, Jodi, and Karen Weise. 2022. "How Two Best Friends Beat Amazon." *The New York Times* (April 14, 2022). Accessed May 8, 2024. www.nytimes.com/2022/04/02/business/amazon-union-christian-smalls.html.

Kapczynski, Amy. 2011. "The Cost of Price: Why and How to Get beyond Intellectual Property Internalism." *UCLA Law Review* 59 (4): 970.

Kaplow, Louis. 1995. "A Fundamental Objection to Tax Equity Norms: A Call for Utilitarianism." *National Tax Journal* 48 (4): 497–514.

1996. "The Optimal Supply of Public Goods and the Distortionary Cost of Taxation." *National Tax Journal* 49 (4): 513–33.

2004. "On the (Ir)relevance of Distribution and Labor Supply Distortion to Government Policy." *Journal of Economic Perspectives* 18 (4): 159–75.

2006. "On the Undesirability of Commodity Taxation Even When Income Taxation Is Not Optimal." *Journal of Public Economics* 90 (6): 1235–50.

2008. *The Theory of Taxation and Public Economics*. Princeton: Princeton University Press.

2012. "On the Choice of Welfare Standards in Competition Law." In *The Goals of Competition Law*, edited by Daniel Zimmer, 3–26. Cheltenham, UK: Edward Elgar.

2021. "Market Power and Income Taxation." *American Economic Journal: Economic Policy* 13 (4): 329–54.

Kaplow, Louis, and Steven Shavell. 1994. "Why the Legal System Is Less Efficient Than the Income Tax in Redistributing Income." *Journal of Legal Studies* 23 (2): 667–81.

1999. "The Conflict between Notions of Fairness and the Pareto Principle." *American Law and Economics Review* 1 (1): 63–77.
2000a. "Notions of Fairness versus the Pareto Principle: On the Role of Logical Consistency." *Yale Law Journal* 110 (2): 237–49.
2000b. "Should Legal Rules Favor the Poor? Clarifying the Role of Legal Rules and the Income Tax in Redistributing Income." *Journal of Legal Studies* 29 (2): 821–35.
2001a. "Any Non-Welfarist Method of Policy Assessment Violates the Pareto Principle." *Journal of Political Economy* 109 (2): 281–86.
2001b. "Fairness versus Welfare." *Harvard Law Review* 114 (4): 961–1388.
2002. *Fairness versus Welfare*. Cambridge, MA: Harvard University Press.
2003. "Fairness versus Welfare: Notes on the Pareto Principle, Preferences, and Distributive Justice." *Journal of Legal Studies* 32 (1): 331–62.
Katz, Michael L. 1984. "Price Discrimination and Monopolistic Competition." *Econometrica* 52 (6): 1453–71.
Kazis, Noah M. 2022. "The Failed Federalism of Affordable Housing: Why States Don't Use Housing Vouchers." *Michigan Law Review* 121 (2): 221–89.
Kelman, Mark. 1987. *A Guide to Critical Legal Studies*. Cambridge, MA: Harvard University Press.
Kennedy, Duncan. 1981. "Distributive and Paternalist Motives in Contract and Tort Law, with Special Reference to Compulsory Terms and Unequal Bargaining Power." *Maryland Law Review* 41 (4): 563–658.
1987. "The Effect of the Warranty of Habitability on Low Income Housing: 'Milking' and Class Violence." *Forida State University Law Review* 15 (3): 485–519.
1991. "The Stakes of Law, or Hale and Foucault!" *Legal Studies Forum* 15 (4): 327.
1998. "Law and Economics from the Perspective of Critical Legal Studies." In *New Palgrave Dictionary of Economics and the Law*, edited by Peter Newman, 2:465–74. New York: Stockton Press.
Khan, Lina M. 2016. "Amazon's Antitrust Paradox." *Yale Law Journal* 126 (3): 710–805.
Klock, Mark. 2002. "Unconscionability and Price Discrimination." *Tennessee Law Review* 69:317.
Komesar, Neil K. 1973. "Return to Slumville: A Critique of the Ackerman Analysis of Housing Code Enforcement and the Poor." *Yale Law Journal* 82 (6): 1175–93.
1983. "Revolution in Landlord-Tenant Law: A Comparative Institutional View." *Cornell Law Review* 69 (3): 612–22.
Kornhauser, Lewis A. 2003. "Preference, Well-Being, and Morality in Social Decisions." *Journal of Legal Studies* 32 (1): 303–29.
Kuziemko, Ilyana, Nicolas Longuet Marx, and Suresh Naidu. 2023. "*Compensate the Losers?*" *Economic Policy and Partisan Realignment in the US*. Working Paper Series 31794. National Bureau of Economic Research. https://doi.org/10.3386/w31794. www.nber.org/papers/w31794%22.
Kwoka, John E. 2017. *U.S. Antitrust and Competition Policy amid the New Merger Wave*. Washington, DC: Washington Center for Equitable Growth. https://equitablegrowth.org/wp-content/uploads/2017/07/072717-kwoka-antitrust-report.pdf.
Lambert, Peter. 2001. *The Distribution and Redistribution of Income*. 3rd. ed. Manchester: Manchester University Press.
Lande, Robert H. 1982. "Wealth Transfers as the Original and Primary Concern of Antitrust: The Efficiency Interpretation Challenged." *Hastings Law Journal* 34 (1): 65–151.
1989. "Chicago's False Foundation: Wealth Transfers (Not Just Efficiency) Should Guide Antitrust." *Antitrust Law Journal* 58 (2): 631–44.

Lang, Kevin. 1987. "Pareto Improving Minimum Wage Laws." *Economic Inquiry* 25 (1): 145–58.
Lee, David. 1999. "Wage Inequality in the United States during the 1980s: Rising Dispersion or Falling Minimum Wage?" *Quarterly Journal of Economics* 114 (3): 977–1023.
Lee, David, and Emmanuel Saez. 2008. *Optimal Minimum Wage Policy in Competitive Labor Markets.* Working Paper Series 14320. National Bureau of Economic Research. doi.org/10.3386/w14320. www.nber.org/papers/w14320.
2012. "Optimal Minimum Wage Policy in Competitive Labor Markets." *Journal of Public Economics* 96 (9): 739–49.
Lee, Emery G., III, and Thomas E. Willging. 2008. *The Impact of the Class Action Fairness Act of 2005 on the Federal Courts.* Washington, DC: Federal Judicial Center, April 1, 2008. www.fjc.gov/content/impact-class-action-fairness-act-2005-federalcourts-fourth-interim-report-judicial-0.
Lewinsohn-Zamir, Daphna. 2006. "In Defense of Redistribution through Private Law." *Minnesota Law Review* 91 (2): 326–97.
Lin, Ken-Hou, and Donald Tomaskovic-Devey. 2013. "Financialization and US Income Inequality, 1970–2008." *American Journal of Sociology* 118 (5): 1284–1329.
Lipsey, Richard G., and Kelvin Lancaster. 1956. "The General Theory of Second Best." *Review of Economic Studies* 24 (1): 11–32.
Liscow, Zachary. 2014. "Reducing Inequality on the Cheap: When Legal Rule Design Should Incorporate Equity as Well as Efficiency." *Yale Law Journal* 123 (7): 2478–510.
2018. "Is Efficiency Biased?" *University of Chicago Law Review* 85 (7): 1649.
Litman, Jessica. 2010. "Real Copyright Reform." *Iowa Law Review* 96 (1): 1–55.
Little, I. M. D. 1952. "Social Choice and Individual Values." *Journal of Political Economy* 60 (5): 422–32.
Manning, Alan. 1987. "An Integration of Trade Union Models in a Sequential Bargaining Framework." *Economic Journal* 97 (385): 121–39.
2004. "Monopsony and the Efficiency of Labour Market Interventions." *Labour Economics* 11 (2): 145–63.
2021. "Monopsony in Labor Markets: A Review." *ILR Review* 74 (1): 3–26.
Marinescu, Ioana, and Herbert Hovenkamp. 2019. "Anticompetitive Mergers in Labor Markets." *Indiana Law Journal* 94 (3): 1031–63.
Markovits, Richard S. 1976. "The Distributive Impact, Allocative Efficiency, and Overall Desirability of Ideal Housing Codes: Some Theoretical Clarifications." *Harvard Law Review*, 89 (8): 1815–46.
1980. "Legal Analysis and the Economic Analysis of Allocative Efficiency." *Hofstra Law Review* 8 (4): 811–903.
2004. "Why Kaplow and Shavell's Double-Distortion Argument Articles Are Wrong." *George Mason Law Review* 13 (3): 511–619.
Mas-Colell, Andreu, Michael D. Whinston, and Jerry R. Green. 1995. *Microeconomic Theory.* Oxford: Oxford University Press.
Mason, J. W. 2019. "Why Rent Control Works." *Jacobin*. November 26. https://jacobin.com/2019/11/rent-controlhousing-crisis-affordability-supply.
McAfee, R. Preston, Hugo M. Mialon, and Michael A. Williams. 2004. "What Is a Barrier to Entry?" *American Economic Review* 94 (2): 461–65.
McCaffery, Edward J. 2005. "A New Understanding of Tax." *Michigan Law Review* 103 (5): 807–938.
McDonald, Ian M., and Robert M. Solow. 1981. "Wage Bargaining and Employment." *American Economic Review* 71 (5): 896–908.

Menezes-Filho, Naercio, and John Van Reenen. 2003. "Unions and Innovation: A Survey of the Theory and Empirical Evidence." In *International Handbook of Trade Unions*, edited by John T Addison and Claus Schnabel, 293–335. Cheltenham: Edward Elgar.

Merges, Robert P., and Richard R. Nelson. 1990. "On the Complex Economics of Patent Scope." *Columbia Law Review* 90 (4): 839–916.

Merkel, Philip L. 2006. "Pain and Suffering Damages at Mid-Twentieth Century: A Retrospective View of the Problem and the Legal Academy's First Responses." *Capital University Law Review* 34 (3): 545–80.

Mian, Atif, and Amir Sufi. 2009. "The Consequences of Mortgage Credit Expansion: Evidence from the US Mortgage Default Crisis." *Quarterly Journal of Economics* 124 (4): 1449–96.

2010. "The Great Recession: Lessons from Microeconomic Data." *American Economic Review* 100 (2): 51–56.

2011. "House Prices, Home Equity–Based Borrowing, and the US Household Leverage Crisis." *American Economic Review* 101 (5): 2132–56.

Minsky, Hyman P. 1986. *Stabilizing an Unstable Economy*. New Haven: Yale University Press.

Mirrlees, James A. 1971. "An Exploration in the Theory of Optimum Income Taxation." *Review of Economic Studies* 38 (2): 175–208.

1990. "Taxing Uncertain Incomes." *Oxford Economic Papers* 42 (1): 34–45.

Moen, Espen R. 1997. "Competitive Search Equilibrium." *Journal of Political Economy* 105 (2): 385–411.

Moene, Karl Ove, and Michael Wallerstein. 1997. "Pay Inequality." *Journal of Labor Economics* 15 (3): 403–30.

Montgomery, James D. 1991. "Equilibrium Wage Dispersion and Interindustry Wage Differentials." *Quarterly Journal of Economics* 106 (1): 163–79.

Mortensen, Dale T. 1982. "Property Rights and Efficiency in Mating, Racing, and Related Games." *American Economic Review* 72 (5): 968–79.

Mortensen, Dale T., and Christopher A. Pissarides. 1999. "New Developments in Models of Search in the Labor Market." In *Handbook of Labor Economics*, edited by Orley Ashenfelter and David E. Card, 3B: 2567–627. Amsterdam: Elsevier.

Murphy, Liam, and Thomas Nagel. 2002. *The Myth of Ownership: Taxes and Justice*. Oxford: Oxford University Press.

Musgrave, Richard A. 1959. *The Theory of Public Finance: A Study in Public Economy*. New York: McGraw-Hill.

Musgrave, Richard A., and Tun Thin. 1948. "Income Tax Progression, 1929–48." *Journal of Political Economy* 56 (6): 498–514.

Nagel, Thomas. 1986. *The View from Nowhere*. New York: Oxford University Press.

Naidu, Suresh, Eric A. Posner, and Glen Weyl. 2018. "Antitrust Remedies for Labor Market Power." *Harvard Law Review* 132 (2): 536–601.

Nelson, Katie. 2009. "Conn. Land Taken from Homeowners Still Undeveloped." *Associated Press* (September 25, 2009).

Neumark, David, and William Wascher. 2000. "Minimum Wages and Employment: A Case Study of the Fast-Food Industry in New Jersey and Pennsylvania: Comment." *American Economic Review* 90 (5): 1362–96.

Odgers, Cameron W, and Julian R Betts. 1997. "Do Unions Reduce Investment? Evidence from Canada." *ILR Review* 51 (1): 18–36.

Oppenheimer, David Benjamin. 2003. "Verdicts Matter: An Empirical Study of California Employment Discrimination and Wrongful Discharge Jury Verdicts Reveals Low Success Rates for Women and Minorities." *U.C. Davis Law Review* 37 (2): 511–66.

Orbach, Barak Y. 2010. "The Antitrust Consumer Welfare Paradox." *Journal of Competition Law and Economics* 7 (1): 133–64.

Philippon, Thomas, and Ariell Reshef. 2012. "Wages and Human Capital in the US Finance Industry: 1909–2006." *Quarterly Journal of Economics* 127 (4): 1551–609.

Piketty, Thomas, and Emmanuel Saez. 2003. "Income Inequality in the United States, 1913–1998." *Quarterly Journal of Economics* 118 (1): 1–41.

2012. *A Theory of Optimal Capital Taxation.* Working Paper Series 17989. National Bureau of Economic Research. https://doi.org/10.3386/w17989. www.nber.org/papers/w17989.

2013. "Optimal Labor Income Taxation." In *Handbook of Public Economics*, edited by Alan J. Auerbach, Raj Chetty, Martin Feldstein, and Emmanuel Saez, 5: 391–474. Amsterdam: Elsevier.

Pissarides, Christopher A. 2000. *Equilibrium Unemployment Theory.* 2nd ed. MIT Press.

Polinsky, A. Mitchell. 1989. *An Introduction to Law and Economics.* 2nd ed. Aspen Publishers.

Polinsky, A. Mitchell, and William P. Rogerson. 1983. "Products Liability, Consumer Misperceptions, and Market Power." *Bell Journal of Economics* 14 (2): 581–89.

Polinsky, A. Mitchell, and Steven Shavell. 2010. "The Uneasy Case for Product Liability." *Harvard Law Review*, 123 (6): 1437–92.

Posner, Eric A. 1995. "Contract Law in the Welfare State: A Defense of the Unconscionability Doctrine, Usury Laws, and Related Limitations on the Freedom to Contract." *Journal of Legal Studies* 24 (2): 283–319.

Posner, Richard A. 1979. "Utilitarianism, Economics, and Legal Theory." *Journal of Legal Studies* 8 (1): 103–40.

1980. "The Ethical and Political Basis of the Efficiency Norm in Common Law Adjudication." *Hofstra Law Review* 8 (3): 487–507.

1984. "Some Economics of Labor Law." *University of Chicago Law Review* 51 (4): 988–1011.

1985. "Wealth Maximization Revisited." *Notre Dame Journal of Law, Ethics & Public Policy* 2 (1): 85–105.

1998. *Economic Analysis of Law.* 5th ed. New York: Aspen.

Quigley, John M. 2008. "Just Suppose: Housing Subsidies for Low-Income Renters." In *Revisiting Rental Housing: Policies, Programs, and Priorities*, edited by Nicolas P Retsinas and Eric S Belsky, 300–18. Washington, DC: Brookings Institution Press.

Rabin, Edward H. 1983. "Revolution in Residential Landlord-Tenant Law: Causes and Consequences." *Cornell Law Review* 69 (3): 517–84.

Rawls, John. 1971. *A Theory of Justice.* Cambridge, MA: Belknap Press of Harvard University Press.

1999. *A Theory of Justice.* Revised edition. Oxford: Oxford University Press.

Rebitzer, James B., and Lowell J. Taylor. 1995. "The Consequences of Minimum Wage Laws: Some New Theoretical Ideas." *Journal of Public Economics* 56 (2): 245–55.

Robbins, Lionel. 1935. *An Essay on the Nature and Significance of Economic Science.* 2nd ed., rev. and extended. London: Macmillan.

1938. "Interpersonal Comparisons of Utility: A Comment." *Economic Journal* 48 (192): 635–41.

Robinson, Joan. 1969. *The Economics of Imperfect Competition.* 2nd ed. London: Macmillan.

Roll, Josh, and Nathan McNeil. 2022. "Race and Income Disparities in Pedestrian Injuries: Factors Influencing Pedestrian Safety Inequity." *Transportation Research Part D: Transport and Environment* 107:103294.

Rolnick, Arthur, and Phil Davies. 2006. "The Cost of Kelo." Federal Reserve Bank of Minneapolis, June 1, 2006. Accessed January 19, 2023. www.minneapolisfed.org/article/2006/the-cost-of-kelo.

Rothschild, Michael, and Joseph E. Stiglitz. 1970. "Increasing Risk: I. A Definition." *Journal of Economic Theory* 2 (3): 225–43.

Rothstein, Jesse. 2010. "Is the EITC as Good as an NIT? Conditional Cash Transfers and Tax Incidence." *American Economic Journal: Economic Policy* 2 (1): 177–208.

Saez, Emmanuel. 2000. *Optimal Income Transfer Programs: Intensive Versus Extensive Labor Supply Responses*. Working Paper Series 7708. National Bureau of Economic Research. https://doi.org/10.3386/w7708. www.nber.org/papers/w7708.

2002a. "Optimal Income Transfer Programs: Intensive versus Extensive Labor Supply Responses." *Quarterly Journal of Economics* 117 (3): 1039–73.

2002b. "The Desirability of Commodity Taxation under Non-Linear Income Taxation and Heterogeneous Tastes." *Journal of Public Economics* 83 (2): 217–30.

2013. "Optimal Progressive Capital Income Taxes in the Infinite Horizon Model." *Journal of Public Economics* 97:61–74.

Salop, Steven. 1977. "The Noisy Monopolist: Imperfect Information, Price Dispersion and Price Discrimination." *Review of Economic Studies* 44 (3): 393–406.

1979. "Monopolistic Competition with Outside Goods." *Bell Journal of Economics* 10 (1): 141–56.

2010. "Question: What is the Real and Proper Antitrust Welfare Standard? Answer: The True Consumer Welfare Standard." *Loyola Consumer Law Review* 22 (3): 336–53.

Salop, Steven, and Joseph E. Stiglitz. 1977. "Bargains and Ripoffs: A Model of Monopolistically Competitive Price Dispersion." *Review of Economic Studies* 44 (3): 493–510.

Sanchirico, Chris William. 2000. "Taxes versus Legal Rules as Instruments for Equity: A More Equitable View." *Journal of Legal Studies* 29 (2): 797–820.

2001. "Deconstructing the New Efficiency Rationale." *Cornell Law Review* 86 (5): 1003–89.

2010. "A Critical Look at the Economic Argument for Taxing Only Labor Income." *Tax Law Review* 63 (4): 867–956.

2011. "Tax Eclecticism." *Tax Law Review* 64 (2): 149–227.

Schmalensee, Richard. 1981. "Output andWelfare Implications of Monopolistic Third-Degree Price Discrimination." *American Economic Review* 71 (1): 242–47.

Schwab, Stewart. 1989. "Coase Defends Coase: Why Lawyers Listen and Economists Do Not." *Michigan Law Review* 87 (6): 1171–2459.

Segal, Ilya, and Michael D. Whinston. 2014. "The Efficiency of Bargaining under Divided Entitlements." *University of Chicago Law Review* 81 (1): 273–89.

2016. "Property Rights and the Efficiency of Bargaining." *Journal of the European Economic Association* 14 (6): 1287–328.

Shavell, Steven. 1979. "On Moral Hazard and Insurance." *Quarterly Journal of Economics* 93 (4): 541–62.

1980. "Strict Liability versus Negligence." *Journal of Legal Studies* 9 (1): 1–25.

1981. "A Note on Efficiency vs. Distributional Equity in Legal Rulemaking: Should Distributional Equity Matter Given Optimal Income Taxation?" *American Economic Review* 71 (2): 414–18.

Shaviro, Daniel. 1997. "The Minimum Wage, the Earned Income Tax Credit, and Optimal Subsidy Policy." *University of Chicago Law Review* 64 (2): 405–81.

Silver-Greenberg, Jessica, and Michael Corkery. 2015. "In Arbitration, a 'Privatization of the Justice System,'" *The New York Times* (November 1, 2015). www.nytimes.com/2015/11/02 %20/business/dealbook/in-arbitration-a-privatization-of-the-justicesystem.html.

Sims, David P. 2007. "Out of Control: What Can We Learn from the End of Massachusetts Rent Control?" *Journal of Urban Economics* 61 (1): 129–51.

Smeeding, Timothy. 2012. *Income, Wealth, and Debt and the Great Recession*. Stanford, CA: Stanford Center on Poverty and Inequality. https://web.stanford.edu/group/recessiontrends-dev/cgi-bin/web/sites/all/themes/barron/pdf/IncomeWealthDebt_fact_sheet.pdf.

Smith, Gary R. 2004. "The Future of Tort Reform: Reforming the Remedy, Re-Balancing the Scales." *Emory Law Journal* 53 (3): 1219.

Somin, Ilya. 2007. "Controlling the Grasping Hand: Economic Development Takings after Kelo." *Supreme Court Economic Review* 15 (1): 183–271.

2016. *The Grasping Hand: "Kelo v. City of New London" and the Limits of Eminent Domain*. University of Chicago Press.

Spence, Michael. 1977. "Consumer Misperceptions, Product Failure and Producer Liability." *Review of Economic Studies* 44 (3): 561–72.

Spence, Muriel Morisey. 1993. "Teaching *Williams v. Walker-Thomas Furniture Co.*" *Temple Political and Civil Rights Law Review* 3:89–105.

Stahl, Konrad. 1985. "Microeconomic Analysis of Housing Markets: Towards a Conceptual Framework." In *Microeconomic Models of Housing Markets*, edited by Konrad Stahl, 1–26. Berlin: Springer-Verlag.

Stark, Kirk J. 2005. "Enslaving the Beachcomber: Some Thoughts on the Liberty Objections to Endowment Taxation." *Canadian Journal of Law & Jurisprudence* 18 (1): 47–68.

Sternlight, Jean R. 2001. "Mandatory Binding Arbitration and the Demise of the Seventh Amendment Right to a Jury Trial." *Ohio State Journal of Dispute Resolution* 16 (3): 669–734.

2011. "Tsunami: *AT&T Mobility LLC v. Concepcion* Impedes Access to Justice." *Oregon Law Review* 90 (3): 703–28.

Stigler, George J., and Gary S. Becker. 1977. "De Gustibus Non Est Disputandum." *American Economic Review* 67 (2): 76–90.

Stiglitz, Joseph E. 1982. "Self-Selection and Pareto Efficient Taxation." *Journal of Public Economics* 17 (2): 213–40.

1987. "Pareto Efficient and Optimal Taxation and the New New Welfare Economics." In *Handbook of Public Economics*, edited by Alan J Auerbach and Martin Feldstein, 2:991–1042. Amsterdam: Elsevier.

2000. *Economics of the Public Sector*. 3rd ed. New York: W. W. Norton & Company.

Stole, Lars A., and Jeffrey Zwiebel. 1996a. "Intra-Firm Bargaining under Non-Binding Contracts." *Review of Economic Studies* 63 (3): 375–410.

1996b. "Organizational Design and Technology Choice under Intrafirm Bargaining." *American Economic Review* 86 (1): 195.

Straub, Ludwig, and Iván Werning. 2020. "Positive Long-Run Capital Taxation: Chamley-Judd Revisited." *American Economic Review* 110 (1): 86–119.

Stucke, Maurice E. 2012. "Reconsidering Antitrust's Goals." *Boston College Law Review* 53 (2): 551–629.

Super, David A. 2011. "The Rise and Fall of the Implied Warranty of Habitability." *California Law Review* 99 (2): 389–463.

Susin, Scott. 2002. "Rent Vouchers and the Price of Low-Income Housing." *Journal of Public Economics* 83 (1): 109–52.

Suzuki, Keishun. 2020. "Patent Protection, Optimal Licensing, and Innovation with Endogenous Entry." *Macroeconomic Dynamics* 24 (8): 2033–2059.

Swinnerton, Kenneth A. 1996. "Minimum Wages in an Equilibrium Search Model with Diminishing Returns to Labor in Production." *Journal of Labor Economics* 14 (2): 340–55.

Thompson, Mark. 1997. "Letting the Air out of Tort Reform." *ABA Journal* 83 (5): 64.

Towers Watson. 2011. *2011 Update on U.S. Tort Cost Trends.* www.casact.org/sites/default/files/old/studynotes_towers-watson-tort-cost-trends.pdf.

Tramposch, A. 2011. "The Global Impact of the America Invents Act." *WIPO Magazine*, no. 6, 6. www.wipo.int/wipo_magazine/en/2011/06/article_0002.html.

Tuomala, Matti. 2016. *Optimal Redistributive Taxation.* Oxford: Oxford University Press.

U.S. Chamber Institute for Legal Reform. 2013. *International Comparisons of Litigation Costs: Canada, Europe, Japan, and the United States.* Washington, DC. https://instituteforlegalreform.com/wp-content/uploads/media/ILR_NERA_Study_International_Liability_Costs-update.pdf.

U.S. Department of Labor, Wage and Hour Division. n.d. *Federal Minimum Wage Rates under the Fair Labor Standards Act.* Accessed February 3, 2022. www.dol.gov/agencies/whd/minimum-wage/history/chart.

Vance, Sarah S. 2005. "A Primer on the Class Action Fairness Act of 2005." *Tulane Law Review* 80 (5 & 6): 1617–44.

Varian, Hal R. 1980. "Redistributive Taxation as Social Insurance." *Journal of Public Economics* 14 (1): 49–68.

1985. "Price Discrimination and Social Welfare." *American Economic Review* 75 (4): 870–75.

1989. "Price Discrimination." In *Handbook of Industrial Organization*, edited by Richard Schmalensee, Mark Armstrong, Robert D Willig, and Robert H Porter, 1:597–654. Amsterdam: North-Holland.

Waldron, Jeremy. 2003. "Locating Distribution." *Journal of Legal Studies* 32 (1): 277–302.

Wallerstein, Michael. 1999. "Wage-Setting Institutions and Pay Inequality in Advanced Industrial Societies." *American Journal of Political Science* 43 (3): 649–80.

Weisbach, David A. 2003. "Should Legal Rules Be Used to Redistribute Income?" *University of Chicago Law Review* 70 (1): 439–53.

2015. "Distributionally Weighted Cost–Benefit Analysis: Welfare Economics Meets Organizational Design." *Journal of Legal Analysis* 7 (1): 151–82.

Western, Bruce, and Jake Rosenfeld. 2011. "Unions, Norms, and the Rise in US Wage Inequality." *American Sociological Review* 76 (4): 513–37.

Wickelgren, Abraham L. 2006. "The Inefficiency of Contractually-Based Liability with Rational Consumers." *Journal of Law, Economics, and Organization* 22 (1): 168–83.

Williamson, Oliver E. 1968. "Economies as an Antitrust Defense: The Welfare Tradeoffs." *American Economic Review* 58 (1): 18–36.

Wolff, Edward N. 1998. "Recent Trends in the Size Distribution of Household Wealth." *Journal of Economic Perspectives* 12 (3): 131–50.

Wright, Joshua D., and Douglas H. Ginsburg. 2012. "The Goals of Antitrust: Welfare Trumps Choice." *Fordham Law Review* 81 (5): 2405–23.

Wu, Tim. 2019. "Antitrust Returns to American Politics." *The New York Times* (March 13, 2019). Accessed May 13, 2024. www.nytimes.com/2019/03/13/opinion/antitrust-2020-campaign.html.

Zelenak, Lawrence. 2006. "Taxing Endowment." *Duke Law Journal* 55 (6): 1145.

Index

Printed by Integrated Books International,
United States of America